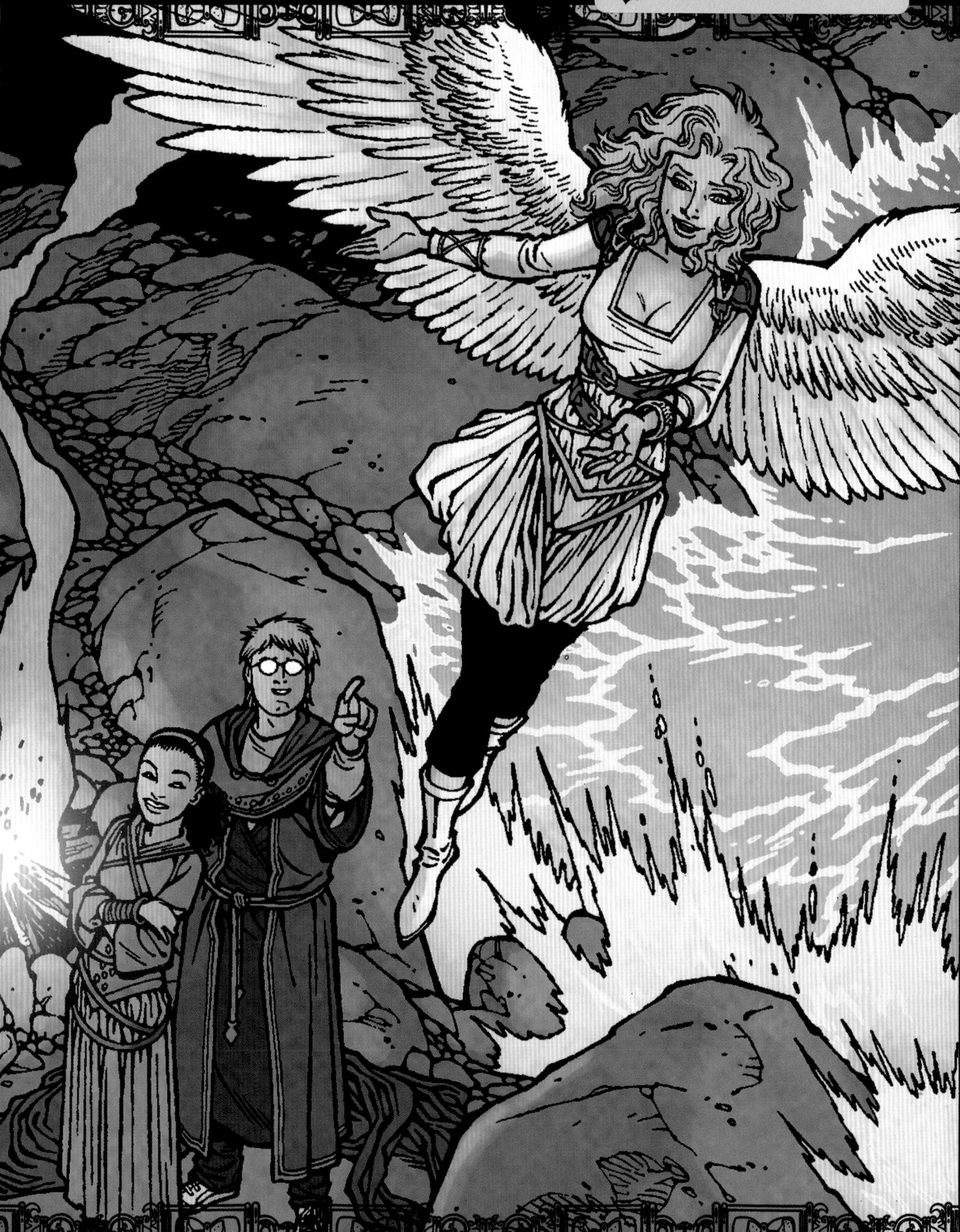

JOE HILL:
For Alan Moore and Neil Gaiman.

GABRIEL RODRIGUEZ:
To my parents, Gabriel and María Eugenia,
with love and gratitude.

-CLOCKWORKS-

CLOCKWORKS
LOCKE & KEY

VOLUME 3

WRITTEN BY

JOE HILL

ART BY

GABRIEL RODRIGUEZ

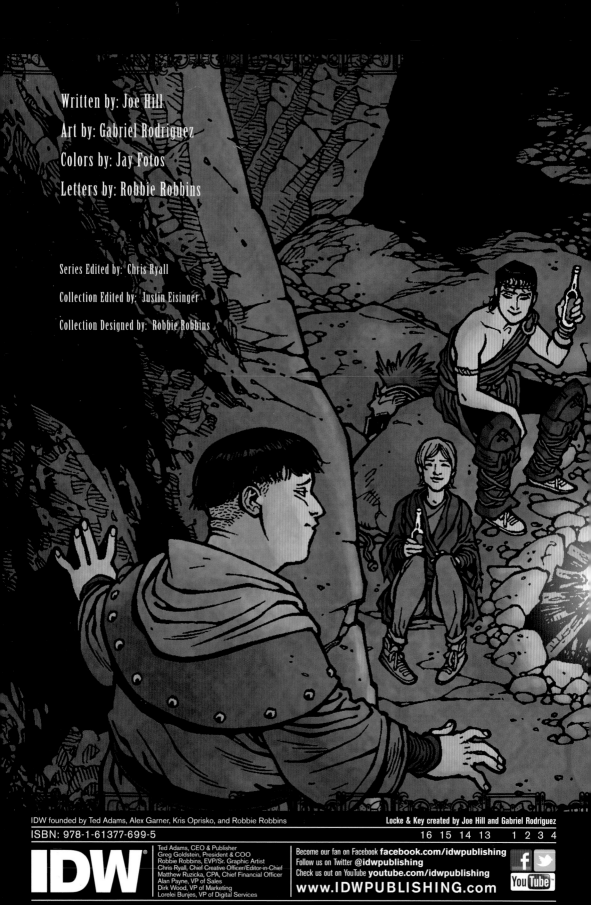

Written by: Joe Hill

Art by: Gabriel Rodriguez

Colors by: Jay Fotos

Letters by: Robbie Robbins

Series Edited by: Chris Ryall

Collection Edited by: Justin Eisinger

Collection Designed by: Robbie Robbins

IDW founded by Ted Adams, Alex Garner, Kris Oprisko, and Robbie Robbins

Locke & Key created by Joe Hill and Gabriel Rodriguez

ISBN: 978-1-61377-699-5

16 15 14 13   1 2 3 4

Ted Adams, CEO & Publisher
Greg Goldstein, President & COO
Robbie Robbins, EVP/Sr. Graphic Artist
Chris Ryall, Chief Creative Officer/Editor-in-Chief
Matthew Ruzicka, CPA, Chief Financial Officer
Alan Payne, VP of Sales
Dirk Wood, VP of Marketing
Lorelei Bunjes, VP of Digital Services

Become our fan on Facebook facebook.com/idwpublishing
Follow us on Twitter @idwpublishing
Check us out on YouTube youtube.com/idwpublishing
www.IDWPUBLISHING.com

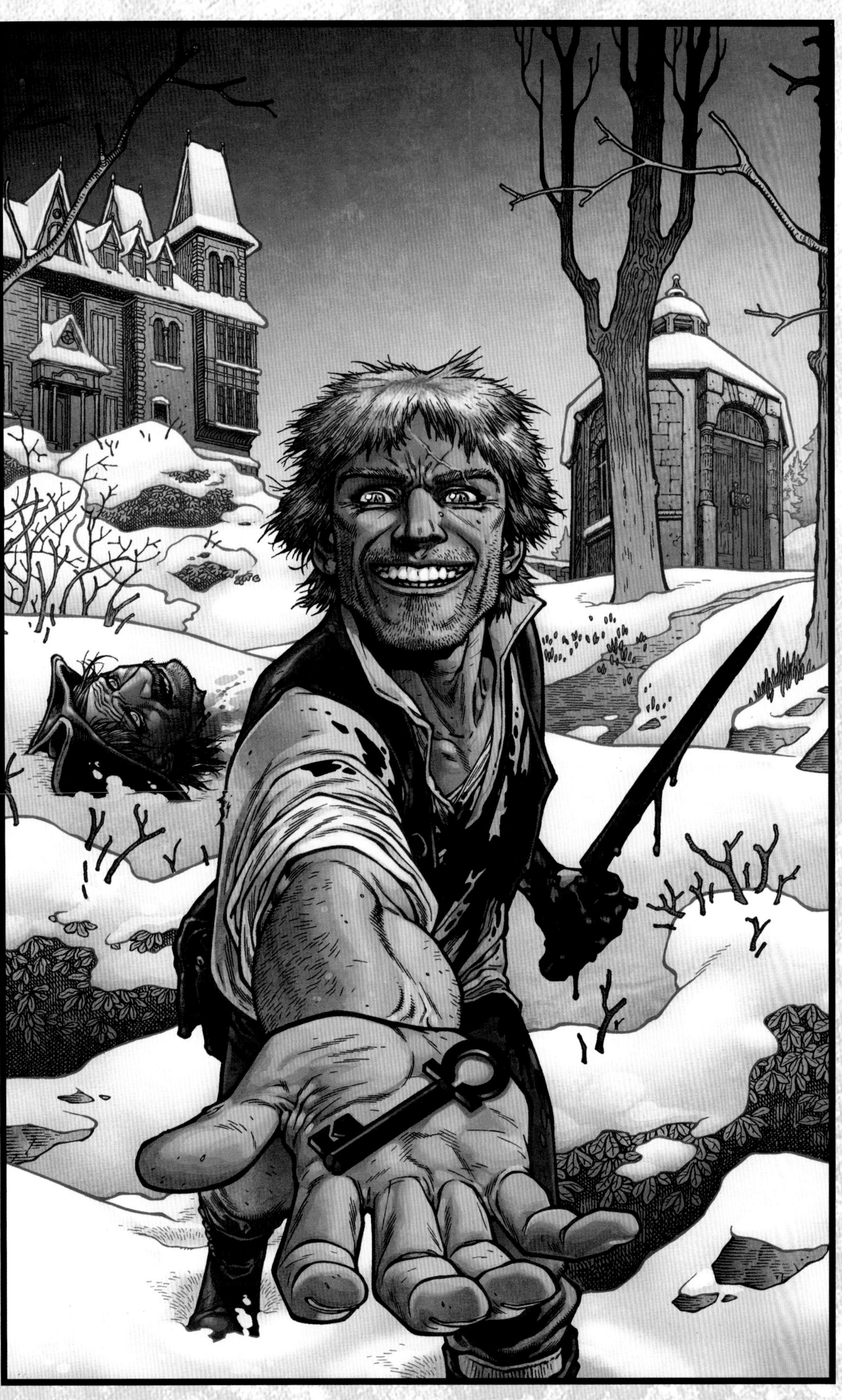

- CLOCKWORKS -

Chapter One

THE LOCKSMITH'S SON

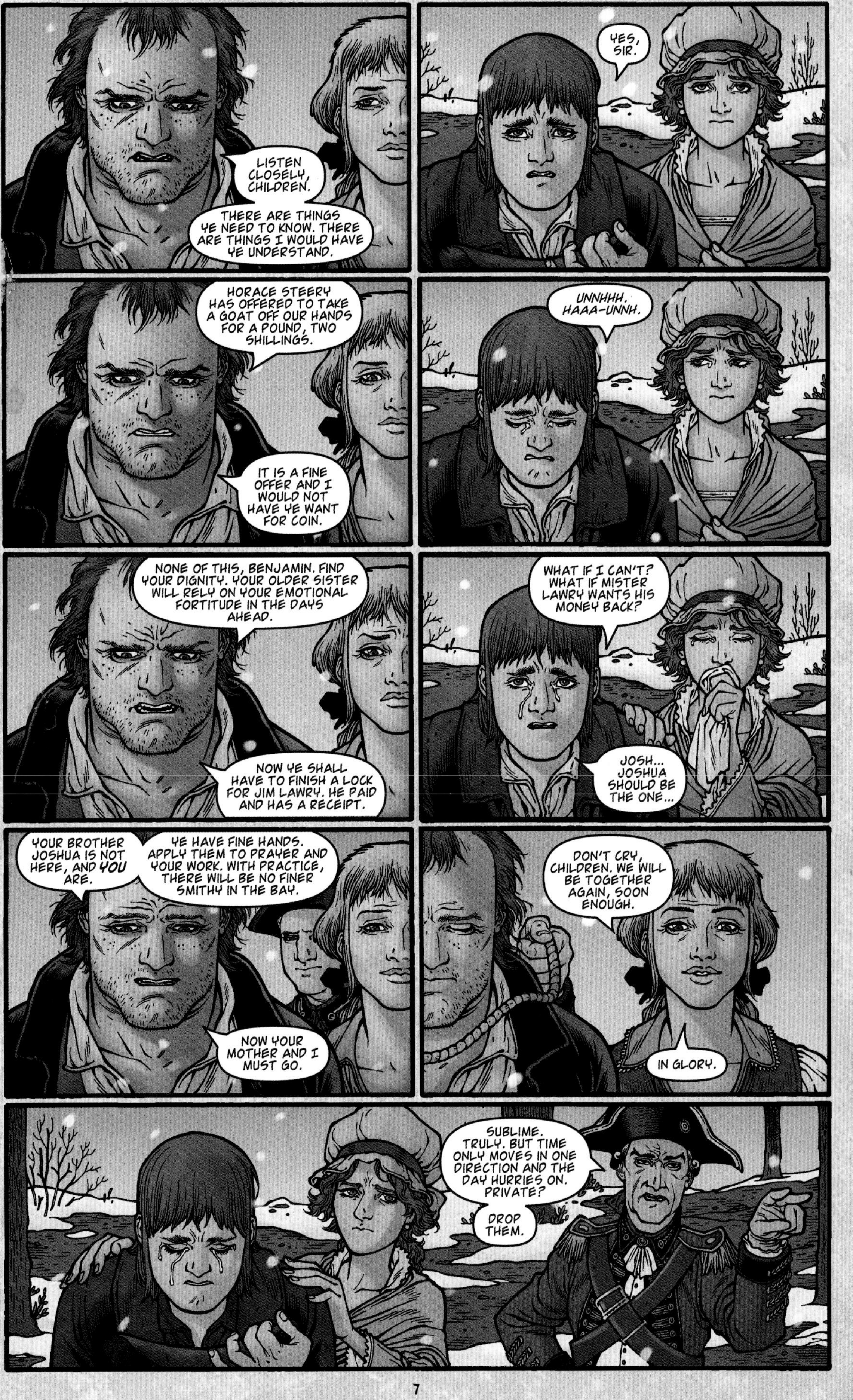

LISTEN CLOSELY, CHILDREN.
THERE ARE THINGS YE NEED TO KNOW. THERE ARE THINGS I WOULD HAVE YE UNDERSTAND.
YES, SIR.
HORACE STEERY HAS OFFERED TO TAKE A GOAT OFF OUR HANDS FOR A POUND, TWO SHILLINGS.
IT IS A FINE OFFER AND I WOULD NOT HAVE YE WANT FOR COIN.
UNNHHH. HAAA-UNNH.
NONE OF THIS, BENJAMIN. FIND YOUR DIGNITY. YOUR OLDER SISTER WILL RELY ON YOUR EMOTIONAL FORTITUDE IN THE DAYS AHEAD.
NOW YE SHALL HAVE TO FINISH A LOCK FOR JIM LAWRY. HE PAID AND HAS A RECEIPT.
WHAT IF I CAN'T? WHAT IF MISTER LAWRY WANTS HIS MONEY BACK?
JOSH... JOSHUA SHOULD BE THE ONE...
YOUR BROTHER JOSHUA IS NOT HERE, AND YOU ARE.
YE HAVE FINE HANDS. APPLY THEM TO PRAYER AND YOUR WORK. WITH PRACTICE, THERE WILL BE NO FINER SMITHY IN THE BAY.
NOW YOUR MOTHER AND I MUST GO.
DON'T CRY, CHILDREN. WE WILL BE TOGETHER AGAIN, SOON ENOUGH.
IN GLORY.
SUBLIME. TRULY. BUT TIME ONLY MOVES IN ONE DIRECTION AND THE DAY HURRIES ON. PRIVATE?
DROP THEM.

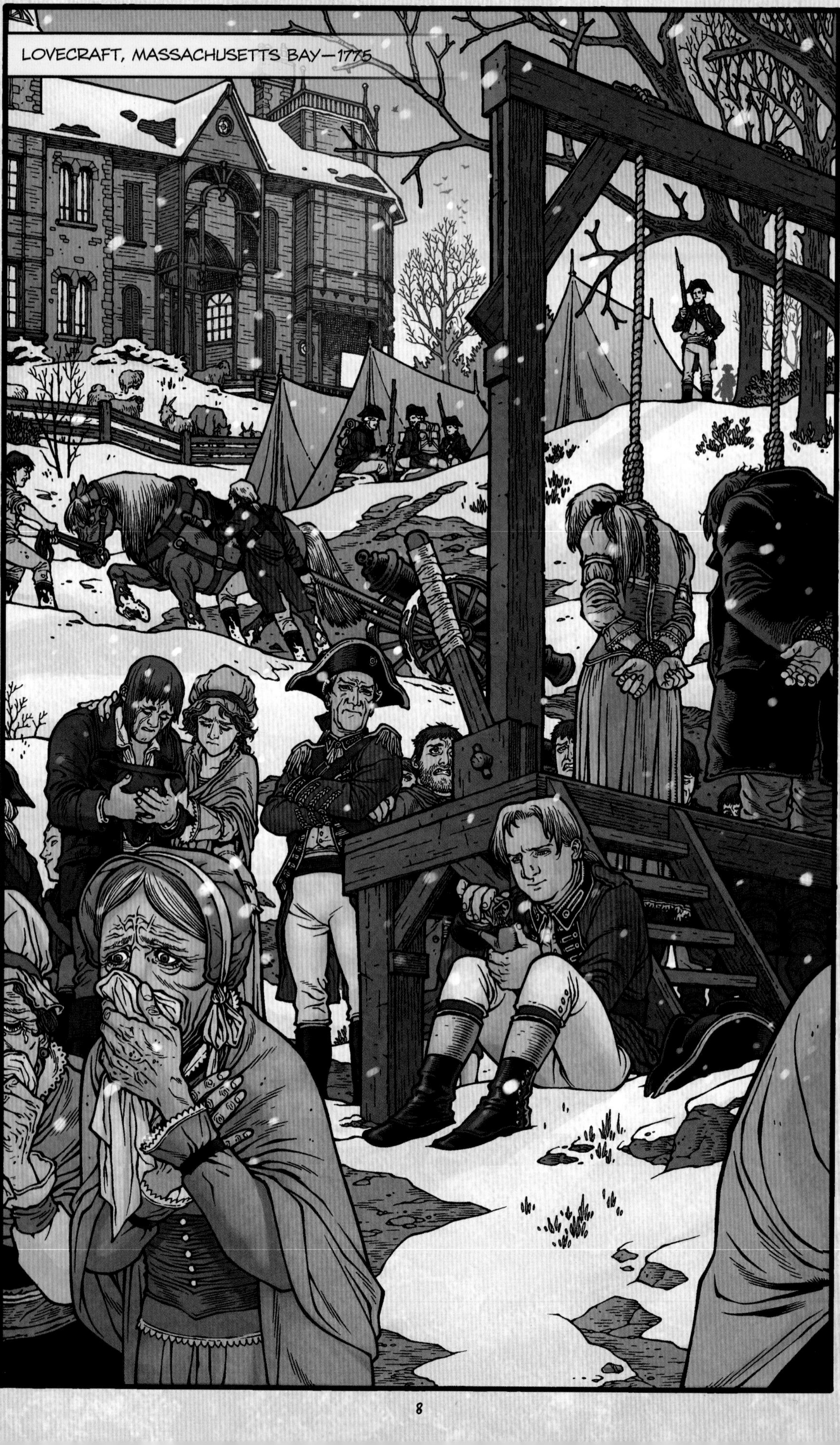
LOVECRAFT, MASSACHUSETTS BAY—1775

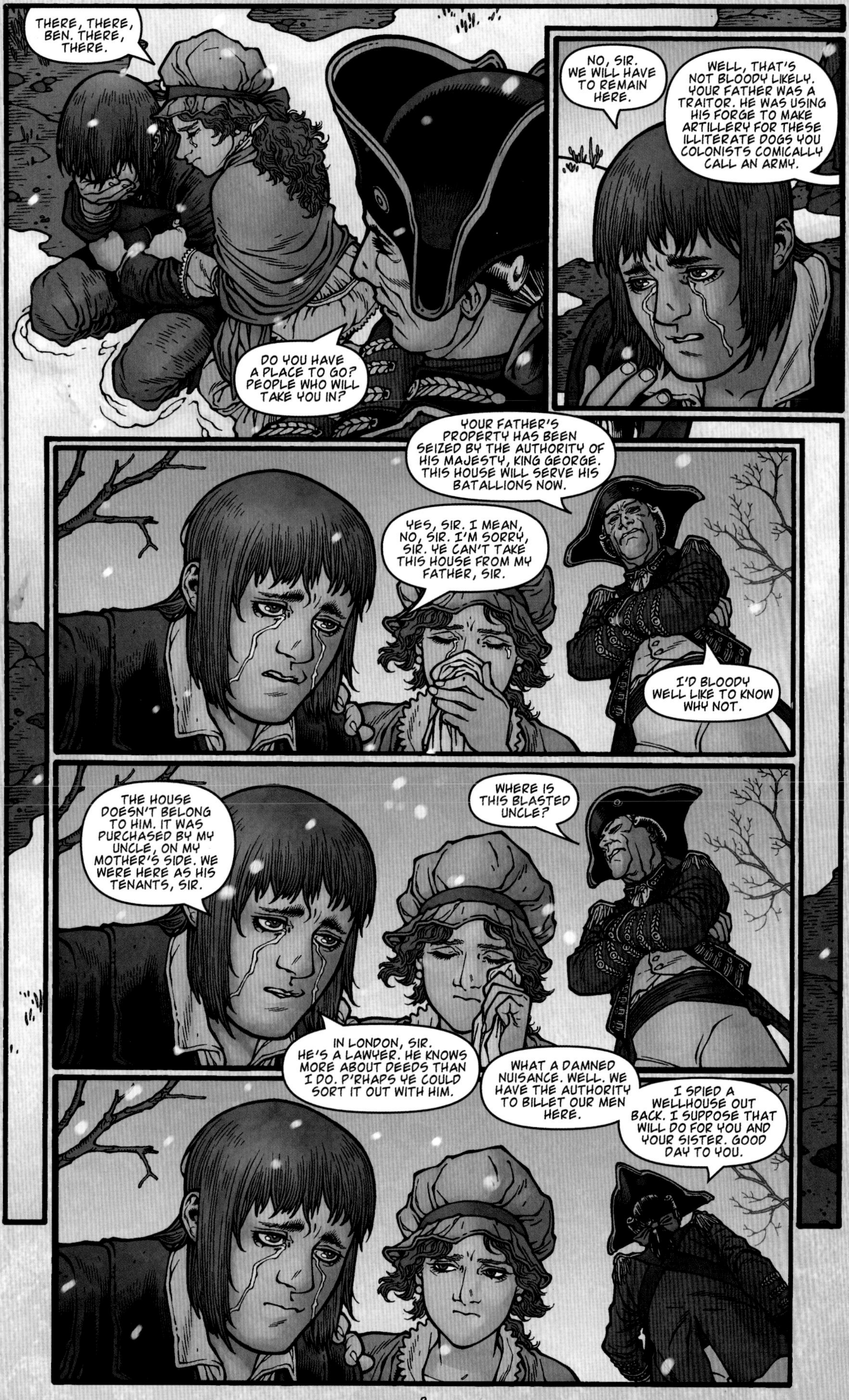

THERE, THERE, BEN. THERE, THERE.
DO YOU HAVE A PLACE TO GO? PEOPLE WHO WILL TAKE YOU IN?
NO, SIR. WE WILL HAVE TO REMAIN HERE.
WELL, THAT'S NOT BLOODY LIKELY. YOUR FATHER WAS A TRAITOR. HE WAS USING HIS FORGE TO MAKE ARTILLERY FOR THESE ILLITERATE DOGS YOU COLONISTS COMICALLY CALL AN ARMY.
YOUR FATHER'S PROPERTY HAS BEEN SEIZED BY THE AUTHORITY OF HIS MAJESTY, KING GEORGE. THIS HOUSE WILL SERVE HIS BATALLIONS NOW.
YES, SIR. I MEAN, NO, SIR. I'M SORRY, SIR. YE CAN'T TAKE THIS HOUSE FROM MY FATHER, SIR.
I'D BLOODY WELL LIKE TO KNOW WHY NOT.
THE HOUSE DOESN'T BELONG TO HIM. IT WAS PURCHASED BY MY UNCLE, ON MY MOTHER'S SIDE. WE WERE HERE AS HIS TENANTS, SIR.
WHERE IS THIS BLASTED UNCLE?
IN LONDON, SIR. HE'S A LAWYER. HE KNOWS MORE ABOUT DEEDS THAN I DO. P'RHAPS YE COULD SORT IT OUT WITH HIM.
WHAT A DAMNED NUISANCE. WELL. WE HAVE THE AUTHORITY TO BILLET OUR MEN HERE.
I SPIED A WELLHOUSE OUT BACK. I SUPPOSE THAT WILL DO FOR YOU AND YOUR SISTER. GOOD DAY TO YOU.

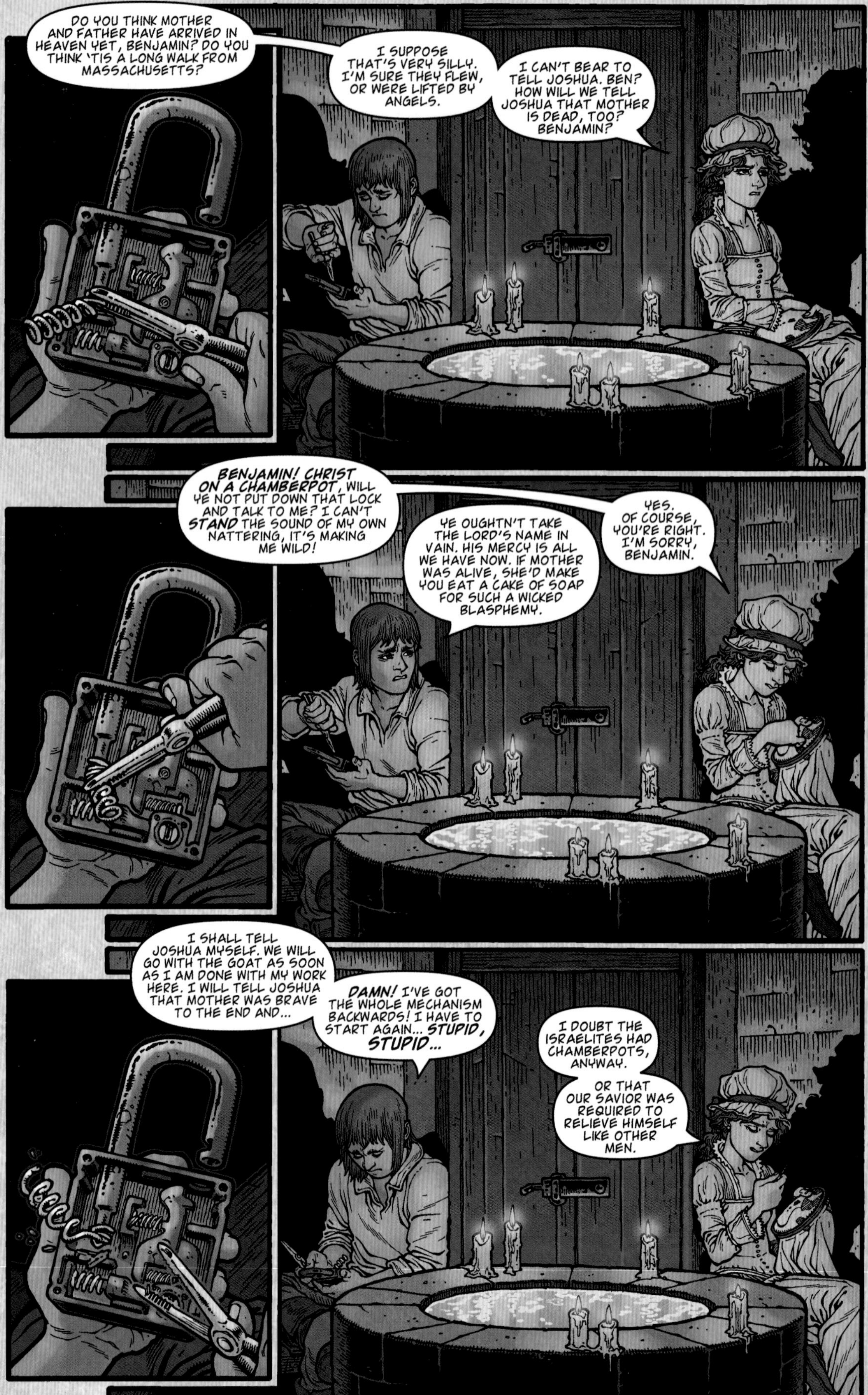

DO YOU THINK MOTHER AND FATHER HAVE ARRIVED IN HEAVEN YET, BENJAMIN? DO YOU THINK 'TIS A LONG WALK FROM MASSACHUSETTS?
I SUPPOSE THAT'S VERY SILLY. I'M SURE THEY FLEW, OR WERE LIFTED BY ANGELS.
I CAN'T BEAR TO TELL JOSHUA. BEN? HOW WILL WE TELL JOSHUA THAT MOTHER IS DEAD, TOO? BENJAMIN?
BENJAMIN! CHRIST ON A CHAMBERPOT, WILL YE NOT PUT DOWN THAT LOCK AND TALK TO ME? I CAN'T STAND THE SOUND OF MY OWN NATTERING, IT'S MAKING ME WILD!
YE OUGHTN'T TAKE THE LORD'S NAME IN VAIN. HIS MERCY IS ALL WE HAVE NOW. IF MOTHER WAS ALIVE, SHE'D MAKE YOU EAT A CAKE OF SOAP FOR SUCH A WICKED BLASPHEMY.
YES. OF COURSE, YOU'RE RIGHT. I'M SORRY, BENJAMIN.
I SHALL TELL JOSHUA MYSELF. WE WILL GO WITH THE GOAT AS SOON AS I AM DONE WITH MY WORK HERE. I WILL TELL JOSHUA THAT MOTHER WAS BRAVE TO THE END AND...
DAMN! I'VE GOT THE WHOLE MECHANISM BACKWARDS! I HAVE TO START AGAIN... STUPID, STUPID...
I DOUBT THE ISRAELITES HAD CHAMBERPOTS, ANYWAY.
OR THAT OUR SAVIOR WAS REQUIRED TO RELIEVE HIMSELF LIKE OTHER MEN.

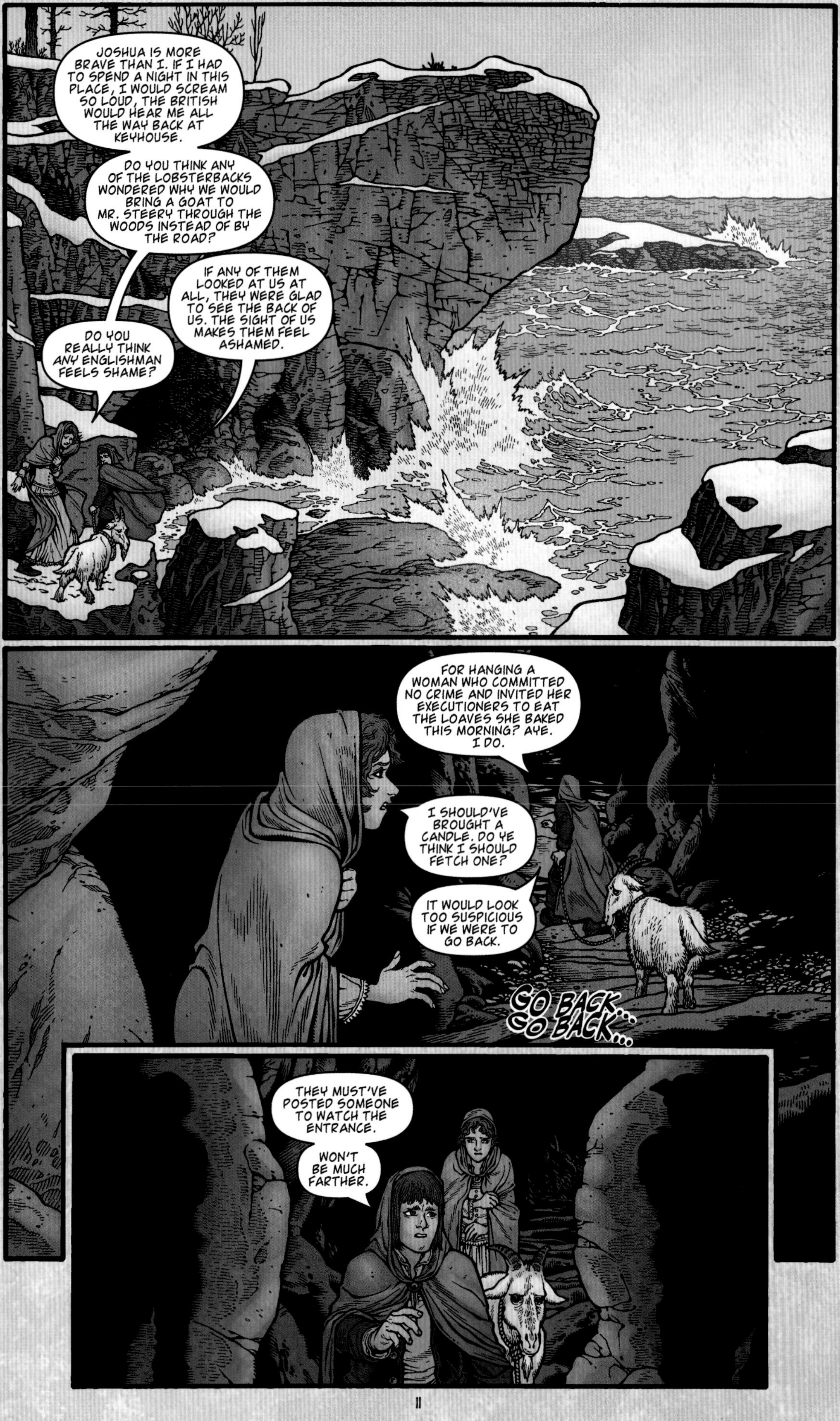
JOSHUA IS MORE BRAVE THAN I. IF I HAD TO SPEND A NIGHT IN THIS PLACE, I WOULD SCREAM SO LOUD, THE BRITISH WOULD HEAR ME ALL THE WAY BACK AT KEYHOUSE.
DO YOU THINK ANY OF THE LOBSTERBACKS WONDERED WHY WE WOULD BRING A GOAT TO MR. STEERY THROUGH THE WOODS INSTEAD OF BY THE ROAD?
IF ANY OF THEM LOOKED AT US AT ALL, THEY WERE GLAD TO SEE THE BACK OF US. THE SIGHT OF US MAKES THEM FEEL ASHAMED.
DO YOU REALLY THINK ANY ENGLISHMAN FEELS SHAME?
FOR HANGING A WOMAN WHO COMMITTED NO CRIME AND INVITED HER EXECUTIONERS TO EAT THE LOAVES SHE BAKED THIS MORNING? AYE. I DO.
I SHOULD'VE BROUGHT A CANDLE. DO YE THINK I SHOULD FETCH ONE?
IT WOULD LOOK TOO SUSPICIOUS IF WE WERE TO GO BACK.
GO BACK... GO BACK...
THEY MUST'VE POSTED SOMEONE TO WATCH THE ENTRANCE.
WON'T BE MUCH FARTHER.

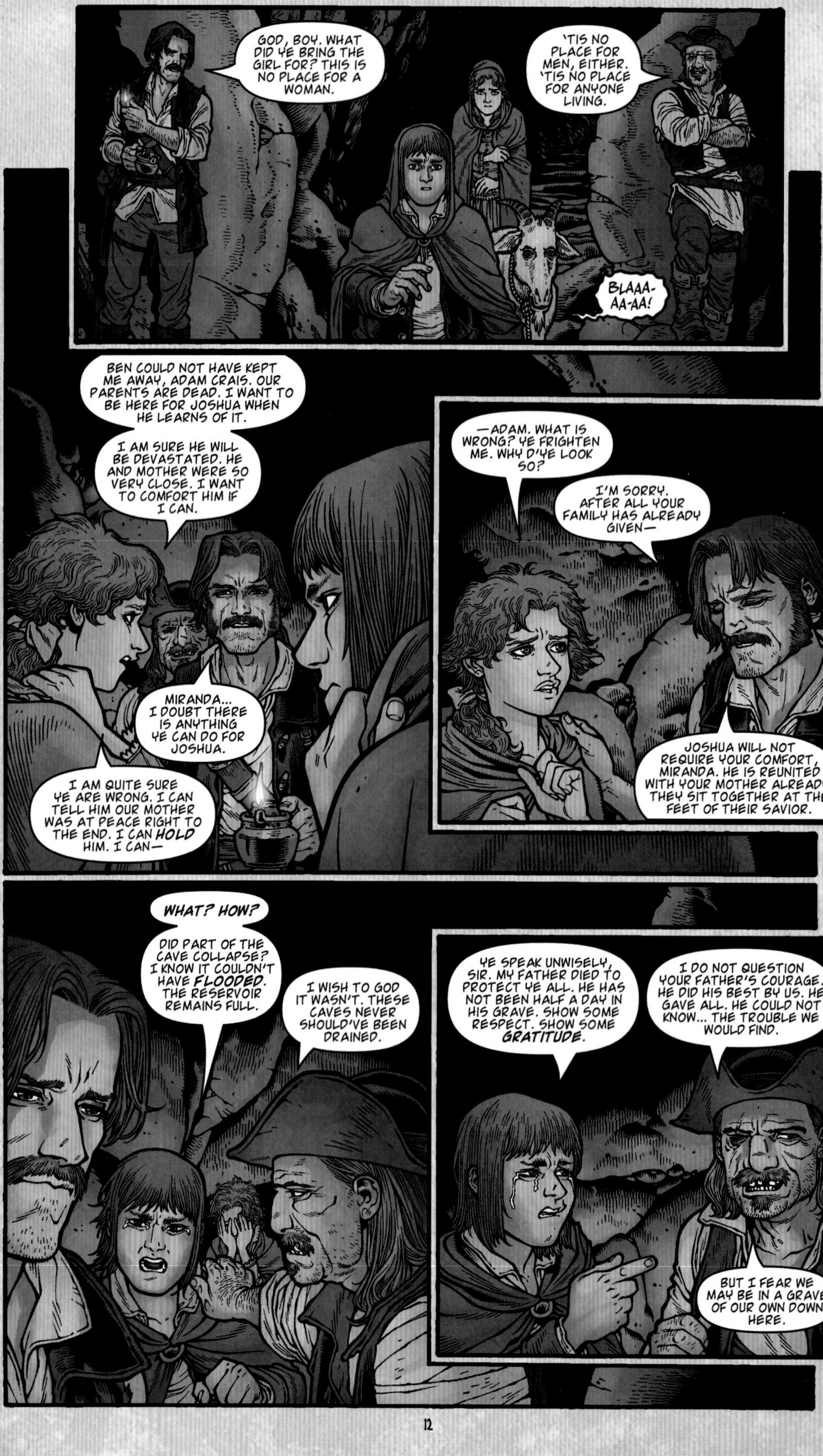
GOD, BOY. WHAT DID YE BRING THE GIRL FOR? THIS IS NO PLACE FOR A WOMAN.
'TIS NO PLACE FOR MEN, EITHER. 'TIS NO PLACE FOR ANYONE LIVING.
BLAAA-AA-AA!
BEN COULD NOT HAVE KEPT ME AWAY, ADAM CRAIS. OUR PARENTS ARE DEAD. I WANT TO BE HERE FOR JOSHUA WHEN HE LEARNS OF IT.
I AM SURE HE WILL BE DEVASTATED. HE AND MOTHER WERE SO VERY CLOSE. I WANT TO COMFORT HIM IF I CAN.
MIRANDA... I DOUBT THERE IS ANYTHING YE CAN DO FOR JOSHUA.
I AM QUITE SURE YE ARE WRONG. I CAN TELL HIM OUR MOTHER WAS AT PEACE RIGHT TO THE END. I CAN HOLD HIM. I CAN—
—ADAM. WHAT IS WRONG? YE FRIGHTEN ME. WHY D'YE LOOK SO?
I'M SORRY. AFTER ALL YOUR FAMILY HAS ALREADY GIVEN—
JOSHUA WILL NOT REQUIRE YOUR COMFORT, MIRANDA. HE IS REUNITED WITH YOUR MOTHER ALREADY. THEY SIT TOGETHER AT THE FEET OF THEIR SAVIOR.
WHAT? HOW?
DID PART OF THE CAVE COLLAPSE? I KNOW IT COULDN'T HAVE FLOODED. THE RESERVOIR REMAINS FULL.
I WISH TO GOD IT WASN'T. THESE CAVES NEVER SHOULD'VE BEEN DRAINED.
YE SPEAK UNWISELY, SIR. MY FATHER DIED TO PROTECT YE ALL. HE HAS NOT BEEN HALF A DAY IN HIS GRAVE. SHOW SOME RESPECT. SHOW SOME GRATITUDE.
I DO NOT QUESTION YOUR FATHER'S COURAGE. HE DID HIS BEST BY US. HE GAVE ALL. HE COULD NOT KNOW... THE TROUBLE WE WOULD FIND.
BUT I FEAR WE MAY BE IN A GRAVE OF OUR OWN DOWN HERE.

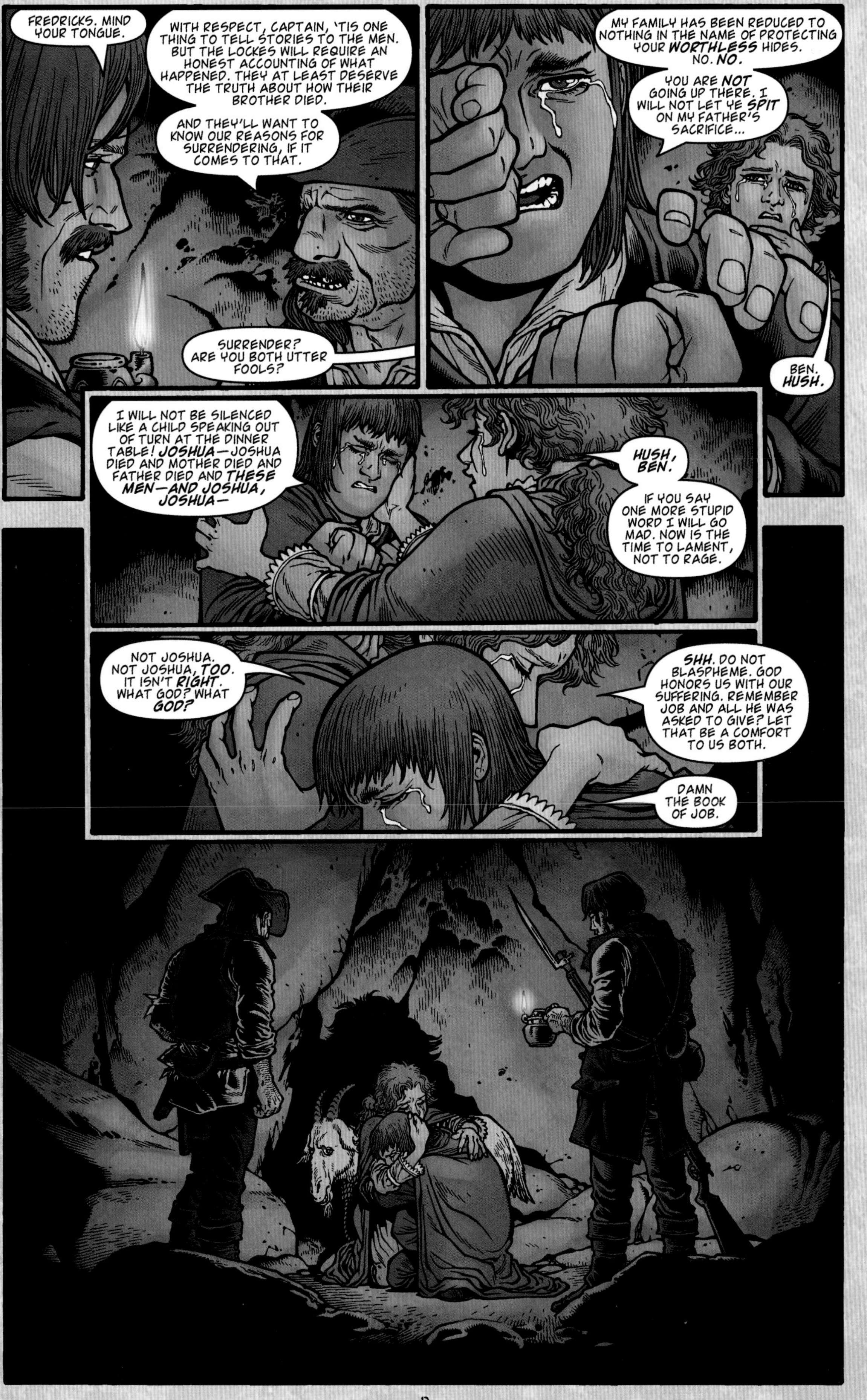
FREDRICKS. MIND YOUR TONGUE.
WITH RESPECT, CAPTAIN, 'TIS ONE THING TO TELL STORIES TO THE MEN. BUT THE LOCKES WILL REQUIRE AN HONEST ACCOUNTING OF WHAT HAPPENED. THEY AT LEAST DESERVE THE TRUTH ABOUT HOW THEIR BROTHER DIED.
AND THEY'LL WANT TO KNOW OUR REASONS FOR SURRENDERING, IF IT COMES TO THAT.
SURRENDER? ARE YOU BOTH UTTER FOOLS?
MY FAMILY HAS BEEN REDUCED TO NOTHING IN THE NAME OF PROTECTING YOUR WORTHLESS HIDES. NO. NO.
YOU ARE NOT GOING UP THERE. I WILL NOT LET YE SPIT ON MY FATHER'S SACRIFICE...
BEN. HUSH.
I WILL NOT BE SILENCED LIKE A CHILD SPEAKING OUT OF TURN AT THE DINNER TABLE! JOSHUA—JOSHUA DIED AND MOTHER DIED AND FATHER DIED AND THESE MEN—AND JOSHUA, JOSHUA—
HUSH, BEN.
IF YOU SAY ONE MORE STUPID WORD I WILL GO MAD. NOW IS THE TIME TO LAMENT, NOT TO RAGE.
NOT JOSHUA. NOT JOSHUA, TOO. IT ISN'T RIGHT. WHAT GOD? WHAT GOD?
SHH. DO NOT BLASPHEME. GOD HONORS US WITH OUR SUFFERING. REMEMBER JOB AND ALL HE WAS ASKED TO GIVE? LET THAT BE A COMFORT TO US BOTH.
DAMN THE BOOK OF JOB.

YOUR MEN SEEM IN GOOD SPIRITS, ADAM.

THEY'RE GLAD TO BE ALIVE. THEY DON'T KNOW THE TROUBLE WE'RE IN.

THEY MUST KNOW THERE ARE THREE HUNDRED BRITISH SOLDIERS WALKING ABOVE THEIR HEADS.

THAT'S NOT THE TROUBLE, THOUGH, IS IT? THEY KNOW ABOUT THE DANGER ABOVE. BUT NOT ABOUT WHAT'S BELOW. THIS WAY.

WE TOLD THE OTHER SOLDIERS A CASK OF GUNPOWDER IGNITED.

WHAT REALLY HAPPENED?

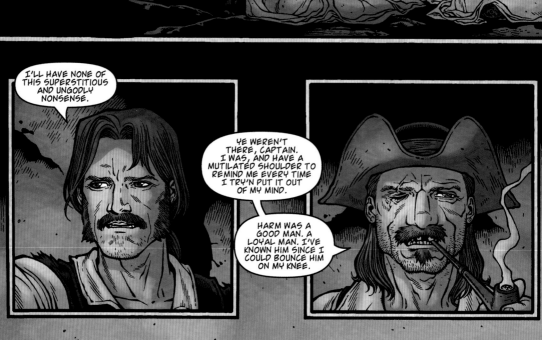

I'LL HAVE NONE OF THIS SUPERSTITIOUS AND UNGODLY NONSENSE.

YE WEREN'T THERE, CAPTAIN. I WAS, AND HAVE A MUTILATED SHOULDER TO REMIND ME EVERY TIME I TRY'N PUT IT OUT OF MY MIND.

HARM WAS A GOOD MAN. A LOYAL MAN. I'VE KNOWN HIM SINCE I COULD BOUNCE HIM ON MY KNEE.

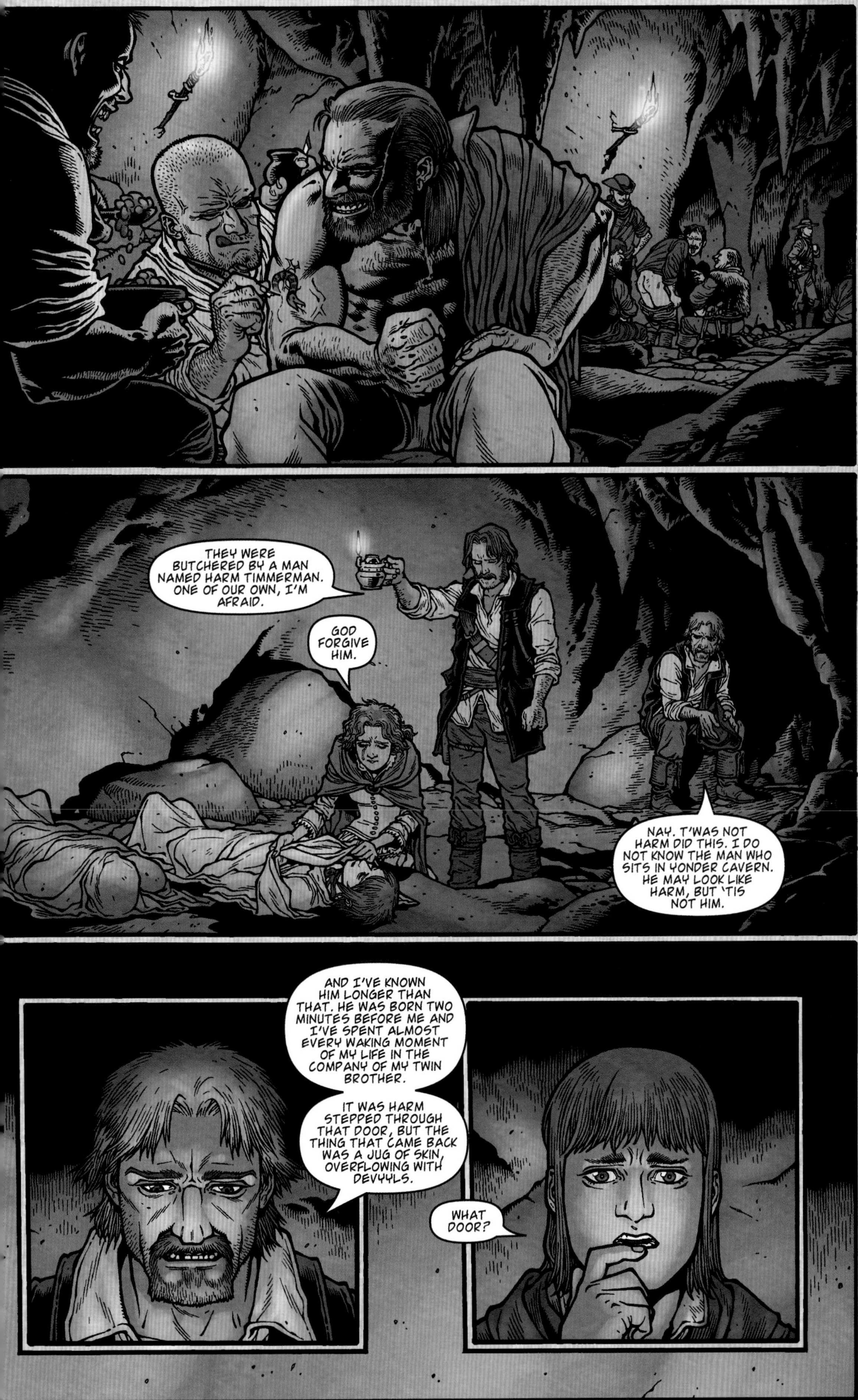
THEY WERE BUTCHERED BY A MAN NAMED HARM TIMMERMAN. ONE OF OUR OWN, I'M AFRAID.
GOD FORGIVE HIM.
NAY. T'WAS NOT HARM DID THIS. I DO NOT KNOW THE MAN WHO SITS IN YONDER CAVERN. HE MAY LOOK LIKE HARM, BUT 'TIS NOT HIM.
AND I'VE KNOWN HIM LONGER THAN THAT. HE WAS BORN TWO MINUTES BEFORE ME AND I'VE SPENT ALMOST EVERY WAKING MOMENT OF MY LIFE IN THE COMPANY OF MY TWIN BROTHER.
IT WAS HARM STEPPED THROUGH THAT DOOR, BUT THE THING THAT CAME BACK WAS A JUG OF SKIN, OVERFLOWING WITH DEVYYLS.
WHAT DOOR?

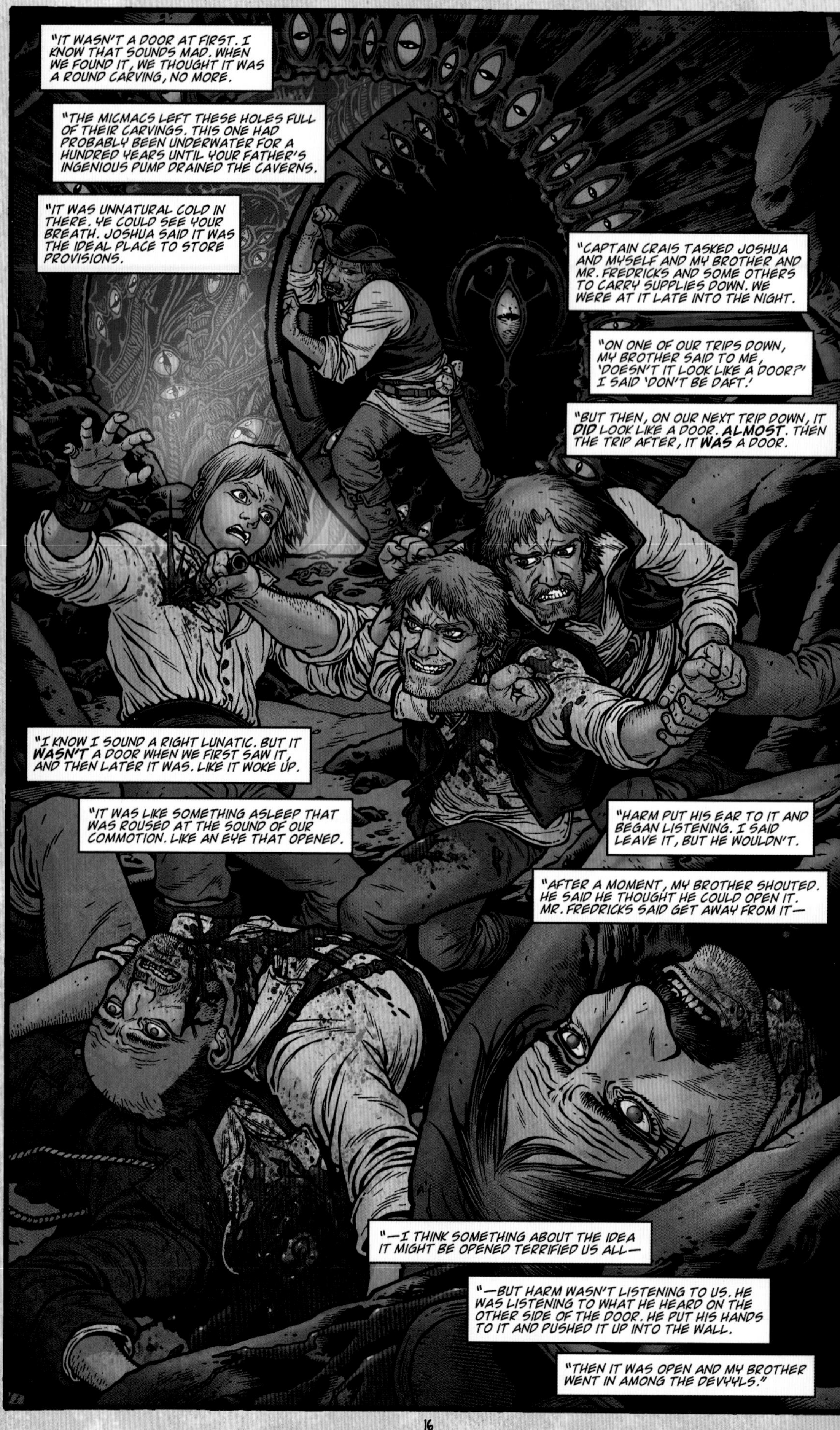
"IT WASN'T A DOOR AT FIRST. I KNOW THAT SOUNDS MAD. WHEN WE FOUND IT, WE THOUGHT IT WAS A ROUND CARVING, NO MORE.
"THE MICMACS LEFT THESE HOLES FULL OF THEIR CARVINGS. THIS ONE HAD PROBABLY BEEN UNDERWATER FOR A HUNDRED YEARS UNTIL YOUR FATHER'S INGENIOUS PUMP DRAINED THE CAVERNS.
"IT WAS UNNATURAL COLD IN THERE. YE COULD SEE YOUR BREATH. JOSHUA SAID IT WAS THE IDEAL PLACE TO STORE PROVISIONS.
"CAPTAIN CRAIS TASKED JOSHUA AND MYSELF AND MY BROTHER AND MR. FREDRICKS AND SOME OTHERS TO CARRY SUPPLIES DOWN. WE WERE AT IT LATE INTO THE NIGHT.
"ON ONE OF OUR TRIPS DOWN, MY BROTHER SAID TO ME, 'DOESN'T IT LOOK LIKE A DOOR?' I SAID 'DON'T BE DAFT.'
"BUT THEN, ON OUR NEXT TRIP DOWN, IT DID LOOK LIKE A DOOR. ALMOST. THEN THE TRIP AFTER, IT WAS A DOOR.
"I KNOW I SOUND A RIGHT LUNATIC. BUT IT WASN'T A DOOR WHEN WE FIRST SAW IT, AND THEN LATER IT WAS. LIKE IT WOKE UP.
"IT WAS LIKE SOMETHING ASLEEP THAT WAS ROUSED AT THE SOUND OF OUR COMMOTION. LIKE AN EYE THAT OPENED.
"HARM PUT HIS EAR TO IT AND BEGAN LISTENING. I SAID LEAVE IT, BUT HE WOULDN'T.
"AFTER A MOMENT, MY BROTHER SHOUTED. HE SAID HE THOUGHT HE COULD OPEN IT. MR. FREDRICKS SAID GET AWAY FROM IT—
"—I THINK SOMETHING ABOUT THE IDEA IT MIGHT BE OPENED TERRIFIED US ALL—
"—BUT HARM WASN'T LISTENING TO US. HE WAS LISTENING TO WHAT HE HEARD ON THE OTHER SIDE OF THE DOOR. HE PUT HIS HANDS TO IT AND PUSHED IT UP INTO THE WALL.
"THEN IT WAS OPEN AND MY BROTHER WENT IN AMONG THE DEVYYLS."

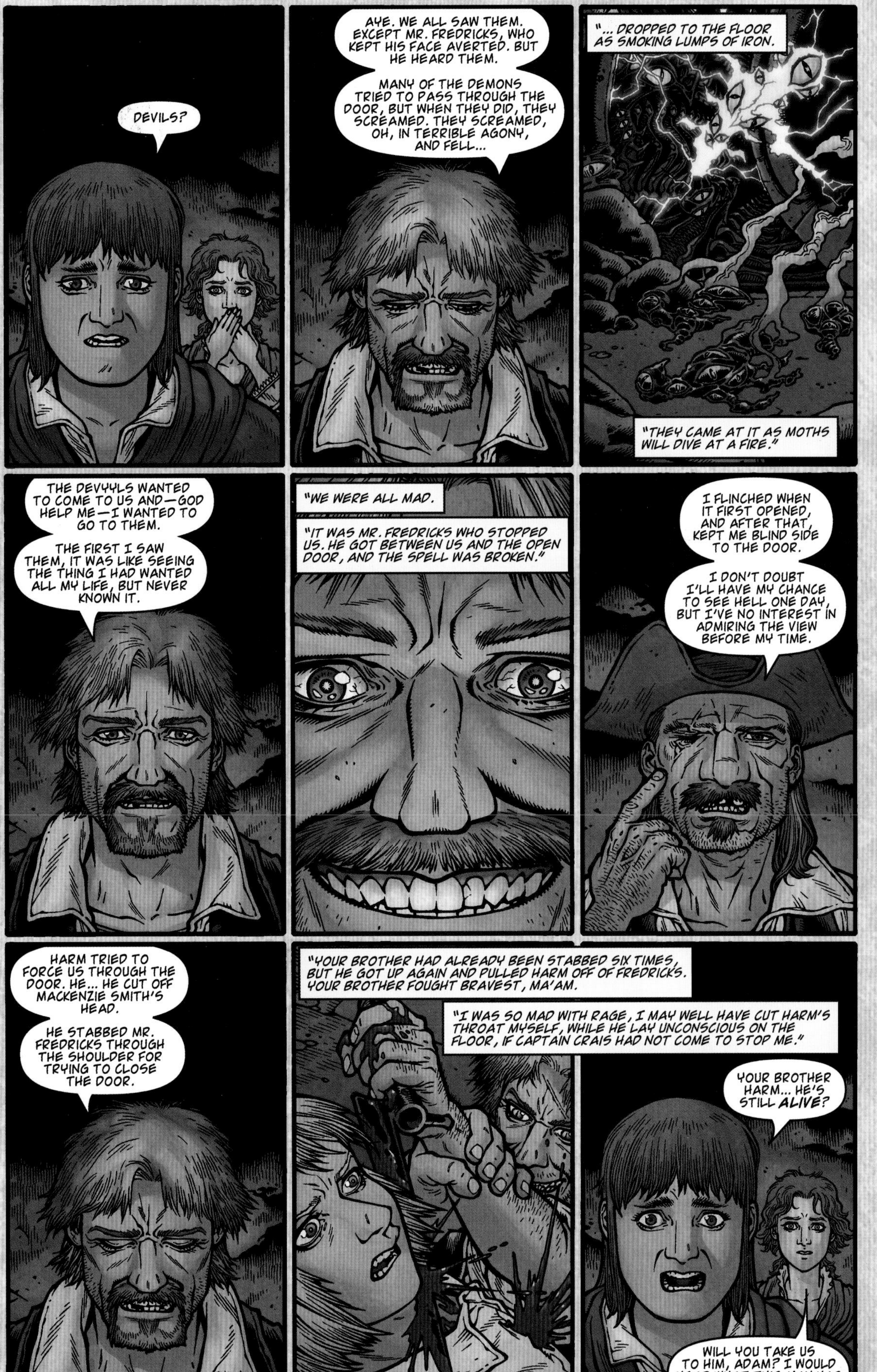

DEVILS?
AYE. WE ALL SAW THEM. EXCEPT MR. FREDRICKS, WHO KEPT HIS FACE AVERTED. BUT HE HEARD THEM.
MANY OF THE DEMONS TRIED TO PASS THROUGH THE DOOR, BUT WHEN THEY DID, THEY SCREAMED. THEY SCREAMED, OH, IN TERRIBLE AGONY, AND FELL...
"...DROPPED TO THE FLOOR AS SMOKING LUMPS OF IRON.
"THEY CAME AT IT AS MOTHS WILL DIVE AT A FIRE."
THE DEVYYLS WANTED TO COME TO US AND—GOD HELP ME—I WANTED TO GO TO THEM.
THE FIRST I SAW THEM, IT WAS LIKE SEEING THE THING I HAD WANTED ALL MY LIFE, BUT NEVER KNOWN IT.
"WE WERE ALL MAD.
"IT WAS MR. FREDRICKS WHO STOPPED US. HE GOT BETWEEN US AND THE OPEN DOOR, AND THE SPELL WAS BROKEN."
I FLINCHED WHEN IT FIRST OPENED, AND AFTER THAT, KEPT ME BLIND SIDE TO THE DOOR.
I DON'T DOUBT I'LL HAVE MY CHANCE TO SEE HELL ONE DAY, BUT I'VE NO INTEREST IN ADMIRING THE VIEW BEFORE MY TIME.
HARM TRIED TO FORCE US THROUGH THE DOOR. HE... HE CUT OFF MACKENZIE SMITH'S HEAD.
HE STABBED MR. FREDRICKS THROUGH THE SHOULDER FOR TRYING TO CLOSE THE DOOR.
"YOUR BROTHER HAD ALREADY BEEN STABBED SIX TIMES, BUT HE GOT UP AGAIN AND PULLED HARM OFF OF FREDRICKS. YOUR BROTHER FOUGHT BRAVEST, MA'AM.
"I WAS SO MAD WITH RAGE, I MAY WELL HAVE CUT HARM'S THROAT MYSELF, WHILE HE LAY UNCONSCIOUS ON THE FLOOR, IF CAPTAIN CRAIS HAD NOT COME TO STOP ME."
YOUR BROTHER HARM... HE'S STILL ALIVE?
WILL YOU TAKE US TO HIM, ADAM? I WOULD HEAR WHAT THIS MAN HAS TO SAY FOR HIMSELF.

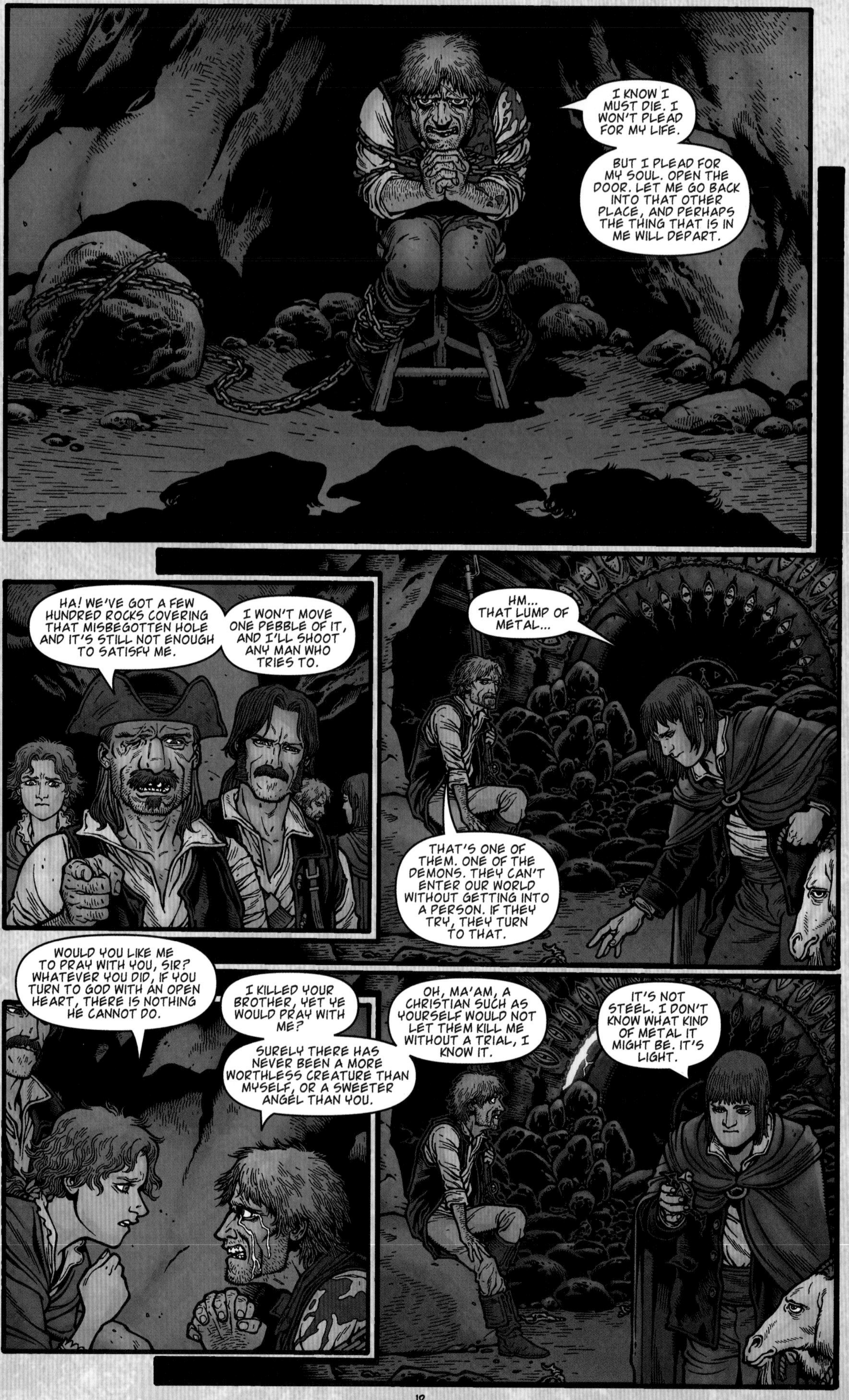

I KNOW I MUST DIE. I WON'T PLEAD FOR MY LIFE.
BUT I PLEAD FOR MY SOUL. OPEN THE DOOR. LET ME GO BACK INTO THAT OTHER PLACE, AND PERHAPS THE THING THAT IS IN ME WILL DEPART.
HA! WE'VE GOT A FEW HUNDRED ROCKS COVERING THAT MISBEGOTTEN HOLE AND IT'S STILL NOT ENOUGH TO SATISFY ME.
I WON'T MOVE ONE PEBBLE OF IT, AND I'LL SHOOT ANY MAN WHO TRIES TO.
HM... THAT LUMP OF METAL...
THAT'S ONE OF THEM. ONE OF THE DEMONS. THEY CAN'T ENTER OUR WORLD WITHOUT GETTING INTO A PERSON. IF THEY TRY, THEY TURN TO THAT.
WOULD YOU LIKE ME TO PRAY WITH YOU, SIR? WHATEVER YOU DID, IF YOU TURN TO GOD WITH AN OPEN HEART, THERE IS NOTHING HE CANNOT DO.
I KILLED YOUR BROTHER, YET YE WOULD PRAY WITH ME?
SURELY THERE HAS NEVER BEEN A MORE WORTHLESS CREATURE THAN MYSELF, OR A SWEETER ANGEL THAN YOU.
OH, MA'AM, A CHRISTIAN SUCH AS YOURSELF WOULD NOT LET THEM KILL ME WITHOUT A TRIAL, I KNOW IT.
IT'S NOT STEEL. I DON'T KNOW WHAT KIND OF METAL IT MIGHT BE. IT'S LIGHT.

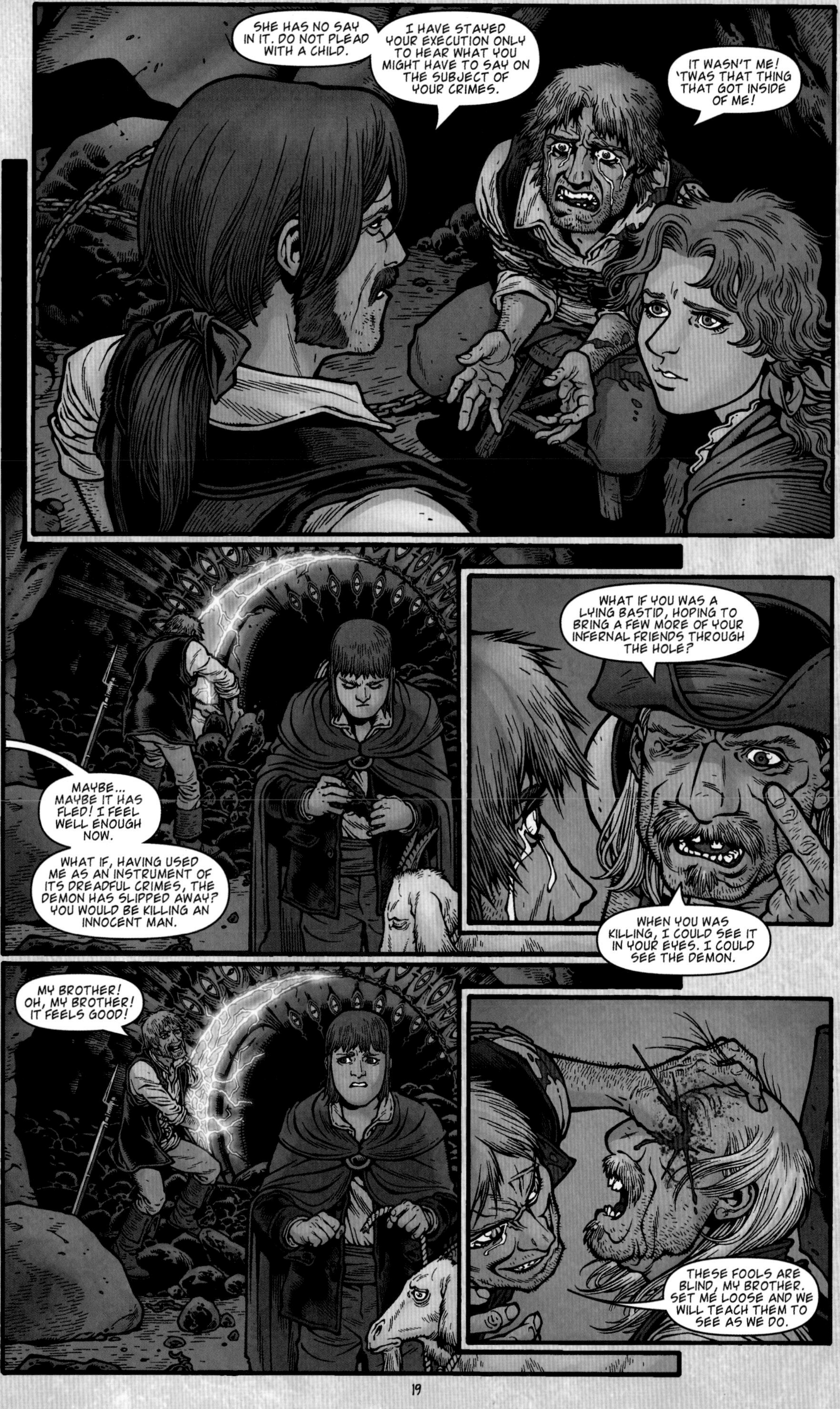
SHE HAS NO SAY IN IT. DO NOT PLEAD WITH A CHILD.
I HAVE STAYED YOUR EXECUTION ONLY TO HEAR WHAT YOU MIGHT HAVE TO SAY ON THE SUBJECT OF YOUR CRIMES.
IT WASN'T ME! 'TWAS THAT THING THAT GOT INSIDE OF ME!
MAYBE... MAYBE IT HAS FLED! I FEEL WELL ENOUGH NOW.
WHAT IF, HAVING USED ME AS AN INSTRUMENT OF ITS DREADFUL CRIMES, THE DEMON HAS SLIPPED AWAY? YOU WOULD BE KILLING AN INNOCENT MAN.
WHAT IF YOU WAS A LYING BASTID, HOPING TO BRING A FEW MORE OF YOUR INFERNAL FRIENDS THROUGH THE HOLE?
WHEN YOU WAS KILLING, I COULD SEE IT IN YOUR EYES. I COULD SEE THE DEMON.
MY BROTHER! OH, MY BROTHER! IT FEELS GOOD!
THESE FOOLS ARE BLIND, MY BROTHER. SET ME LOOSE AND WE WILL TEACH THEM TO SEE AS WE DO.

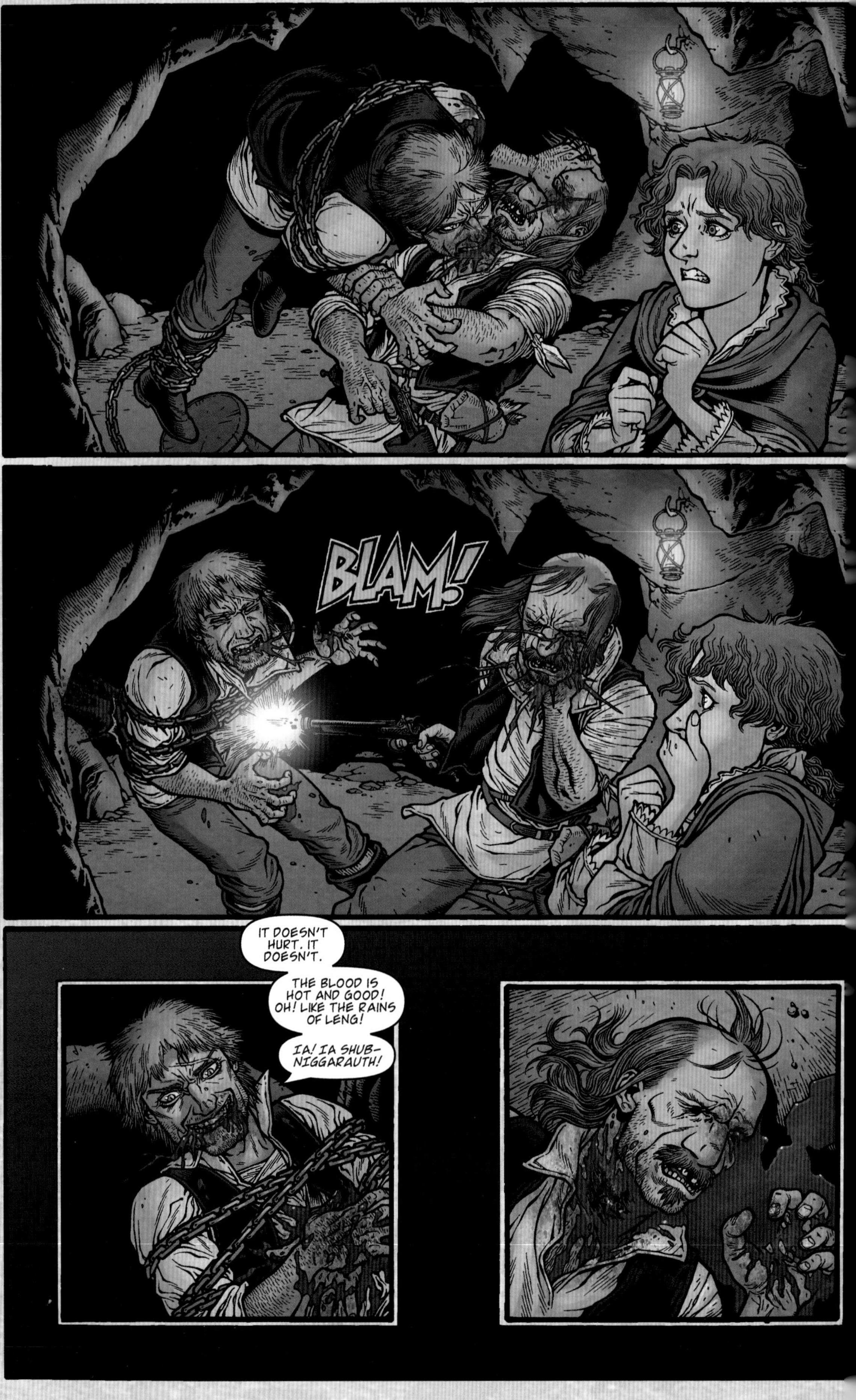

BLAM!
IT DOESN'T HURT. IT DOESN'T.
THE BLOOD IS HOT AND GOOD! OH! LIKE THE RAINS OF LENG!
IA! IA SHUB-NIGGARAUTH!

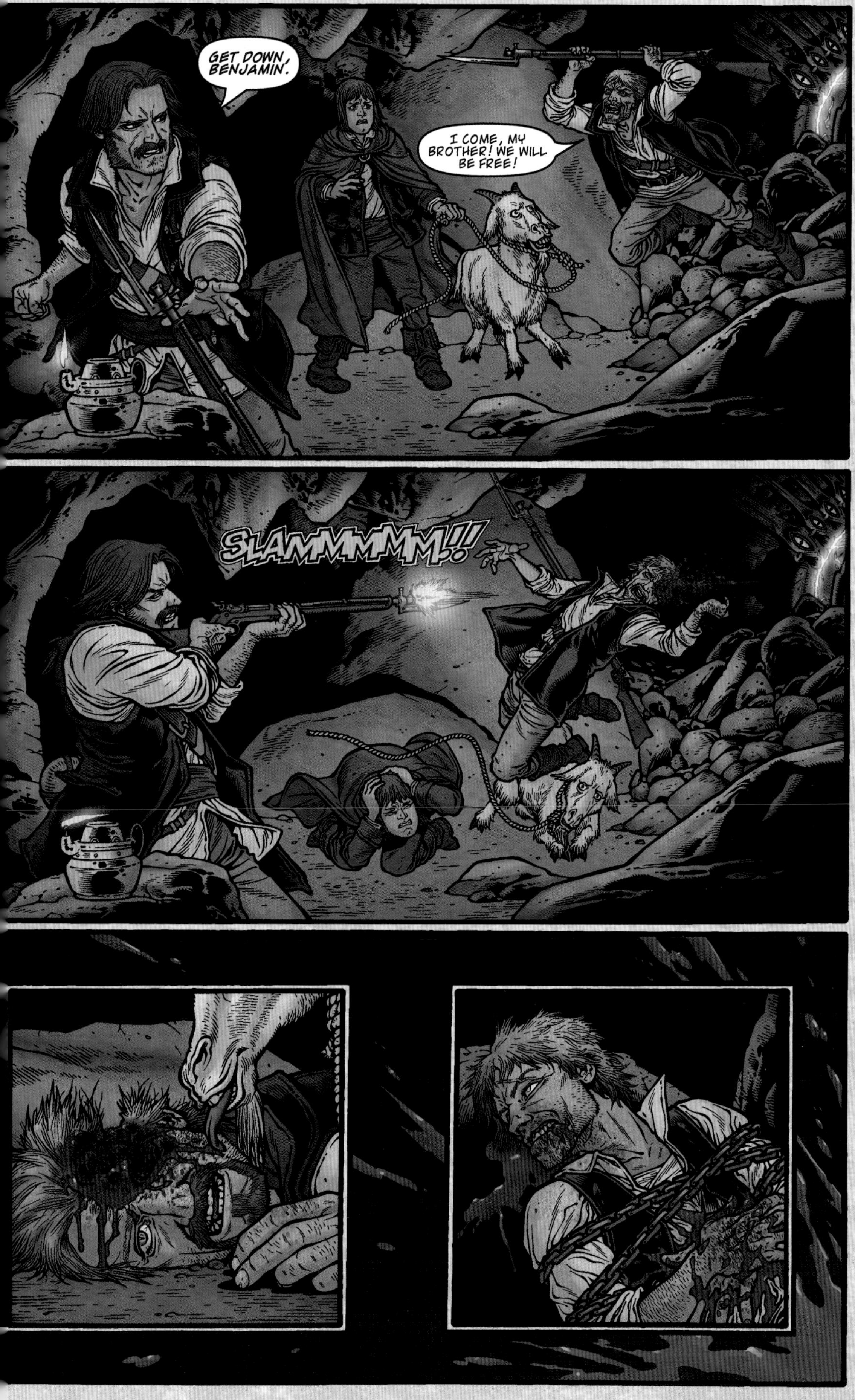
GET DOWN, BENJAMIN!
I COME, MY BROTHER! WE WILL BE FREE!
SLAMMMMMM!!

COVER THAT DOOR WITH STONES, BOY. AND FOR GOD'S SAKE, DON'T LOOK THROUGH IT WHILE YOU'RE DOING IT.

WE HAVE TO GET OUT OF THIS PLACE.

YES. ALL OF US. NOW.

THERE. I'VE PUSHED THE DOOR SHUT.

THESE STONES AREN'T DOING A DAMNED THING TO KEEP IT CLOSED.

NO? I'M SURE 20,000 TONS OF SEA WATER WILL DO THE TRICK.

IF YOU FLOOD THE CAVE, THERE'S NO PLACE FOR YOUR MEN TO HIDE. THE BRITISH WILL KILL EVERY ONE OF YOU.

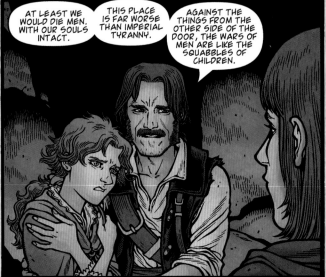

AT LEAST WE WOULD DIE MEN. WITH OUR SOULS INTACT.

THIS PLACE IS FAR WORSE THAN IMPERIAL TYRANNY.

AGAINST THE THINGS FROM THE OTHER SIDE OF THE DOOR, THE WARS OF MEN ARE LIKE THE SQUABBLES OF CHILDREN.

22

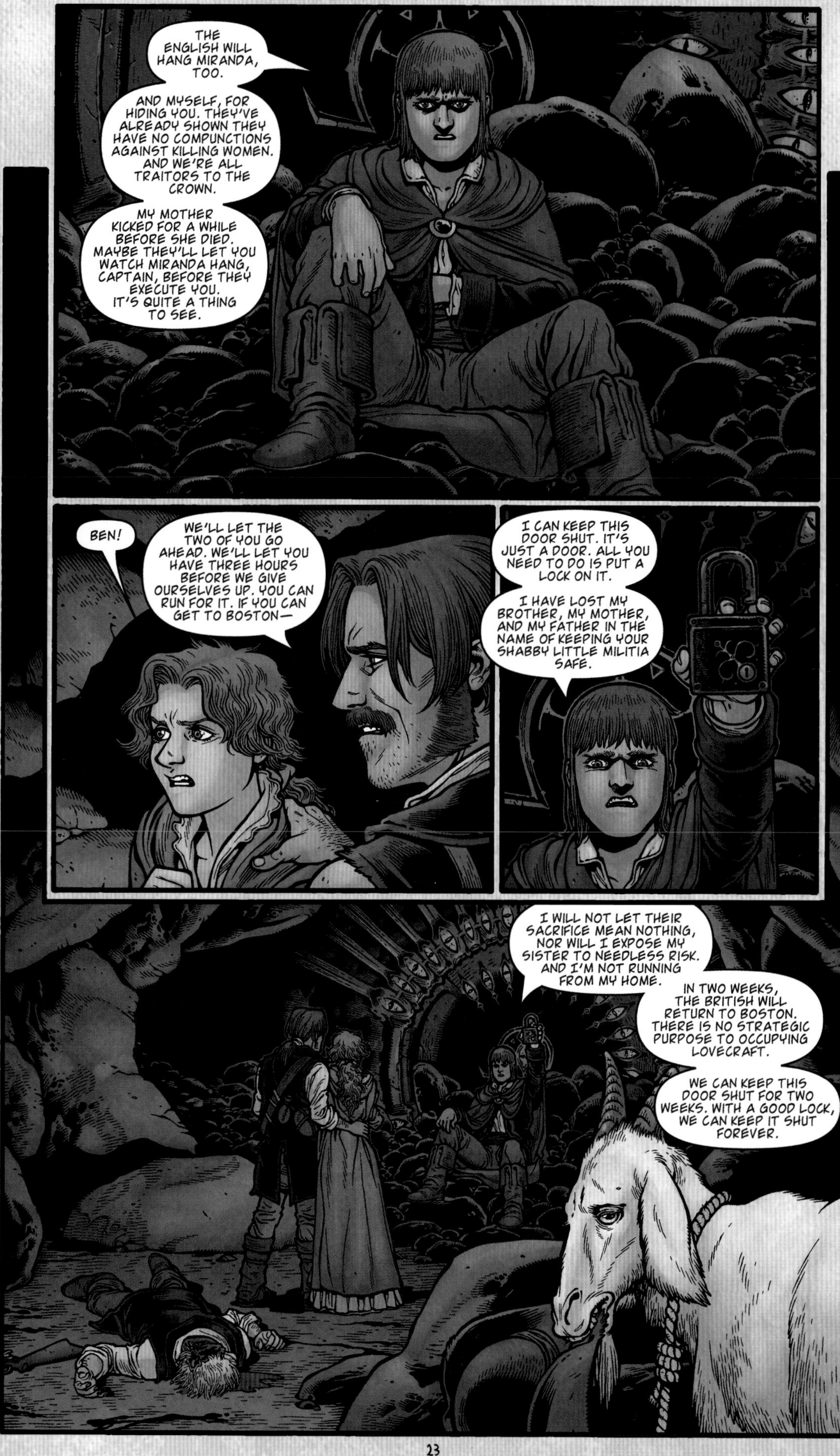
THE ENGLISH WILL HANG MIRANDA, TOO.
AND MYSELF, FOR HIDING YOU. THEY'VE ALREADY SHOWN THEY HAVE NO COMPUNCTIONS AGAINST KILLING WOMEN. AND WE'RE ALL TRAITORS TO THE CROWN.
MY MOTHER KICKED FOR A WHILE BEFORE SHE DIED. MAYBE THEY'LL LET YOU WATCH MIRANDA HANG, CAPTAIN, BEFORE THEY EXECUTE YOU. IT'S QUITE A THING TO SEE.
BEN!
WE'LL LET THE TWO OF YOU GO AHEAD. WE'LL LET YOU HAVE THREE HOURS BEFORE WE GIVE OURSELVES UP. YOU CAN RUN FOR IT. IF YOU CAN GET TO BOSTON—
I CAN KEEP THIS DOOR SHUT. IT'S JUST A DOOR. ALL YOU NEED TO DO IS PUT A LOCK ON IT.
I HAVE LOST MY BROTHER, MY MOTHER, AND MY FATHER IN THE NAME OF KEEPING YOUR SHABBY LITTLE MILITIA SAFE.
I WILL NOT LET THEIR SACRIFICE MEAN NOTHING, NOR WILL I EXPOSE MY SISTER TO NEEDLESS RISK. AND I'M NOT RUNNING FROM MY HOME.
IN TWO WEEKS, THE BRITISH WILL RETURN TO BOSTON. THERE IS NO STRATEGIC PURPOSE TO OCCUPYING LOVECRAFT.
WE CAN KEEP THIS DOOR SHUT FOR TWO WEEKS. WITH A GOOD LOCK, WE CAN KEEP IT SHUT FOREVER.

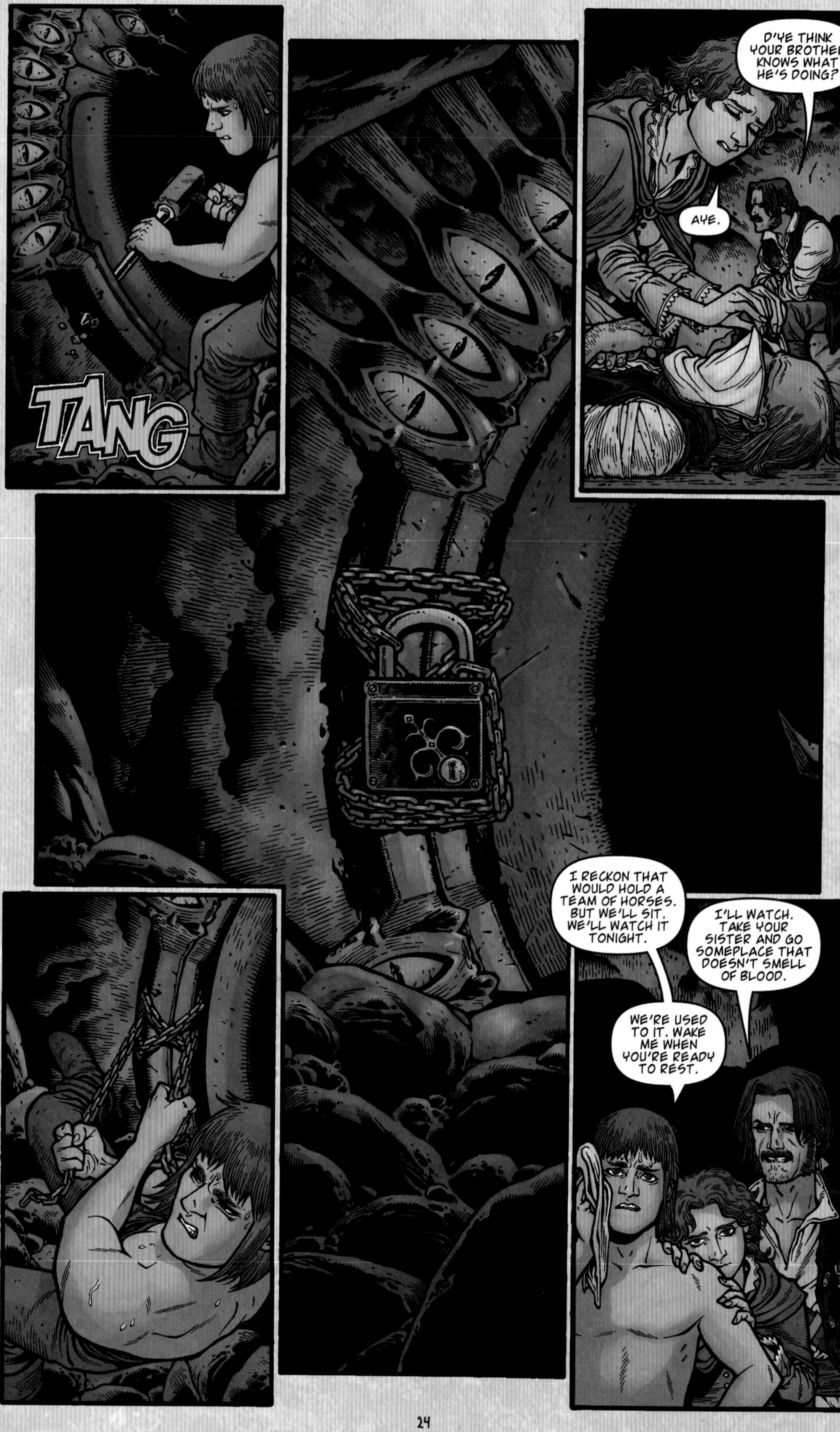
TANG
D'YE THINK YOUR BROTHER KNOWS WHAT HE'S DOING?
AYE.
I RECKON THAT WOULD HOLD A TEAM OF HORSES. BUT WE'LL SIT. WE'LL WATCH IT TONIGHT.
I'LL WATCH. TAKE YOUR SISTER AND GO SOMEPLACE THAT DOESN'T SMELL OF BLOOD.
WE'RE USED TO IT. WAKE ME WHEN YOU'RE READY TO REST.

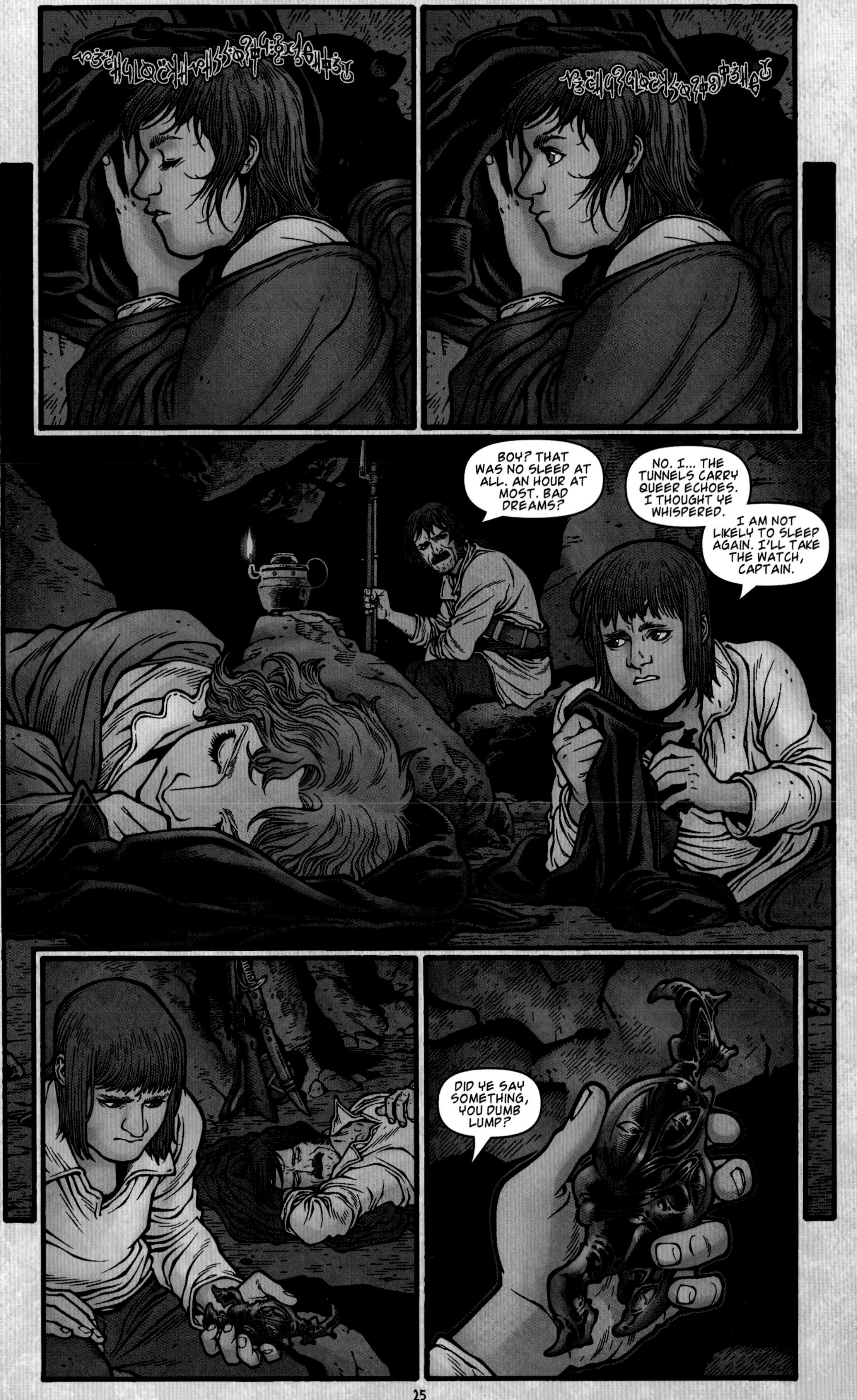
BOY? THAT WAS NO SLEEP AT ALL. AN HOUR AT MOST. BAD DREAMS?
NO. I... THE TUNNELS CARRY QUEER ECHOES. I THOUGHT YE WHISPERED.
I AM NOT LIKELY TO SLEEP AGAIN. I'LL TAKE THE WATCH, CAPTAIN.
DID YE SAY SOMETHING, YOU DUMB LUMP?

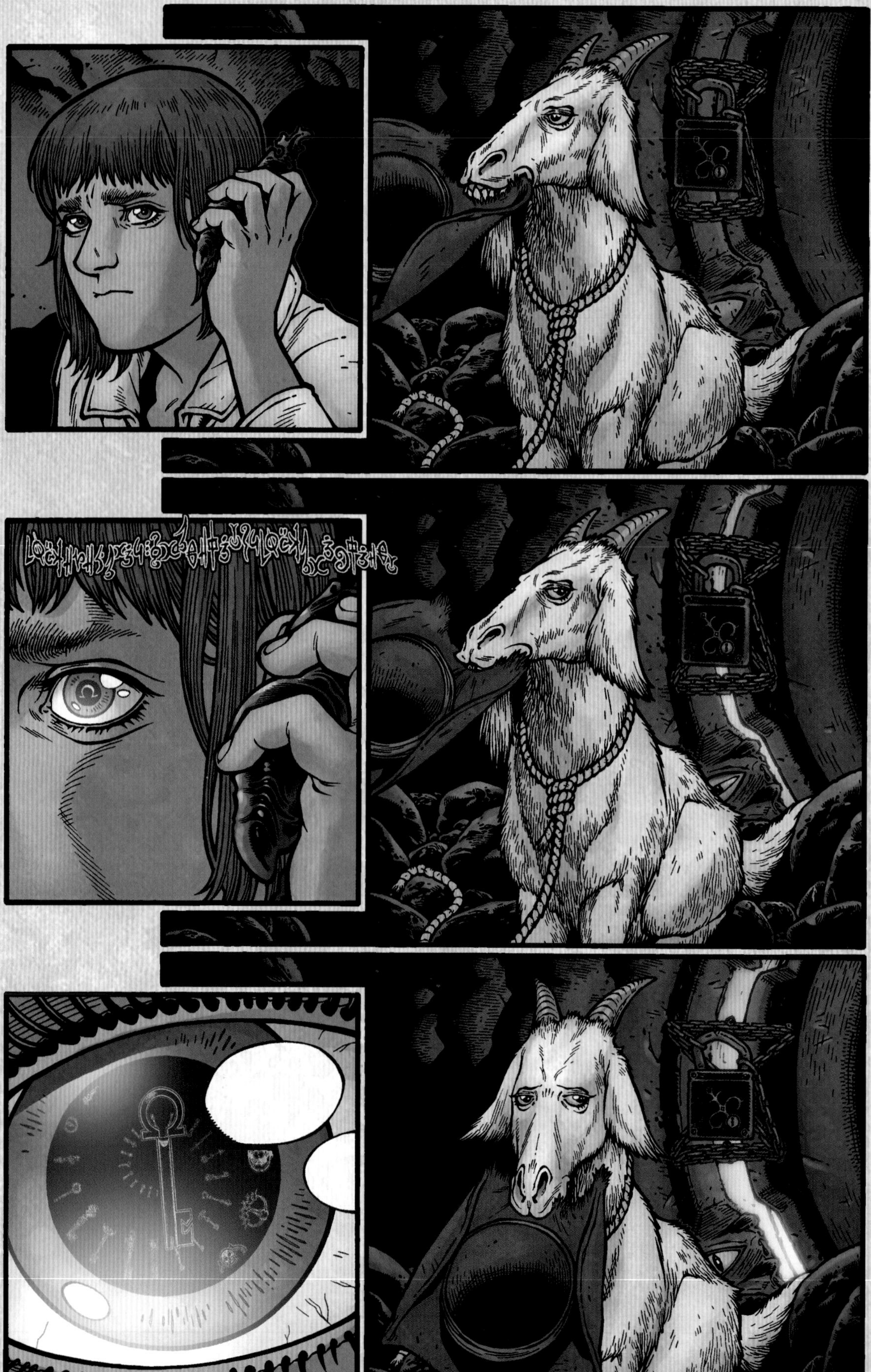

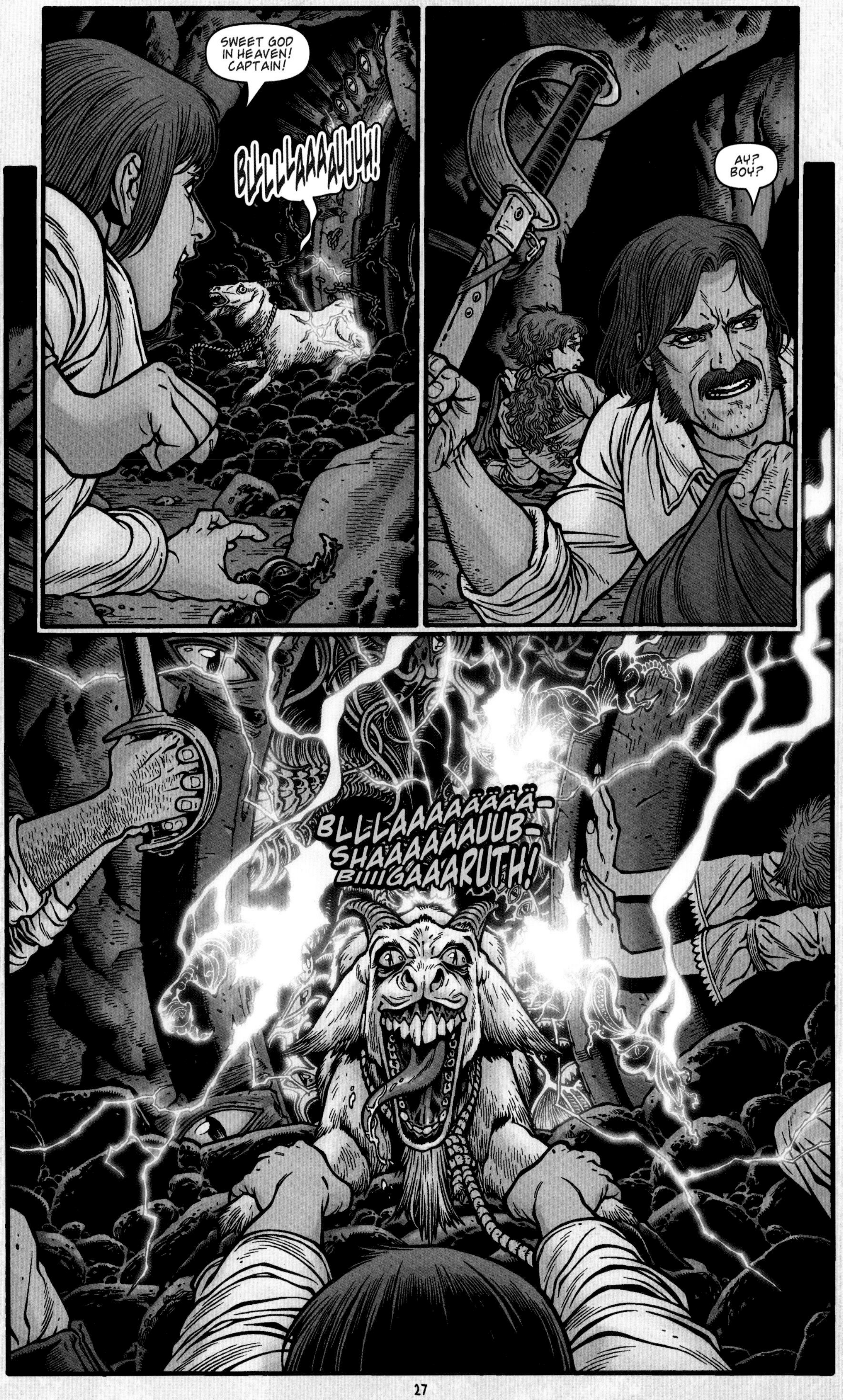
SWEET GOD IN HEAVEN! CAPTAIN!
BLLLLAAAAUUH!
AY? BOY?
BLLLAAAAAAAÄ-SHAAAAAAAUUB-BIIIIGAAARUTH!

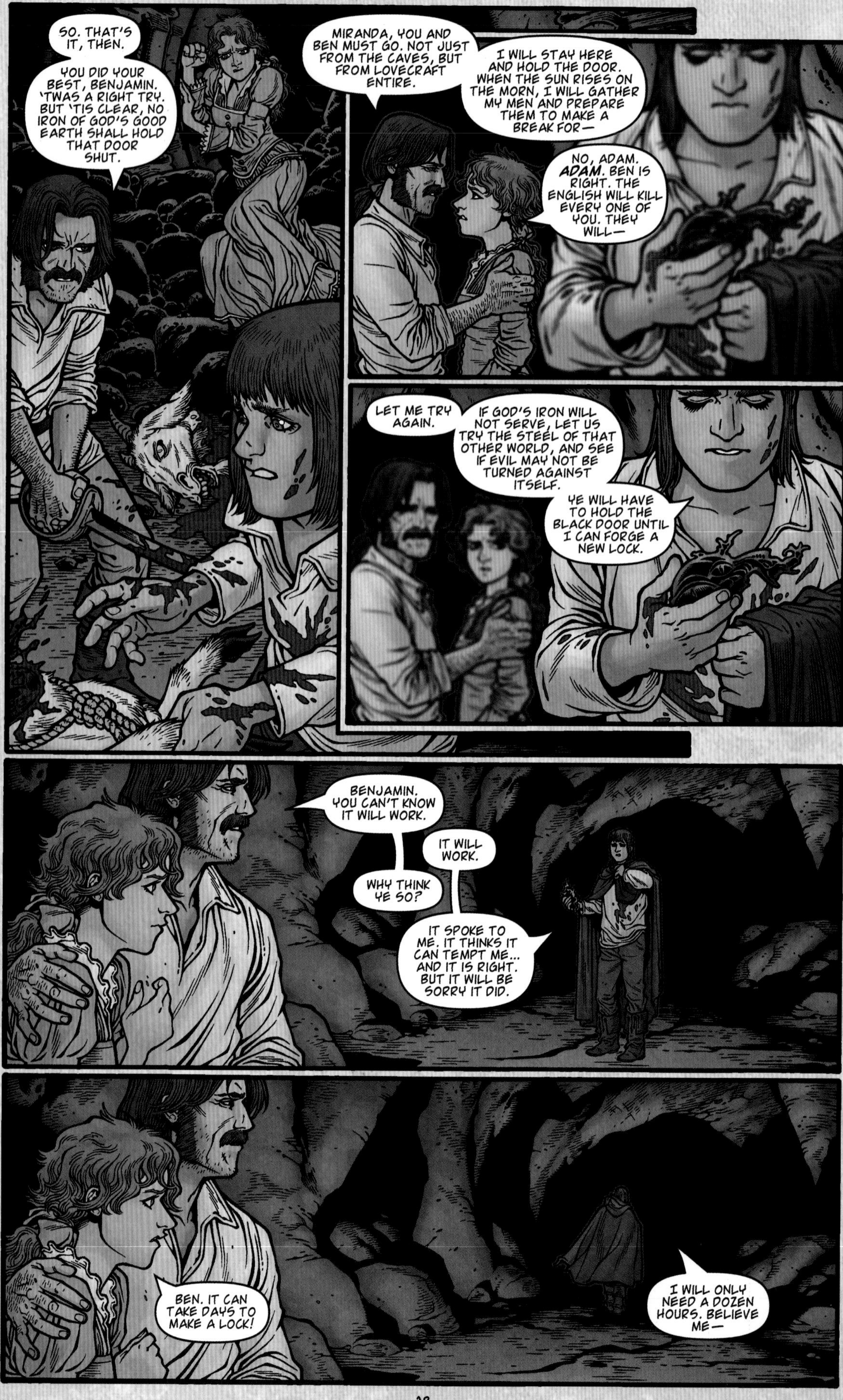
SO. THAT'S IT, THEN.
YOU DID YOUR BEST, BENJAMIN. 'TWAS A RIGHT TRY. BUT 'TIS CLEAR, NO IRON OF GOD'S GOOD EARTH SHALL HOLD THAT DOOR SHUT.
MIRANDA, YOU AND BEN MUST GO. NOT JUST FROM THE CAVES, BUT FROM LOVECRAFT ENTIRE.
I WILL STAY HERE AND HOLD THE DOOR. WHEN THE SUN RISES ON THE MORN, I WILL GATHER MY MEN AND PREPARE THEM TO MAKE A BREAK FOR—
NO, ADAM. ADAM. BEN IS RIGHT. THE ENGLISH WILL KILL EVERY ONE OF YOU. THEY WILL—
LET ME TRY AGAIN.
IF GOD'S IRON WILL NOT SERVE, LET US TRY THE STEEL OF THAT OTHER WORLD, AND SEE IF EVIL MAY NOT BE TURNED AGAINST ITSELF.
YE WILL HAVE TO HOLD THE BLACK DOOR UNTIL I CAN FORGE A NEW LOCK.
BENJAMIN. YOU CAN'T KNOW IT WILL WORK.
IT WILL WORK.
WHY THINK YE SO?
IT SPOKE TO ME. IT THINKS IT CAN TEMPT ME... AND IT IS RIGHT. BUT IT WILL BE SORRY IT DID.
BEN. IT CAN TAKE DAYS TO MAKE A LOCK!
I WILL ONLY NEED A DOZEN HOURS. BELIEVE ME—

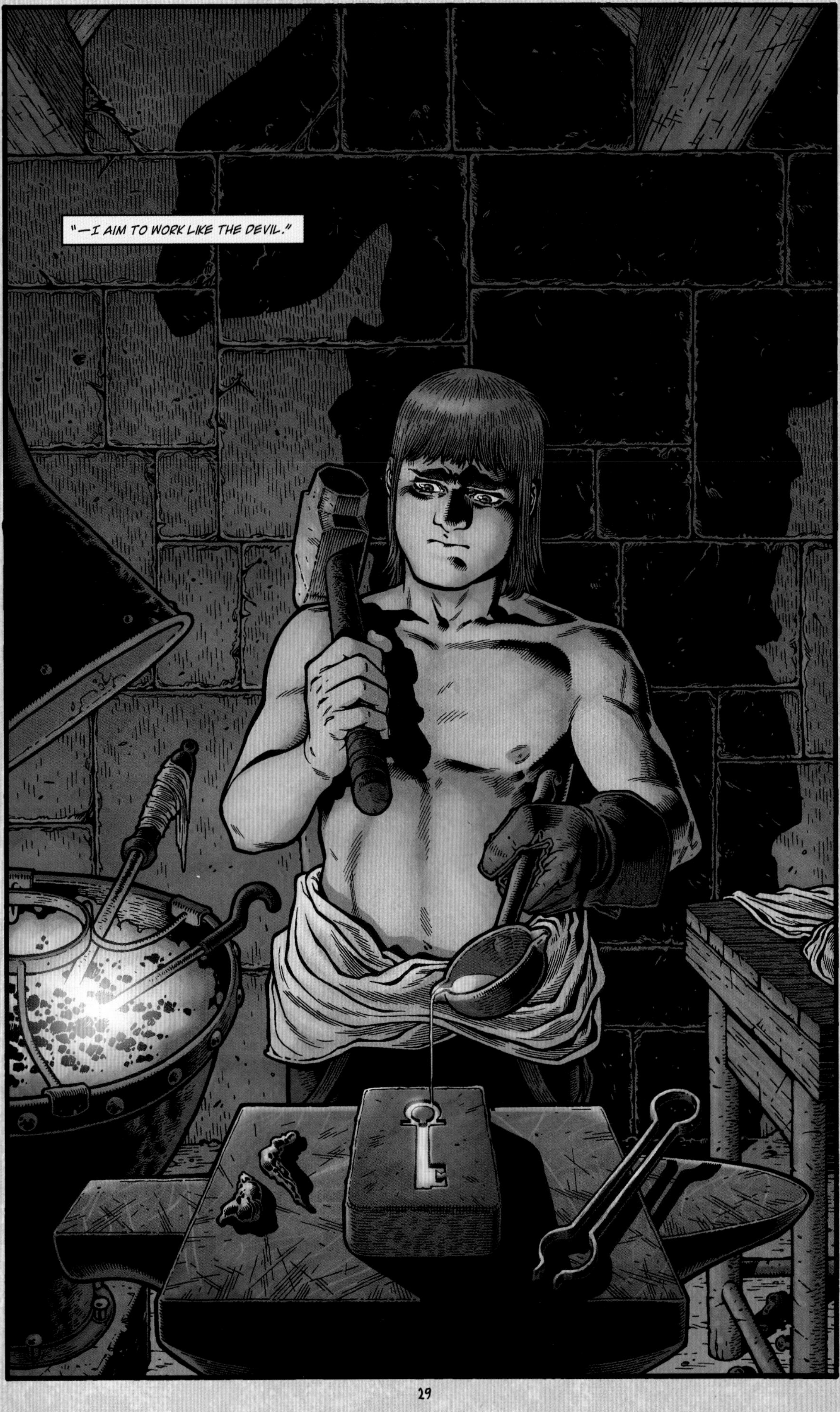
"—I AIM TO WORK LIKE THE DEVIL."

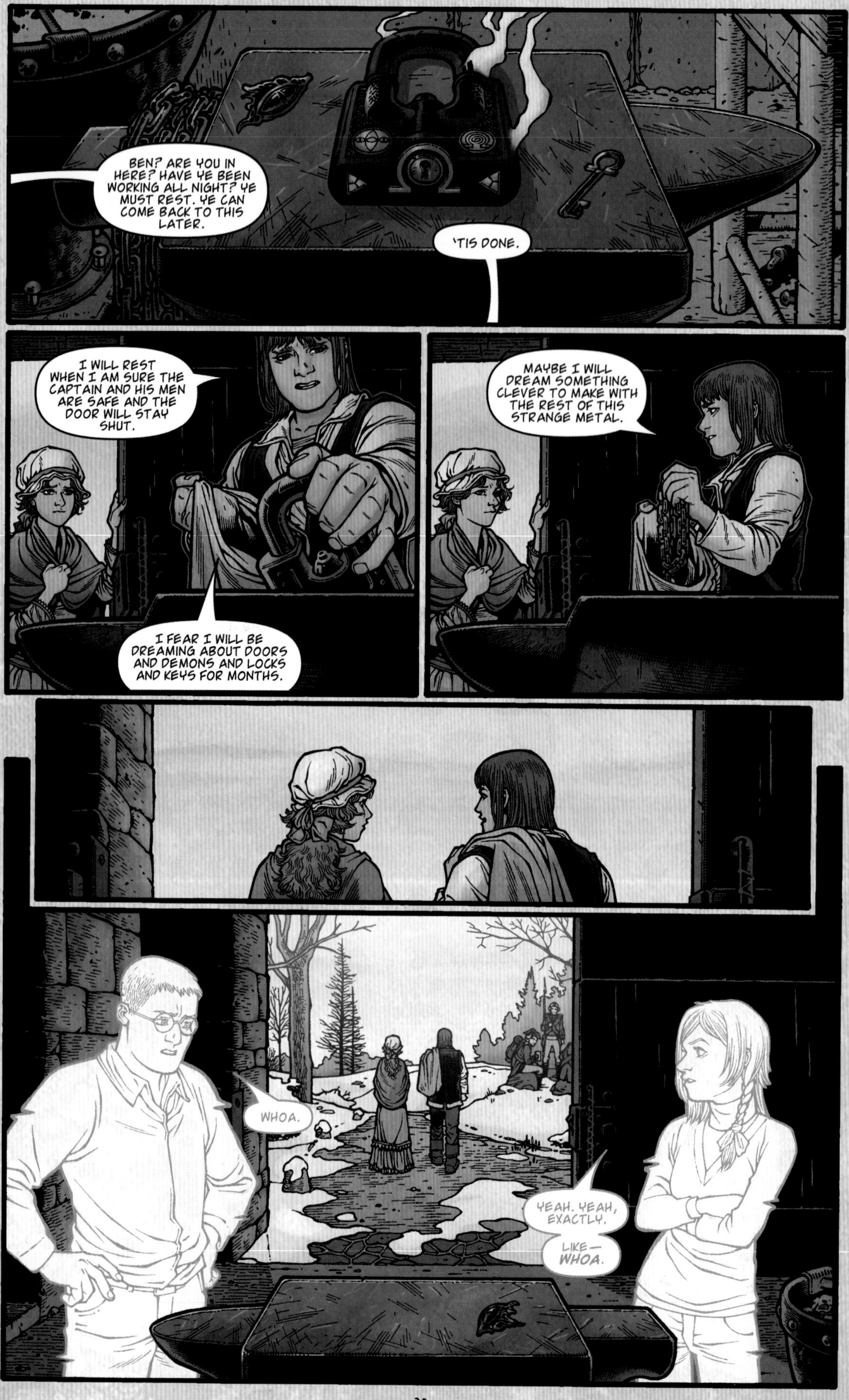

BEN? ARE YOU IN HERE? HAVE YE BEEN WORKING ALL NIGHT? YE MUST REST. YE CAN COME BACK TO THIS LATER.
'TIS DONE.
I WILL REST WHEN I AM SURE THE CAPTAIN AND HIS MEN ARE SAFE AND THE DOOR WILL STAY SHUT.
I FEAR I WILL BE DREAMING ABOUT DOORS AND DEMONS AND LOCKS AND KEYS FOR MONTHS.
MAYBE I WILL DREAM SOMETHING CLEVER TO MAKE WITH THE REST OF THIS STRANGE METAL.
WHOA.
YEAH. YEAH, EXACTLY.
LIKE— WHOA.

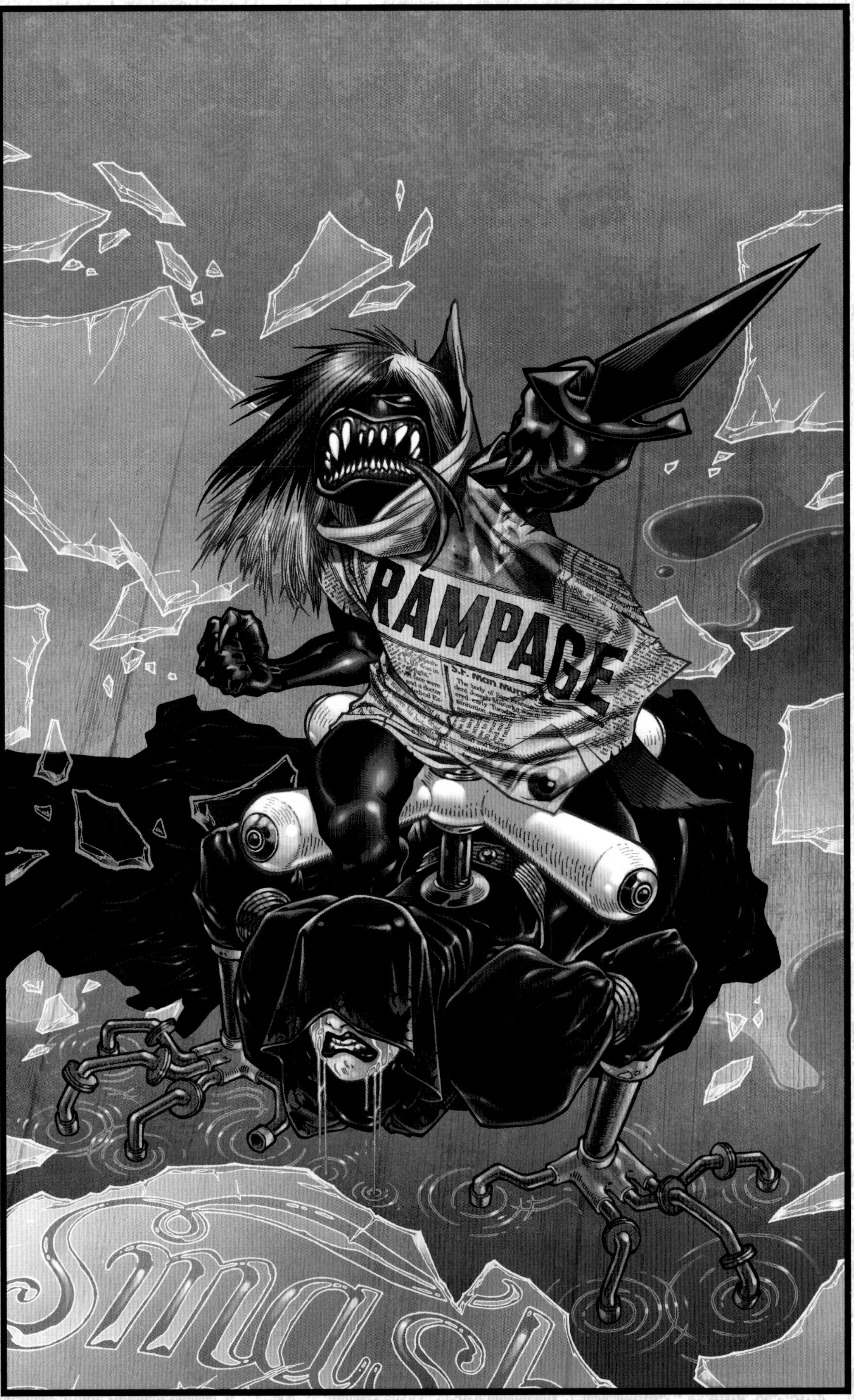
RAMPAGE
Smash

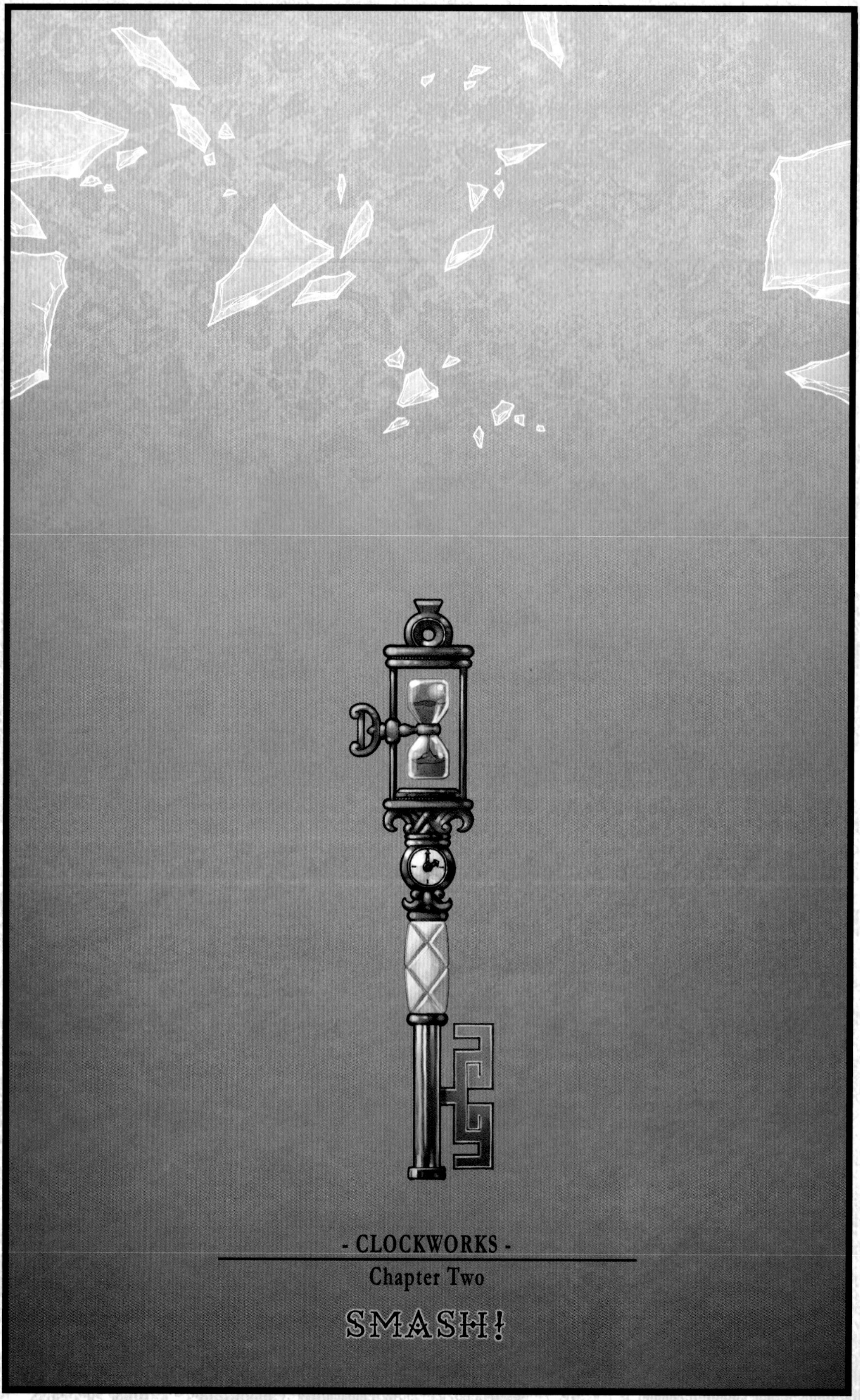

- CLOCKWORKS -

Chapter Two

SMASH!

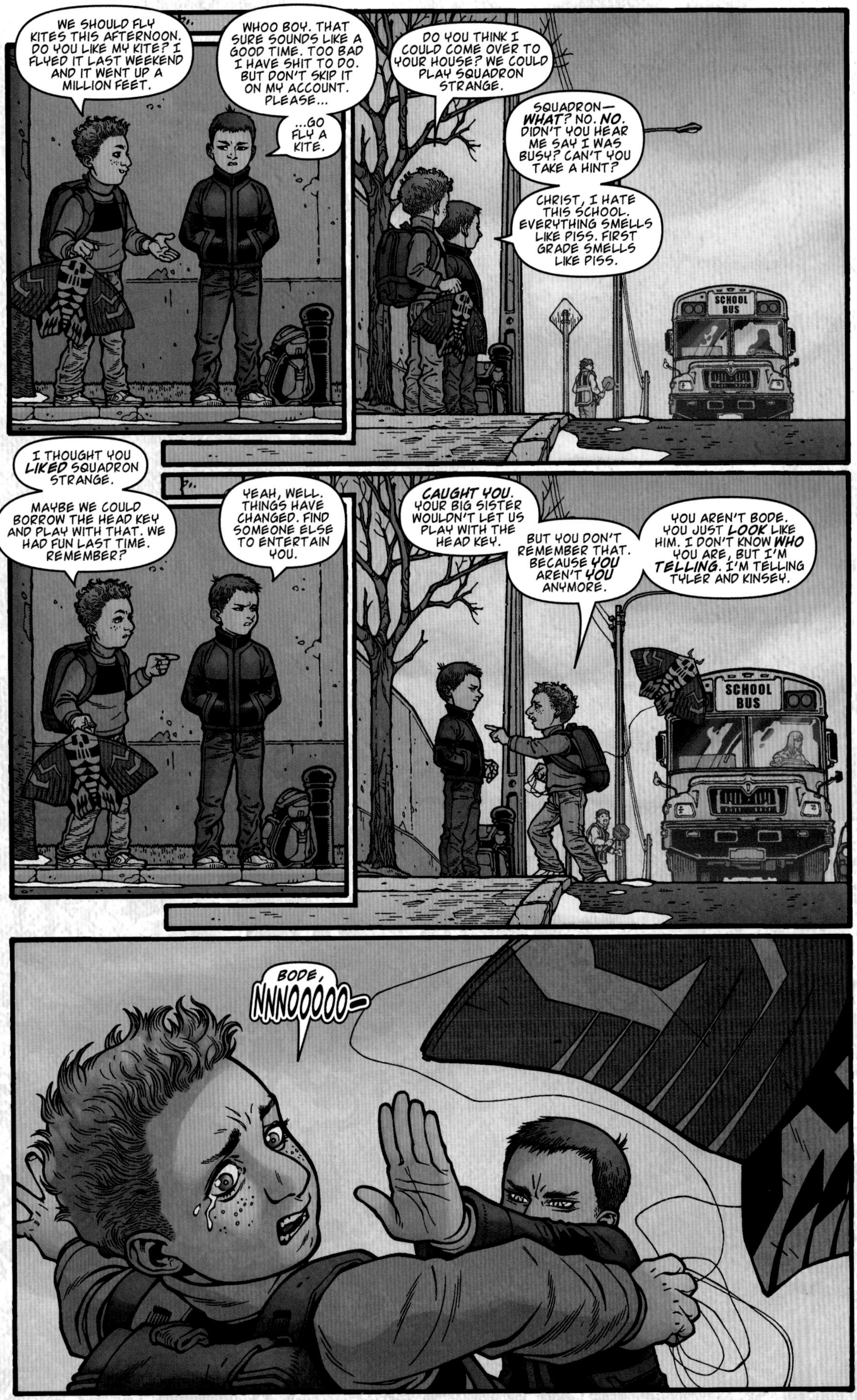

WE SHOULD FLY KITES THIS AFTERNOON. DO YOU LIKE MY KITE? I FLYED IT LAST WEEKEND AND IT WENT UP A MILLION FEET.
WHOO BOY. THAT SURE SOUNDS LIKE A GOOD TIME. TOO BAD I HAVE SHIT TO DO. BUT DON'T SKIP IT ON MY ACCOUNT. PLEASE...
...GO FLY A KITE.
DO YOU THINK I COULD COME OVER TO YOUR HOUSE? WE COULD PLAY SQUADRON STRANGE.
SQUADRON—WHAT? NO. NO. DIDN'T YOU HEAR ME SAY I WAS BUSY? CAN'T YOU TAKE A HINT?
CHRIST, I HATE THIS SCHOOL. EVERYTHING SMELLS LIKE PISS. FIRST GRADE SMELLS LIKE PISS.
SCHOOL BUS
I THOUGHT YOU LIKED SQUADRON STRANGE.
MAYBE WE COULD BORROW THE HEAD KEY AND PLAY WITH THAT. WE HAD FUN LAST TIME. REMEMBER?
YEAH, WELL. THINGS HAVE CHANGED. FIND SOMEONE ELSE TO ENTERTAIN YOU.
CAUGHT YOU. YOUR BIG SISTER WOULDN'T LET US PLAY WITH THE HEAD KEY.
BUT YOU DON'T REMEMBER THAT. BECAUSE YOU AREN'T YOU ANYMORE.
YOU AREN'T BODE. YOU JUST LOOK LIKE HIM. I DON'T KNOW WHO YOU ARE, BUT I'M TELLING. I'M TELLING TYLER AND KINSEY.
SCHOOL BUS
BODE, NNNOOOOO-

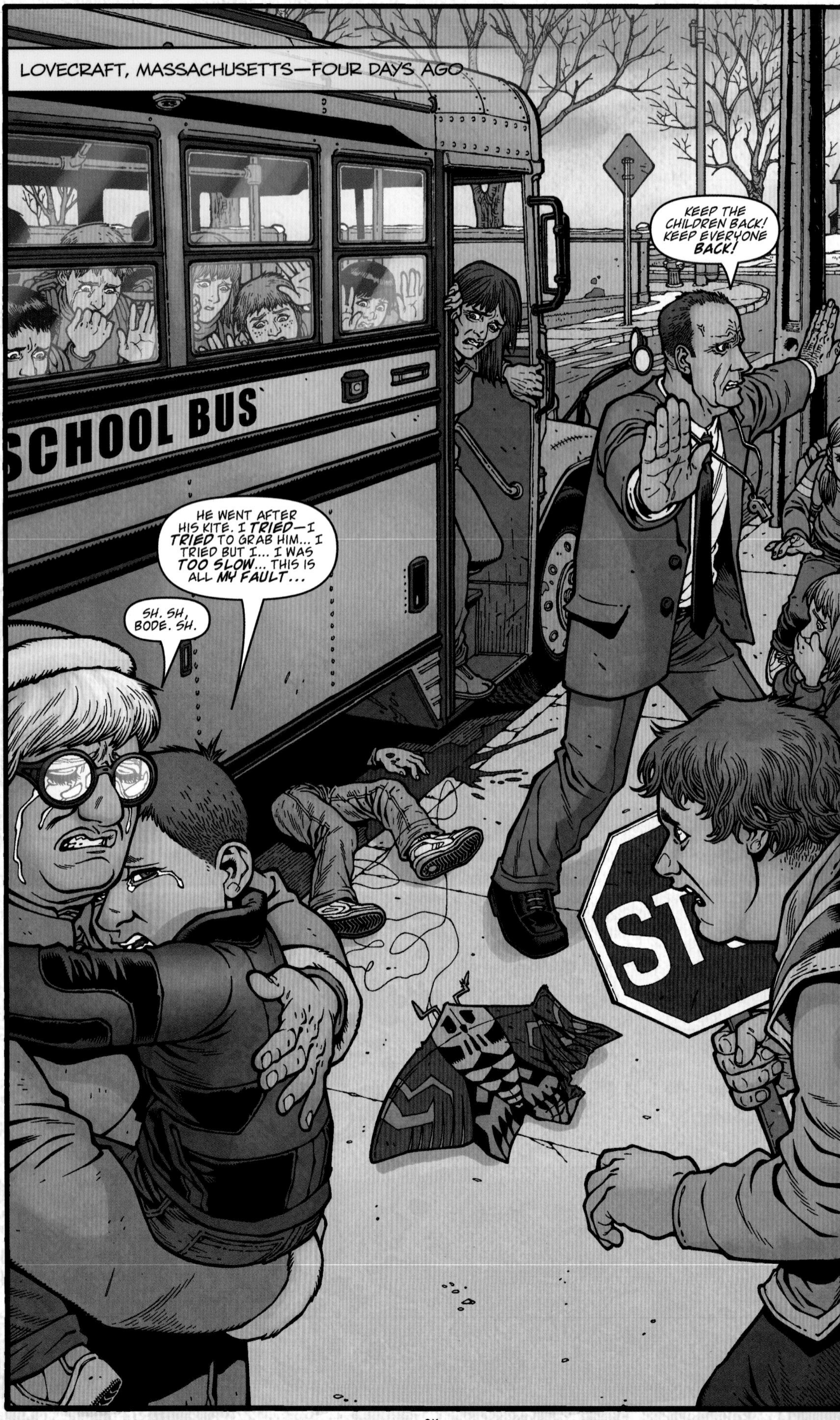
LOVECRAFT, MASSACHUSETTS—FOUR DAYS AGO
KEEP THE CHILDREN BACK! KEEP EVERYONE BACK!
SCHOOL BUS
HE WENT AFTER HIS KITE. I TRIED—I TRIED TO GRAB HIM... I TRIED BUT I... I WAS TOO SLOW... THIS IS ALL MY FAULT...
SH. SH, BODE. SH.
ST

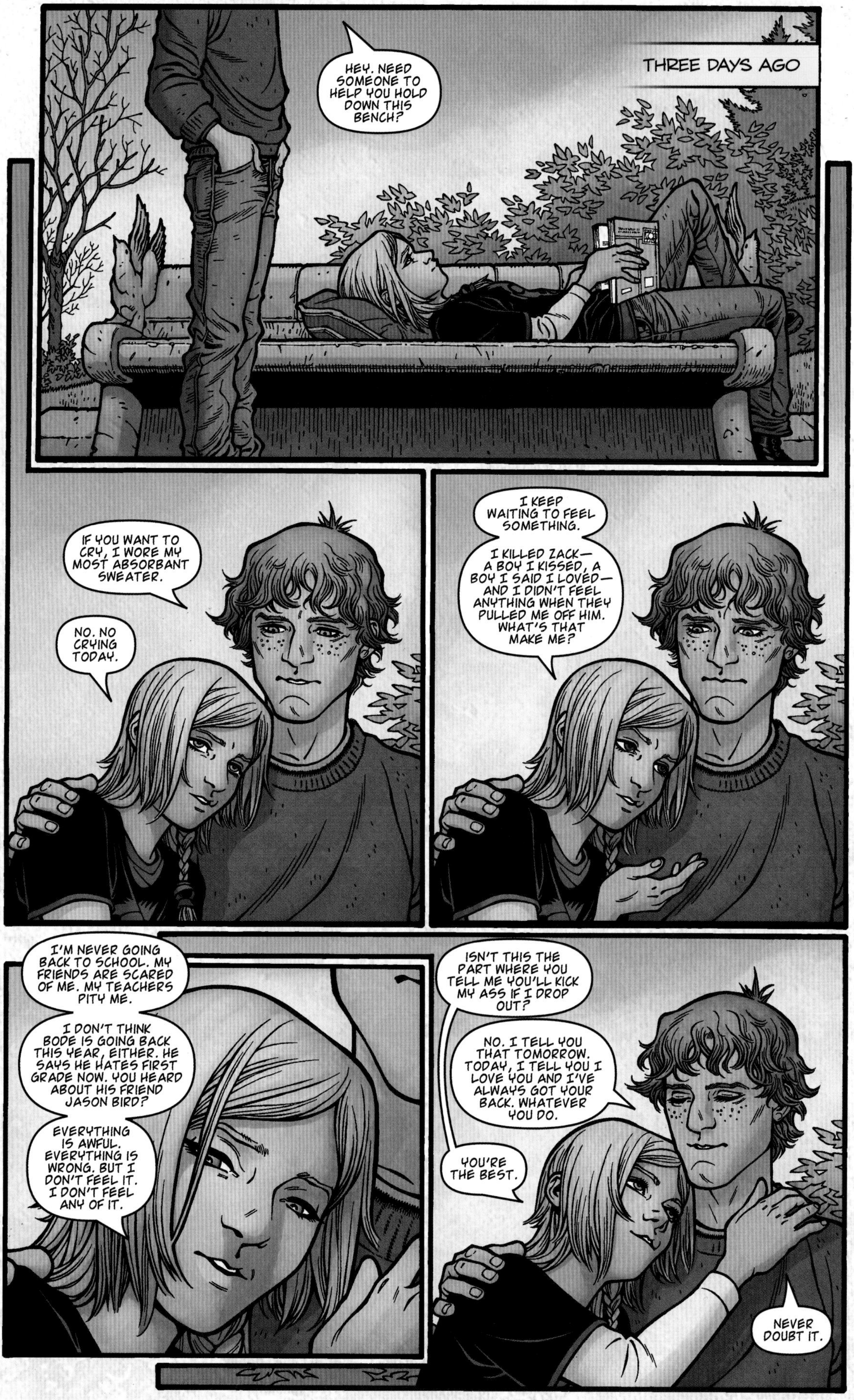
THREE DAYS AGO
HEY. NEED SOMEONE TO HELP YOU HOLD DOWN THIS BENCH?
IF YOU WANT TO CRY, I WORE MY MOST ABSORBANT SWEATER.
NO. NO CRYING TODAY.
I KEEP WAITING TO FEEL SOMETHING.
I KILLED ZACK— A BOY I KISSED, A BOY I SAID I LOVED— AND I DIDN'T FEEL ANYTHING WHEN THEY PULLED ME OFF HIM. WHAT'S THAT MAKE ME?
I'M NEVER GOING BACK TO SCHOOL. MY FRIENDS ARE SCARED OF ME. MY TEACHERS PITY ME.
I DON'T THINK BODE IS GOING BACK THIS YEAR, EITHER. HE SAYS HE HATES FIRST GRADE NOW. YOU HEARD ABOUT HIS FRIEND JASON BIRD?
EVERYTHING IS AWFUL. EVERYTHING IS WRONG. BUT I DON'T FEEL IT. I DON'T FEEL ANY OF IT.
ISN'T THIS THE PART WHERE YOU TELL ME YOU'LL KICK MY ASS IF I DROP OUT?
NO. I TELL YOU THAT TOMORROW. TODAY, I TELL YOU I LOVE YOU AND I'VE ALWAYS GOT YOUR BACK. WHATEVER YOU DO.
YOU'RE THE BEST.
NEVER DOUBT IT.

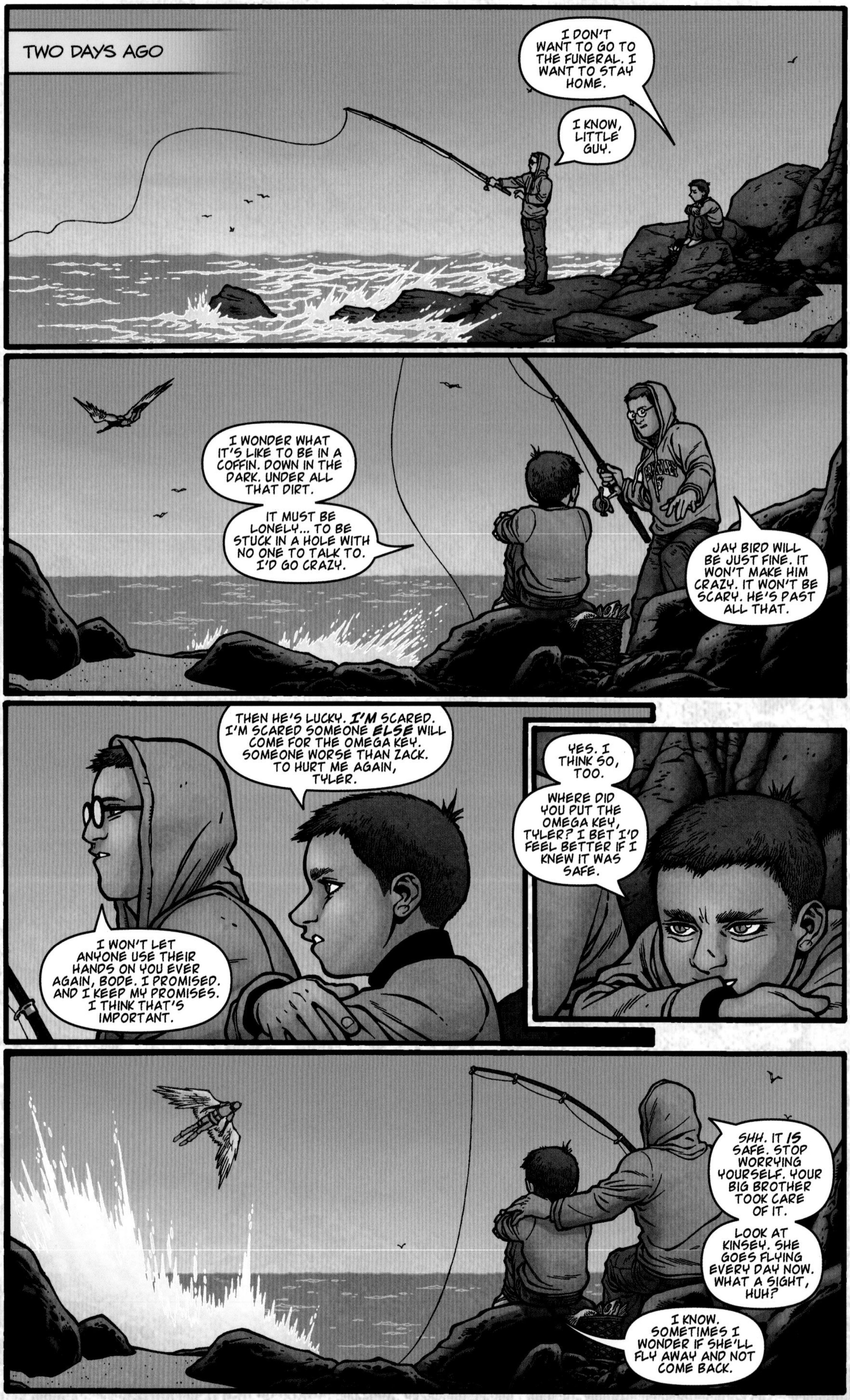
TWO DAYS AGO
I DON'T WANT TO GO TO THE FUNERAL. I WANT TO STAY HOME.
I KNOW, LITTLE GUY.
I WONDER WHAT IT'S LIKE TO BE IN A COFFIN. DOWN IN THE DARK. UNDER ALL THAT DIRT.
IT MUST BE LONELY... TO BE STUCK IN A HOLE WITH NO ONE TO TALK TO. I'D GO CRAZY.
JAY BIRD WILL BE JUST FINE. IT WON'T MAKE HIM CRAZY. IT WON'T BE SCARY. HE'S PAST ALL THAT.
THEN HE'S LUCKY. I'M SCARED. I'M SCARED SOMEONE ELSE WILL COME FOR THE OMEGA KEY. SOMEONE WORSE THAN ZACK. TO HURT ME AGAIN, TYLER.
I WON'T LET ANYONE USE THEIR HANDS ON YOU EVER AGAIN, BODE. I PROMISED. AND I KEEP MY PROMISES. I THINK THAT'S IMPORTANT.
YES. I THINK SO, TOO.
WHERE DID YOU PUT THE OMEGA KEY, TYLER? I BET I'D FEEL BETTER IF I KNEW IT WAS SAFE.
SHH. IT IS SAFE. STOP WORRYING YOURSELF. YOUR BIG BROTHER TOOK CARE OF IT.
LOOK AT KINSEY. SHE GOES FLYING EVERY DAY NOW. WHAT A SIGHT, HUH?
I KNOW. SOMETIMES I WONDER IF SHE'LL FLY AWAY AND NOT COME BACK.

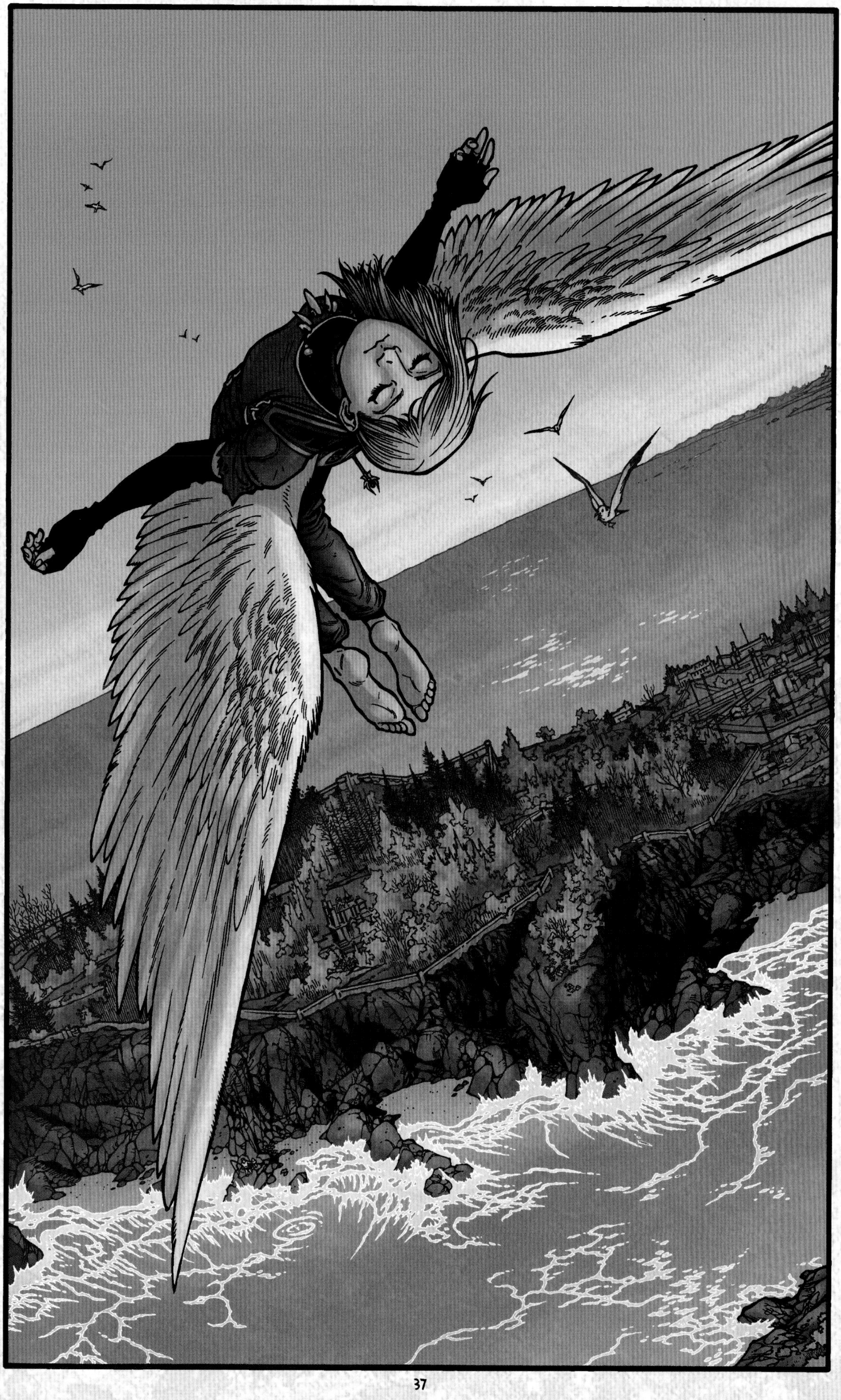

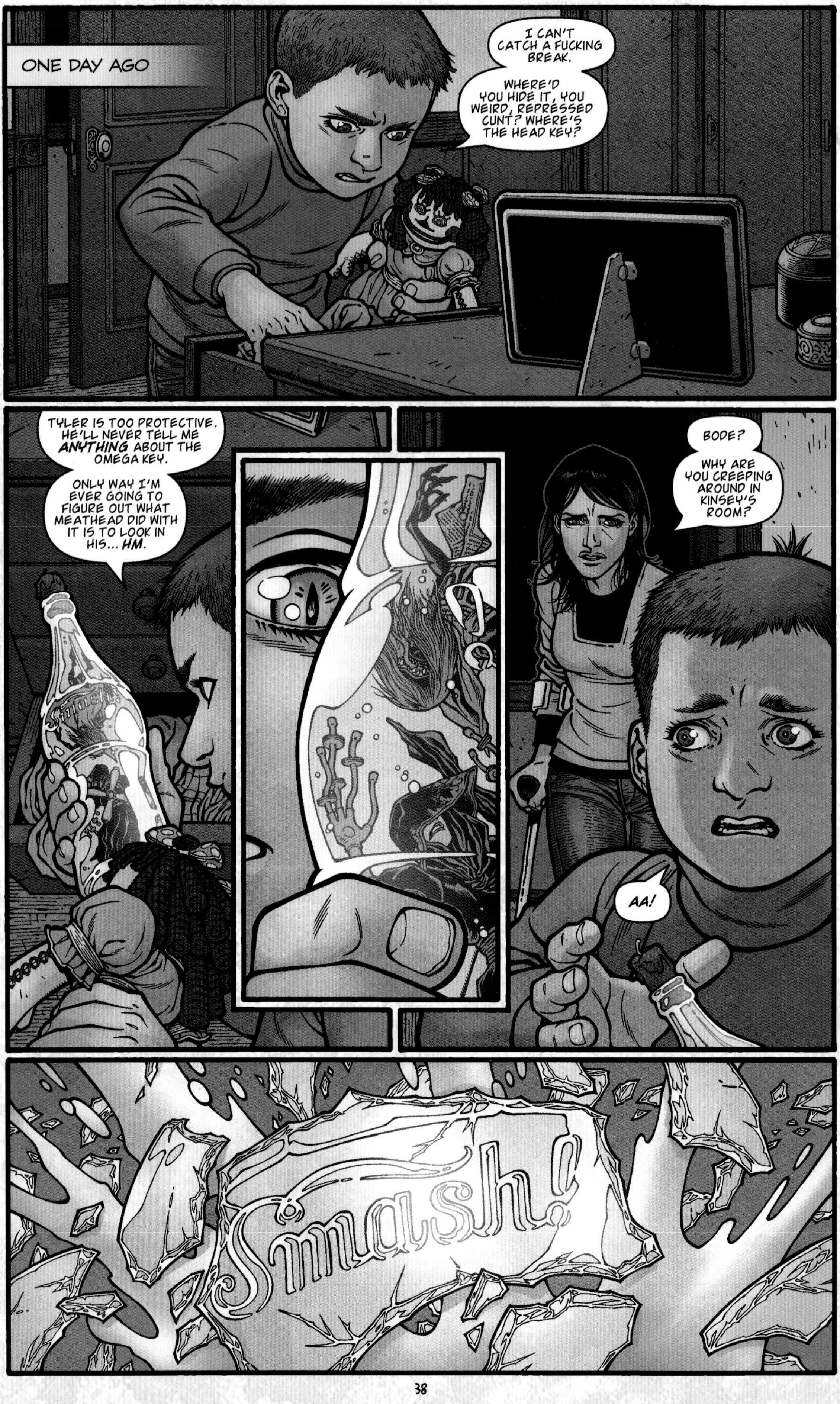
ONE DAY AGO
I CAN'T CATCH A FUCKING BREAK.
WHERE'D YOU HIDE IT, YOU WEIRD, REPRESSED CUNT? WHERE'S THE HEAD KEY?
TYLER IS TOO PROTECTIVE. HE'LL NEVER TELL ME ANYTHING ABOUT THE OMEGA KEY.
ONLY WAY I'M EVER GOING TO FIGURE OUT WHAT MEATHEAD DID WITH IT IS TO LOOK IN HIS... HM.
Smash!
BODE?
WHY ARE YOU CREEPING AROUND IN KINSEY'S ROOM?
AA!
Smash!

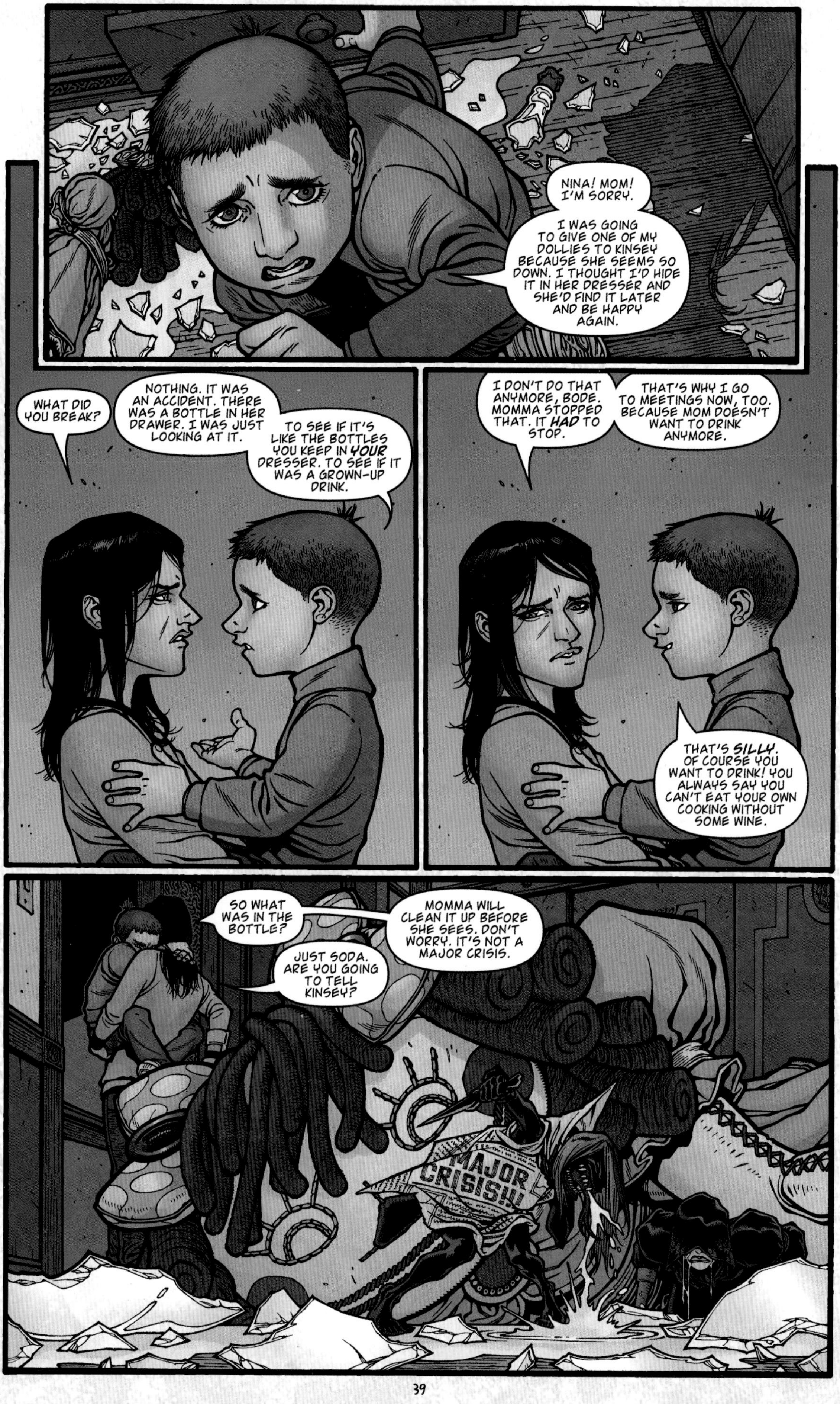

NINA! MOM! I'M SORRY.
I WAS GOING TO GIVE ONE OF MY DOLLIES TO KINSEY BECAUSE SHE SEEMS SO DOWN. I THOUGHT I'D HIDE IT IN HER DRESSER AND SHE'D FIND IT LATER AND BE HAPPY AGAIN.
WHAT DID YOU BREAK?
NOTHING. IT WAS AN ACCIDENT. THERE WAS A BOTTLE IN HER DRAWER. I WAS JUST LOOKING AT IT.
TO SEE IF IT'S LIKE THE BOTTLES YOU KEEP IN *YOUR* DRESSER. TO SEE IF IT WAS A GROWN-UP DRINK.
I DON'T DO THAT ANYMORE, BODE. MOMMA STOPPED THAT. IT *HAD* TO STOP.
THAT'S WHY I GO TO MEETINGS NOW, TOO. BECAUSE MOM DOESN'T WANT TO DRINK ANYMORE.
THAT'S *SILLY*. OF COURSE YOU WANT TO DRINK! YOU ALWAYS SAY YOU CAN'T EAT YOUR OWN COOKING WITHOUT SOME WINE.
SO WHAT WAS IN THE BOTTLE?
JUST SODA. ARE YOU GOING TO TELL KINSEY?
MOMMA WILL CLEAN IT UP BEFORE SHE SEES. DON'T WORRY. IT'S NOT A MAJOR CRISIS.
MAJOR CRISIS!!

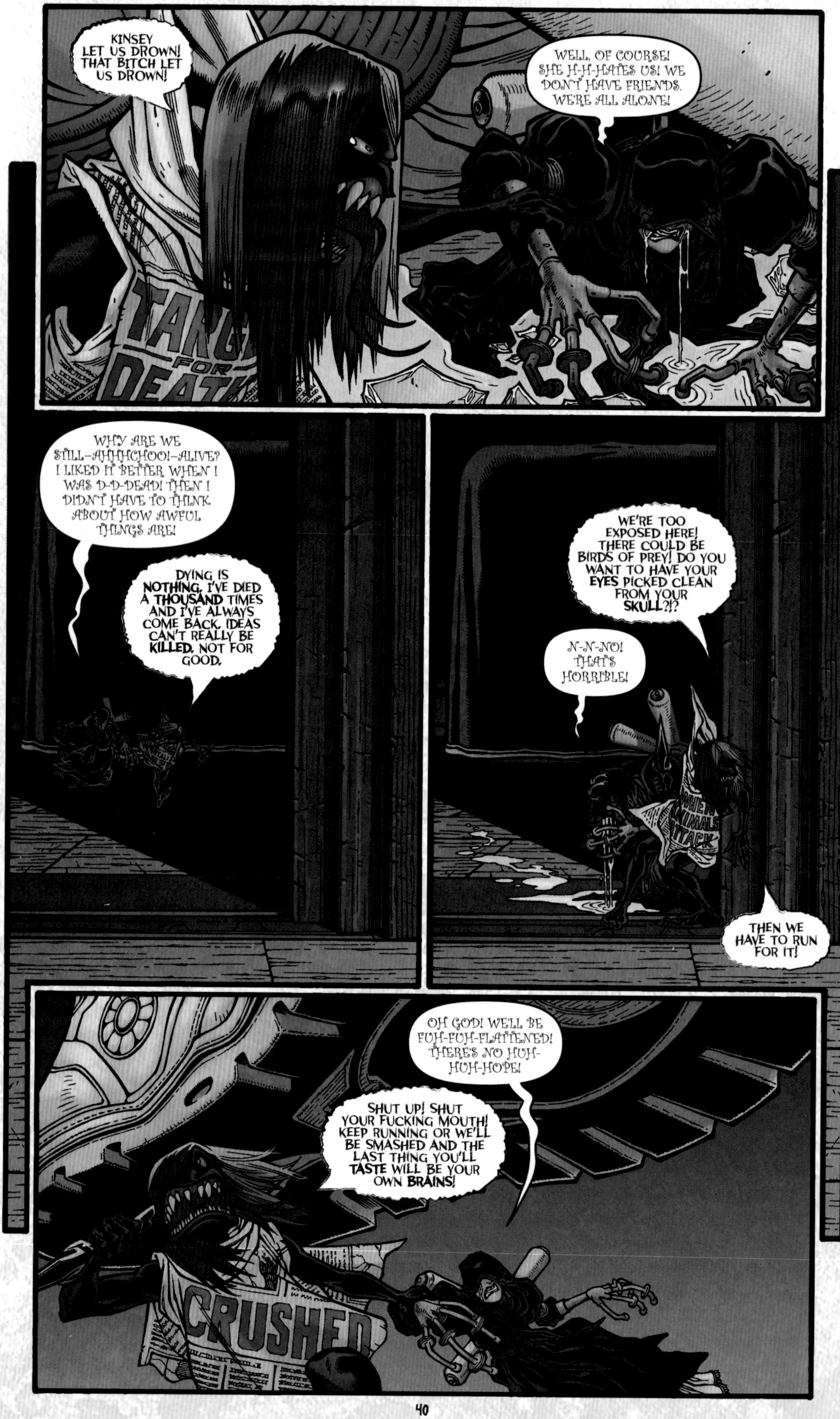
KINSEY LET US DROWN! THAT BITCH LET US DROWN!
WELL, OF COURSE! SHE H-H-HATES US! WE DON'T HAVE FRIENDS. WE'RE ALL ALONE!
TARGET FOR DEATH
WHY ARE WE STILL--AHHHCHOO!--ALIVE? I LIKED IT BETTER WHEN I WAS D-D-DEAD! THEN I DIDN'T HAVE TO THINK ABOUT HOW AWFUL THINGS ARE!
DYING IS NOTHING. I'VE DIED A THOUSAND TIMES AND I'VE ALWAYS COME BACK. IDEAS CAN'T REALLY BE KILLED. NOT FOR GOOD.
WE'RE TOO EXPOSED HERE! THERE COULD BE BIRDS OF PREY! DO YOU WANT TO HAVE YOUR EYES PICKED CLEAN FROM YOUR SKULL?!?
N-N-NO! THAT'S HORRIBLE!
WHEN ANIMALS ATTACK
THEN WE HAVE TO RUN FOR IT!
OH GOD! WE'LL BE FUH-FUH-FLATTENED! THERE'S NO HUH-HUH-HOPE!
SHUT UP! SHUT YOUR FUCKING MOUTH! KEEP RUNNING OR WE'LL BE SMASHED AND THE LAST THING YOU'LL TASTE WILL BE YOUR OWN BRAINS!
CRUSHED

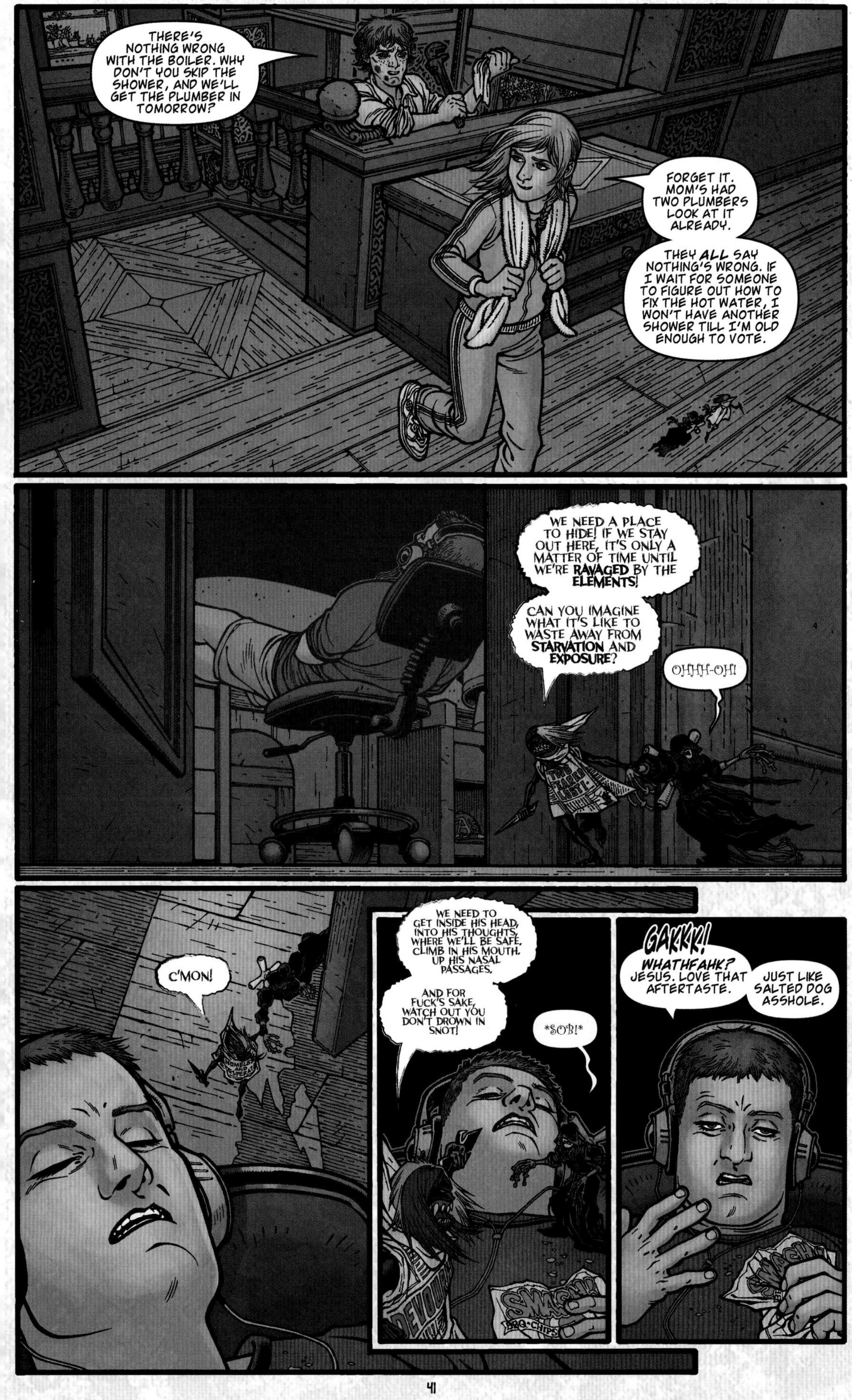
THERE'S NOTHING WRONG WITH THE BOILER. WHY DON'T YOU SKIP THE SHOWER, AND WE'LL GET THE PLUMBER IN TOMORROW?
FORGET IT. MOM'S HAD TWO PLUMBERS LOOK AT IT ALREADY.
THEY ALL SAY NOTHING'S WRONG. IF I WAIT FOR SOMEONE TO FIGURE OUT HOW TO FIX THE HOT WATER, I WON'T HAVE ANOTHER SHOWER TILL I'M OLD ENOUGH TO VOTE.
WE NEED A PLACE TO HIDE! IF WE STAY OUT HERE, IT'S ONLY A MATTER OF TIME UNTIL WE'RE RAVAGED BY THE ELEMENTS!
CAN YOU IMAGINE WHAT IT'S LIKE TO WASTE AWAY FROM STARVATION AND EXPOSURE?
OHHH-OH!
C'MON!
WE NEED TO GET INSIDE HIS HEAD, INTO HIS THOUGHTS, WHERE WE'LL BE SAFE. CLIMB IN HIS MOUTH, UP HIS NASAL PASSAGES.
AND FOR FUCK'S SAKE, WATCH OUT YOU DON'T DROWN IN SNOT!
SOB!
GAKKK!
WHATHFAHK? JESUS. LOVE THAT AFTERTASTE.
JUST LIKE SALTED DOG ASSHOLE.

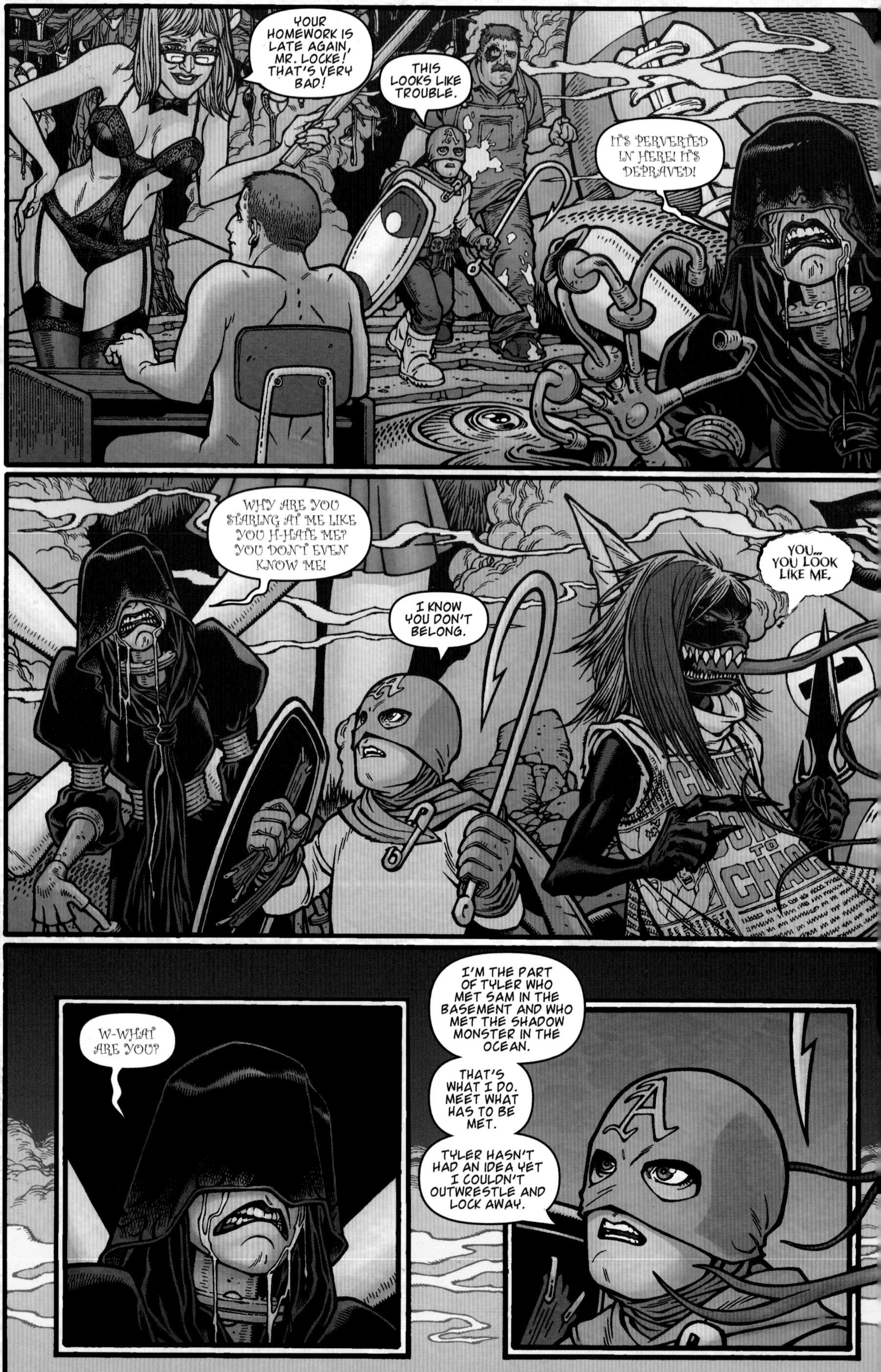

YOUR HOMEWORK IS LATE AGAIN, MR. LOCKE! THAT'S VERY BAD!
THIS LOOKS LIKE TROUBLE.
IT'S PERVERTED IN HERE! IT'S DEPRAVED!
WHY ARE YOU STARING AT ME LIKE YOU H-HATE ME? YOU DON'T EVEN KNOW ME!
I KNOW YOU DON'T BELONG.
YOU... YOU LOOK LIKE ME.
W-WHAT ARE YOU?
I'M THE PART OF TYLER WHO MET SAM IN THE BASEMENT AND WHO MET THE SHADOW MONSTER IN THE OCEAN.
THAT'S WHAT I DO. MEET WHAT HAS TO BE MET.
TYLER HASN'T HAD AN IDEA YET I COULDN'T OUTWRESTLE AND LOCK AWAY.

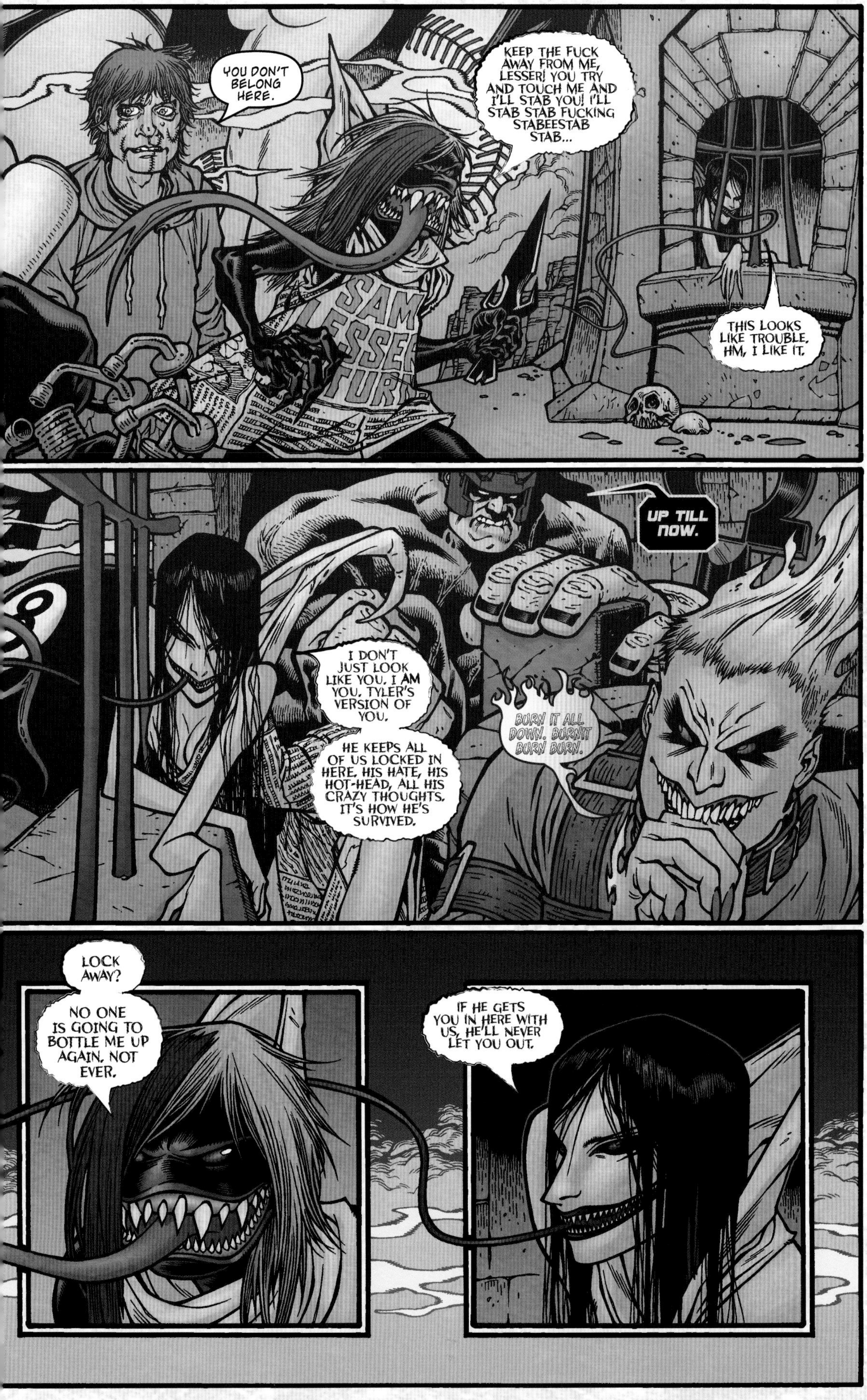
YOU DON'T BELONG HERE.
KEEP THE FUCK AWAY FROM ME, LESSER! YOU TRY AND TOUCH ME AND I'LL STAB YOU! I'LL STAB STAB FUCKING STABEESTAB STAB...
THIS LOOKS LIKE TROUBLE. HM, I LIKE IT.
UP TILL NOW.
I DON'T JUST LOOK LIKE YOU. I AM YOU. TYLER'S VERSION OF YOU.
HE KEEPS ALL OF US LOCKED IN HERE. HIS HATE, HIS HOT-HEAD, ALL HIS CRAZY THOUGHTS. IT'S HOW HE'S SURVIVED.
BURN IT ALL DOWN. BURNIT BURN BURN.
LOCK AWAY?
NO ONE IS GOING TO BOTTLE ME UP AGAIN. NOT EVER.
IF HE GETS YOU IN HERE WITH US, HE'LL NEVER LET YOU OUT.

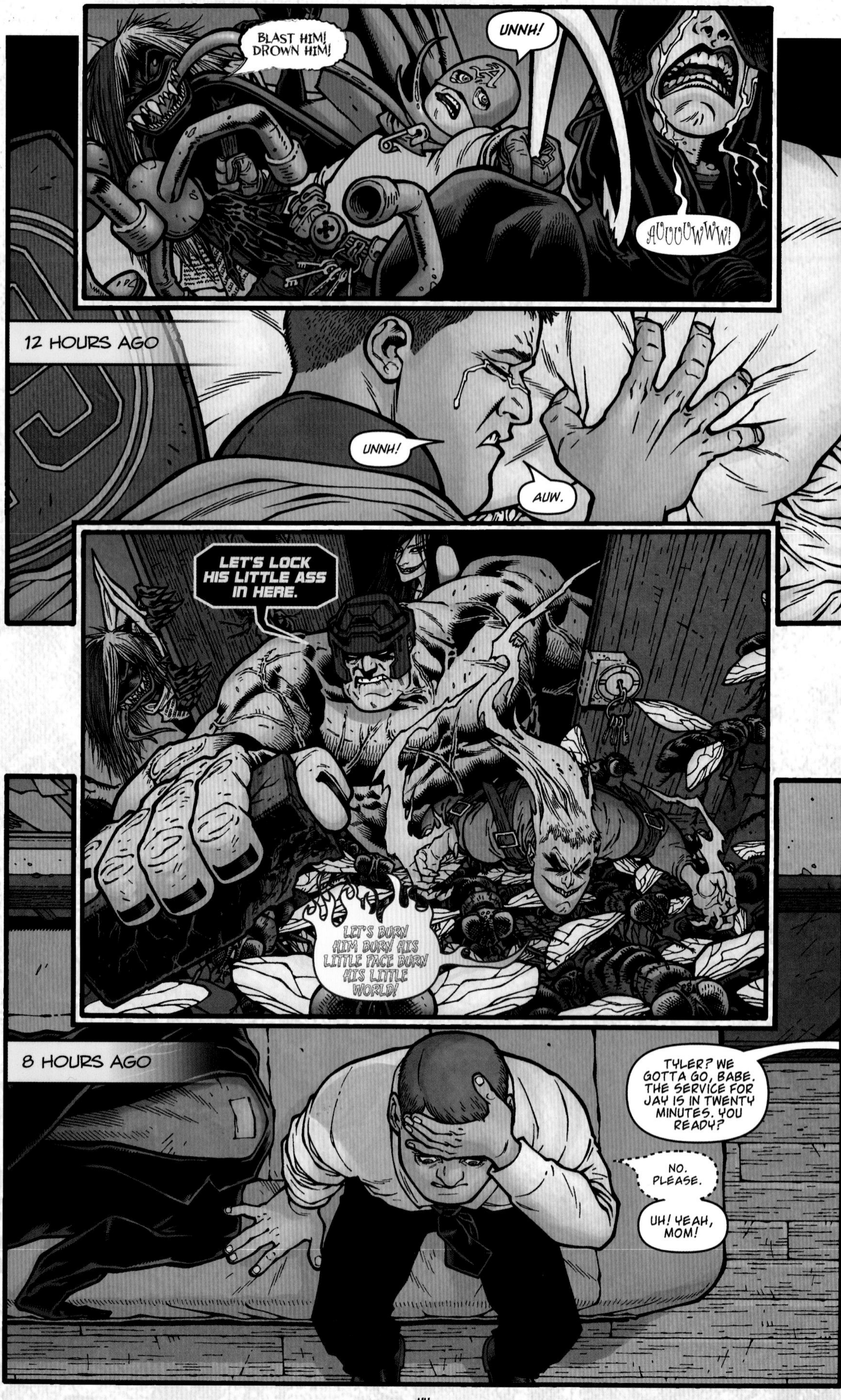
BLAST HIM! DROWN HIM!
UNNH!
AUUUUWWW!
12 HOURS AGO
UNNH!
AUW.
LET'S LOCK HIS LITTLE ASS IN HERE.
LET'S BURN HIM BURN HIS LITTLE FACE BURN HIS LITTLE WORLD!
8 HOURS AGO
TYLER? WE GOTTA GO, BABE. THE SERVICE FOR JAY IS IN TWENTY MINUTES. YOU READY?
NO. PLEASE.
UH! YEAH, MOM!

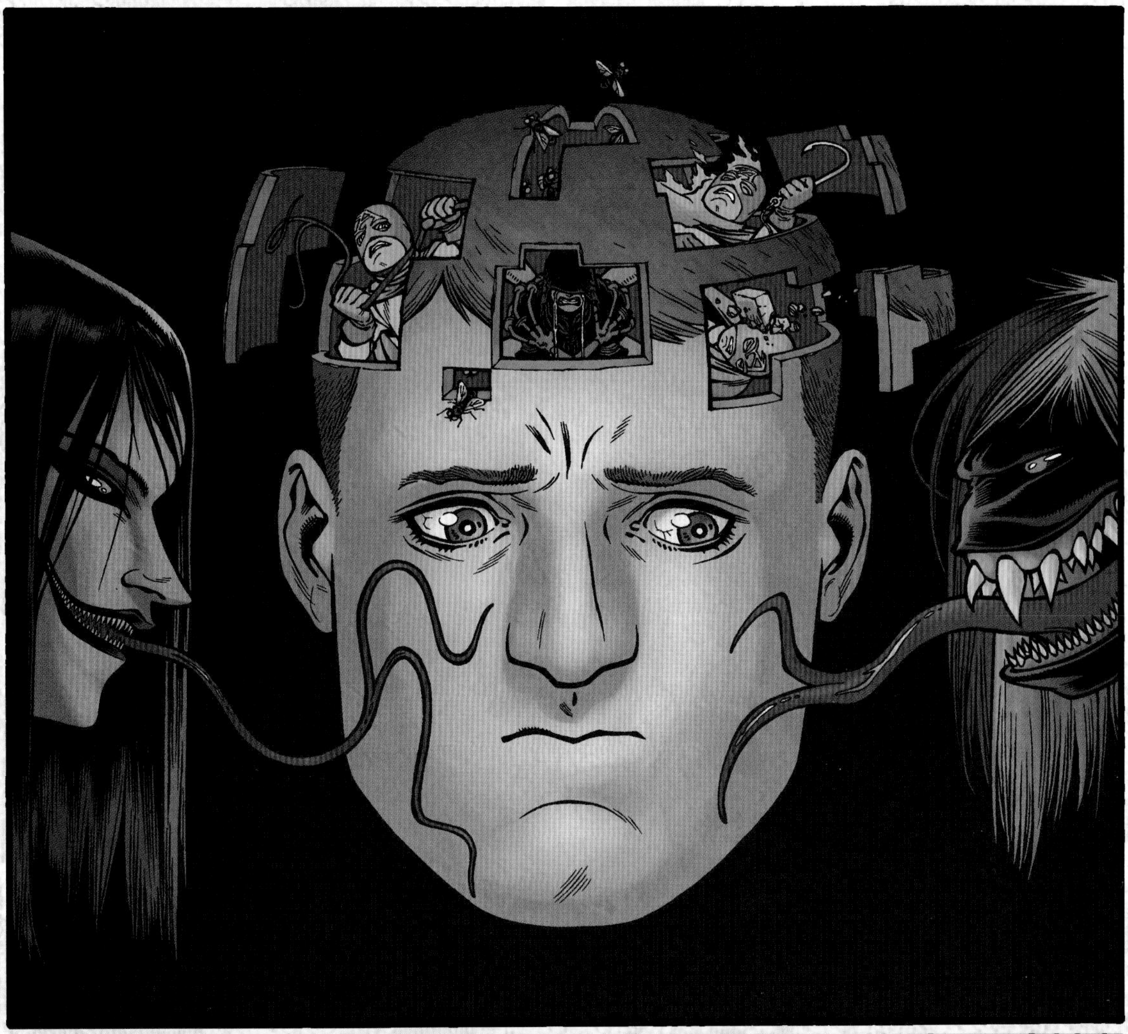

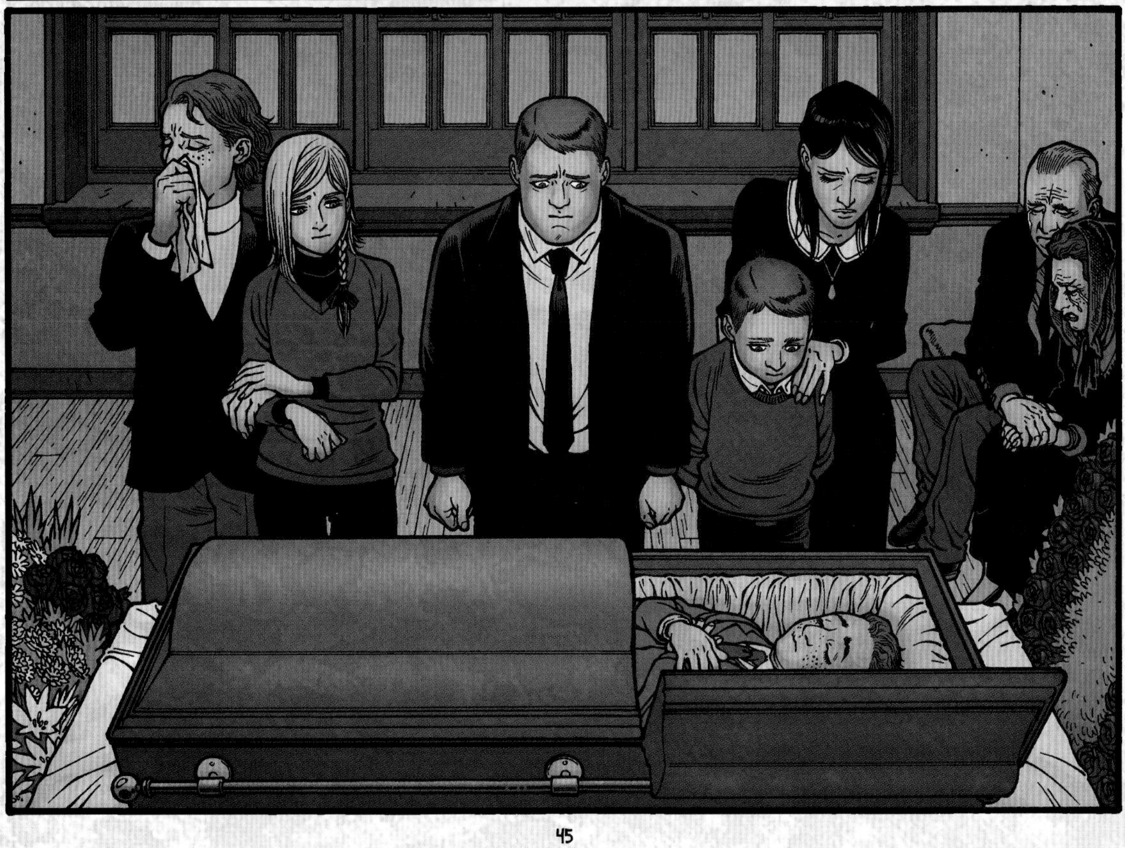

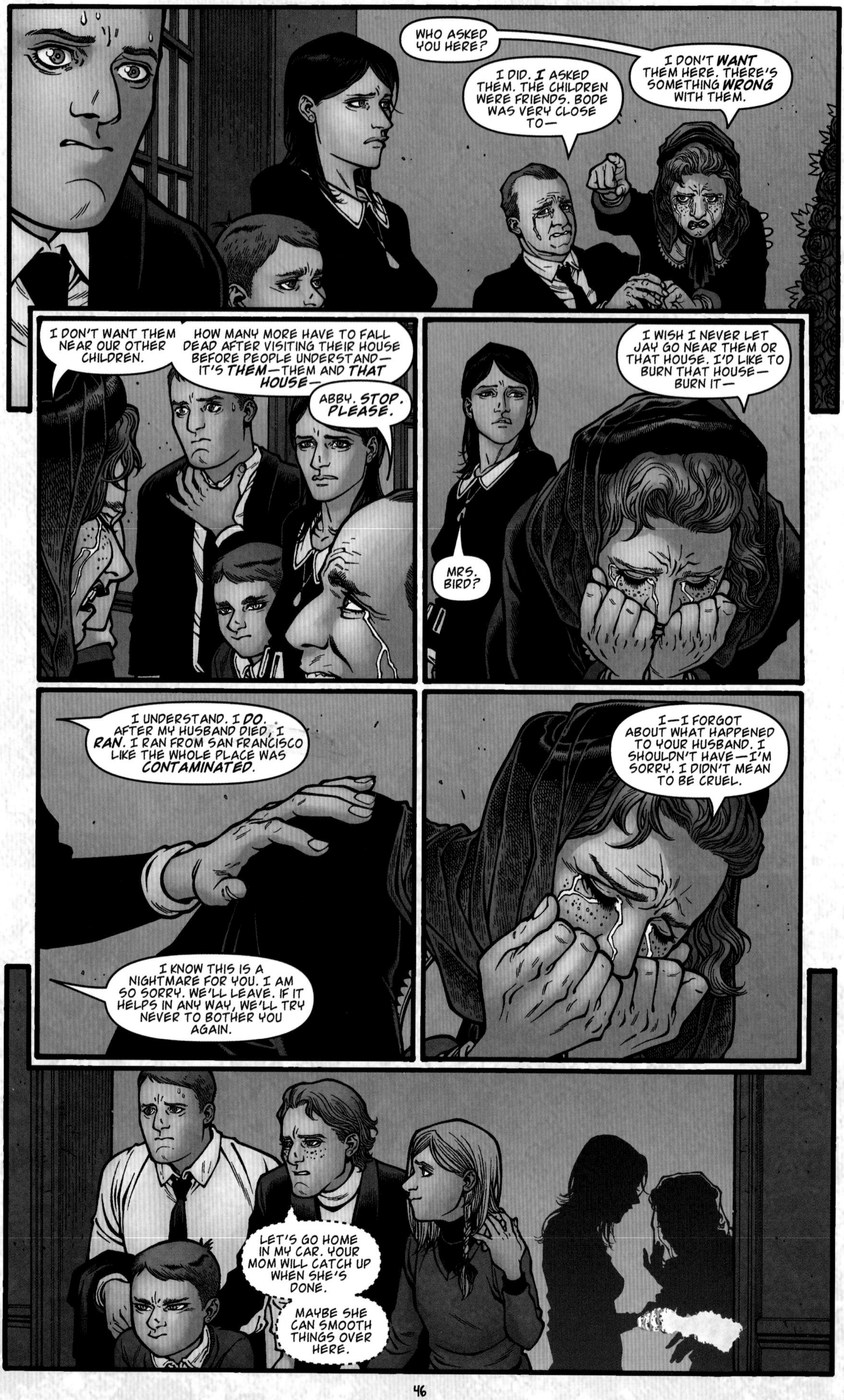
WHO ASKED YOU HERE?
I DON'T WANT THEM HERE. THERE'S SOMETHING WRONG WITH THEM.
I DID. I ASKED THEM. THE CHILDREN WERE FRIENDS. BODE WAS VERY CLOSE TO—
I DON'T WANT THEM NEAR OUR OTHER CHILDREN.
HOW MANY MORE HAVE TO FALL DEAD AFTER VISITING THEIR HOUSE BEFORE PEOPLE UNDERSTAND—IT'S THEM—THEM AND THAT HOUSE—
ABBY. STOP. PLEASE.
I WISH I NEVER LET JAY GO NEAR THEM OR THAT HOUSE. I'D LIKE TO BURN THAT HOUSE—BURN IT—
MRS. BIRD?
I UNDERSTAND. I DO. AFTER MY HUSBAND DIED, I RAN. I RAN FROM SAN FRANCISCO LIKE THE WHOLE PLACE WAS CONTAMINATED.
I KNOW THIS IS A NIGHTMARE FOR YOU. I AM SO SORRY. WE'LL LEAVE. IF IT HELPS IN ANY WAY, WE'LL TRY NEVER TO BOTHER YOU AGAIN.
I—I FORGOT ABOUT WHAT HAPPENED TO YOUR HUSBAND. I SHOULDN'T HAVE—I'M SORRY. I DIDN'T MEAN TO BE CRUEL.
LET'S GO HOME IN MY CAR. YOUR MOM WILL CATCH UP WHEN SHE'S DONE.
MAYBE SHE CAN SMOOTH THINGS OVER HERE.

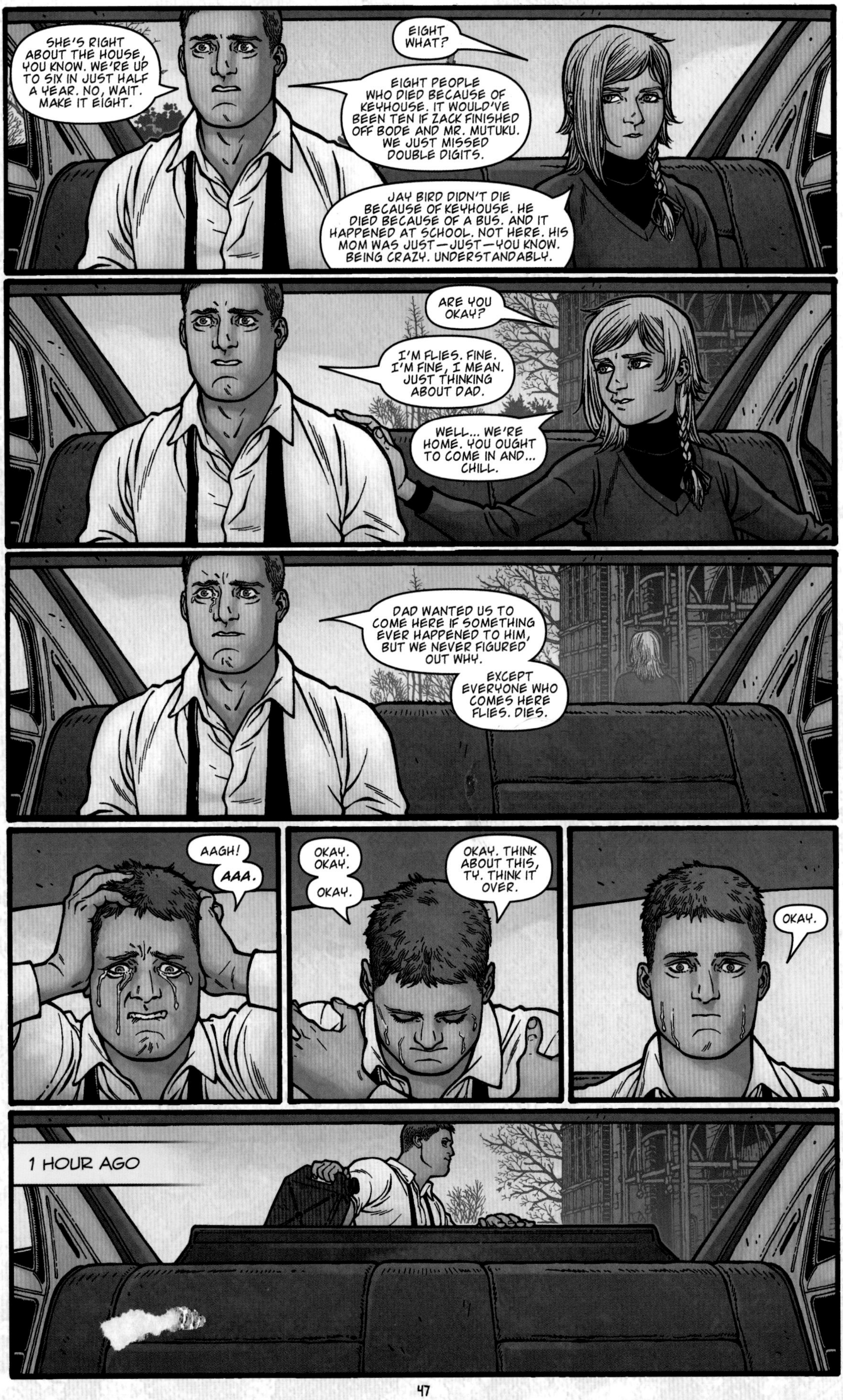

SHE'S RIGHT ABOUT THE HOUSE, YOU KNOW. WE'RE UP TO SIX IN JUST HALF A YEAR. NO, WAIT. MAKE IT EIGHT.
EIGHT WHAT?
EIGHT PEOPLE WHO DIED BECAUSE OF KEYHOUSE. IT WOULD'VE BEEN TEN IF ZACK FINISHED OFF BODE AND MR. MUTUKU. WE JUST MISSED DOUBLE DIGITS.
JAY BIRD DIDN'T DIE BECAUSE OF KEYHOUSE. HE DIED BECAUSE OF A BUS. AND IT HAPPENED AT SCHOOL. NOT HERE. HIS MOM WAS JUST—JUST—YOU KNOW. BEING CRAZY. UNDERSTANDABLY.
ARE YOU OKAY?
I'M FLIES. FINE. I'M FINE, I MEAN. JUST THINKING ABOUT DAD.
WELL... WE'RE HOME. YOU OUGHT TO COME IN AND... CHILL.
DAD WANTED US TO COME HERE IF SOMETHING EVER HAPPENED TO HIM, BUT WE NEVER FIGURED OUT WHY.
EXCEPT EVERYONE WHO COMES HERE FLIES. DIES.
AAGH!
AAA.
OKAY. OKAY.
OKAY.
OKAY. THINK ABOUT THIS, TY. THINK IT OVER.
OKAY.
1 HOUR AGO

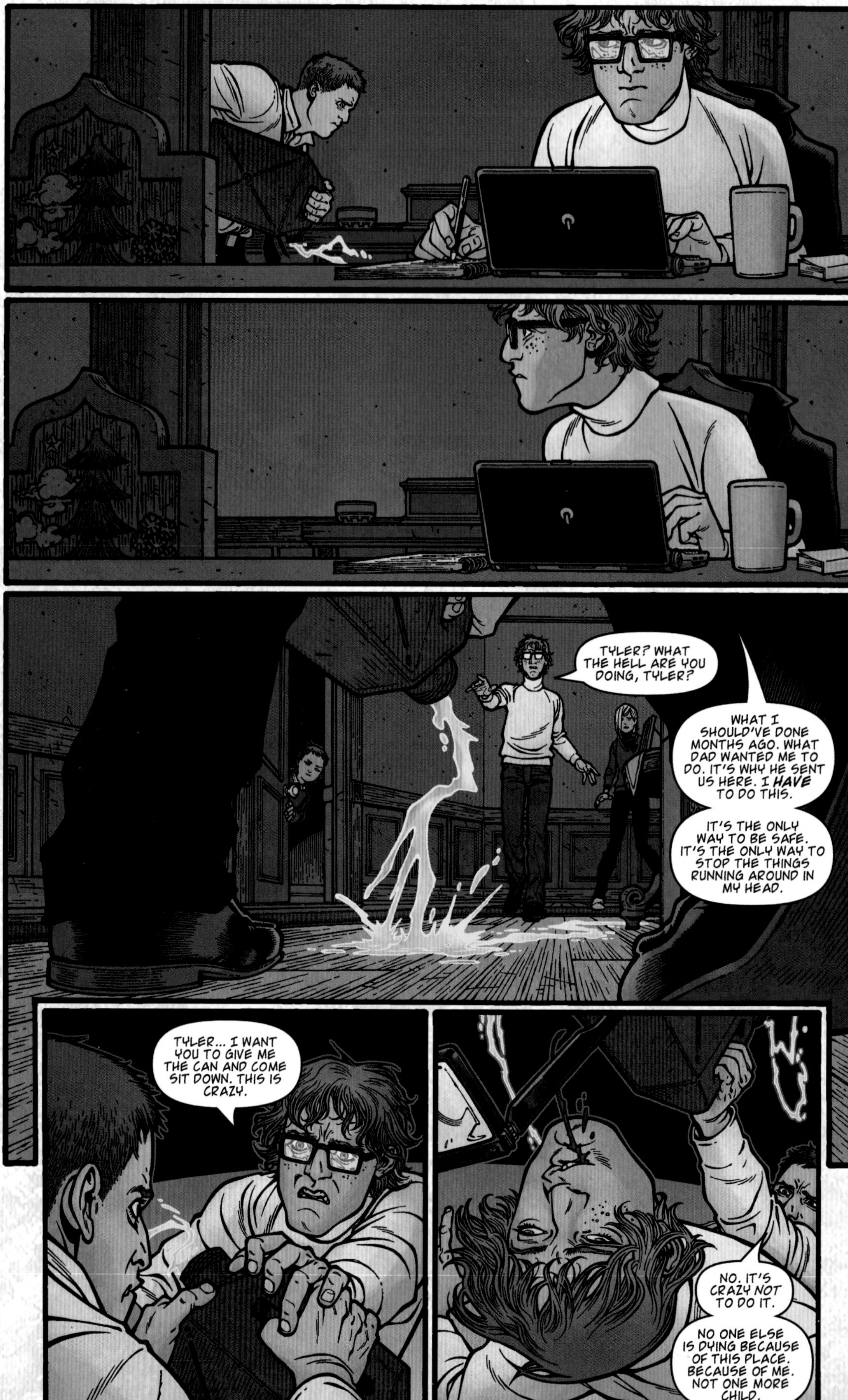

TYLER? WHAT THE HELL ARE YOU DOING, TYLER?
WHAT I SHOULD'VE DONE MONTHS AGO. WHAT DAD WANTED ME TO DO. IT'S WHY HE SENT US HERE. I *HAVE* TO DO THIS.
IT'S THE ONLY WAY TO BE SAFE. IT'S THE ONLY WAY TO STOP THE THINGS RUNNING AROUND IN MY HEAD.
TYLER... I WANT YOU TO GIVE ME THE CAN AND COME SIT DOWN. THIS IS CRAZY.
NO. IT'S CRAZY NOT TO DO IT.
NO ONE ELSE IS DYING BECAUSE OF THIS PLACE. BECAUSE OF ME. NOT ONE MORE CHILD.

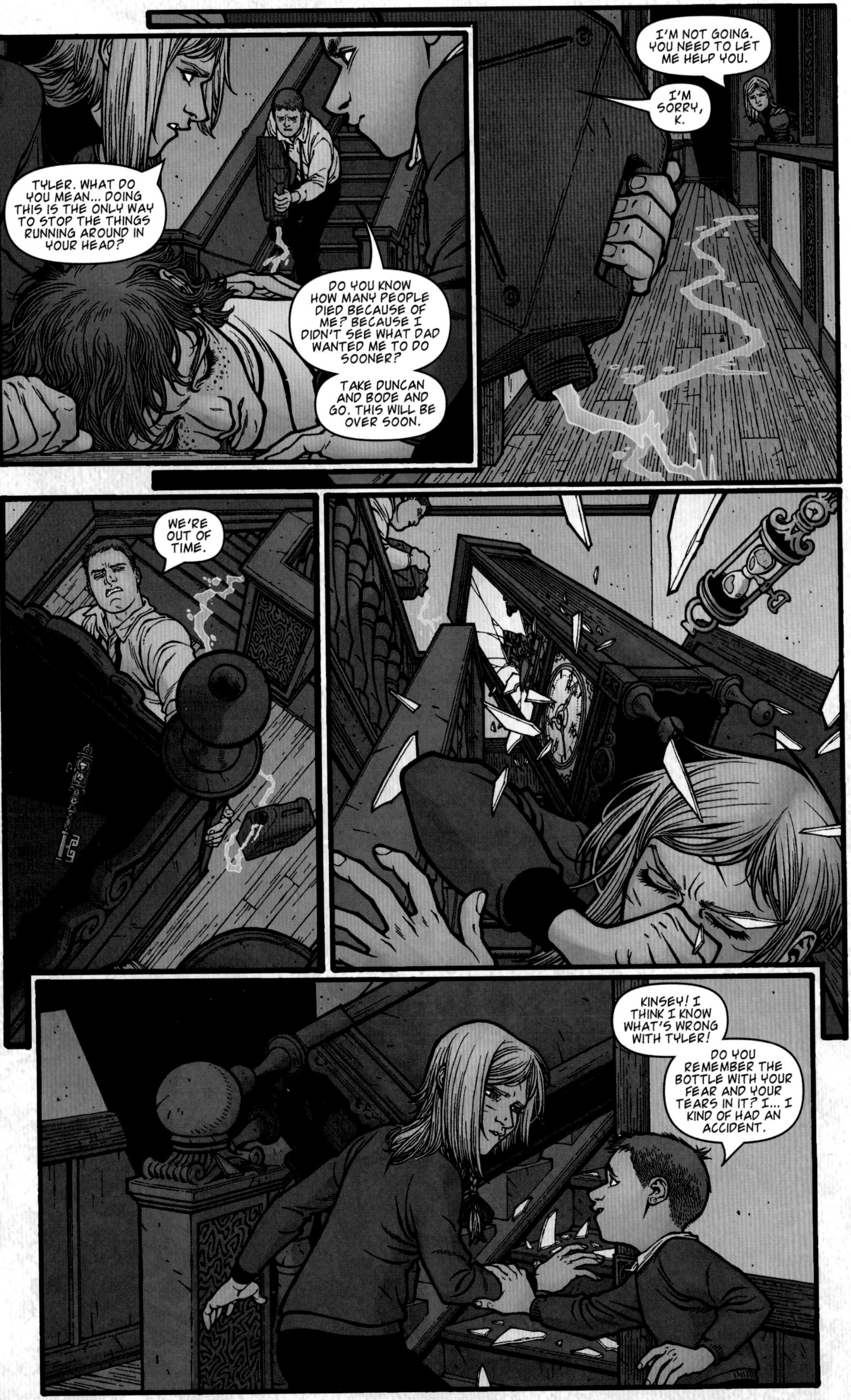

TYLER. WHAT DO YOU MEAN... DOING THIS IS THE ONLY WAY TO STOP THE THINGS RUNNING AROUND IN YOUR HEAD?
DO YOU KNOW HOW MANY PEOPLE DIED BECAUSE OF ME? BECAUSE I DIDN'T SEE WHAT DAD WANTED ME TO DO SOONER?
TAKE DUNCAN AND BODE AND GO. THIS WILL BE OVER SOON.
I'M NOT GOING. YOU NEED TO LET ME HELP YOU.
I'M SORRY, K.
WE'RE OUT OF TIME.
KINSEY! I THINK I KNOW WHAT'S WRONG WITH TYLER!
DO YOU REMEMBER THE BOTTLE WITH YOUR FEAR AND YOUR TEARS IN IT? I... I KIND OF HAD AN ACCIDENT.

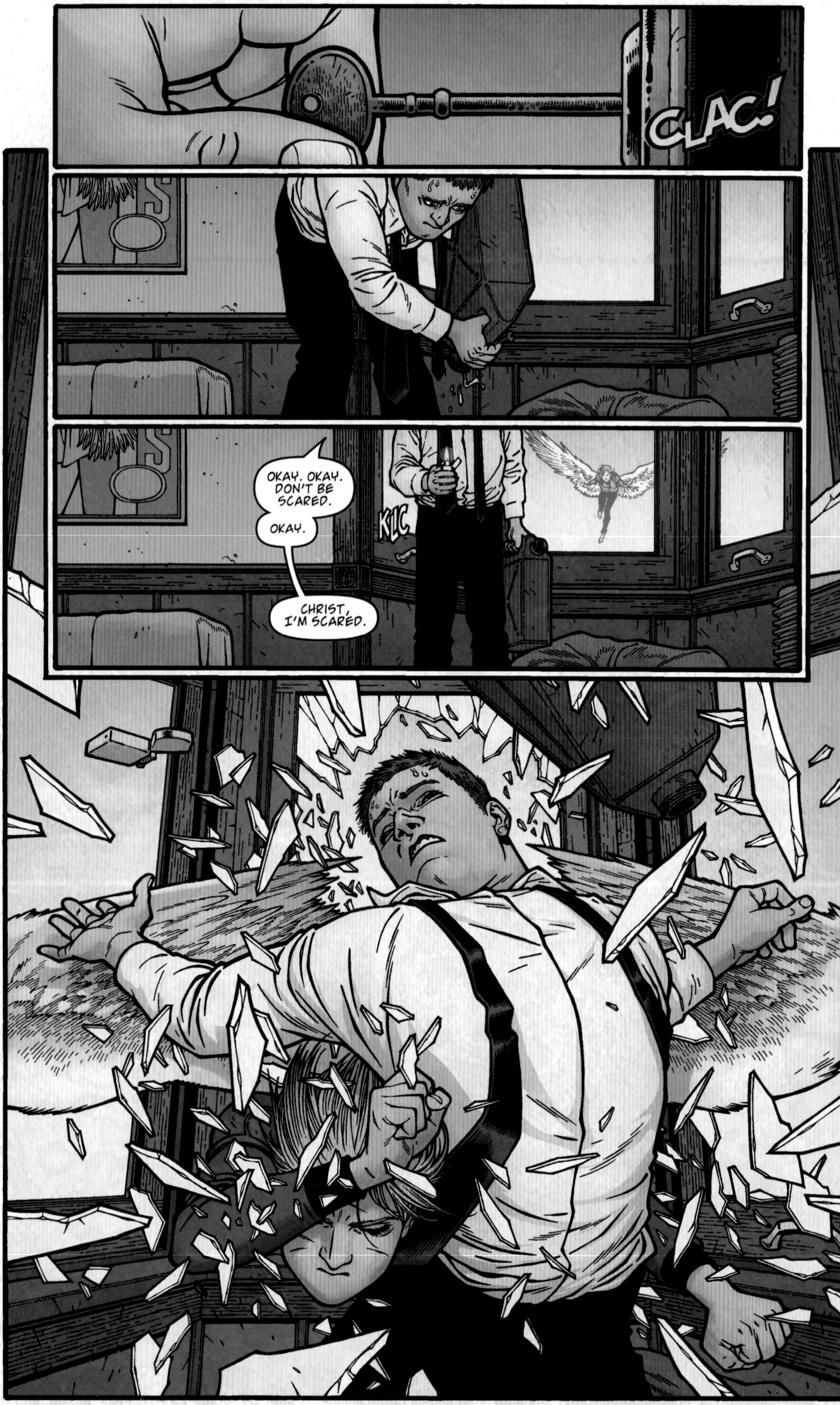
CLAC!
OKAY. OKAY. DON'T BE SCARED.
OKAY.
KLIC
CHRIST, I'M SCARED.

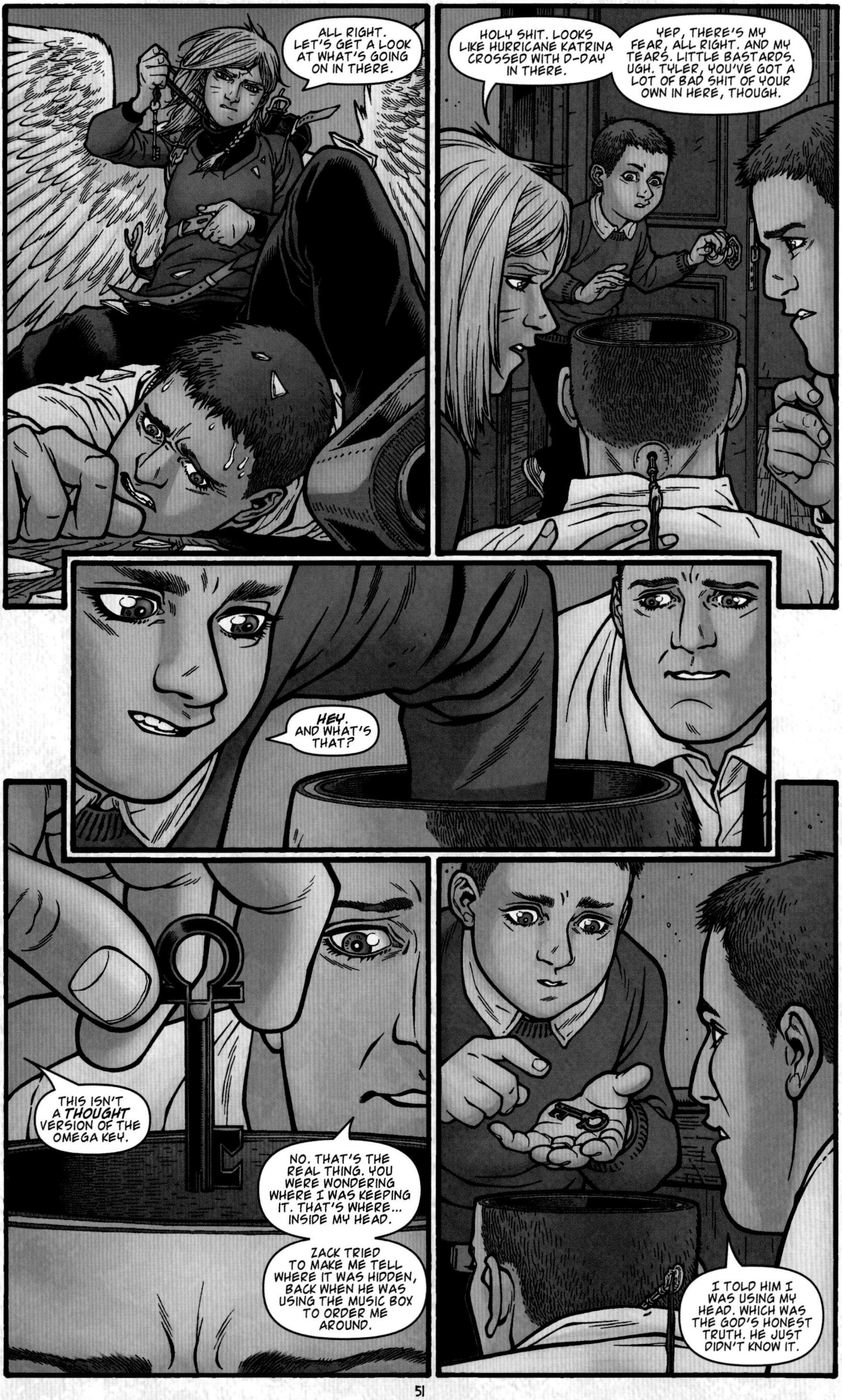

ALL RIGHT. LET'S GET A LOOK AT WHAT'S GOING ON IN THERE.
HOLY SHIT. LOOKS LIKE HURRICANE KATRINA CROSSED WITH D-DAY IN THERE.
YEP, THERE'S MY FEAR, ALL RIGHT. AND MY TEARS. LITTLE BASTARDS. UGH. TYLER, YOU'VE GOT A LOT OF BAD SHIT OF YOUR OWN IN HERE, THOUGH.
HEY. AND WHAT'S THAT?
THIS ISN'T A THOUGHT VERSION OF THE OMEGA KEY.
NO. THAT'S THE REAL THING. YOU WERE WONDERING WHERE I WAS KEEPING IT. THAT'S WHERE... INSIDE MY HEAD.
ZACK TRIED TO MAKE ME TELL WHERE IT WAS HIDDEN, BACK WHEN HE WAS USING THE MUSIC BOX TO ORDER ME AROUND.
I TOLD HIM I WAS USING MY HEAD. WHICH WAS THE GOD'S HONEST TRUTH. HE JUST DIDN'T KNOW IT.

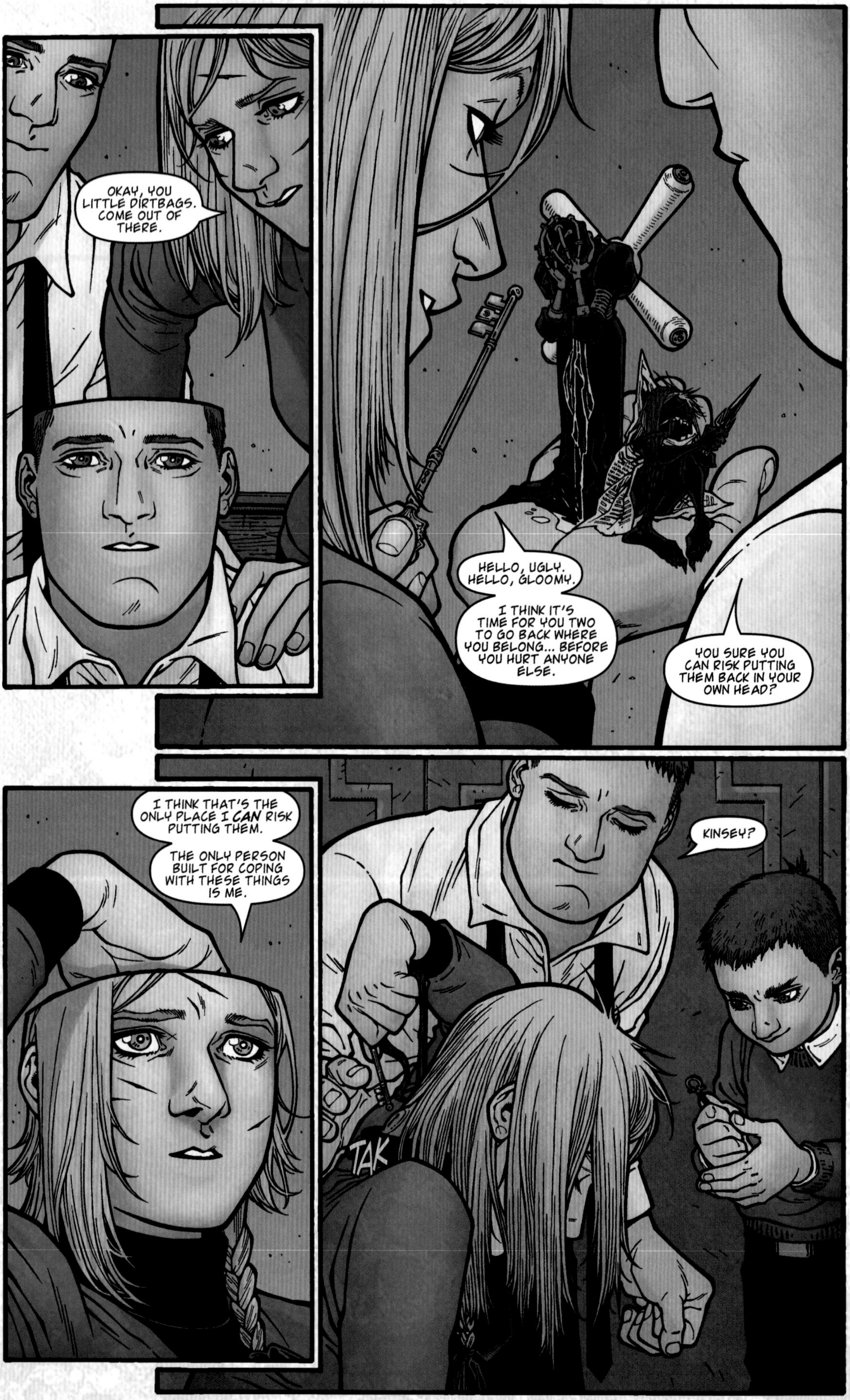
OKAY, YOU LITTLE DIRTBAGS. COME OUT OF THERE.
HELLO, UGLY. HELLO, GLOOMY.
I THINK IT'S TIME FOR YOU TWO TO GO BACK WHERE YOU BELONG... BEFORE YOU HURT ANYONE ELSE.
YOU SURE YOU CAN RISK PUTTING THEM BACK IN YOUR OWN HEAD?
I THINK THAT'S THE ONLY PLACE I CAN RISK PUTTING THEM.
THE ONLY PERSON BUILT FOR COPING WITH THESE THINGS IS ME.
KINSEY?
TAK

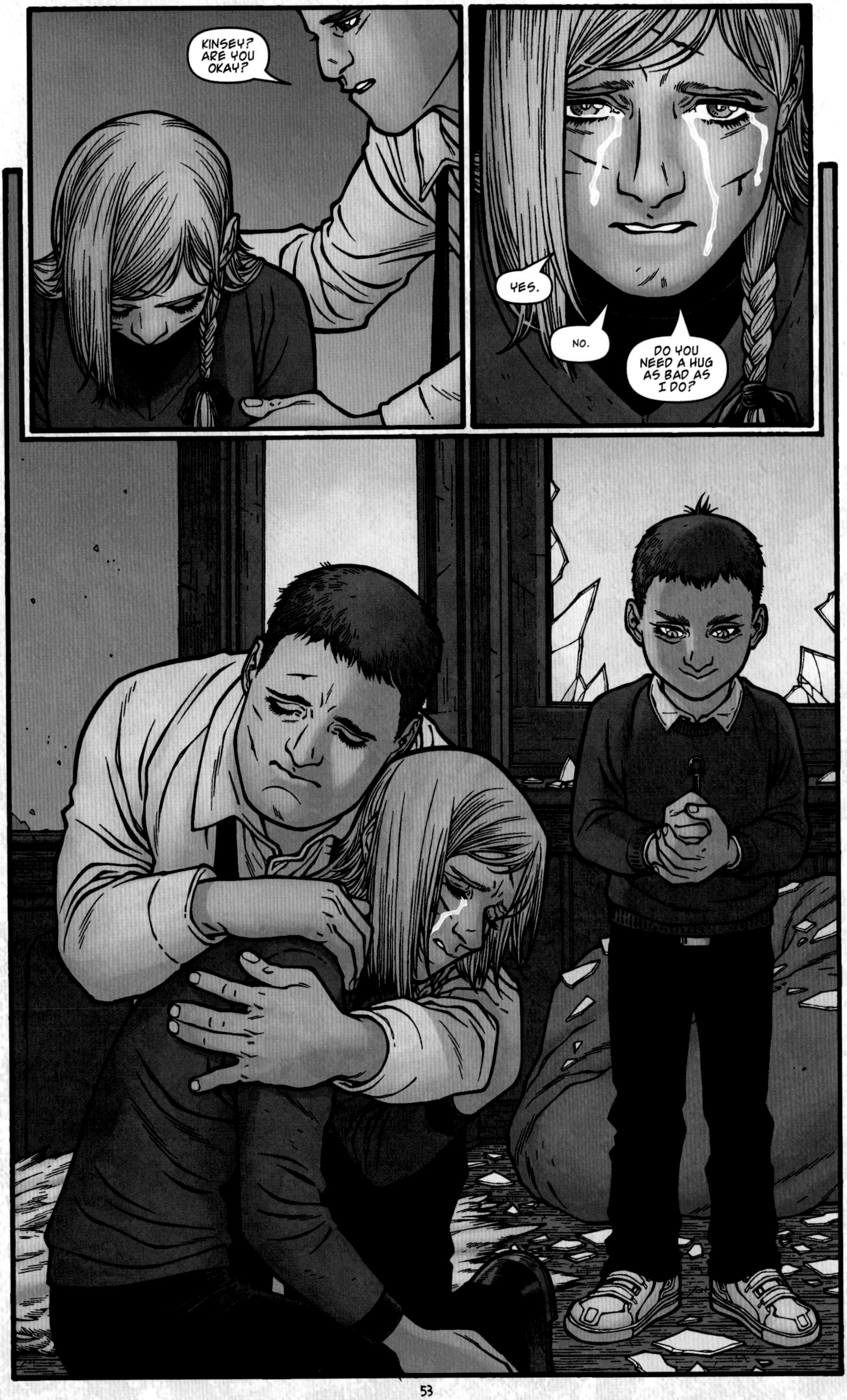
KINSEY? ARE YOU OKAY?
YES.
NO.
DO YOU NEED A HUG AS BAD AS I DO?

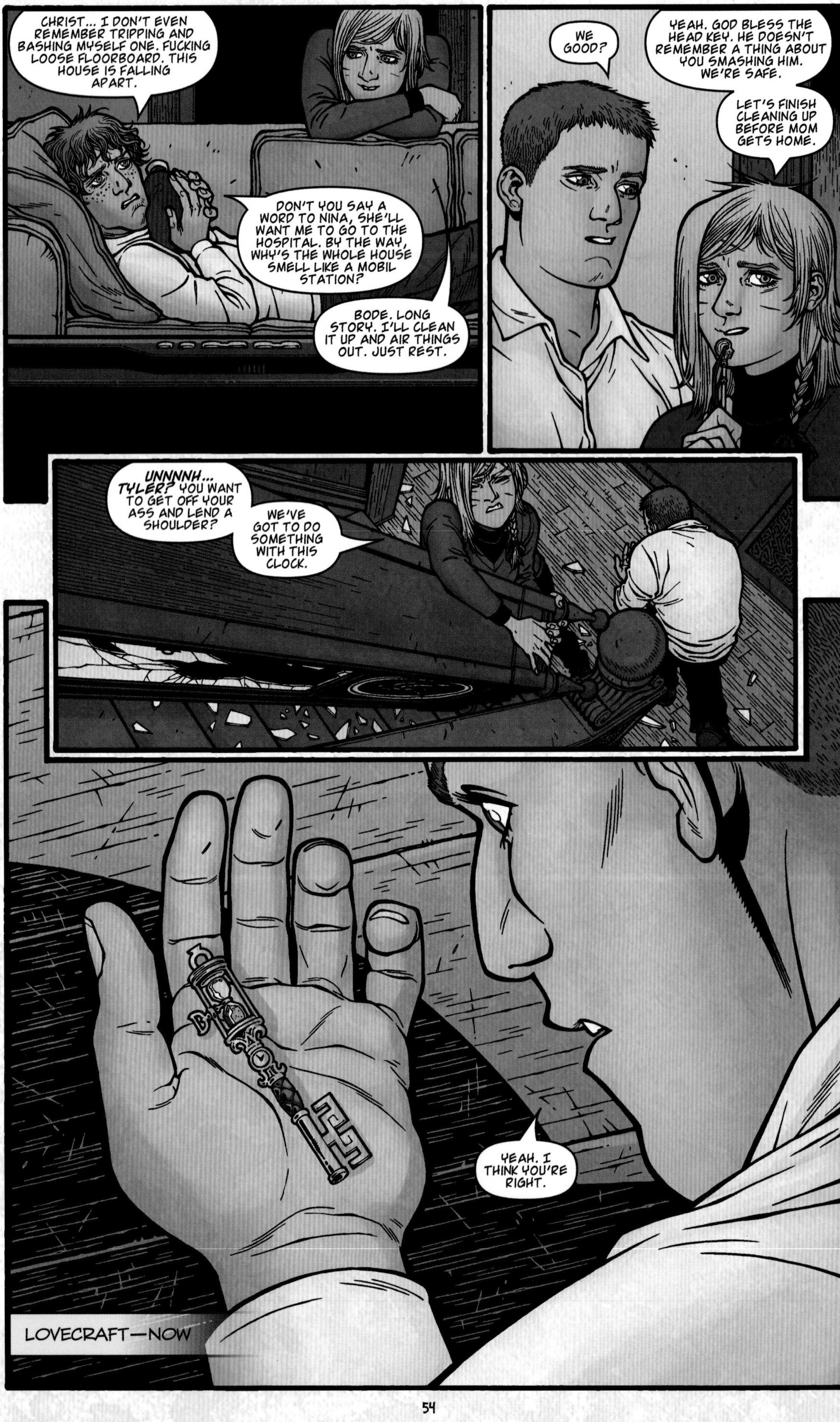
CHRIST... I DON'T EVEN REMEMBER TRIPPING AND BASHING MYSELF ONE. FUCKING LOOSE FLOORBOARD. THIS HOUSE IS FALLING APART.
DON'T YOU SAY A WORD TO NINA, SHE'LL WANT ME TO GO TO THE HOSPITAL. BY THE WAY, WHY'S THE WHOLE HOUSE SMELL LIKE A MOBIL STATION?
BODE. LONG STORY. I'LL CLEAN IT UP AND AIR THINGS OUT. JUST REST.
WE GOOD?
YEAH. GOD BLESS THE HEAD KEY. HE DOESN'T REMEMBER A THING ABOUT YOU SMASHING HIM. WE'RE SAFE.
LET'S FINISH CLEANING UP BEFORE MOM GETS HOME.
UNNNNH... TYLER? YOU WANT TO GET OFF YOUR ASS AND LEND A SHOULDER?
WE'VE GOT TO DO SOMETHING WITH THIS CLOCK.
YEAH. I THINK YOU'RE RIGHT.
LOVECRAFT—NOW

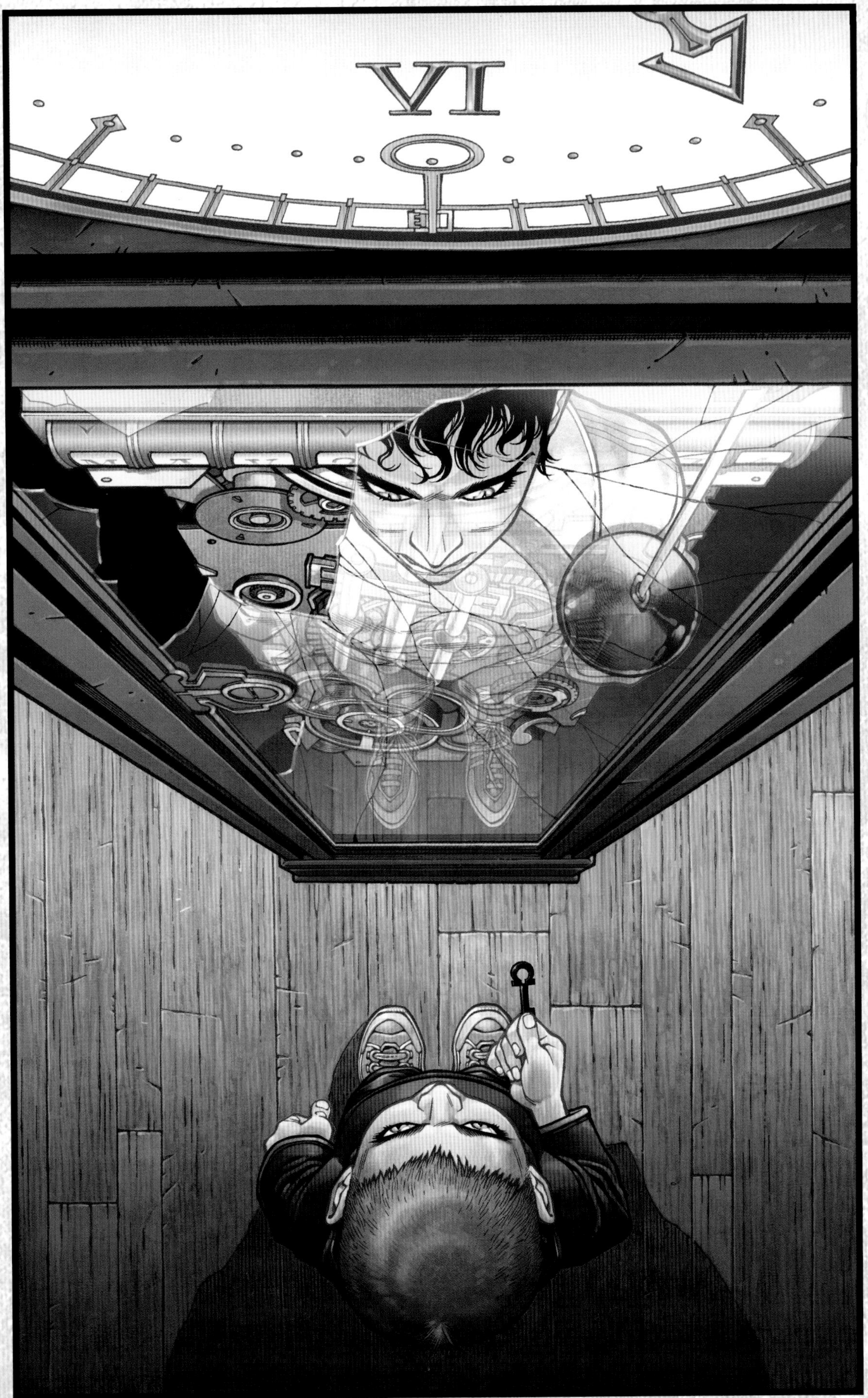

- CLOCKWORKS -

Chapter Three

THE TAMERS OF THE TEMPEST

NOW DOES MY PROJECT GATHER TO A HEAD:

MY CHARMS CRACK NOT; MY SPIRITS OBEY.

AND TIME GOES UPRIGHT WITH HIS CARRIAGE.

HOW'S THE DAY?

'TIS THE SIXTH HOUR, MY LORD, AT WHICH TIME YOU SAID OUR WORK WOULD CEASE.

I DID SAY SO... WHEN FIRST I RAISED THIS TEMPEST.

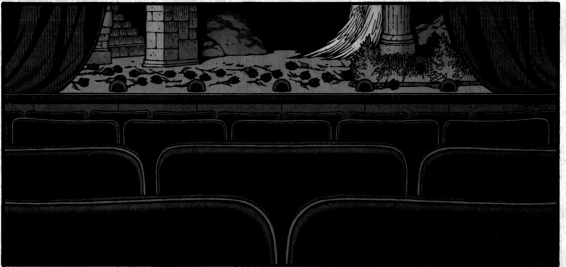

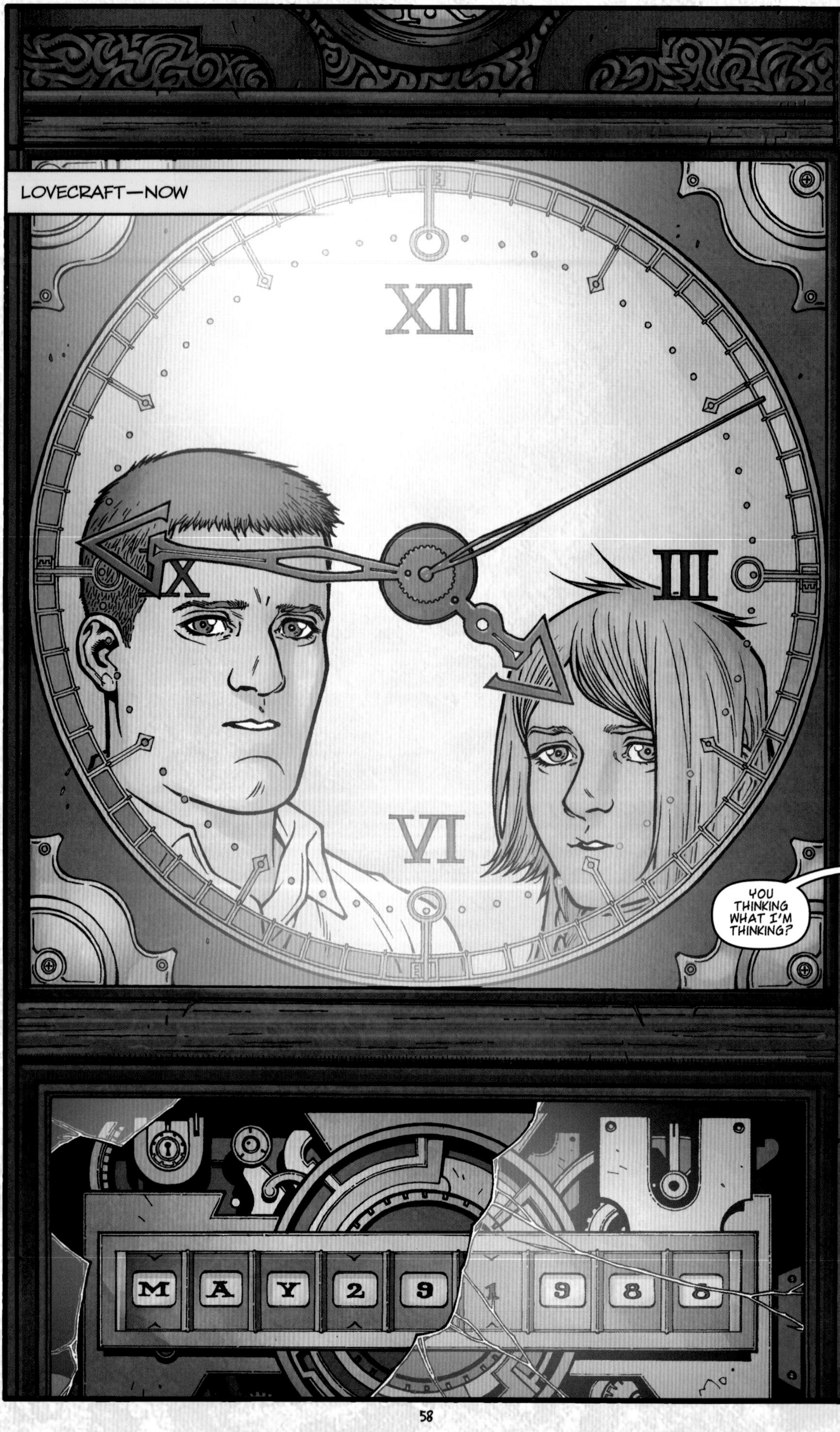
LOVECRAFT—NOW
YOU THINKING WHAT I'M THINKING?
MAY 29 1988

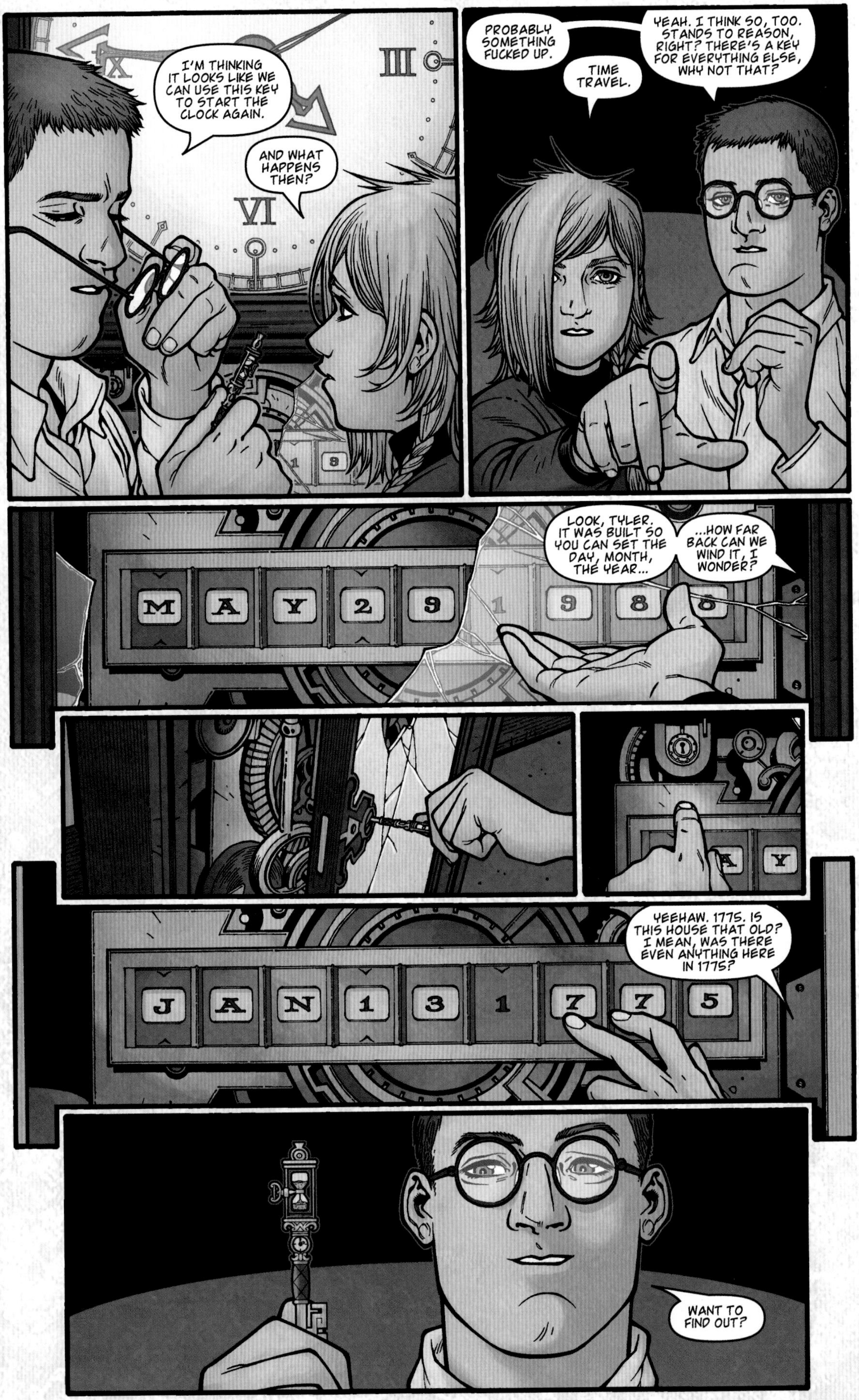
I'M THINKING IT LOOKS LIKE WE CAN USE THIS KEY TO START THE CLOCK AGAIN.
AND WHAT HAPPENS THEN?
PROBABLY SOMETHING FUCKED UP.
TIME TRAVEL.
YEAH. I THINK SO, TOO. STANDS TO REASON, RIGHT? THERE'S A KEY FOR EVERYTHING ELSE, WHY NOT THAT?
MAY 29 1988
LOOK, TYLER. IT WAS BUILT SO YOU CAN SET THE DAY, MONTH, THE YEAR...
...HOW FAR BACK CAN WE WIND IT, I WONDER?
JAN 13 1775
YEEHAW. 1775. IS THIS HOUSE THAT OLD? I MEAN, WAS THERE EVEN ANYTHING HERE IN 1775?
WANT TO FIND OUT?

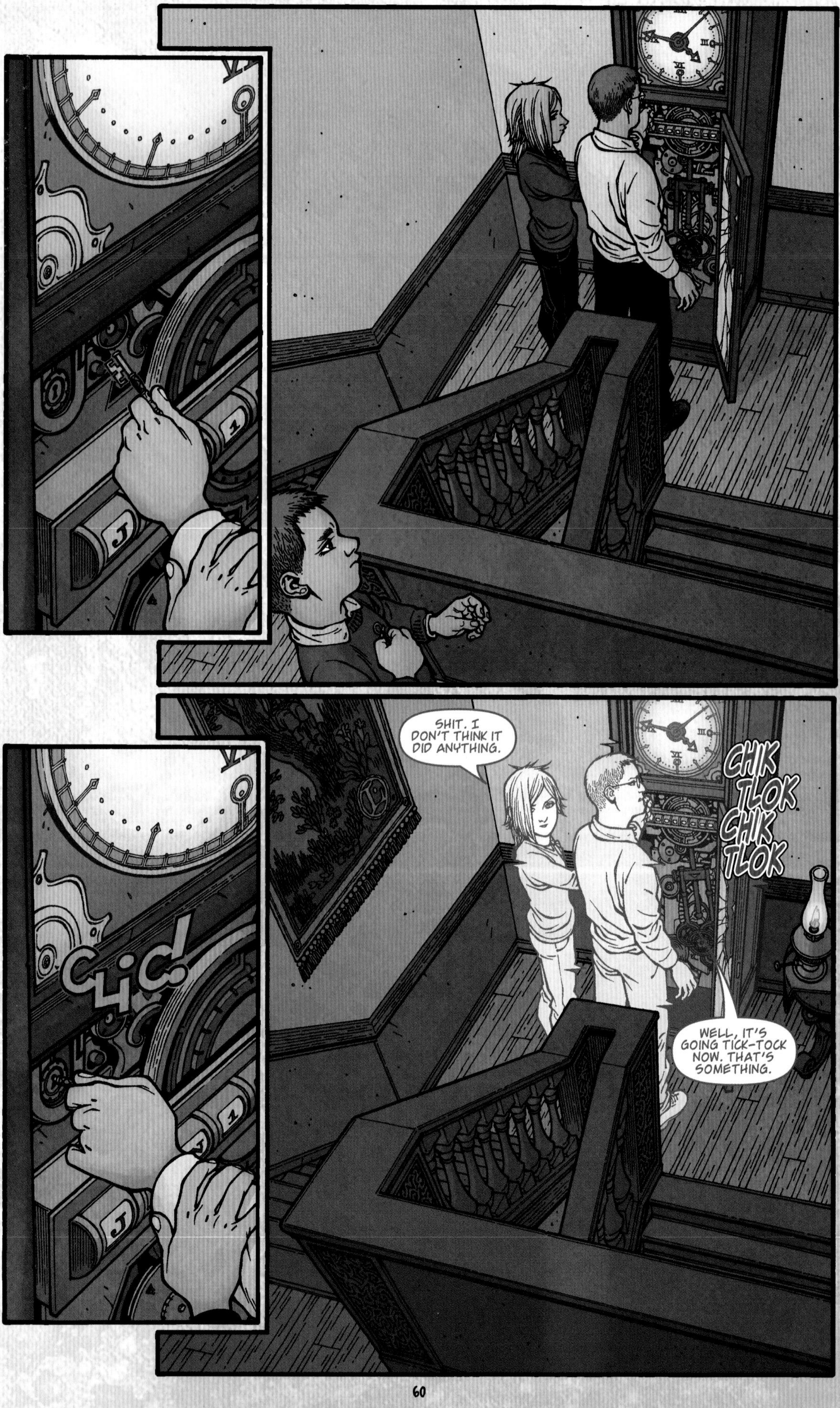
CLIC!
SHIT. I DON'T THINK IT DID ANYTHING.
CHIK TLOK CHIK TLOK
WELL, IT'S GOING TICK-TOCK NOW. THAT'S SOMETHING.

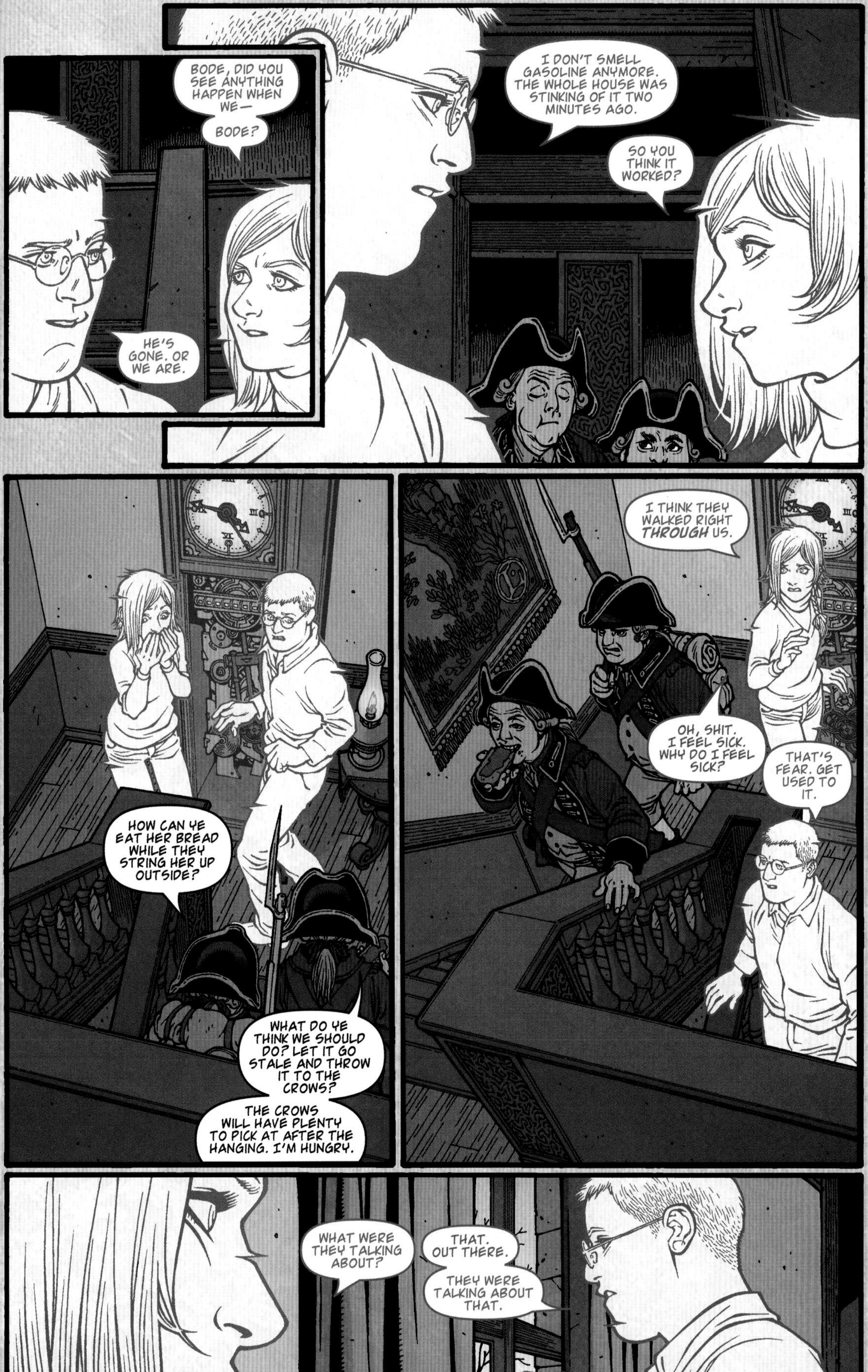

BODE, DID YOU SEE ANYTHING HAPPEN WHEN WE—
BODE?
HE'S GONE. OR WE ARE.
I DON'T SMELL GASOLINE ANYMORE. THE WHOLE HOUSE WAS STINKING OF IT TWO MINUTES AGO.
SO YOU THINK IT WORKED?
HOW CAN YE EAT HER BREAD WHILE THEY STRING HER UP OUTSIDE?
WHAT DO YE THINK WE SHOULD DO? LET IT GO STALE AND THROW IT TO THE CROWS?
THE CROWS WILL HAVE PLENTY TO PICK AT AFTER THE HANGING. I'M HUNGRY.
I THINK THEY WALKED RIGHT *THROUGH* US.
OH, SHIT. I FEEL SICK. WHY DO I FEEL SICK?
THAT'S FEAR. GET USED TO IT.
WHAT WERE THEY TALKING ABOUT?
THAT. OUT THERE.
THEY WERE TALKING ABOUT THAT.

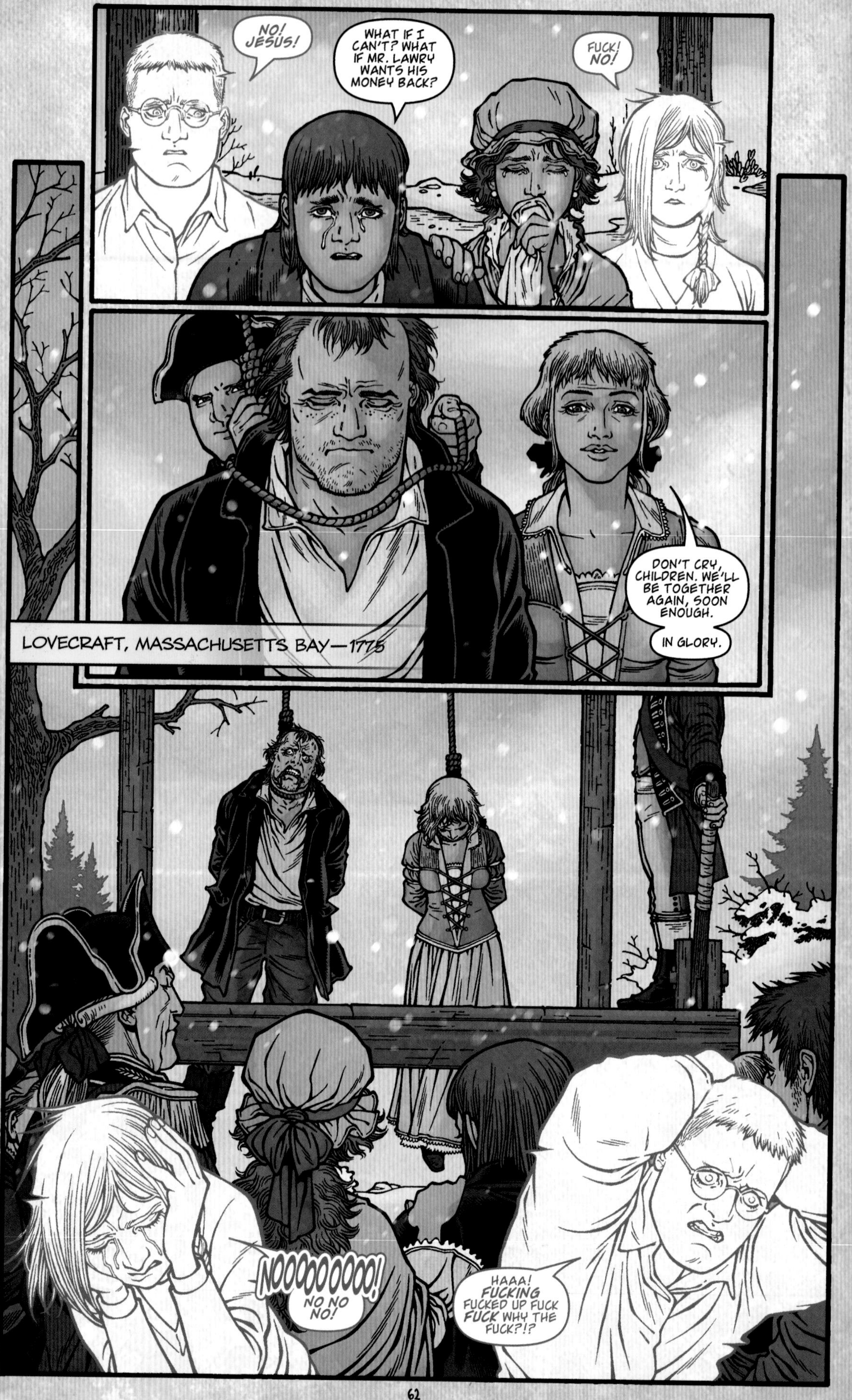
NO! JESUS!
WHAT IF I CAN'T? WHAT IF MR. LAWRY WANTS HIS MONEY BACK?
FUCK! NO!
LOVECRAFT, MASSACHUSETTS BAY—1775
DON'T CRY, CHILDREN. WE'LL BE TOGETHER AGAIN, SOON ENOUGH.
IN GLORY.
NOOOOOOOOO! NO NO NO!
HAAA! FUCKING FUCKED UP FUCK FUCK WHY THE FUCK?!?

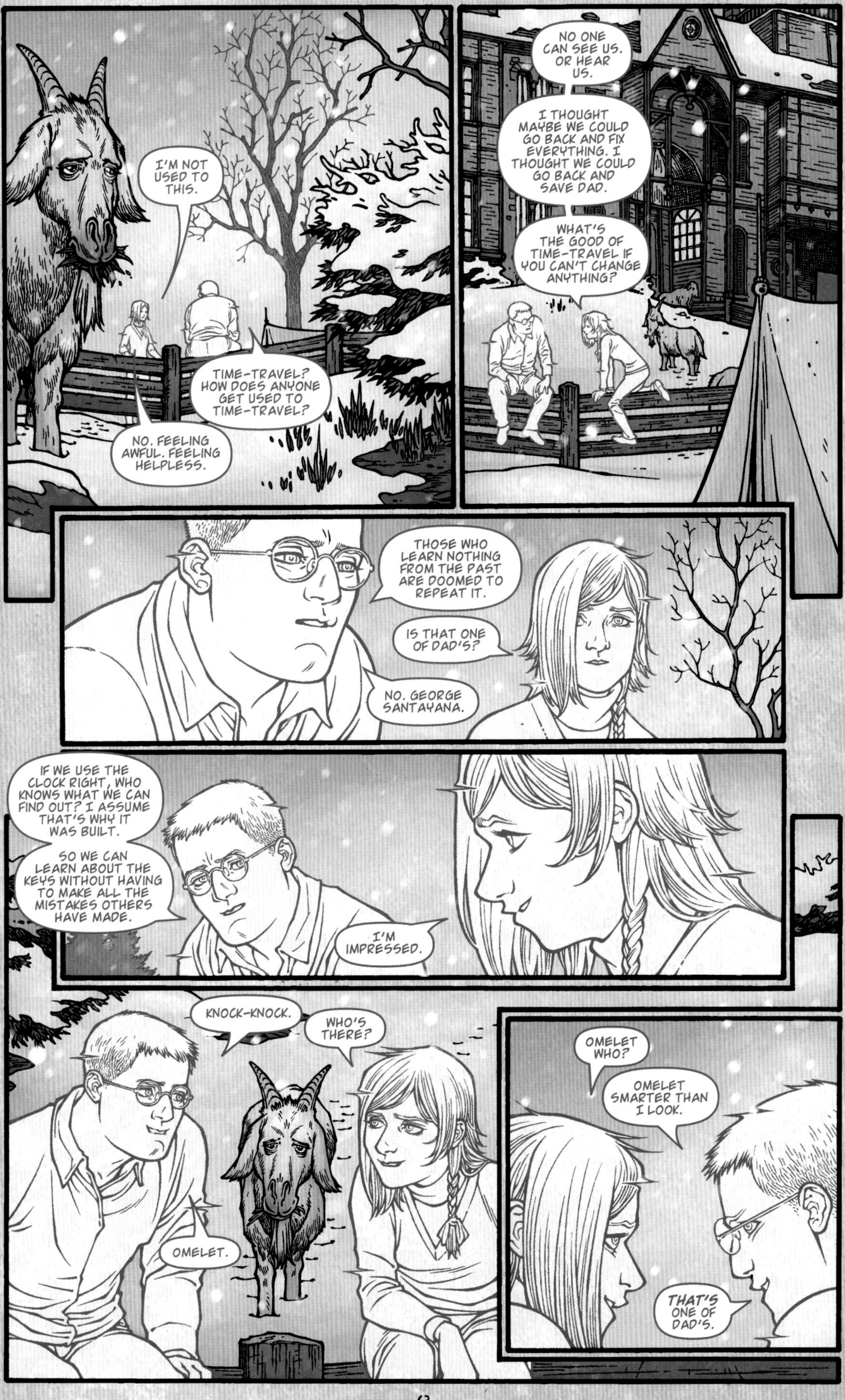

I'M NOT USED TO THIS.
TIME-TRAVEL? HOW DOES ANYONE GET USED TO TIME-TRAVEL?
NO. FEELING AWFUL. FEELING HELPLESS.
NO ONE CAN SEE US. OR HEAR US.
I THOUGHT MAYBE WE COULD GO BACK AND FIX EVERYTHING. I THOUGHT WE COULD GO BACK AND SAVE DAD.
WHAT'S THE GOOD OF TIME-TRAVEL IF YOU CAN'T CHANGE ANYTHING?
THOSE WHO LEARN NOTHING FROM THE PAST ARE DOOMED TO REPEAT IT.
IS THAT ONE OF DAD'S?
NO. GEORGE SANTAYANA.
IF WE USE THE CLOCK RIGHT, WHO KNOWS WHAT WE CAN FIND OUT? I ASSUME THAT'S WHY IT WAS BUILT.
SO WE CAN LEARN ABOUT THE KEYS WITHOUT HAVING TO MAKE ALL THE MISTAKES OTHERS HAVE MADE.
I'M IMPRESSED.
KNOCK-KNOCK.
WHO'S THERE?
OMELET.
OMELET WHO?
OMELET SMARTER THAN I LOOK.
THAT'S ONE OF DAD'S.

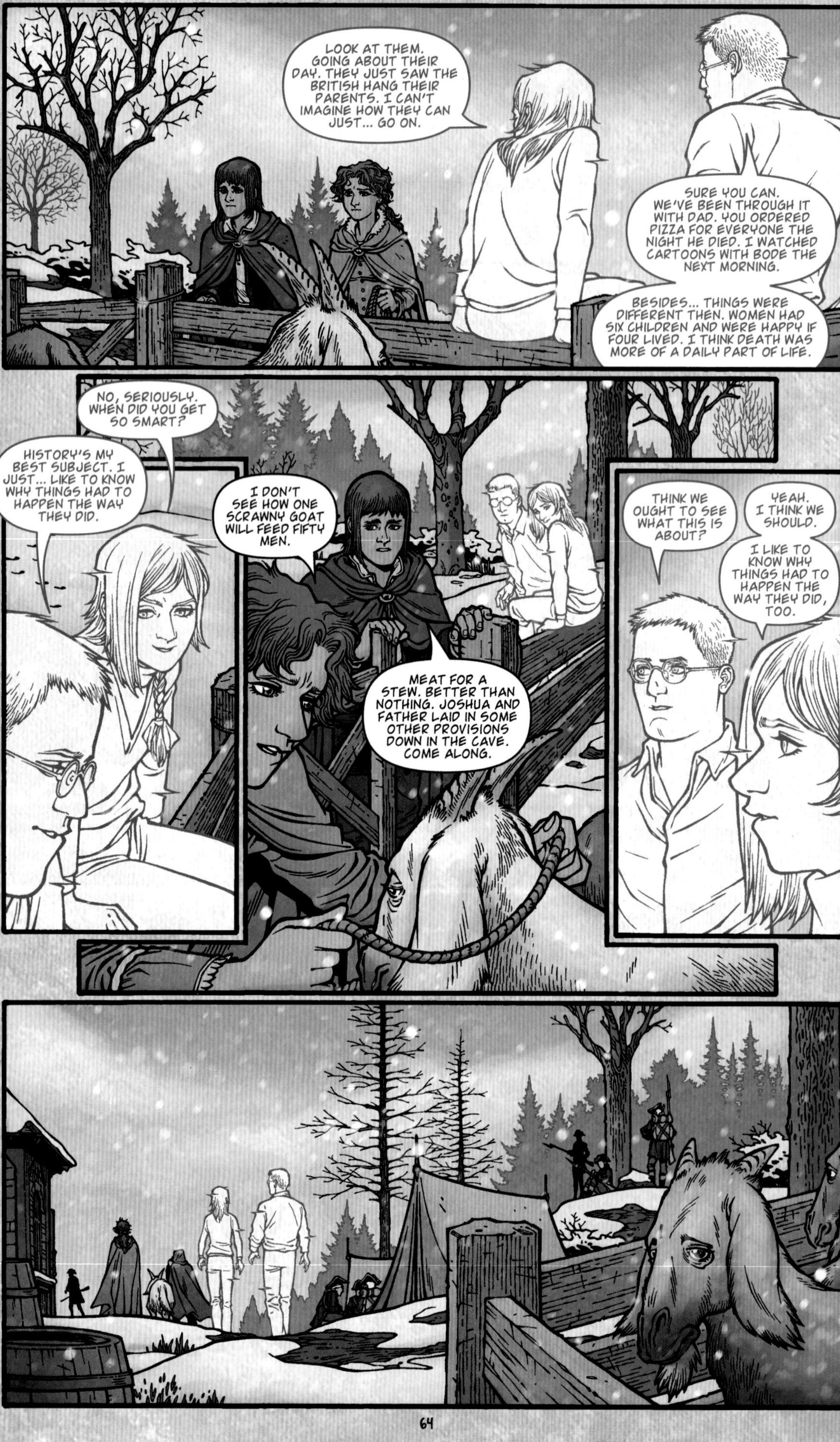

LOOK AT THEM. GOING ABOUT THEIR DAY. THEY JUST SAW THE BRITISH HANG THEIR PARENTS. I CAN'T IMAGINE HOW THEY CAN JUST... GO ON.
SURE YOU CAN. WE'VE BEEN THROUGH IT WITH DAD. YOU ORDERED PIZZA FOR EVERYONE THE NIGHT HE DIED. I WATCHED CARTOONS WITH BODE THE NEXT MORNING.
BESIDES... THINGS WERE DIFFERENT THEN. WOMEN HAD SIX CHILDREN AND WERE HAPPY IF FOUR LIVED. I THINK DEATH WAS MORE OF A DAILY PART OF LIFE.
NO, SERIOUSLY. WHEN DID YOU GET SO SMART?
HISTORY'S MY BEST SUBJECT. I JUST... LIKE TO KNOW WHY THINGS HAD TO HAPPEN THE WAY THEY DID.
I DON'T SEE HOW ONE SCRAWNY GOAT WILL FEED FIFTY MEN.
MEAT FOR A STEW. BETTER THAN NOTHING. JOSHUA AND FATHER LAID IN SOME OTHER PROVISIONS DOWN IN THE CAVE. COME ALONG.
THINK WE OUGHT TO SEE WHAT THIS IS ABOUT?
YEAH. I THINK WE SHOULD.
I LIKE TO KNOW WHY THINGS HAD TO HAPPEN THE WAY THEY DID, TOO.

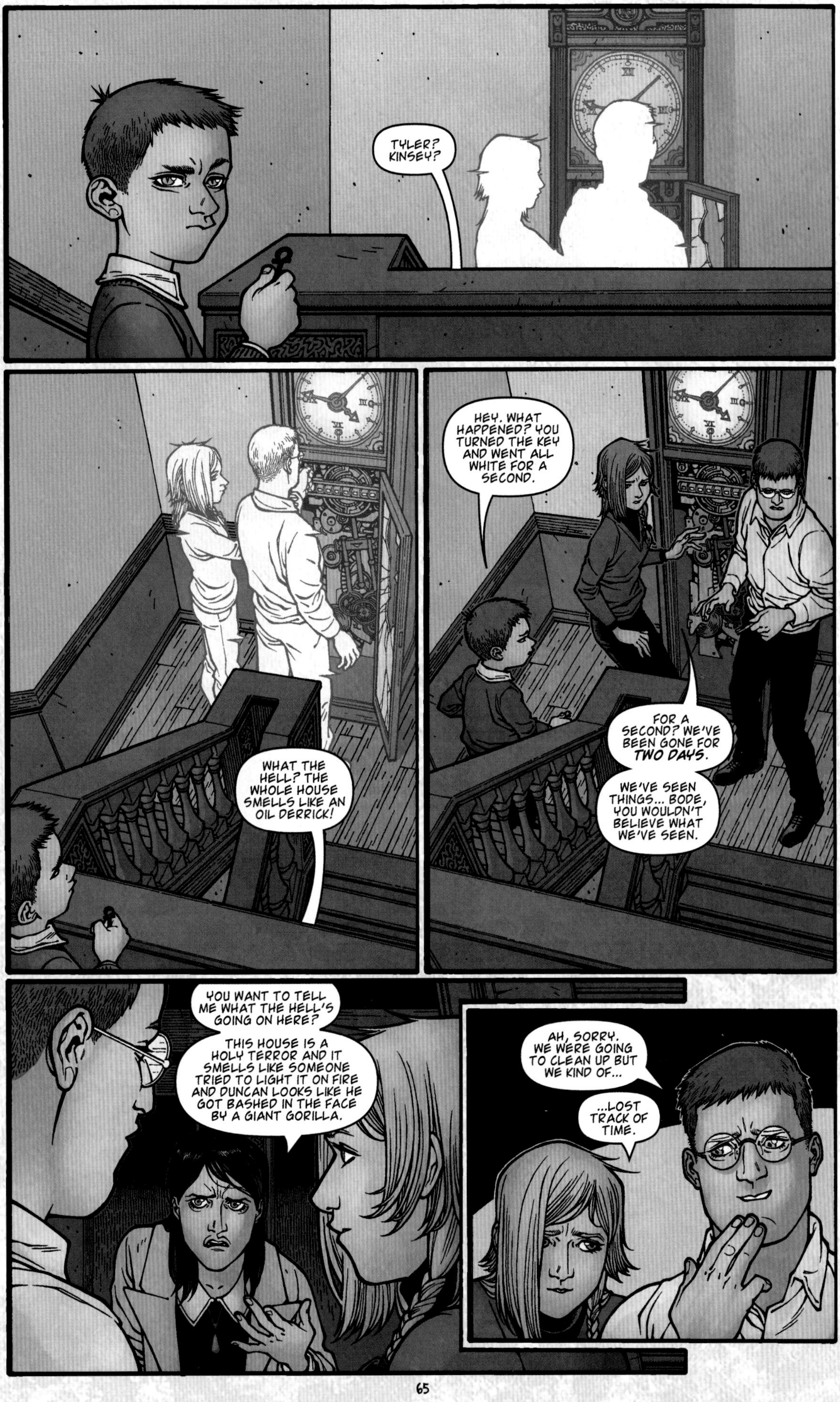
TYLER? KINSEY?
WHAT THE HELL? THE WHOLE HOUSE SMELLS LIKE AN OIL DERRICK!
HEY. WHAT HAPPENED? YOU TURNED THE KEY AND WENT ALL WHITE FOR A SECOND.
FOR A SECOND? WE'VE BEEN GONE FOR TWO DAYS.
WE'VE SEEN THINGS... BODE, YOU WOULDN'T BELIEVE WHAT WE'VE SEEN.
YOU WANT TO TELL ME WHAT THE HELL'S GOING ON HERE?
THIS HOUSE IS A HOLY TERROR AND IT SMELLS LIKE SOMEONE TRIED TO LIGHT IT ON FIRE AND DUNCAN LOOKS LIKE HE GOT BASHED IN THE FACE BY A GIANT GORILLA.
AH, SORRY. WE WERE GOING TO CLEAN UP BUT WE KIND OF...
...LOST TRACK OF TIME.

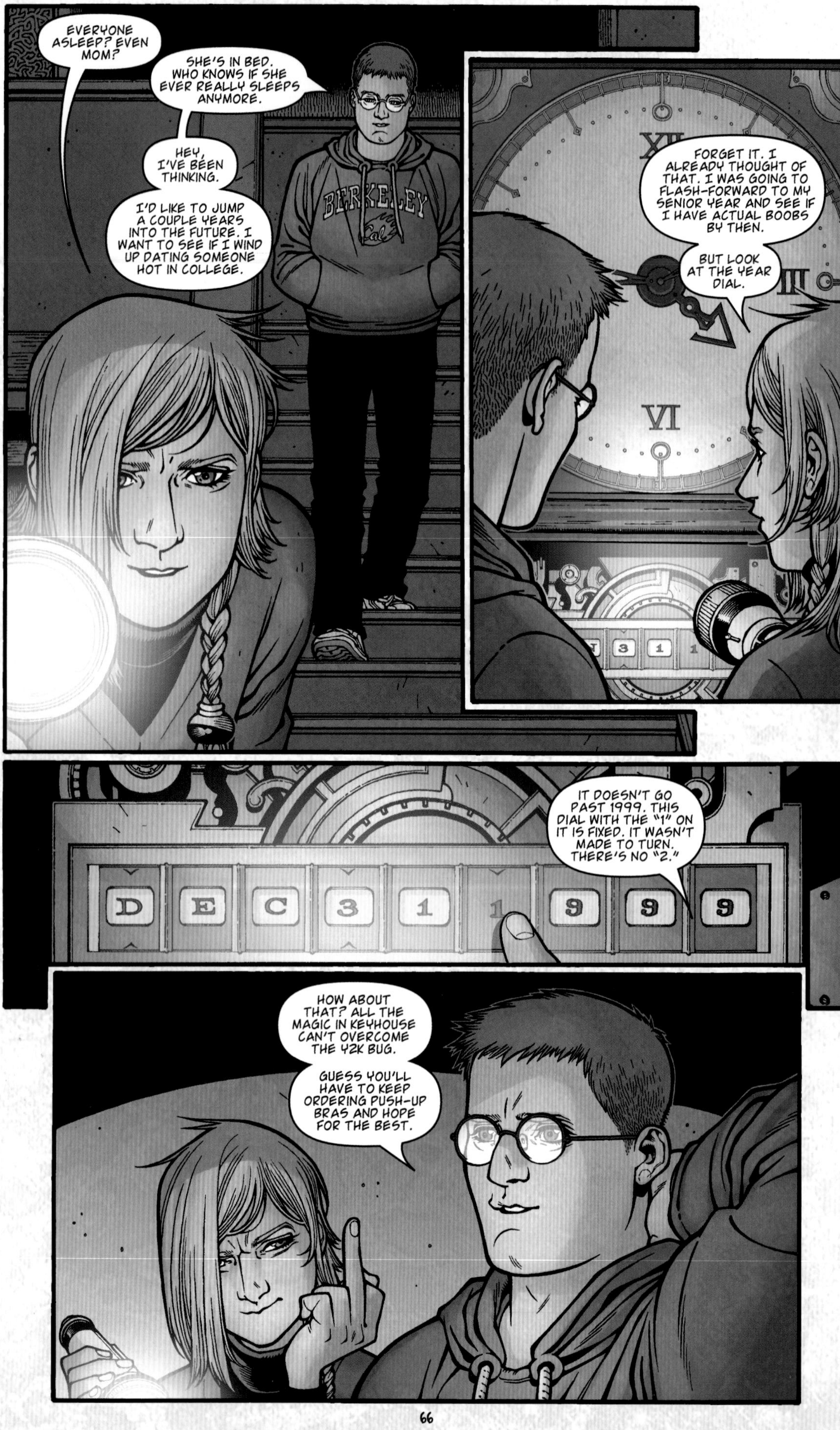
EVERYONE ASLEEP? EVEN MOM?
SHE'S IN BED. WHO KNOWS IF SHE EVER REALLY SLEEPS ANYMORE.
HEY, I'VE BEEN THINKING.
I'D LIKE TO JUMP A COUPLE YEARS INTO THE FUTURE. I WANT TO SEE IF I WIND UP DATING SOMEONE HOT IN COLLEGE.
BERKELEY
FORGET IT. I ALREADY THOUGHT OF THAT. I WAS GOING TO FLASH-FORWARD TO MY SENIOR YEAR AND SEE IF I HAVE ACTUAL BOOBS BY THEN.
BUT LOOK AT THE YEAR DIAL.
IT DOESN'T GO PAST 1999. THIS DIAL WITH THE "1" ON IT IS FIXED. IT WASN'T MADE TO TURN. THERE'S NO "2."
D E C 3 1 1 9 9 9
HOW ABOUT THAT? ALL THE MAGIC IN KEYHOUSE CAN'T OVERCOME THE Y2K BUG.
GUESS YOU'LL HAVE TO KEEP ORDERING PUSH-UP BRAS AND HOPE FOR THE BEST.

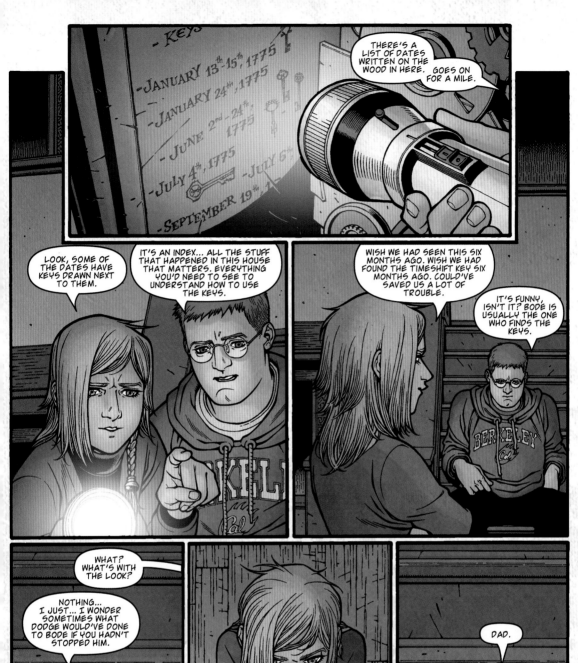

- Keys

-JANUARY 13th-15th, 1775

-JANUARY 24th, 1775

-JUNE 2nd-24th, 1775

-JULY 4th, 1775

-SEPTEMBER 19th, 1

THERE'S A LIST OF DATES WRITTEN ON THE WOOD IN HERE. GOES ON FOR A MILE.

LOOK, SOME OF THE DATES HAVE KEYS DRAWN NEXT TO THEM.

IT'S AN INDEX... ALL THE STUFF THAT HAPPENED IN THIS HOUSE THAT MATTERS. EVERYTHING YOU'D NEED TO SEE TO UNDERSTAND HOW TO USE THE KEYS.

WISH WE HAD SEEN THIS SIX MONTHS AGO. WISH WE HAD FOUND THE TIMESHIFT KEY SIX MONTHS AGO. COULD'VE SAVED US A LOT OF TROUBLE.

IT'S FUNNY, ISN'T IT? BODE IS USUALLY THE ONE WHO FINDS THE KEYS.

WHAT? WHAT'S WITH THE LOOK?

NOTHING... I JUST... I WONDER SOMETIMES WHAT DODGE WOULD'VE DONE TO BODE IF YOU HADN'T STOPPED HIM.

I WISH WE COULD GO BACK TO SEE WHAT DODGE DID WHEN HE GOT TO THE HOUSE. RIGHT BEFORE HE DIED. BUT... Y2K BUG, HUH?

SO WHAT DO WE CHECK OUT FIRST? MORE OF BEN LOCKE IN THE REVOLUTIONARY WAR? WHAT ABOUT GREAT-GRANDMA JEAN RAY IN WORLD WAR II? I STILL KIND OF REMEMBER HER. SHE WAS COOL.

WHO DO YOU WANT TO GO BACK AND SEE NOW?

DAD.

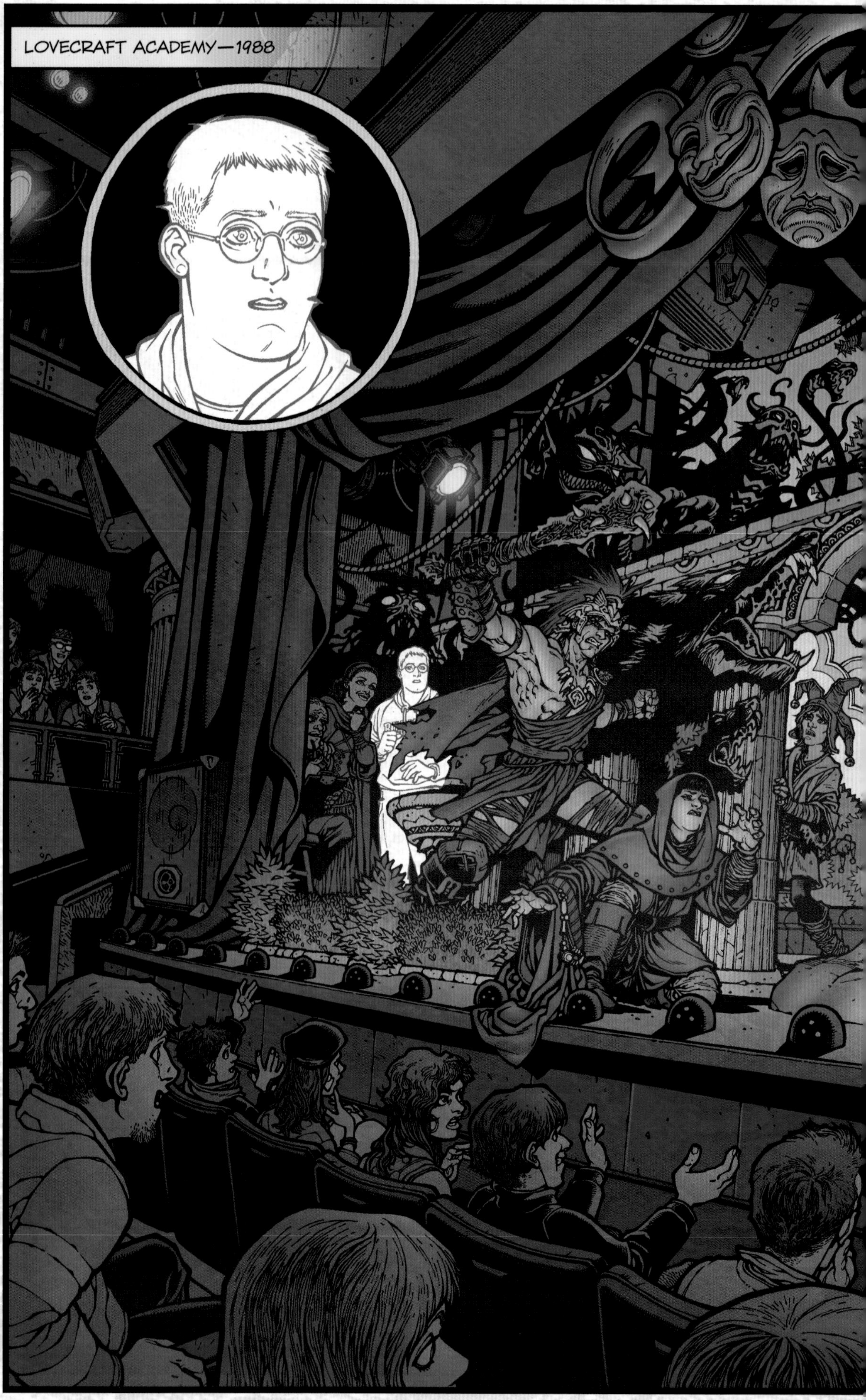
LOVECRAFT ACADEMY—1988

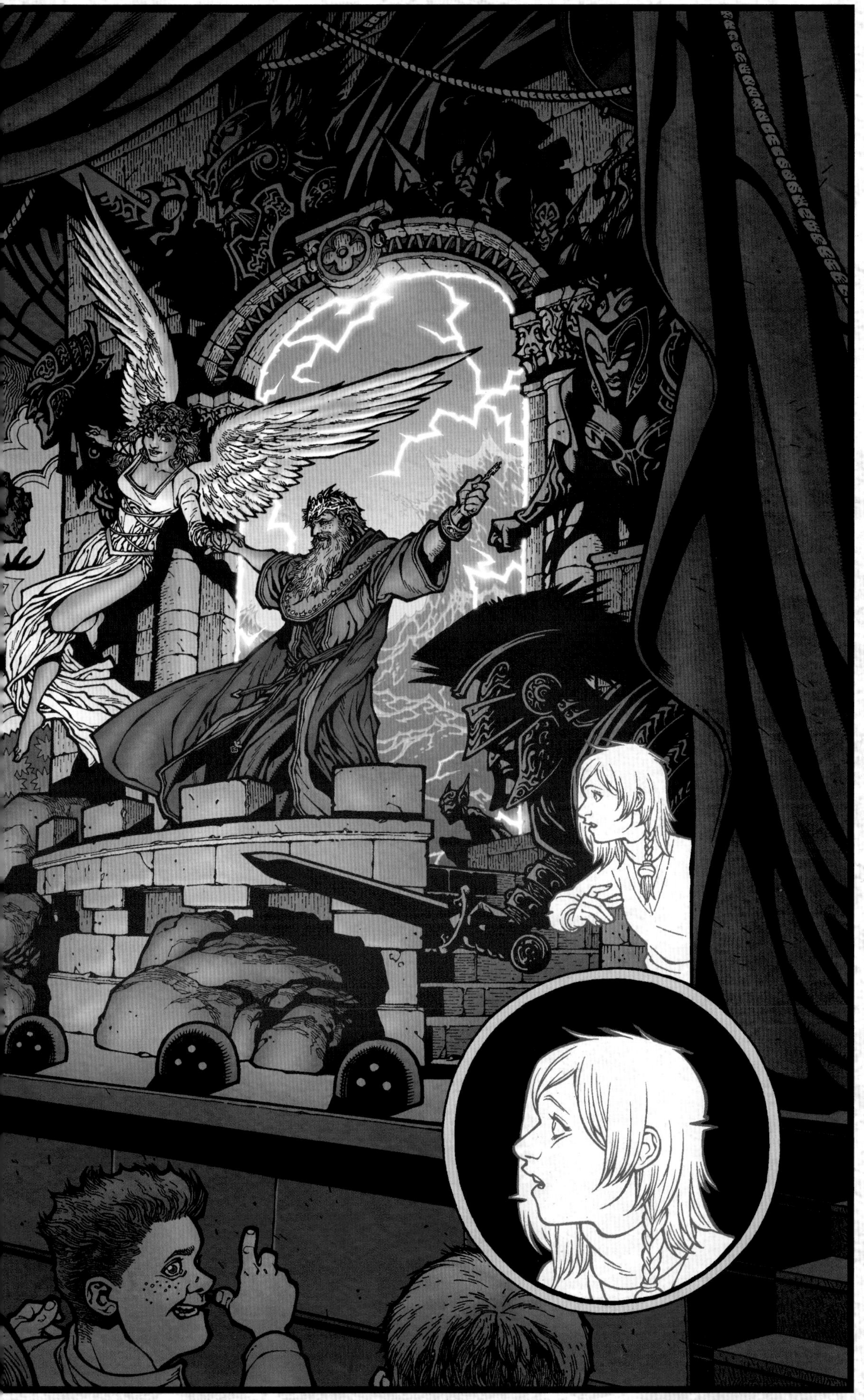

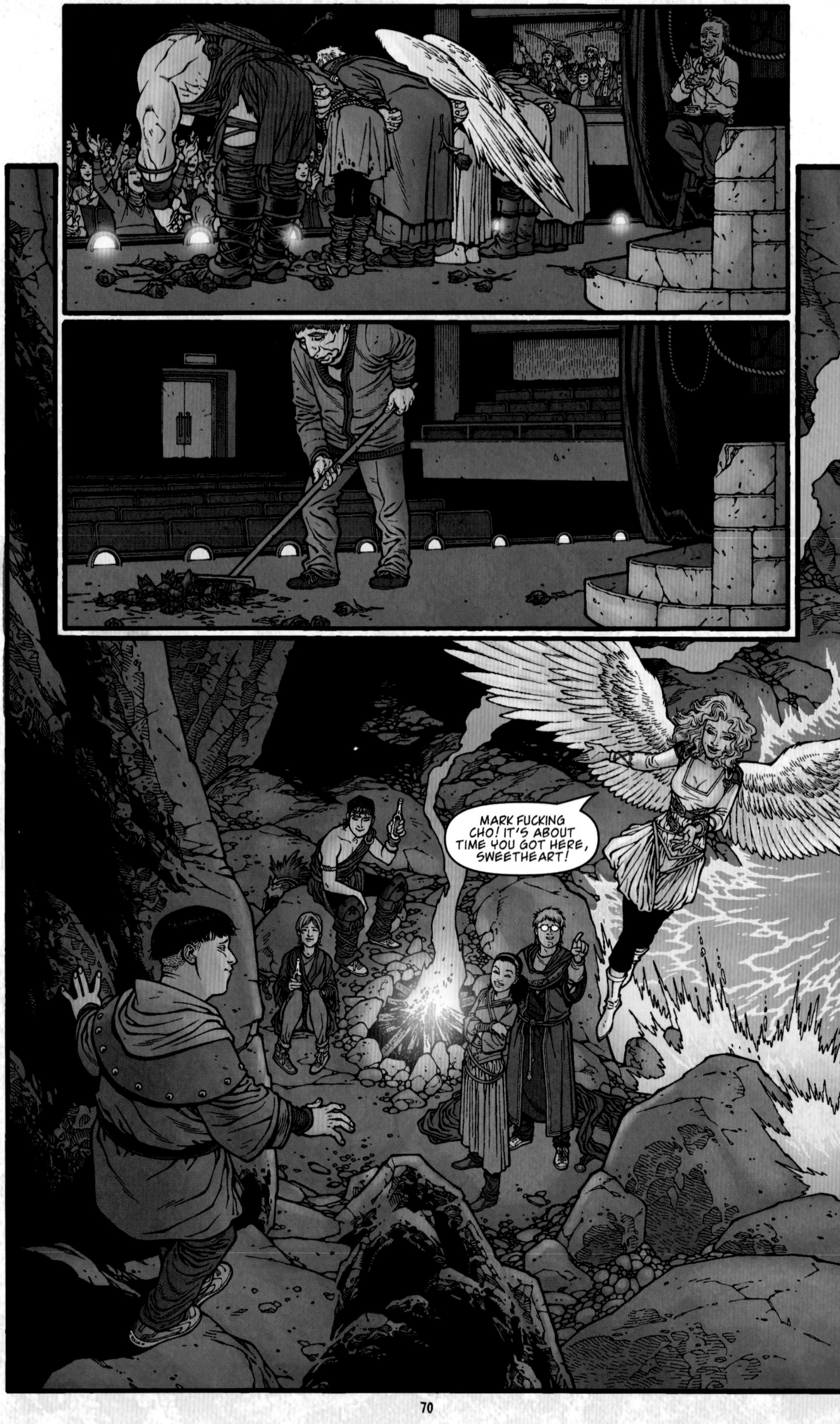
MARK FUCKING CHO! IT'S ABOUT TIME YOU GOT HERE, SWEETHEART!

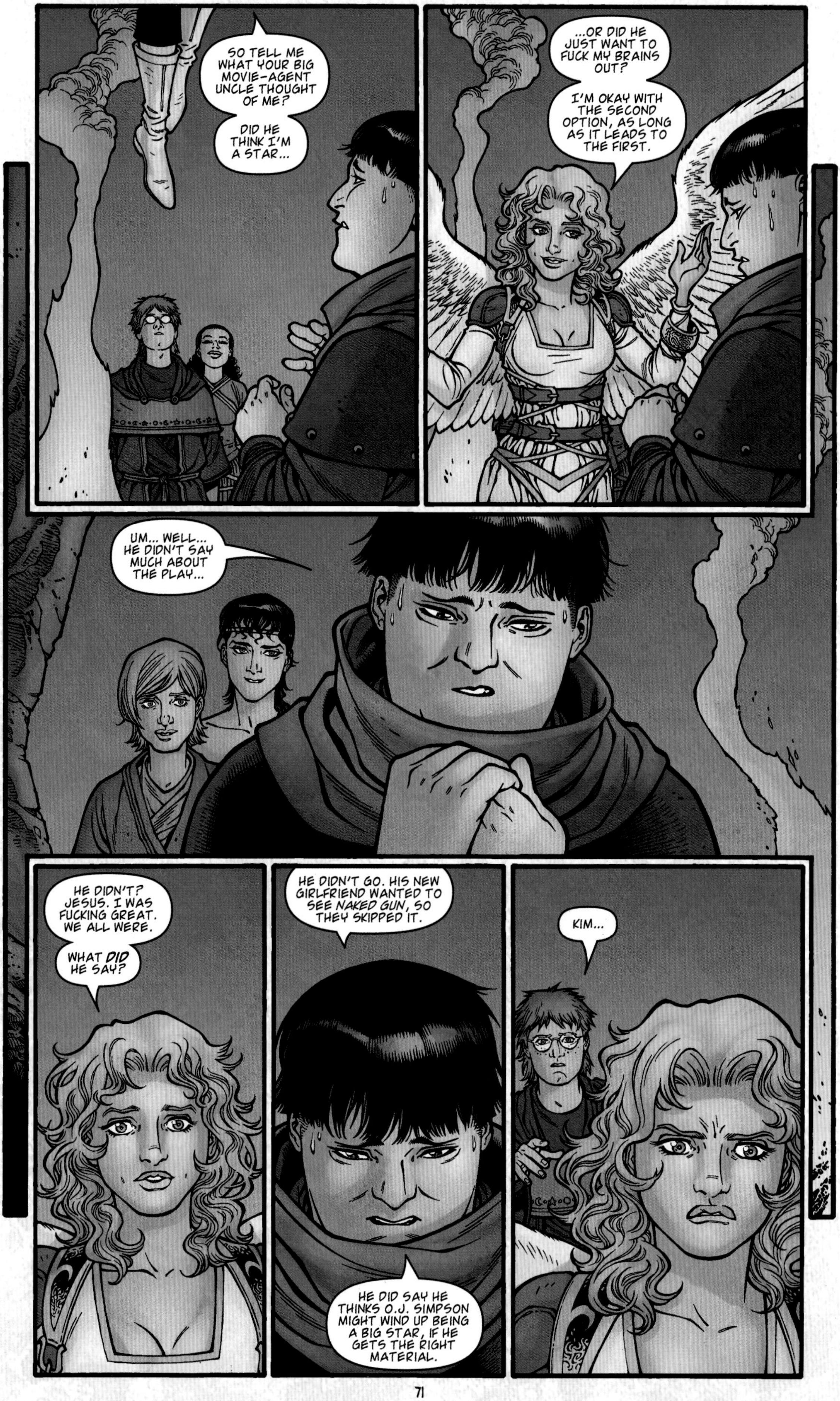
SO TELL ME WHAT YOUR BIG MOVIE-AGENT UNCLE THOUGHT OF ME?
DID HE THINK I'M A STAR...
...OR DID HE JUST WANT TO FUCK MY BRAINS OUT?
I'M OKAY WITH THE SECOND OPTION, AS LONG AS IT LEADS TO THE FIRST.
UM... WELL... HE DIDN'T SAY MUCH ABOUT THE PLAY...
HE DIDN'T? JESUS. I WAS FUCKING GREAT. WE ALL WERE.
WHAT *DID* HE SAY?
HE DIDN'T GO. HIS NEW GIRLFRIEND WANTED TO SEE *NAKED GUN*, SO THEY SKIPPED IT.
HE DID SAY HE THINKS O.J. SIMPSON MIGHT WIND UP BEING A BIG STAR, IF HE GETS THE RIGHT MATERIAL.
KIM...

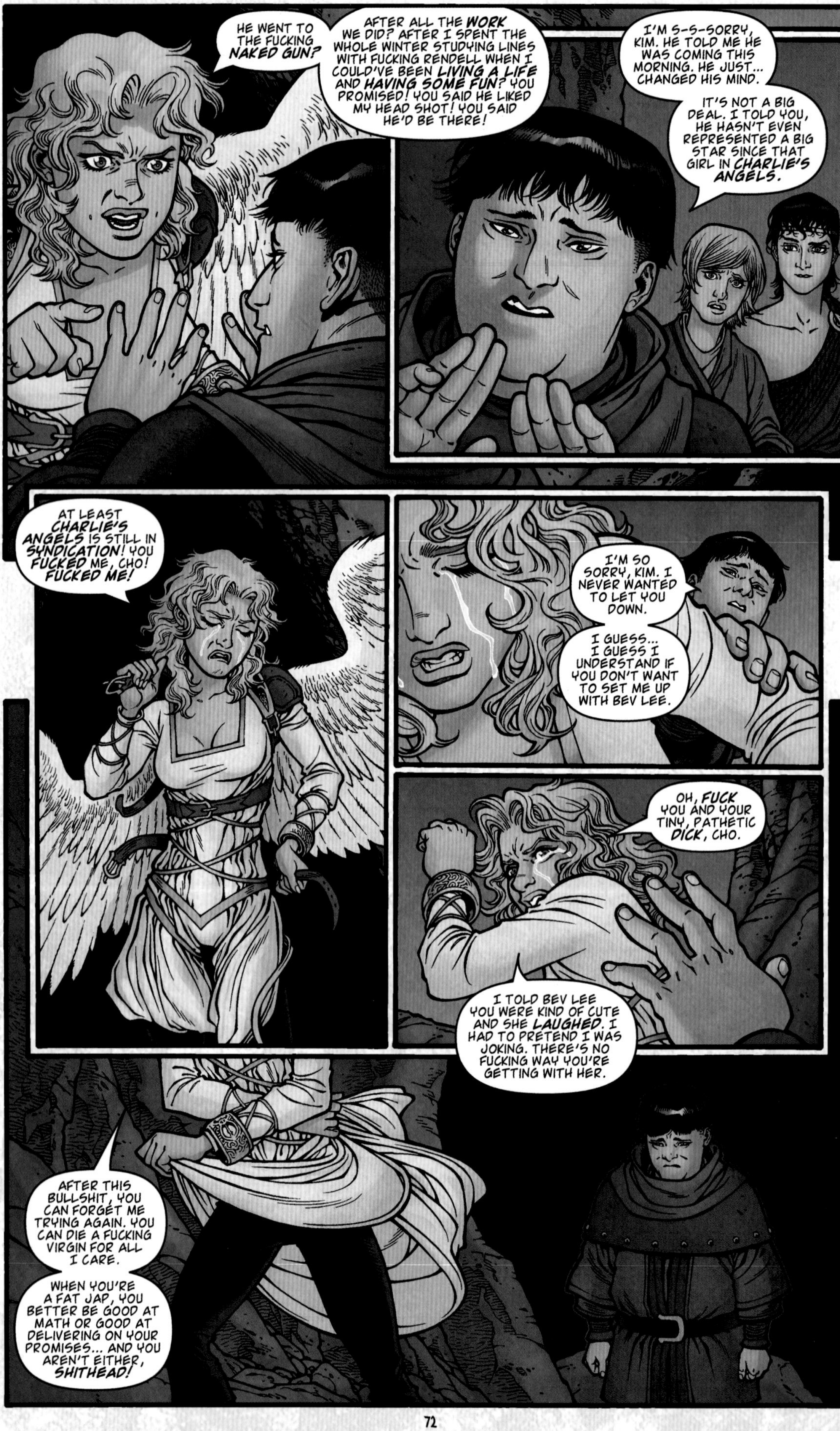
HE WENT TO THE FUCKING NAKED GUN?
AFTER ALL THE WORK WE DID? AFTER I SPENT THE WHOLE WINTER STUDYING LINES WITH FUCKING RENDELL WHEN I COULD'VE BEEN LIVING A LIFE AND HAVING SOME FUN? YOU PROMISED! YOU SAID HE LIKED MY HEAD SHOT! YOU SAID HE'D BE THERE!
I'M S-S-SORRY, KIM. HE TOLD ME HE WAS COMING THIS MORNING. HE JUST... CHANGED HIS MIND.
IT'S NOT A BIG DEAL. I TOLD YOU, HE HASN'T EVEN REPRESENTED A BIG STAR SINCE THAT GIRL IN CHARLIE'S ANGELS.
AT LEAST CHARLIE'S ANGELS IS STILL IN SYNDICATION! YOU FUCKED ME, CHO! FUCKED ME!
I'M SO SORRY, KIM. I NEVER WANTED TO LET YOU DOWN.
I GUESS... I GUESS I UNDERSTAND IF YOU DON'T WANT TO SET ME UP WITH BEV LEE.
OH, FUCK YOU AND YOUR TINY, PATHETIC DICK, CHO.
I TOLD BEV LEE YOU WERE KIND OF CUTE AND SHE LAUGHED. I HAD TO PRETEND I WAS JOKING. THERE'S NO FUCKING WAY YOU'RE GETTING WITH HER.
AFTER THIS BULLSHIT, YOU CAN FORGET ME TRYING AGAIN. YOU CAN DIE A FUCKING VIRGIN FOR ALL I CARE.
WHEN YOU'RE A FAT JAP, YOU BETTER BE GOOD AT MATH OR GOOD AT DELIVERING ON YOUR PROMISES... AND YOU AREN'T EITHER, SHITHEAD!

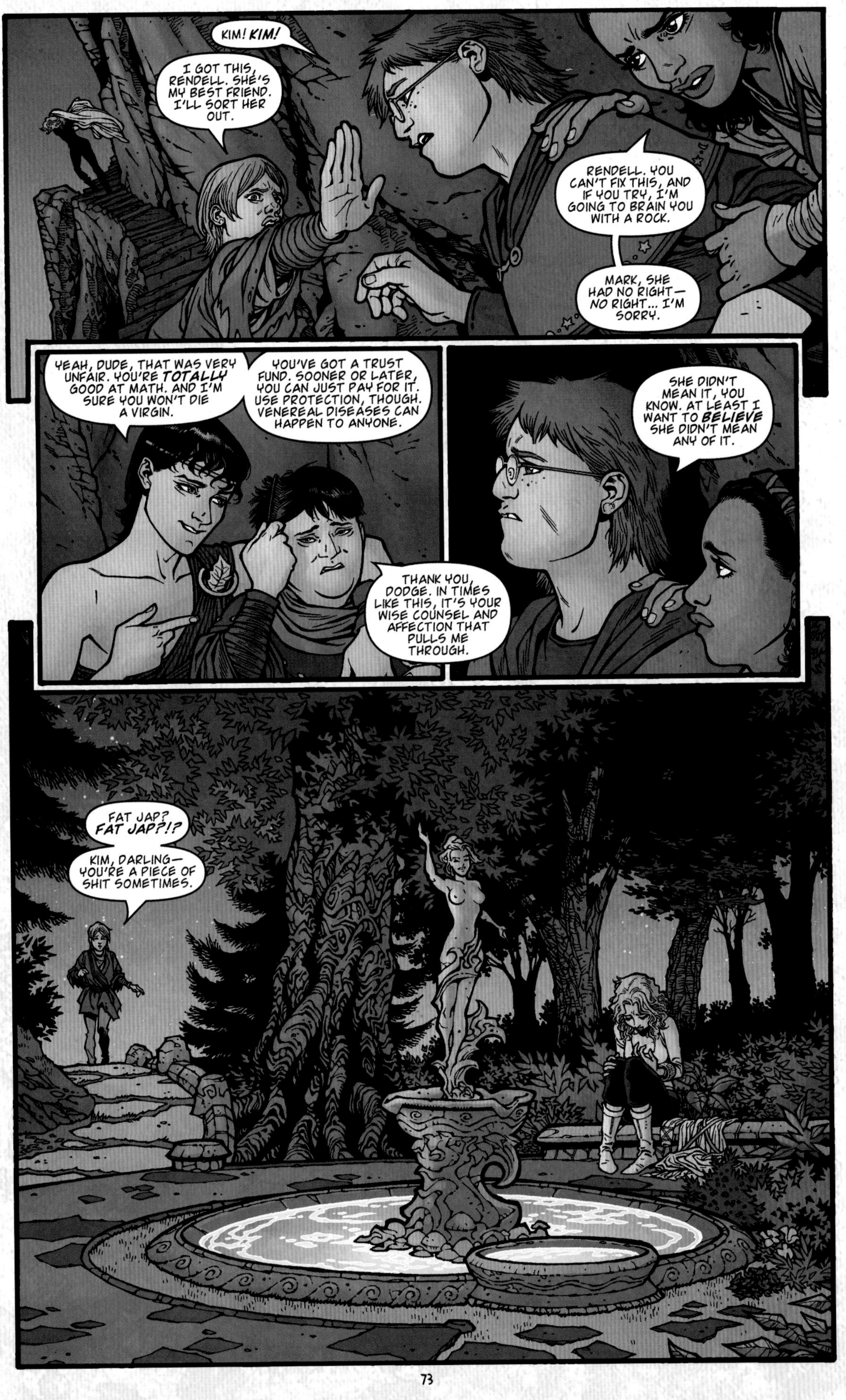
KIM! KIM!
I GOT THIS, RENDELL. SHE'S MY BEST FRIEND. I'LL SORT HER OUT.
RENDELL. YOU CAN'T FIX THIS, AND IF YOU TRY, I'M GOING TO BRAIN YOU WITH A ROCK.
MARK, SHE HAD NO RIGHT— NO RIGHT... I'M SORRY.
YEAH, DUDE, THAT WAS VERY UNFAIR. YOU'RE TOTALLY GOOD AT MATH. AND I'M SURE YOU WON'T DIE A VIRGIN.
YOU'VE GOT A TRUST FUND. SOONER OR LATER, YOU CAN JUST PAY FOR IT. USE PROTECTION, THOUGH. VENEREAL DISEASES CAN HAPPEN TO ANYONE.
THANK YOU, DODGE. IN TIMES LIKE THIS, IT'S YOUR WISE COUNSEL AND AFFECTION THAT PULLS ME THROUGH.
SHE DIDN'T MEAN IT, YOU KNOW. AT LEAST I WANT TO BELIEVE SHE DIDN'T MEAN ANY OF IT.
FAT JAP? FAT JAP?!?
KIM, DARLING— YOU'RE A PIECE OF SHIT SOMETIMES.

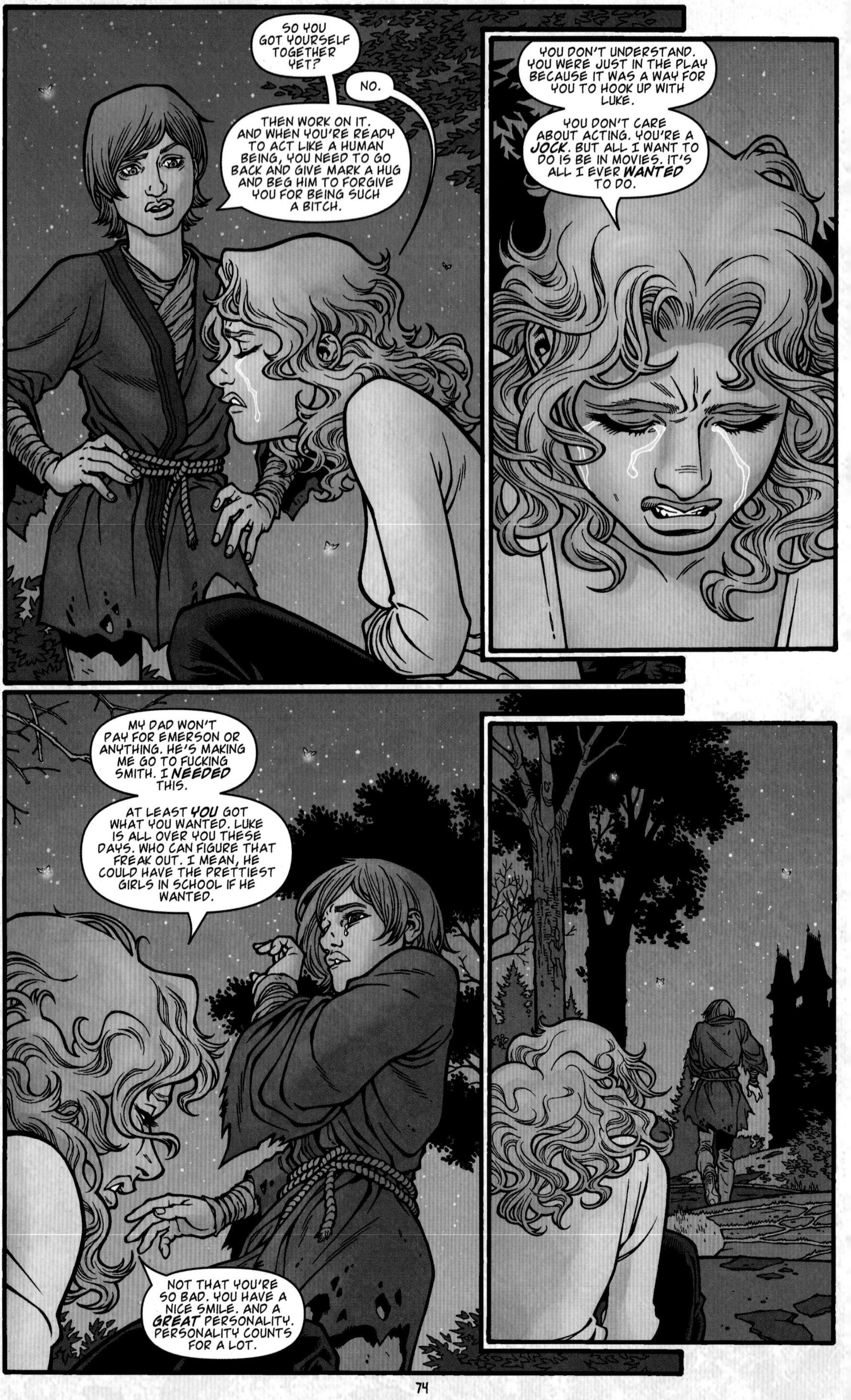
SO YOU GOT YOURSELF TOGETHER YET?
NO.
THEN WORK ON IT. AND WHEN YOU'RE READY TO ACT LIKE A HUMAN BEING, YOU NEED TO GO BACK AND GIVE MARK A HUG AND BEG HIM TO FORGIVE YOU FOR BEING SUCH A BITCH.
YOU DON'T UNDERSTAND. YOU WERE JUST IN THE PLAY BECAUSE IT WAS A WAY FOR YOU TO HOOK UP WITH LUKE.
YOU DON'T CARE ABOUT ACTING. YOU'RE A JOCK. BUT ALL I WANT TO DO IS BE IN MOVIES. IT'S ALL I EVER WANTED TO DO.
MY DAD WON'T PAY FOR EMERSON OR ANYTHING. HE'S MAKING ME GO TO FUCKING SMITH. I NEEDED THIS.
AT LEAST YOU GOT WHAT YOU WANTED. LUKE IS ALL OVER YOU THESE DAYS. WHO CAN FIGURE THAT FREAK OUT. I MEAN, HE COULD HAVE THE PRETTIEST GIRLS IN SCHOOL IF HE WANTED.
NOT THAT YOU'RE SO BAD. YOU HAVE A NICE SMILE. AND A GREAT PERSONALITY. PERSONALITY COUNTS FOR A LOT.

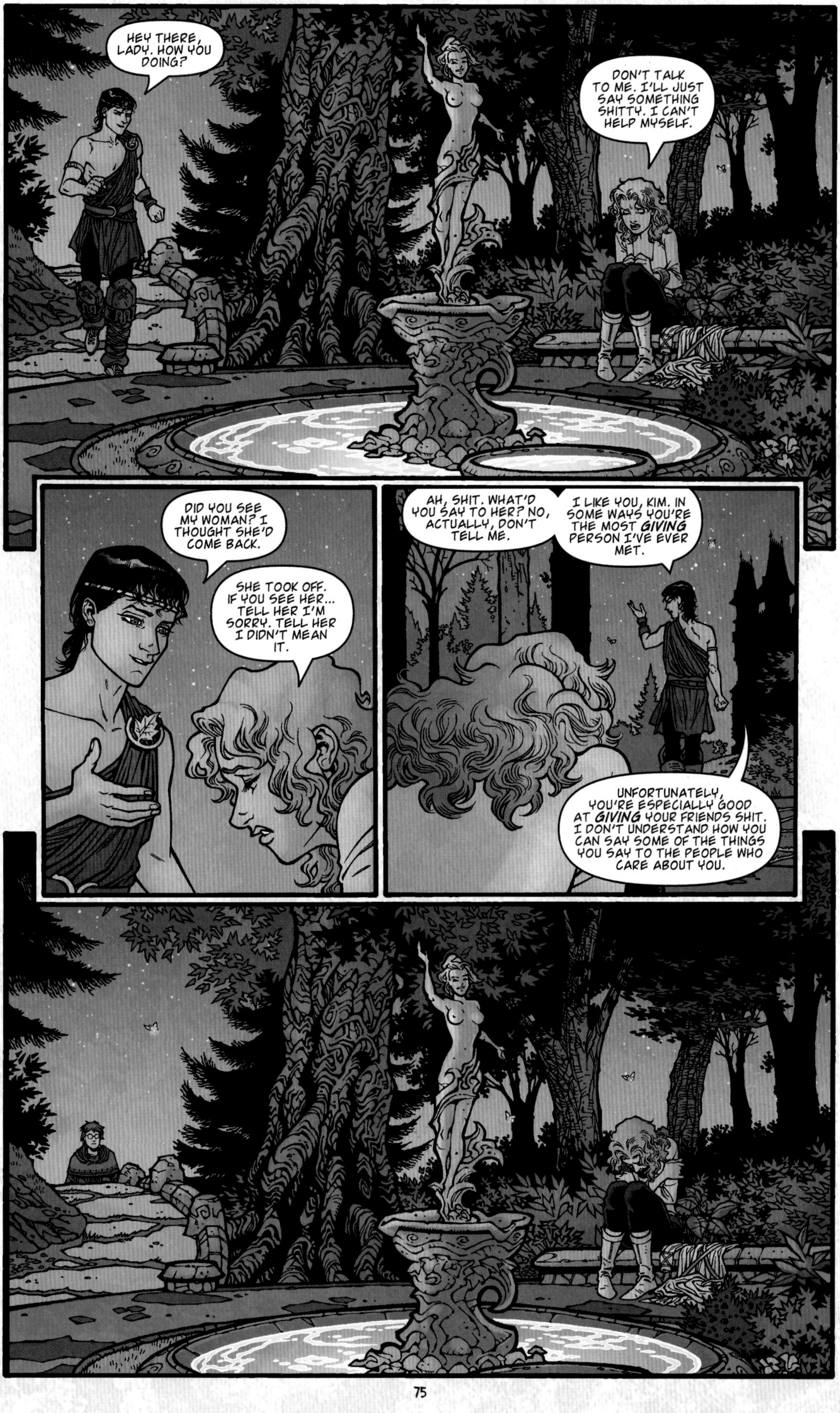
HEY THERE, LADY. HOW YOU DOING?
DON'T TALK TO ME. I'LL JUST SAY SOMETHING SHITTY. I CAN'T HELP MYSELF.
DID YOU SEE MY WOMAN? I THOUGHT SHE'D COME BACK.
SHE TOOK OFF. IF YOU SEE HER... TELL HER I'M SORRY. TELL HER I DIDN'T MEAN IT.
AH, SHIT. WHAT'D YOU SAY TO HER? NO, ACTUALLY, DON'T TELL ME.
I LIKE YOU, KIM. IN SOME WAYS YOU'RE THE MOST GIVING PERSON I'VE EVER MET.
UNFORTUNATELY, YOU'RE ESPECIALLY GOOD AT GIVING YOUR FRIENDS SHIT. I DON'T UNDERSTAND HOW YOU CAN SAY SOME OF THE THINGS YOU SAY TO THE PEOPLE WHO CARE ABOUT YOU.

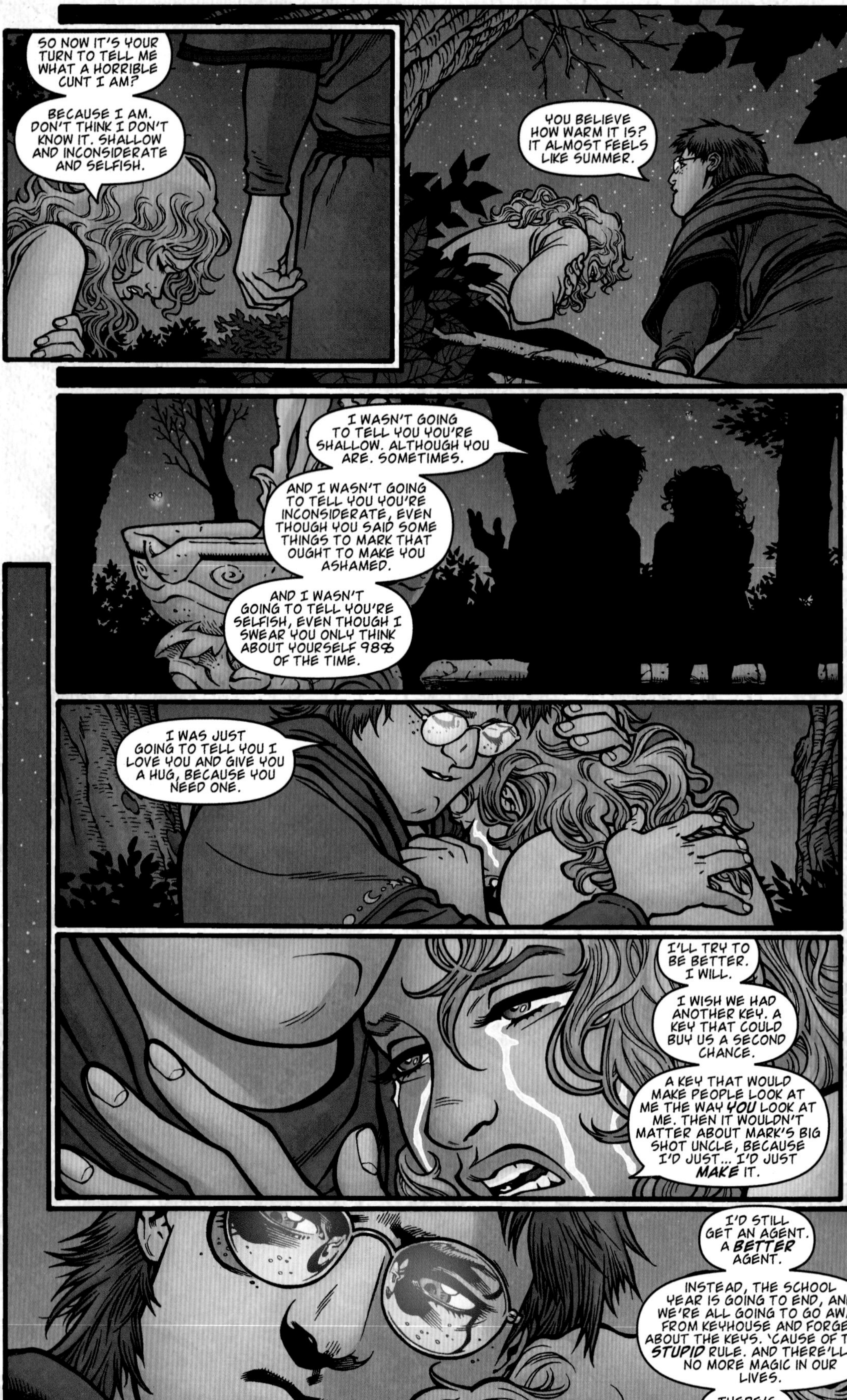
SO NOW IT'S YOUR TURN TO TELL ME WHAT A HORRIBLE CUNT I AM?
BECAUSE I AM. DON'T THINK I DON'T KNOW IT. SHALLOW AND INCONSIDERATE AND SELFISH.
YOU BELIEVE HOW WARM IT IS? IT ALMOST FEELS LIKE SUMMER.
I WASN'T GOING TO TELL YOU YOU'RE SHALLOW. ALTHOUGH YOU ARE. SOMETIMES.
AND I WASN'T GOING TO TELL YOU YOU'RE INCONSIDERATE, EVEN THOUGH YOU SAID SOME THINGS TO MARK THAT OUGHT TO MAKE YOU ASHAMED.
AND I WASN'T GOING TO TELL YOU'RE SELFISH, EVEN THOUGH I SWEAR YOU ONLY THINK ABOUT YOURSELF 98% OF THE TIME.
I WAS JUST GOING TO TELL YOU I LOVE YOU AND GIVE YOU A HUG, BECAUSE YOU NEED ONE.
I'LL TRY TO BE BETTER. I WILL.
I WISH WE HAD ANOTHER KEY. A KEY THAT COULD BUY US A SECOND CHANCE.
A KEY THAT WOULD MAKE PEOPLE LOOK AT ME THE WAY YOU LOOK AT ME. THEN IT WOULDN'T MATTER ABOUT MARK'S BIG SHOT UNCLE, BECAUSE I'D JUST... I'D JUST MAKE IT.
I'D STILL GET AN AGENT. A BETTER AGENT.
INSTEAD, THE SCHOOL YEAR IS GOING TO END, AND WE'RE ALL GOING TO GO AWAY FROM KEYHOUSE AND FORGET ABOUT THE KEYS. 'CAUSE OF THAT STUPID RULE. AND THERE'LL BE NO MORE MAGIC IN OUR LIVES.
THERE'S NO HOPE, IS THERE?

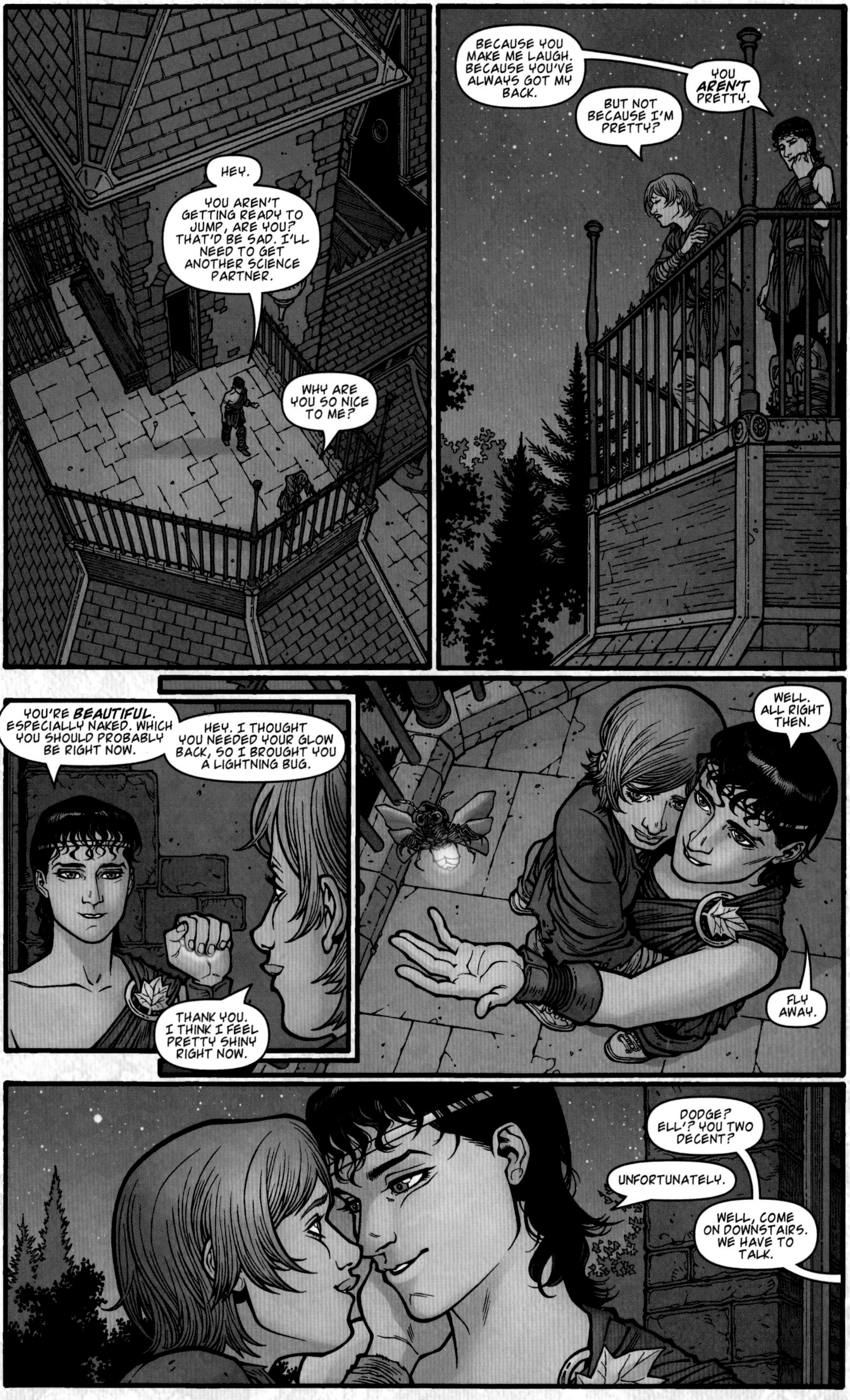
HEY.
YOU AREN'T GETTING READY TO JUMP, ARE YOU? THAT'D BE SAD. I'LL NEED TO GET ANOTHER SCIENCE PARTNER.
WHY ARE YOU SO NICE TO ME?
BECAUSE YOU MAKE ME LAUGH. BECAUSE YOU'VE ALWAYS GOT MY BACK.
BUT NOT BECAUSE I'M PRETTY?
YOU AREN'T PRETTY.
YOU'RE BEAUTIFUL. ESPECIALLY NAKED. WHICH YOU SHOULD PROBABLY BE RIGHT NOW.
HEY. I THOUGHT YOU NEEDED YOUR GLOW BACK, SO I BROUGHT YOU A LIGHTNING BUG.
THANK YOU. I THINK I FEEL PRETTY SHINY RIGHT NOW.
WELL. ALL RIGHT THEN.
FLY AWAY.
DODGE? ELL'? YOU TWO DECENT?
UNFORTUNATELY.
WELL, COME ON DOWNSTAIRS. WE HAVE TO TALK.

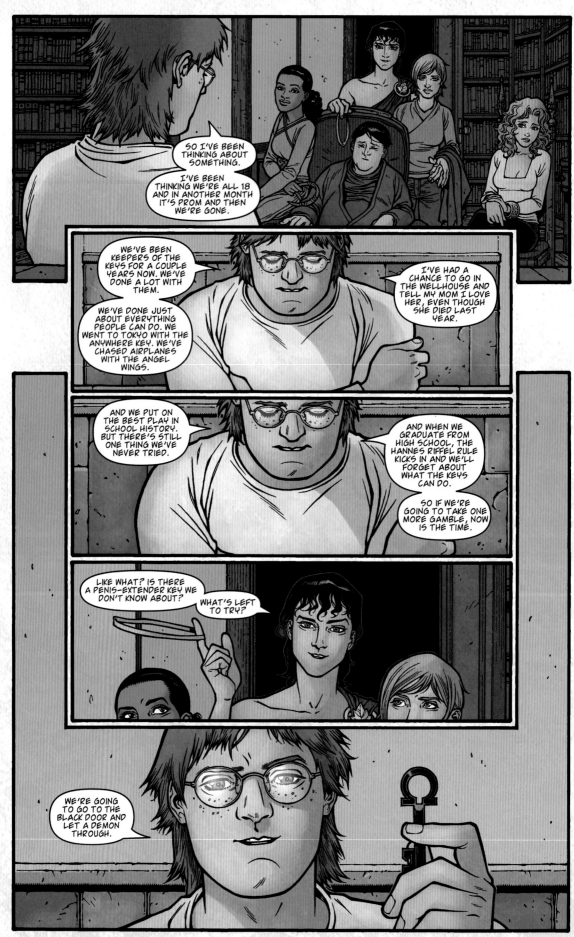

SO I'VE BEEN THINKING ABOUT SOMETHING.

I'VE BEEN THINKING WE'RE ALL 18 AND IN ANOTHER MONTH IT'S PROM AND THEN WE'RE GONE.

WE'VE BEEN KEEPERS OF THE KEYS FOR A COUPLE YEARS NOW. WE'VE DONE A LOT WITH THEM.

WE'VE DONE JUST ABOUT EVERYTHING PEOPLE CAN DO. WE WENT TO TOKYO WITH THE ANYWHERE KEY. WE'VE CHASED AIRPLANES WITH THE ANGEL WINGS.

I'VE HAD A CHANCE TO GO IN THE WELLHOUSE AND TELL MY MOM I LOVE HER, EVEN THOUGH SHE DIED LAST YEAR.

AND WE PUT ON THE BEST PLAY IN SCHOOL HISTORY. BUT THERE'S STILL ONE THING WE'VE NEVER TRIED.

AND WHEN WE GRADUATE FROM HIGH SCHOOL, THE HANNES RIFFEL RULE KICKS IN AND WE'LL FORGET ABOUT WHAT THE KEYS CAN DO.

SO IF WE'RE GOING TO TAKE ONE MORE GAMBLE, NOW IS THE TIME.

LIKE WHAT? IS THERE A PENIS-EXTENDER KEY WE DON'T KNOW ABOUT?

WHAT'S LEFT TO TRY?

WE'RE GOING TO GO TO THE BLACK DOOR AND LET A DEMON THROUGH.

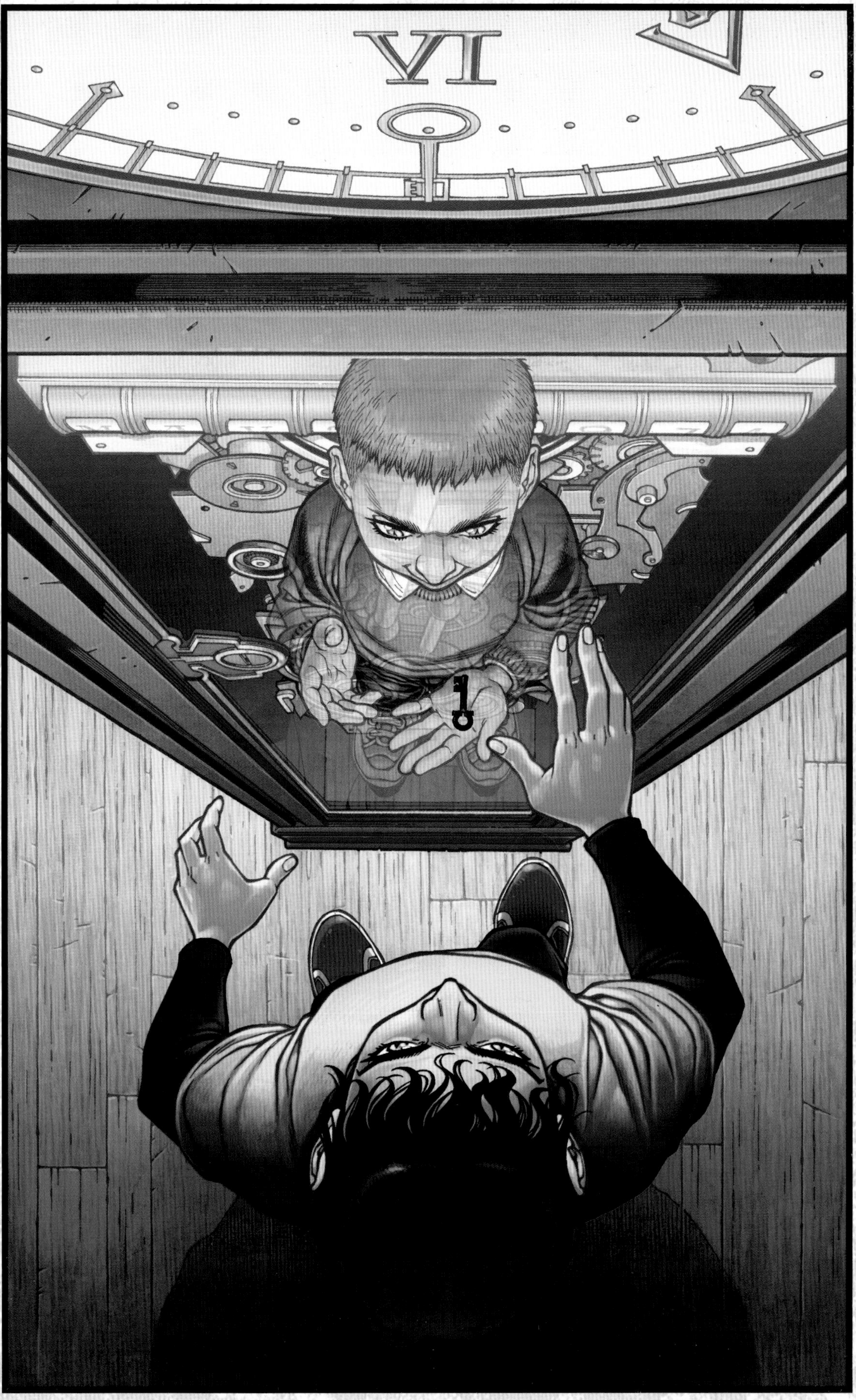

- CLOCKWORKS -
Chapter Four

THE WHISPERING IRON

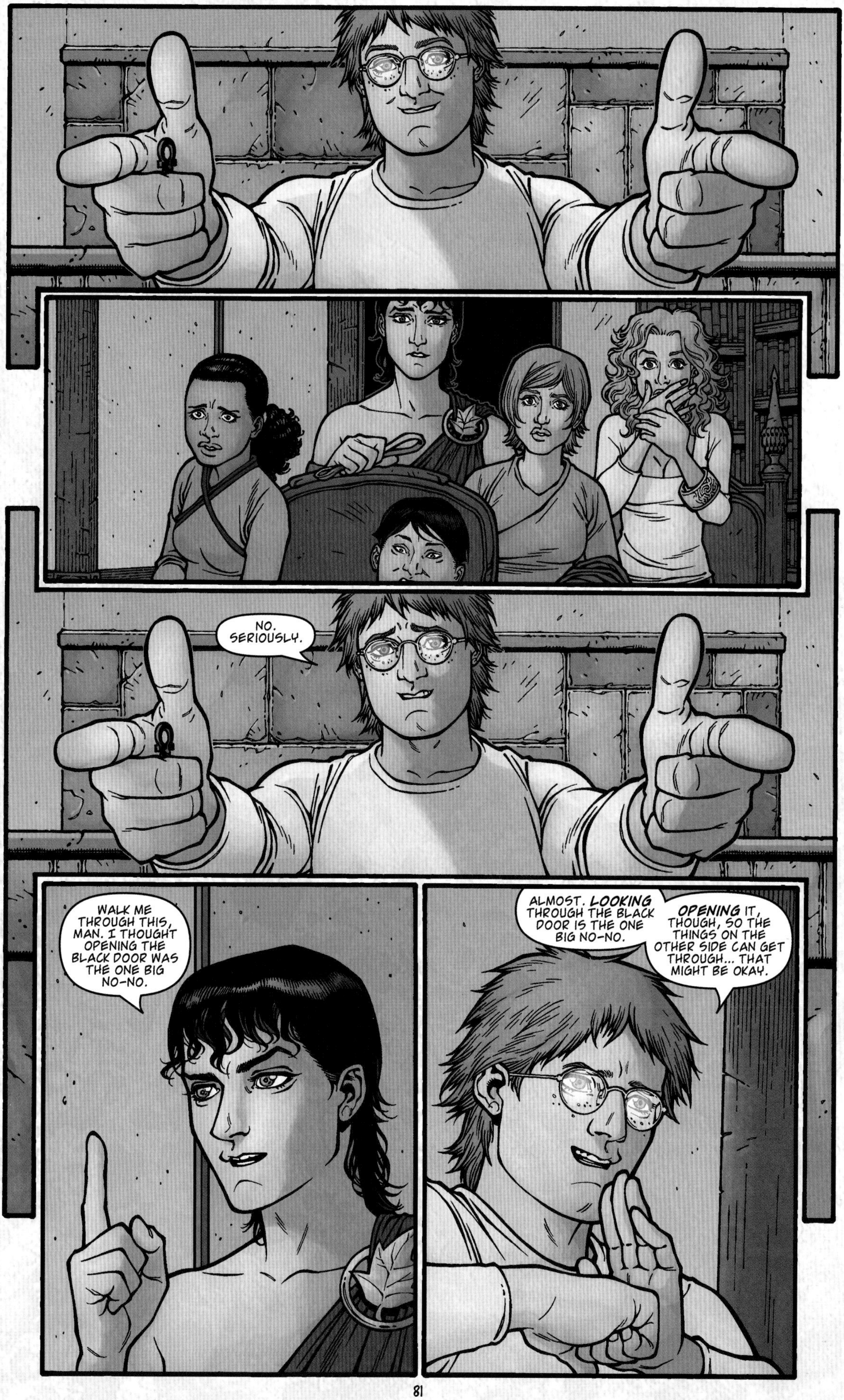
NO. SERIOUSLY.
WALK ME THROUGH THIS, MAN. I THOUGHT OPENING THE BLACK DOOR WAS THE ONE BIG NO-NO.
ALMOST. LOOKING THROUGH THE BLACK DOOR IS THE ONE BIG NO-NO.
OPENING IT, THOUGH, SO THE THINGS ON THE OTHER SIDE CAN GET THROUGH... THAT MIGHT BE OKAY.

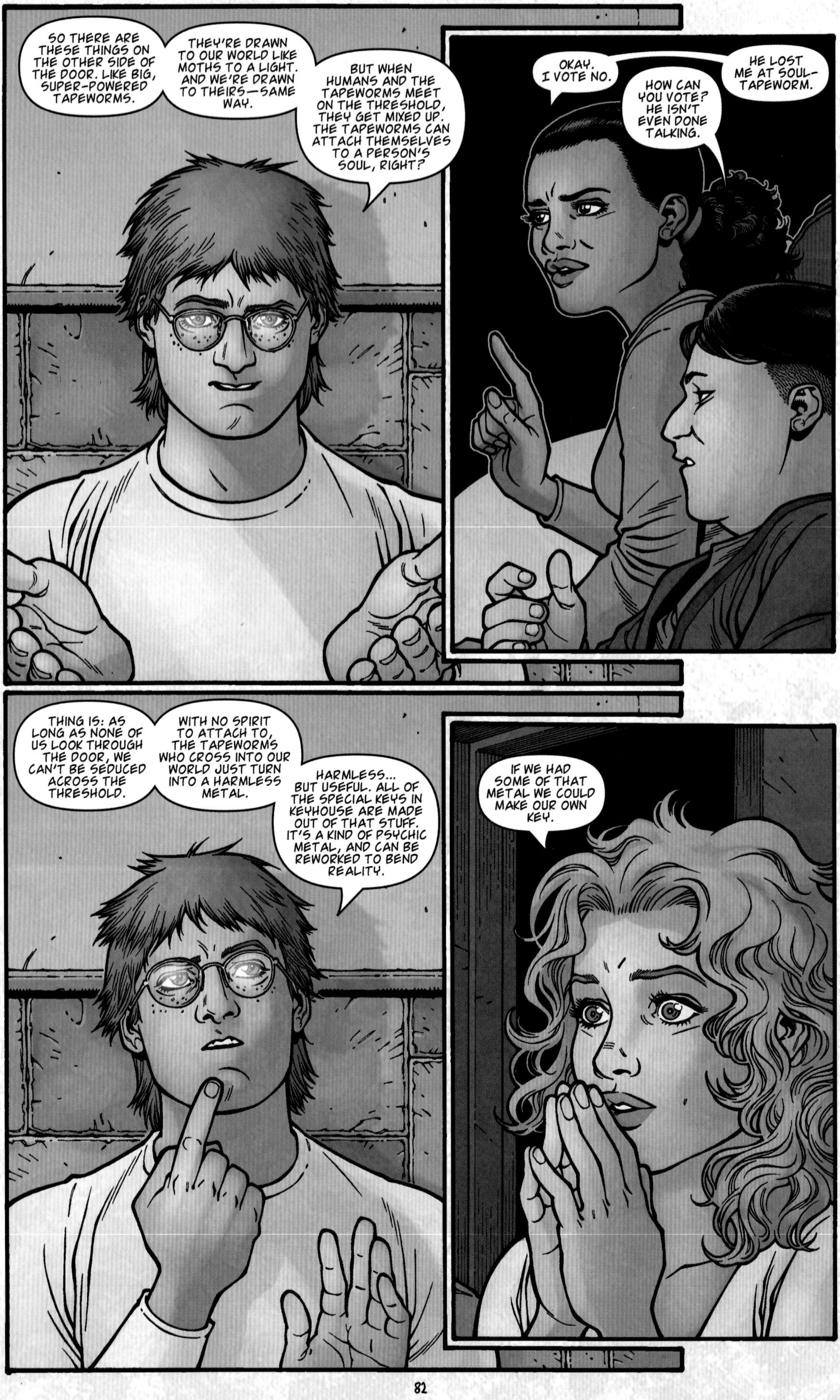

SO THERE ARE THESE THINGS ON THE OTHER SIDE OF THE DOOR. LIKE BIG, SUPER-POWERED TAPEWORMS.
THEY'RE DRAWN TO OUR WORLD LIKE MOTHS TO A LIGHT. AND WE'RE DRAWN TO THEIRS—SAME WAY.
BUT WHEN HUMANS AND THE TAPEWORMS MEET ON THE THRESHOLD, THEY GET MIXED UP. THE TAPEWORMS CAN ATTACH THEMSELVES TO A PERSON'S SOUL, RIGHT?
OKAY. I VOTE NO.
HOW CAN YOU VOTE? HE ISN'T EVEN DONE TALKING.
HE LOST ME AT SOUL-TAPEWORM.
THING IS: AS LONG AS NONE OF US LOOK THROUGH THE DOOR, WE CAN'T BE SEDUCED ACROSS THE THRESHOLD.
WITH NO SPIRIT TO ATTACH TO, THE TAPEWORMS WHO CROSS INTO OUR WORLD JUST TURN INTO A HARMLESS METAL.
HARMLESS... BUT USEFUL. ALL OF THE SPECIAL KEYS IN KEYHOUSE ARE MADE OUT OF THAT STUFF. IT'S A KIND OF PSYCHIC METAL, AND CAN BE REWORKED TO BEND REALITY.
IF WE HAD SOME OF THAT METAL WE COULD MAKE OUR OWN KEY.

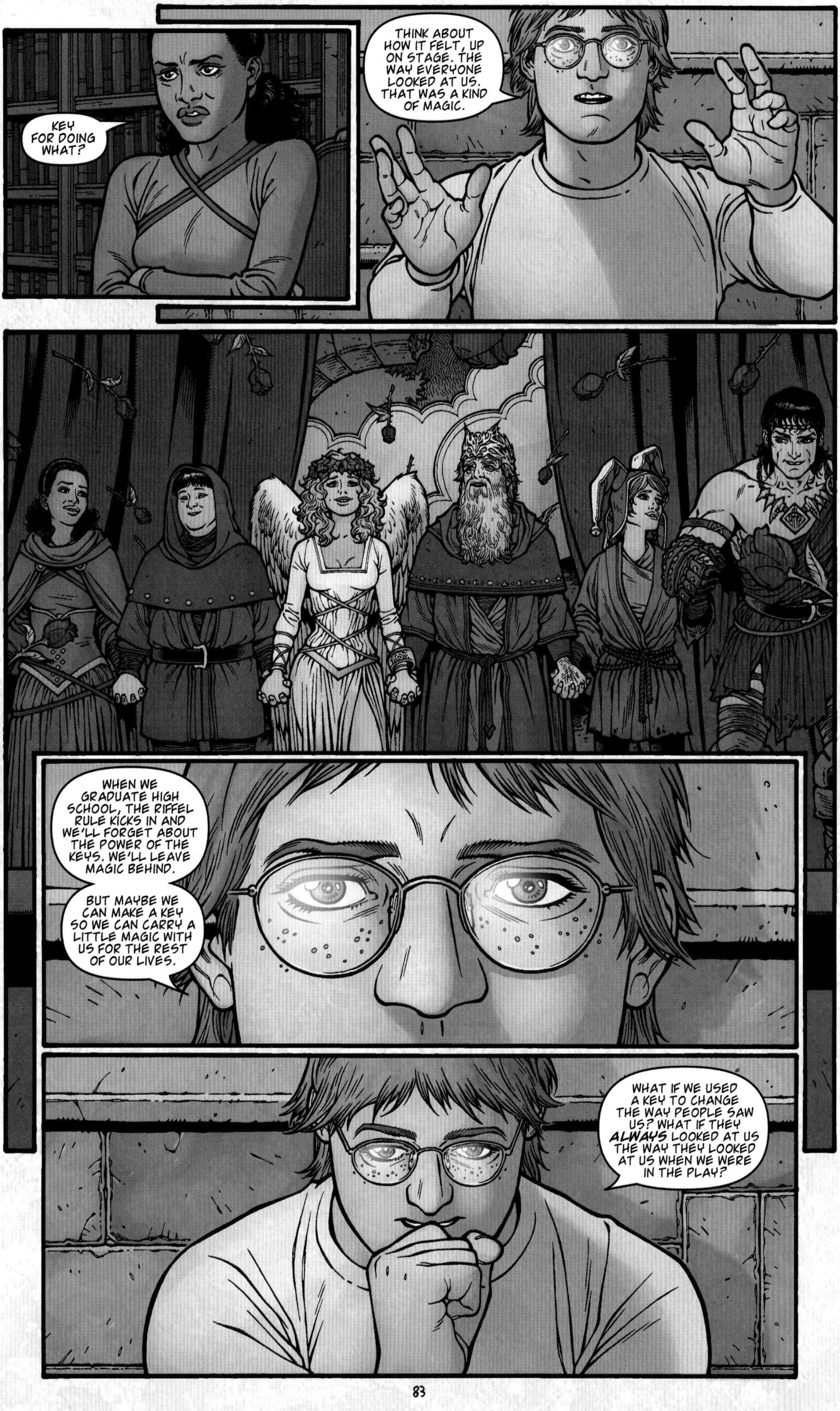
KEY FOR DOING WHAT?
THINK ABOUT HOW IT FELT, UP ON STAGE. THE WAY EVERYONE LOOKED AT US. THAT WAS A KIND OF MAGIC.
WHEN WE GRADUATE HIGH SCHOOL, THE RIFFEL RULE KICKS IN AND WE'LL FORGET ABOUT THE POWER OF THE KEYS. WE'LL LEAVE MAGIC BEHIND.
BUT MAYBE WE CAN MAKE A KEY SO WE CAN CARRY A LITTLE MAGIC WITH US FOR THE REST OF OUR LIVES.
WHAT IF WE USED A KEY TO CHANGE THE WAY PEOPLE SAW US? WHAT IF THEY *ALWAYS* LOOKED AT US THE WAY THEY LOOKED AT US WHEN WE WERE IN THE PLAY?

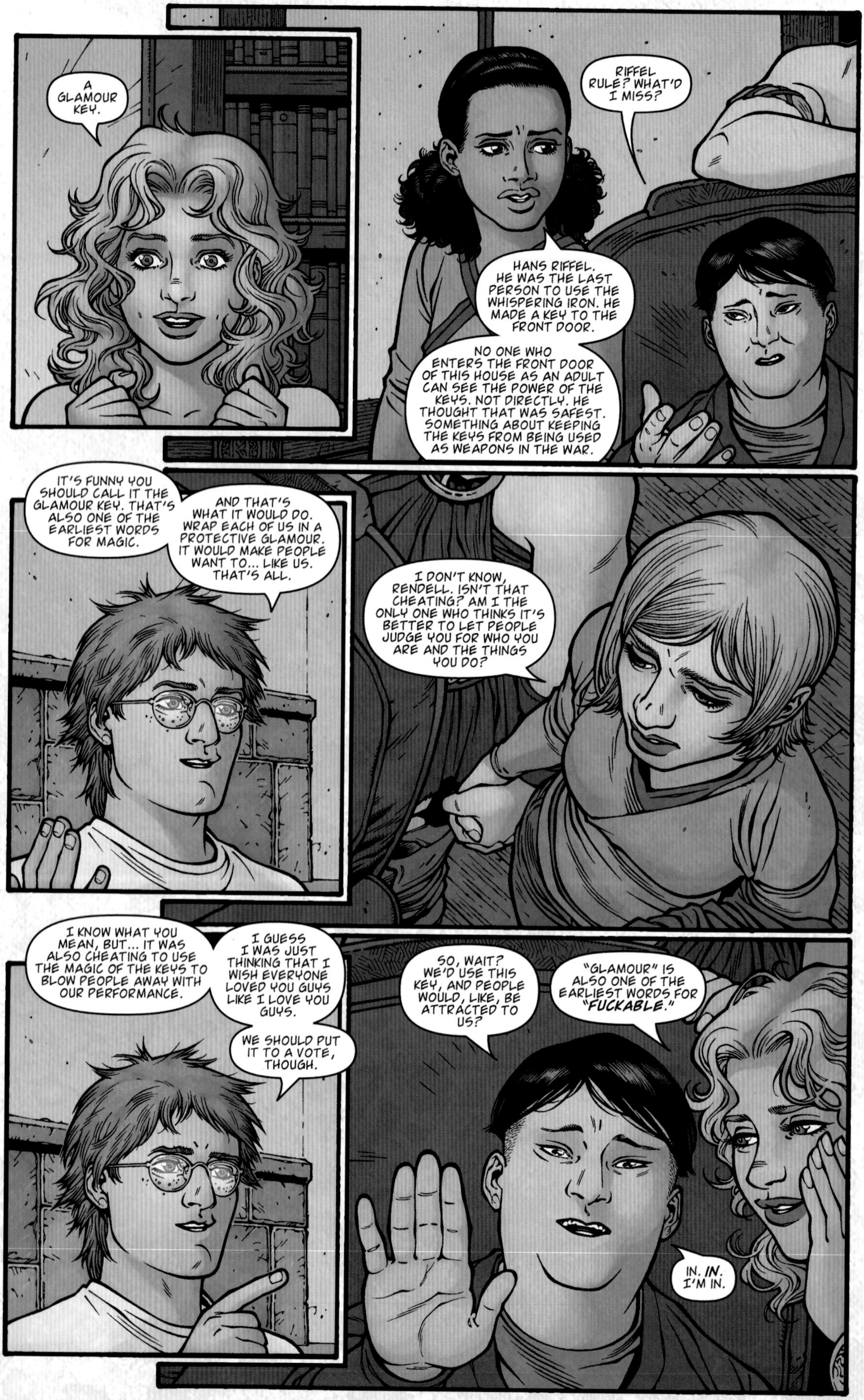
A GLAMOUR KEY.
RIFFEL RULE? WHAT'D I MISS?
HANS RIFFEL. HE WAS THE LAST PERSON TO USE THE WHISPERING IRON. HE MADE A KEY TO THE FRONT DOOR.
NO ONE WHO ENTERS THE FRONT DOOR OF THIS HOUSE AS AN ADULT CAN SEE THE POWER OF THE KEYS. NOT DIRECTLY. HE THOUGHT THAT WAS SAFEST. SOMETHING ABOUT KEEPING THE KEYS FROM BEING USED AS WEAPONS IN THE WAR.
IT'S FUNNY YOU SHOULD CALL IT THE GLAMOUR KEY. THAT'S ALSO ONE OF THE EARLIEST WORDS FOR MAGIC.
AND THAT'S WHAT IT WOULD DO. WRAP EACH OF US IN A PROTECTIVE GLAMOUR. IT WOULD MAKE PEOPLE WANT TO... LIKE US. THAT'S ALL.
I DON'T KNOW, RENDELL. ISN'T THAT CHEATING? AM I THE ONLY ONE WHO THINKS IT'S BETTER TO LET PEOPLE JUDGE YOU FOR WHO YOU ARE AND THE THINGS YOU DO?
I KNOW WHAT YOU MEAN, BUT... IT WAS ALSO CHEATING TO USE THE MAGIC OF THE KEYS TO BLOW PEOPLE AWAY WITH OUR PERFORMANCE.
I GUESS I WAS JUST THINKING THAT I WISH EVERYONE LOVED YOU GUYS LIKE I LOVE YOU GUYS.
WE SHOULD PUT IT TO A VOTE, THOUGH.
SO, WAIT? WE'D USE THIS KEY, AND PEOPLE WOULD, LIKE, BE ATTRACTED TO US?
"GLAMOUR" IS ALSO ONE OF THE EARLIEST WORDS FOR "*FUCKABLE*."
IN. *IN*. I'M IN.

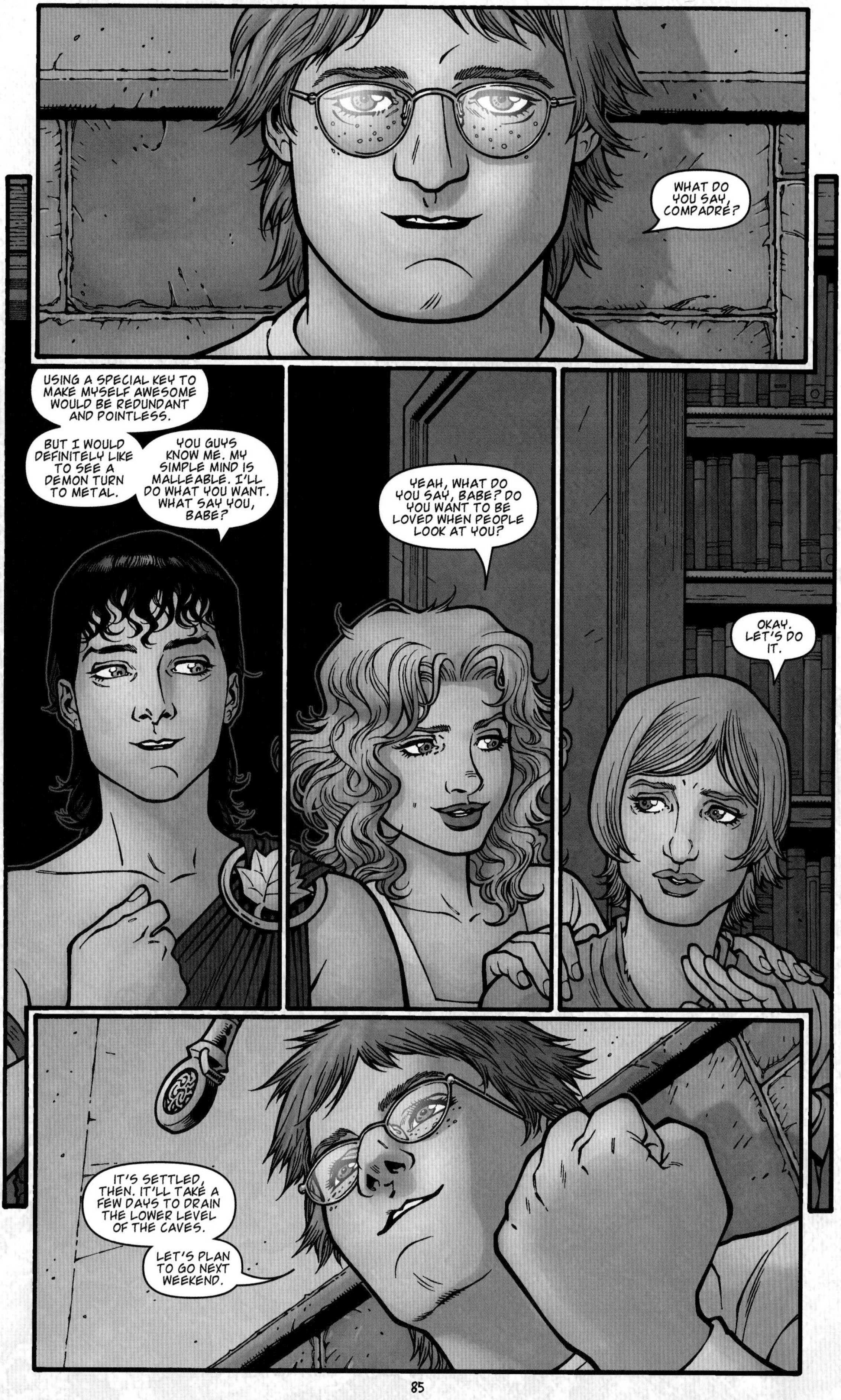
WHAT DO YOU SAY, COMPADRE?
USING A SPECIAL KEY TO MAKE MYSELF AWESOME WOULD BE REDUNDANT AND POINTLESS.
BUT I WOULD DEFINITELY LIKE TO SEE A DEMON TURN TO METAL.
YOU GUYS KNOW ME. MY SIMPLE MIND IS MALLEABLE. I'LL DO WHAT YOU WANT. WHAT SAY YOU, BABE?
YEAH, WHAT DO YOU SAY, BABE? DO YOU WANT TO BE LOVED WHEN PEOPLE LOOK AT YOU?
OKAY. LET'S DO IT.
IT'S SETTLED, THEN. IT'LL TAKE A FEW DAYS TO DRAIN THE LOWER LEVEL OF THE CAVES.
LET'S PLAN TO GO NEXT WEEKEND.

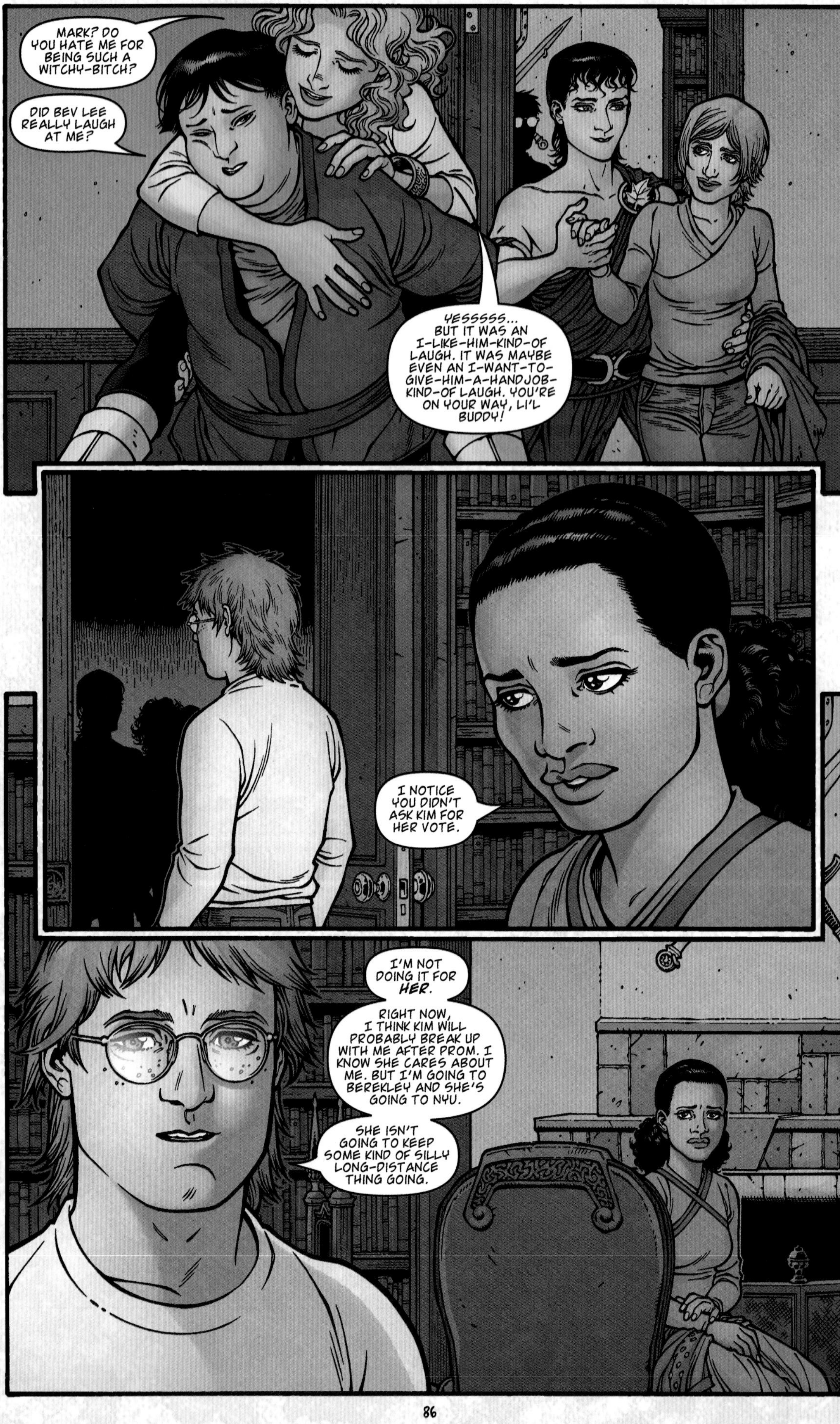

MARK? DO YOU HATE ME FOR BEING SUCH A WITCHY-BITCH?
DID BEV LEE REALLY LAUGH AT ME?
YESSSSS... BUT IT WAS AN I-LIKE-HIM-KIND-OF LAUGH. IT WAS MAYBE EVEN AN I-WANT-TO-GIVE-HIM-A-HANDJOB-KIND-OF LAUGH. YOU'RE ON YOUR WAY, LI'L BUDDY!
I NOTICE YOU DIDN'T ASK KIM FOR HER VOTE.
I'M NOT DOING IT FOR ***HER***.
RIGHT NOW, I THINK KIM WILL PROBABLY BREAK UP WITH ME AFTER PROM. I KNOW SHE CARES ABOUT ME. BUT I'M GOING TO BEREKLEY AND SHE'S GOING TO NYU.
SHE ISN'T GOING TO KEEP SOME KIND OF SILLY LONG-DISTANCE THING GOING.

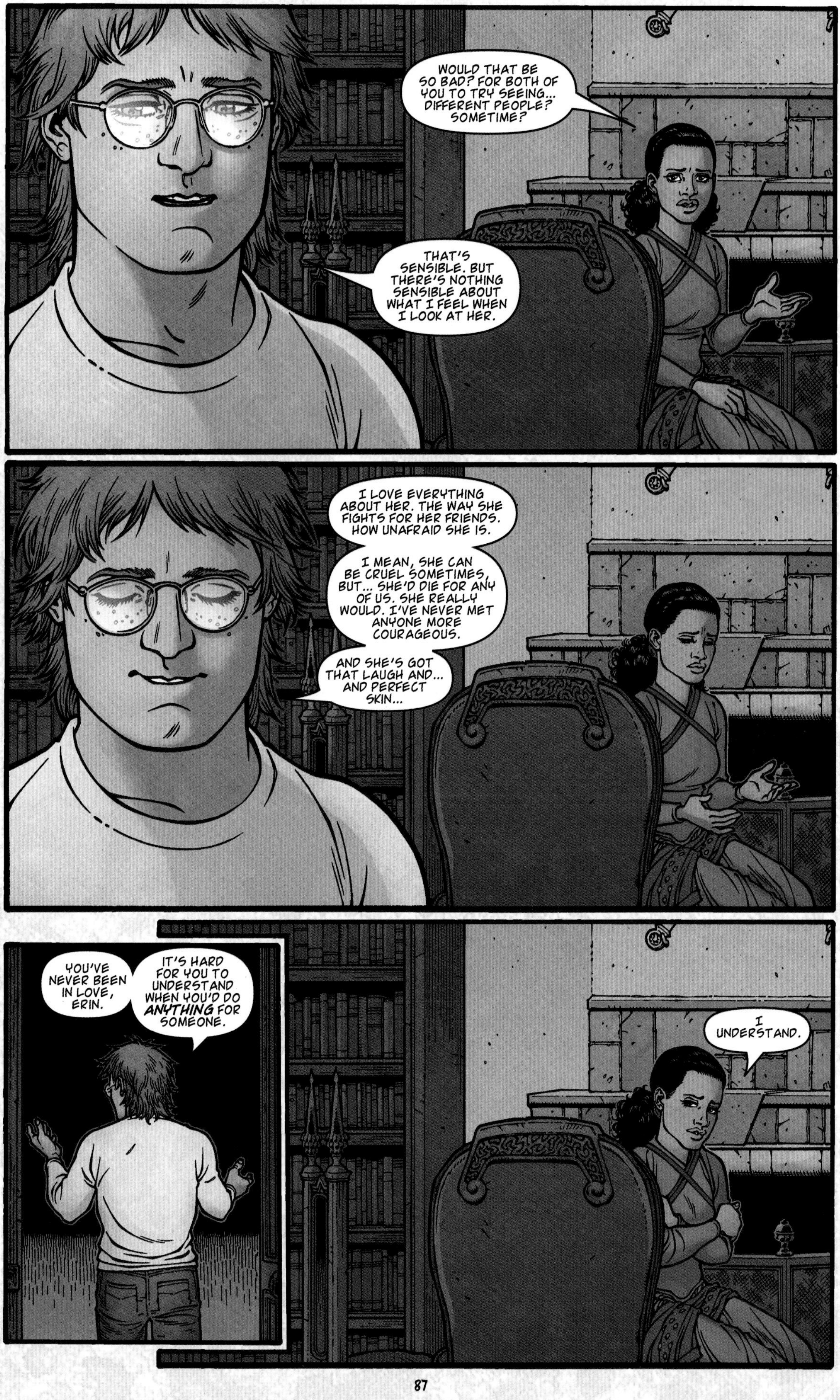
WOULD THAT BE SO BAD? FOR BOTH OF YOU TO TRY SEEING... DIFFERENT PEOPLE? SOMETIME?
THAT'S SENSIBLE. BUT THERE'S NOTHING SENSIBLE ABOUT WHAT I FEEL WHEN I LOOK AT HER.
I LOVE EVERYTHING ABOUT HER. THE WAY SHE FIGHTS FOR HER FRIENDS. HOW UNAFRAID SHE IS.
I MEAN, SHE CAN BE CRUEL SOMETIMES, BUT... SHE'D DIE FOR ANY OF US. SHE REALLY WOULD. I'VE NEVER MET ANYONE MORE COURAGEOUS.
AND SHE'S GOT THAT LAUGH AND... AND PERFECT SKIN...
YOU'VE NEVER BEEN IN LOVE, ERIN.
IT'S HARD FOR YOU TO UNDERSTAND WHEN YOU'D DO *ANYTHING* FOR SOMEONE.
I UNDERSTAND.

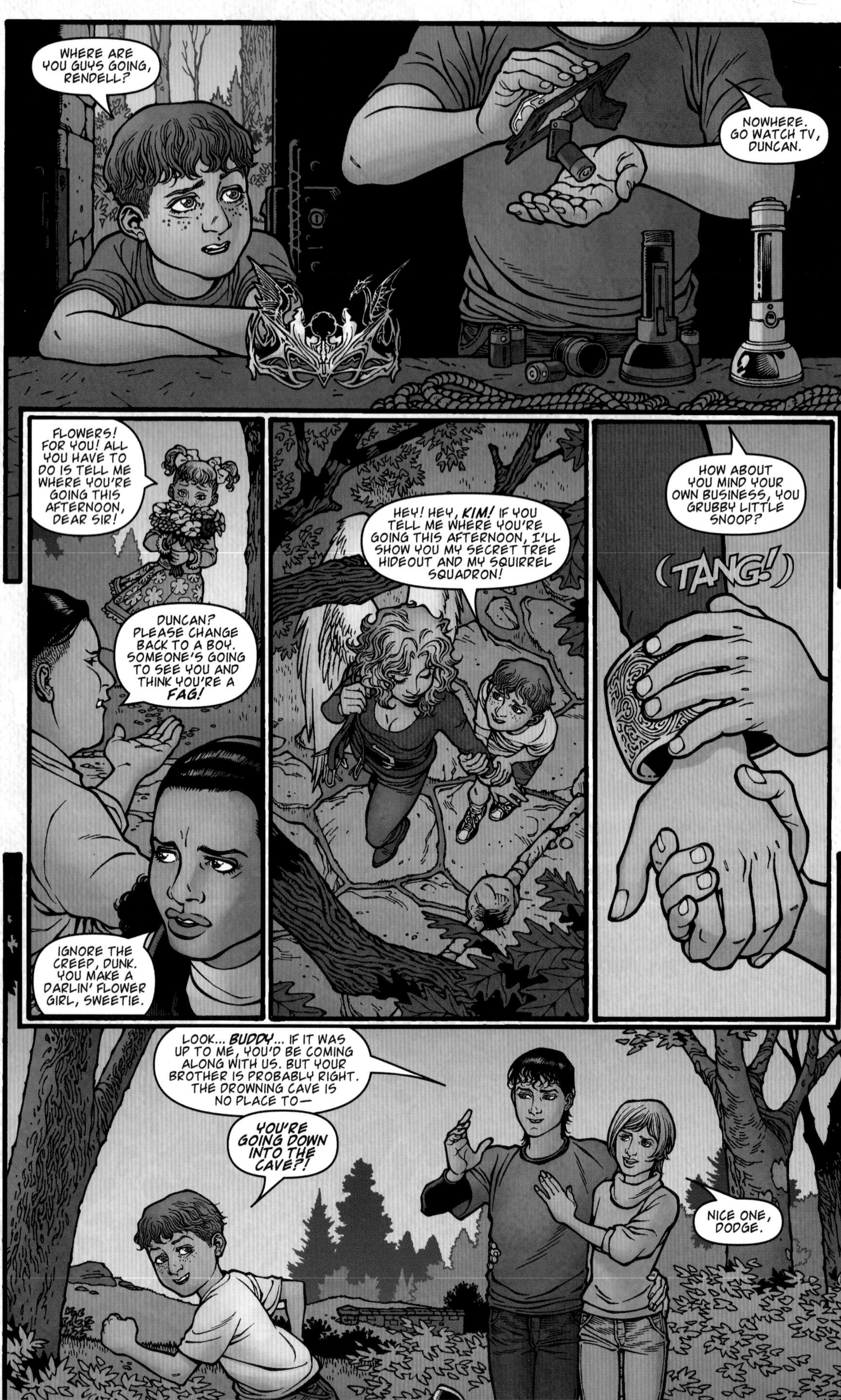
WHERE ARE YOU GUYS GOING, RENDELL?
NOWHERE. GO WATCH TV, DUNCAN.
FLOWERS! FOR YOU! ALL YOU HAVE TO DO IS TELL ME WHERE YOU'RE GOING THIS AFTERNOON, DEAR SIR!
DUNCAN? PLEASE CHANGE BACK TO A BOY. SOMEONE'S GOING TO SEE YOU AND THINK YOU'RE A FAG!
IGNORE THE CREEP, DUNK. YOU MAKE A DARLIN' FLOWER GIRL, SWEETIE.
HEY! HEY, KIM! IF YOU TELL ME WHERE YOU'RE GOING THIS AFTERNOON, I'LL SHOW YOU MY SECRET TREE HIDEOUT AND MY SQUIRREL SQUADRON!
HOW ABOUT YOU MIND YOUR OWN BUSINESS, YOU GRUBBY LITTLE SNOOP?
(TANG!)
LOOK... BUDDY... IF IT WAS UP TO ME, YOU'D BE COMING ALONG WITH US. BUT YOUR BROTHER IS PROBABLY RIGHT. THE DROWNING CAVE IS NO PLACE TO—
YOU'RE GOING DOWN INTO THE CAVE?!
NICE ONE, DODGE.

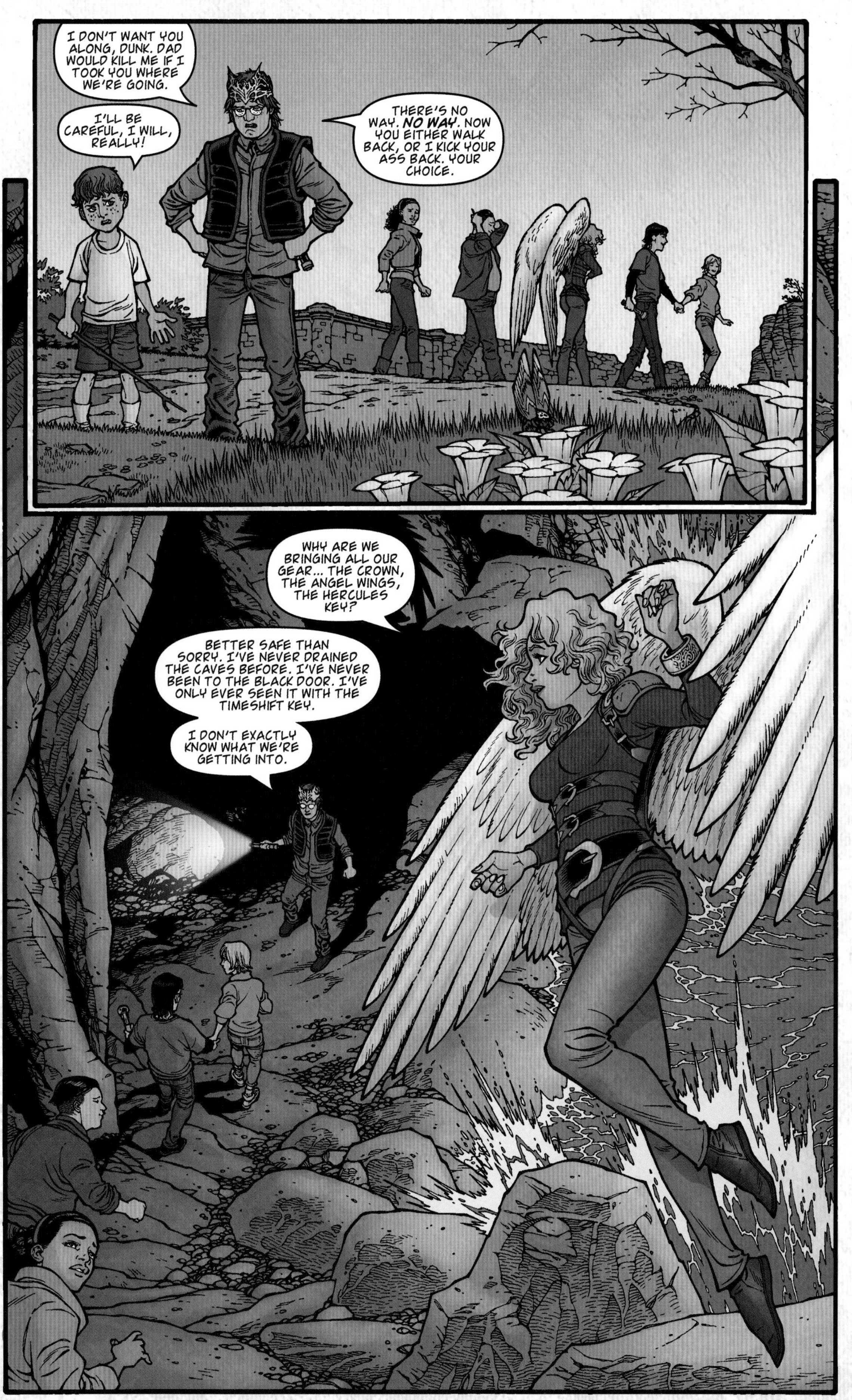

I DON'T WANT YOU ALONG, DUNK. DAD WOULD KILL ME IF I TOOK YOU WHERE WE'RE GOING.
I'LL BE CAREFUL, I WILL, REALLY!
THERE'S NO WAY. NO WAY. NOW YOU EITHER WALK BACK, OR I KICK YOUR ASS BACK. YOUR CHOICE.
WHY ARE WE BRINGING ALL OUR GEAR... THE CROWN, THE ANGEL WINGS, THE HERCULES KEY?
BETTER SAFE THAN SORRY. I'VE NEVER DRAINED THE CAVES BEFORE. I'VE NEVER BEEN TO THE BLACK DOOR. I'VE ONLY EVER SEEN IT WITH THE TIMESHIFT KEY.
I DON'T EXACTLY KNOW WHAT WE'RE GETTING INTO.

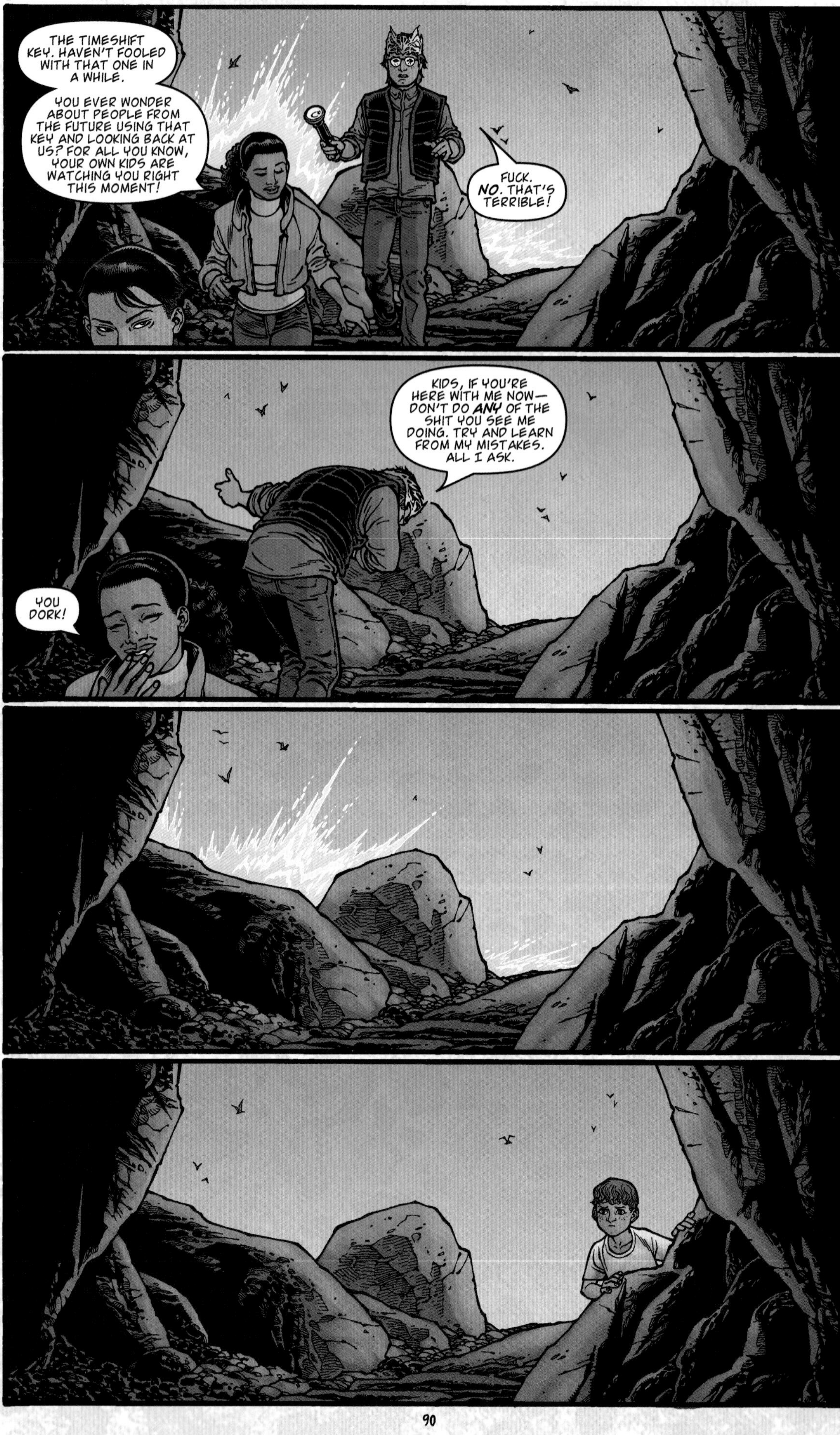

THE TIMESHIFT KEY. HAVEN'T FOOLED WITH THAT ONE IN A WHILE.
YOU EVER WONDER ABOUT PEOPLE FROM THE FUTURE USING THAT KEY AND LOOKING BACK AT US? FOR ALL YOU KNOW, YOUR OWN KIDS ARE WATCHING YOU RIGHT THIS MOMENT!
FUCK. NO. THAT'S TERRIBLE!
KIDS, IF YOU'RE HERE WITH ME NOW—DON'T DO ANY OF THE SHIT YOU SEE ME DOING. TRY AND LEARN FROM MY MISTAKES. ALL I ASK.
YOU DORK!

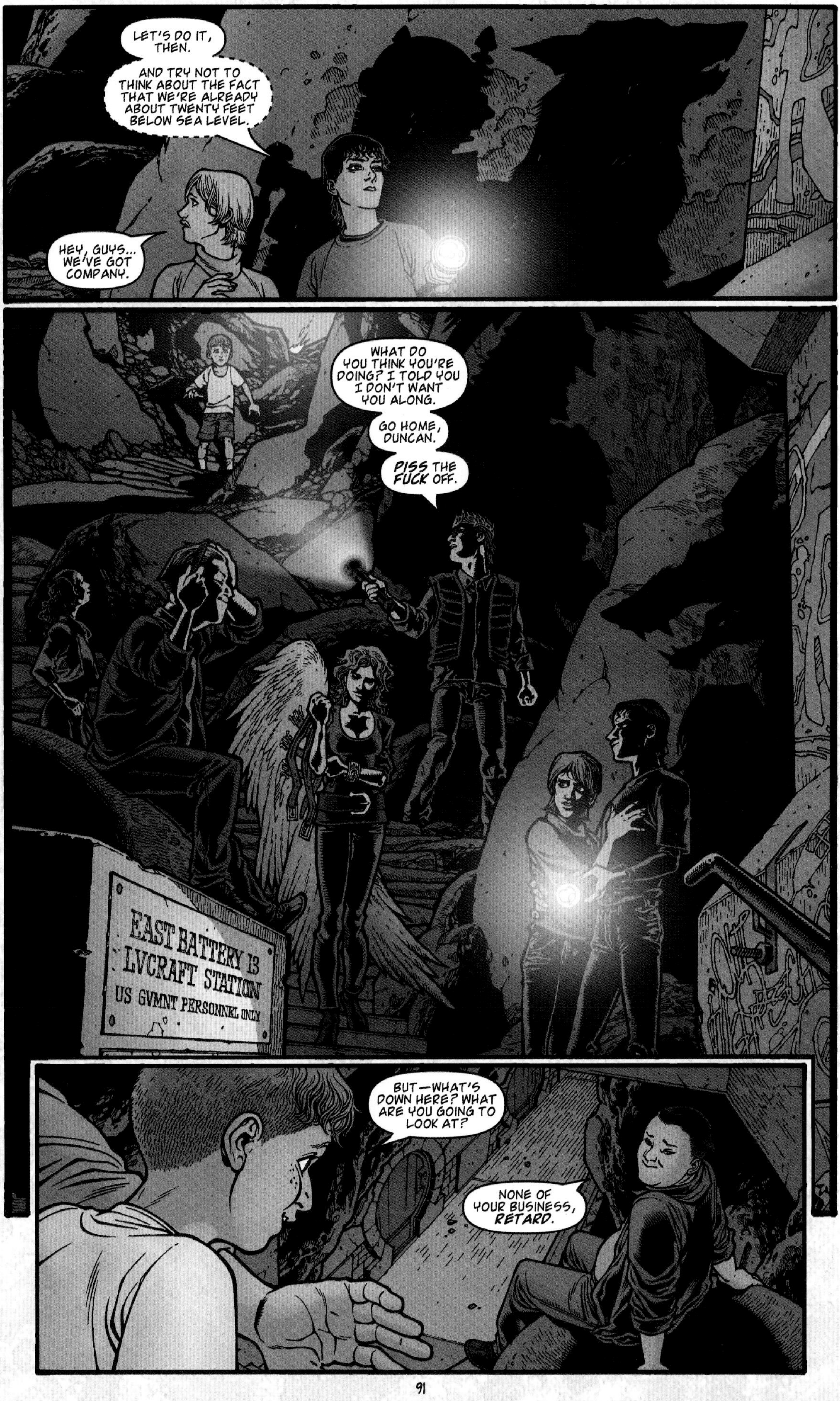

LET'S DO IT, THEN.
AND TRY NOT TO THINK ABOUT THE FACT THAT WE'RE ALREADY ABOUT TWENTY FEET BELOW SEA LEVEL.
HEY, GUYS... WE'VE GOT COMPANY.
WHAT DO YOU THINK YOU'RE DOING? I TOLD YOU I DON'T WANT YOU ALONG.
GO HOME, DUNCAN.
PISS THE FUCK OFF.
EAST BATTERY 13
LVCRAFT STATION
US GVMNT PERSONNEL ONLY
BUT—WHAT'S DOWN HERE? WHAT ARE YOU GOING TO LOOK AT?
NONE OF YOUR BUSINESS, RETARD.

GIVE THE LITTLE GUY A BREAK. HE'S CURIOUS.

HE'S GOING TO FUCK THINGS UP. IT'S WHAT HE ALWAYS DOES!

I GOT THIS. CHILL.

TAKE IT FROM YOUR BUDDY, DODGE. IT WOULDN'T BE FUN IF SOMETHING HAPPENED TO YOU. HEAD ON BACK, OKAY?

OH, AND HEY, IF ANYONE ASKS WHERE WE WENT, FORGET YOU SAW US HERE, OKAY?

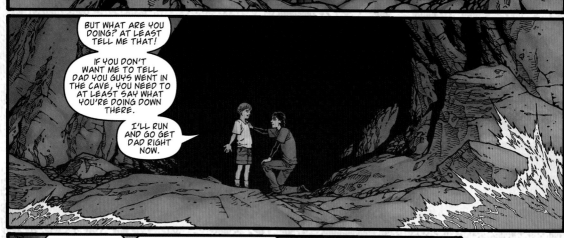

BUT WHAT ARE YOU DOING? AT LEAST TELL ME THAT!

IF YOU DON'T WANT ME TO TELL DAD YOU GUYS WENT IN THE CAVE, YOU NEED TO AT LEAST SAY WHAT YOU'RE DOING DOWN THERE.

I'LL RUN AND GO GET DAD RIGHT NOW.

NOW DARN IT, KID, THAT'S JUST NOT FAIR.

TELL. TELL AND I PROMISE— I *PROMISE*— I WON'T WALK BACK DOWN THOSE STEPS AFTER YOU.

OKAY. BUT YOU LISTEN UP, BUDDY. PROMISES ARE *IMPORTANT.*

YOU MAKE A PROMISE, YOU HAVE TO KEEP IT, NO MATTER WHAT. THAT'S HOW WE CAN TELL THE BAD GUYS FROM THE GOOD GUYS.

THE GOOD GUYS *ALWAYS* KEEP THEIR PROMISES.

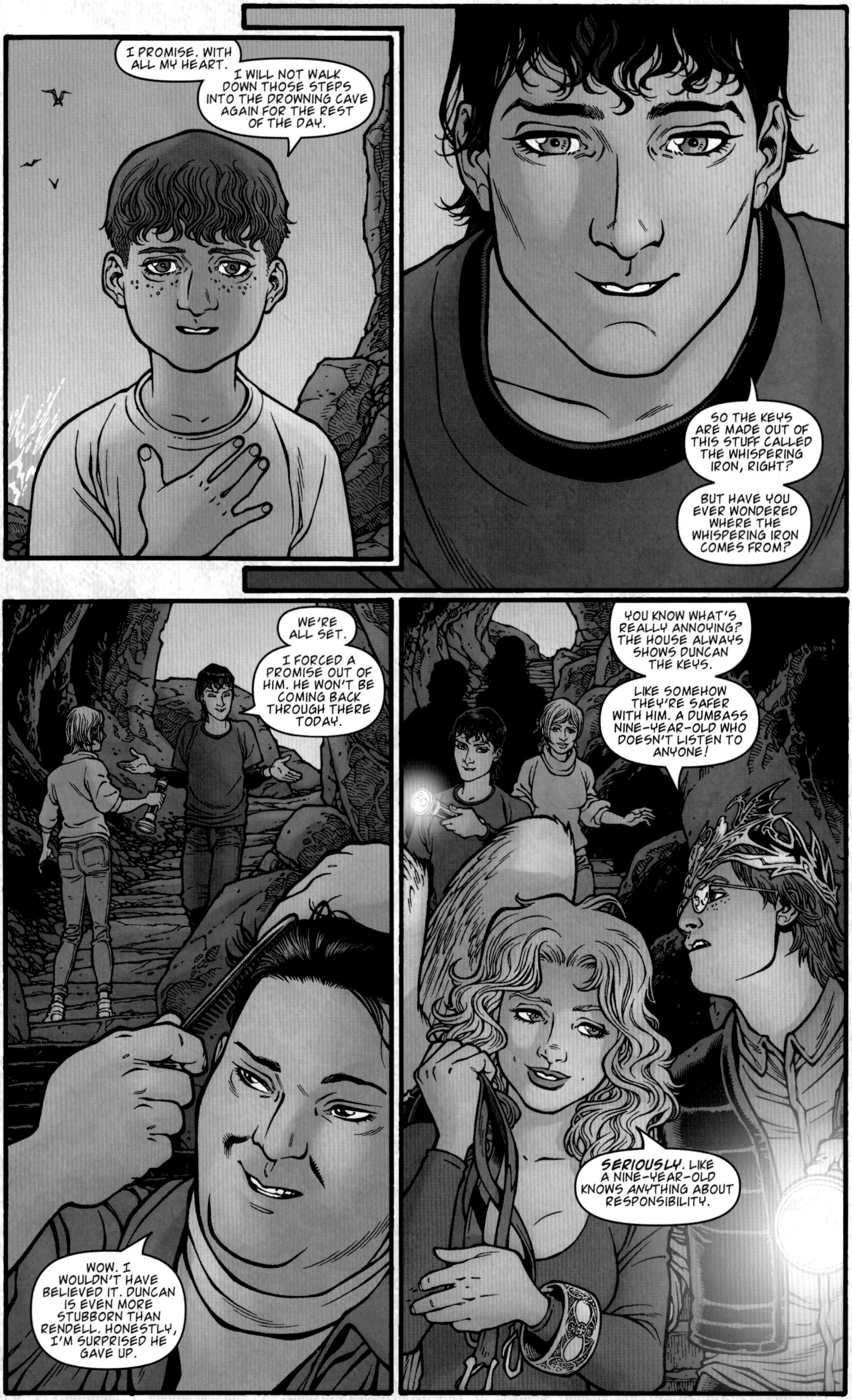
I PROMISE. WITH ALL MY HEART.
I WILL NOT WALK DOWN THOSE STEPS INTO THE DROWNING CAVE AGAIN FOR THE REST OF THE DAY.
SO THE KEYS ARE MADE OUT OF THIS STUFF CALLED THE WHISPERING IRON, RIGHT?
BUT HAVE YOU EVER WONDERED WHERE THE WHISPERING IRON COMES FROM?
WE'RE ALL SET.
I FORCED A PROMISE OUT OF HIM. HE WON'T BE COMING BACK THROUGH THERE TODAY.
WOW. I WOULDN'T HAVE BELIEVED IT. DUNCAN IS EVEN MORE STUBBORN THAN RENDELL. HONESTLY, I'M SURPRISED HE GAVE UP.
YOU KNOW WHAT'S REALLY ANNOYING? THE HOUSE ALWAYS SHOWS DUNCAN THE KEYS.
LIKE SOMEHOW THEY'RE SAFER WITH HIM. A DUMBASS NINE-YEAR-OLD WHO DOESN'T LISTEN TO ANYONE!
SERIOUSLY. LIKE A NINE-YEAR-OLD KNOWS ANYTHING ABOUT RESPONSIBILITY.

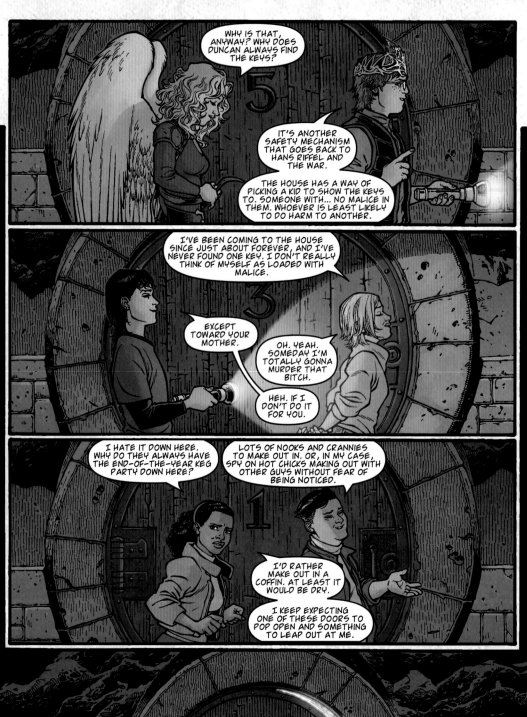

WHY IS THAT, ANYWAY? WHY DOES DUNCAN ALWAYS FIND THE KEYS?

IT'S ANOTHER SAFETY MECHANISM THAT GOES BACK TO HANS RIFFEL AND THE WAR.

THE HOUSE HAS A WAY OF PICKING A KID TO SHOW THE KEYS TO. SOMEONE WITH... NO MALICE IN THEM. WHOEVER IS LEAST LIKELY TO DO HARM TO ANOTHER.

I'VE BEEN COMING TO THE HOUSE SINCE JUST ABOUT FOREVER, AND I'VE NEVER FOUND ONE KEY. I DON'T REALLY THINK OF MYSELF AS LOADED WITH MALICE.

EXCEPT TOWARD YOUR MOTHER.

OH. YEAH. SOMEDAY I'M TOTALLY GONNA MURDER THAT BITCH.

HEH. IF I DON'T DO IT FOR YOU.

I HATE IT DOWN HERE. WHY DO THEY ALWAYS HAVE THE END-OF-THE-YEAR KEG PARTY DOWN HERE?

LOTS OF NOOKS AND CRANNIES TO MAKE OUT IN. OR, IN MY CASE, SPY ON HOT CHICKS MAKING OUT WITH OTHER GUYS WITHOUT FEAR OF BEING NOTICED.

I'D RATHER MAKE OUT IN A COFFIN. AT LEAST IT WOULD BE DRY.

I KEEP EXPECTING ONE OF THESE DOORS TO POP OPEN AND SOMETHING TO LEAP OUT AT ME.

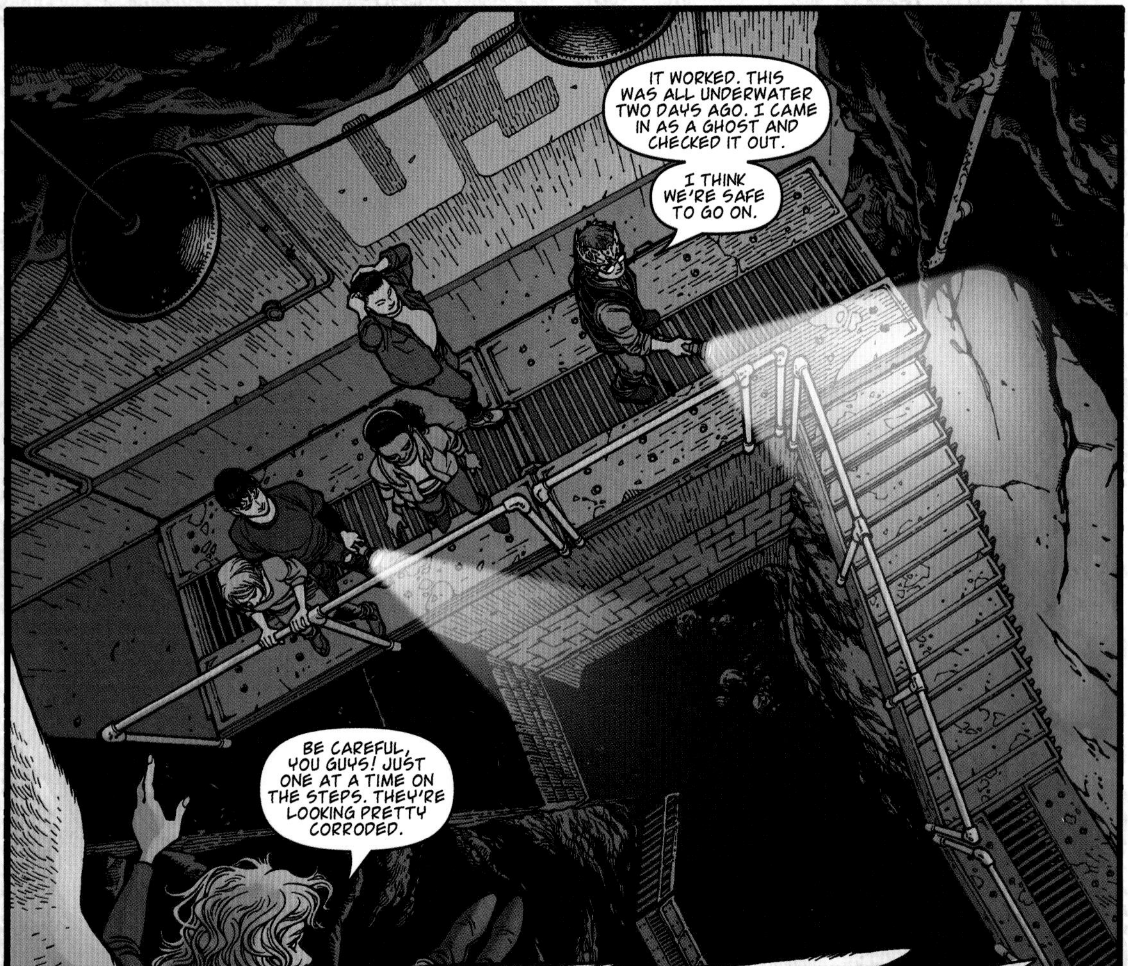
IT WORKED. THIS WAS ALL UNDERWATER TWO DAYS AGO. I CAME IN AS A GHOST AND CHECKED IT OUT.
I THINK WE'RE SAFE TO GO ON.
BE CAREFUL, YOU GUYS! JUST ONE AT A TIME ON THE STEPS. THEY'RE LOOKING PRETTY CORRODED.

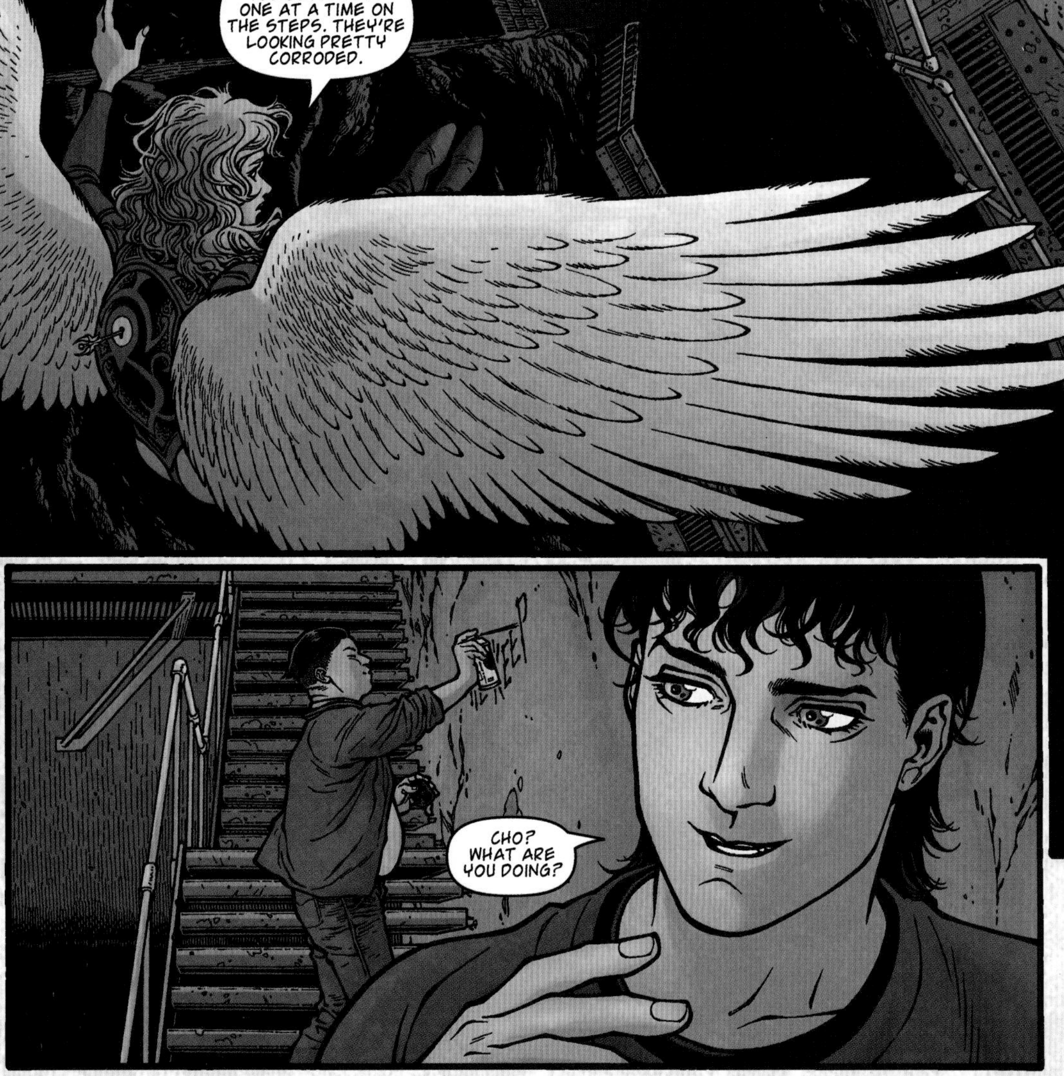
CHO? WHAT ARE YOU DOING?

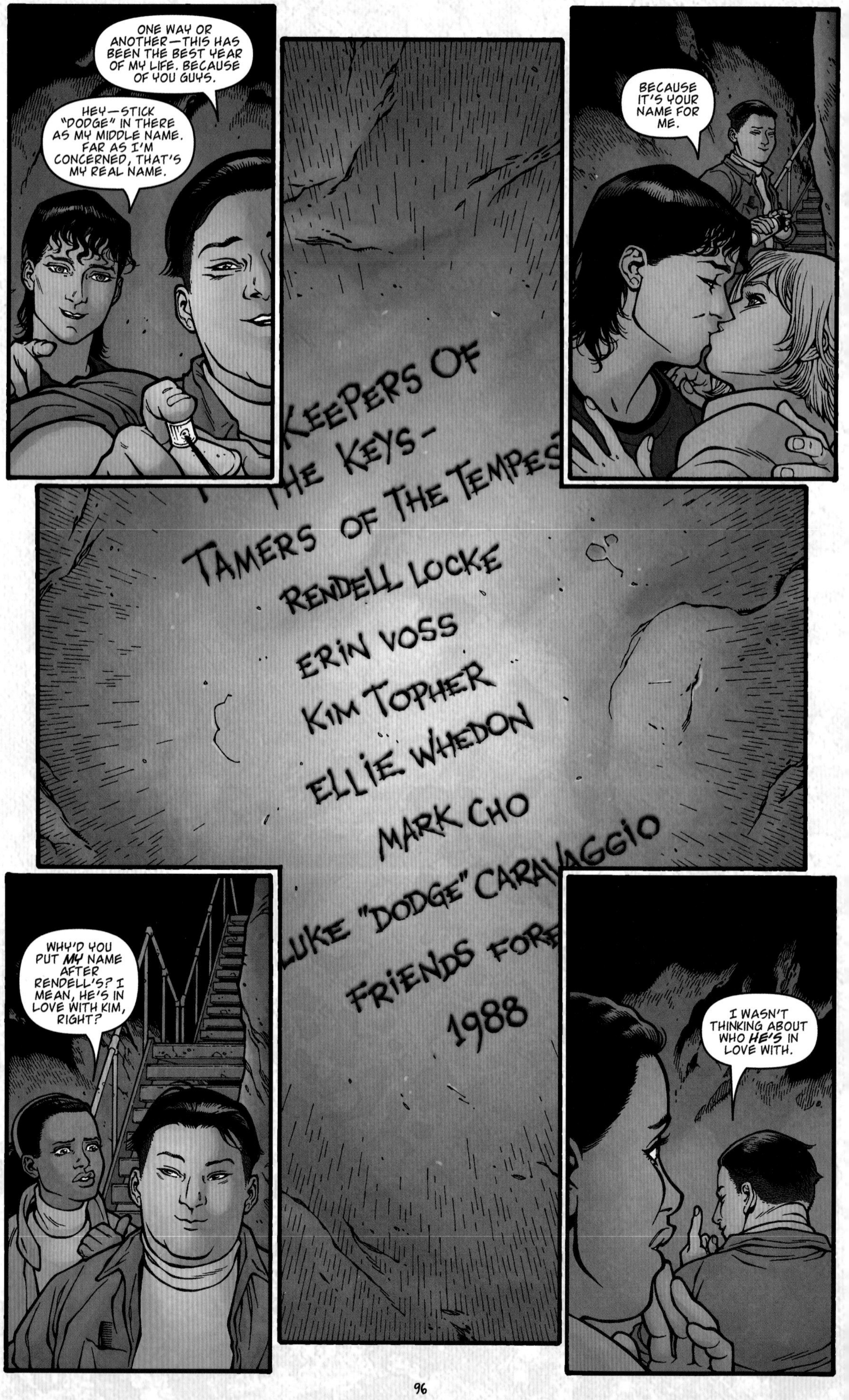

ONE WAY OR ANOTHER—THIS HAS BEEN THE BEST YEAR OF MY LIFE. BECAUSE OF YOU GUYS.
HEY—STICK "DODGE" IN THERE AS MY MIDDLE NAME. FAR AS I'M CONCERNED, THAT'S MY REAL NAME.
BECAUSE IT'S YOUR NAME FOR ME.
KEEPERS OF THE KEYS-
TAMERS OF THE TEMPES
RENDELL LOCKE
ERIN VOSS
KIM TOPHER
ELLIE WHEDON
MARK CHO
LUKE "DODGE" CARAVAGGIO
FRIENDS FORE
1988
WHY'D YOU PUT MY NAME AFTER RENDELL'S? I MEAN, HE'S IN LOVE WITH KIM, RIGHT?
I WASN'T THINKING ABOUT WHO HE'S IN LOVE WITH.

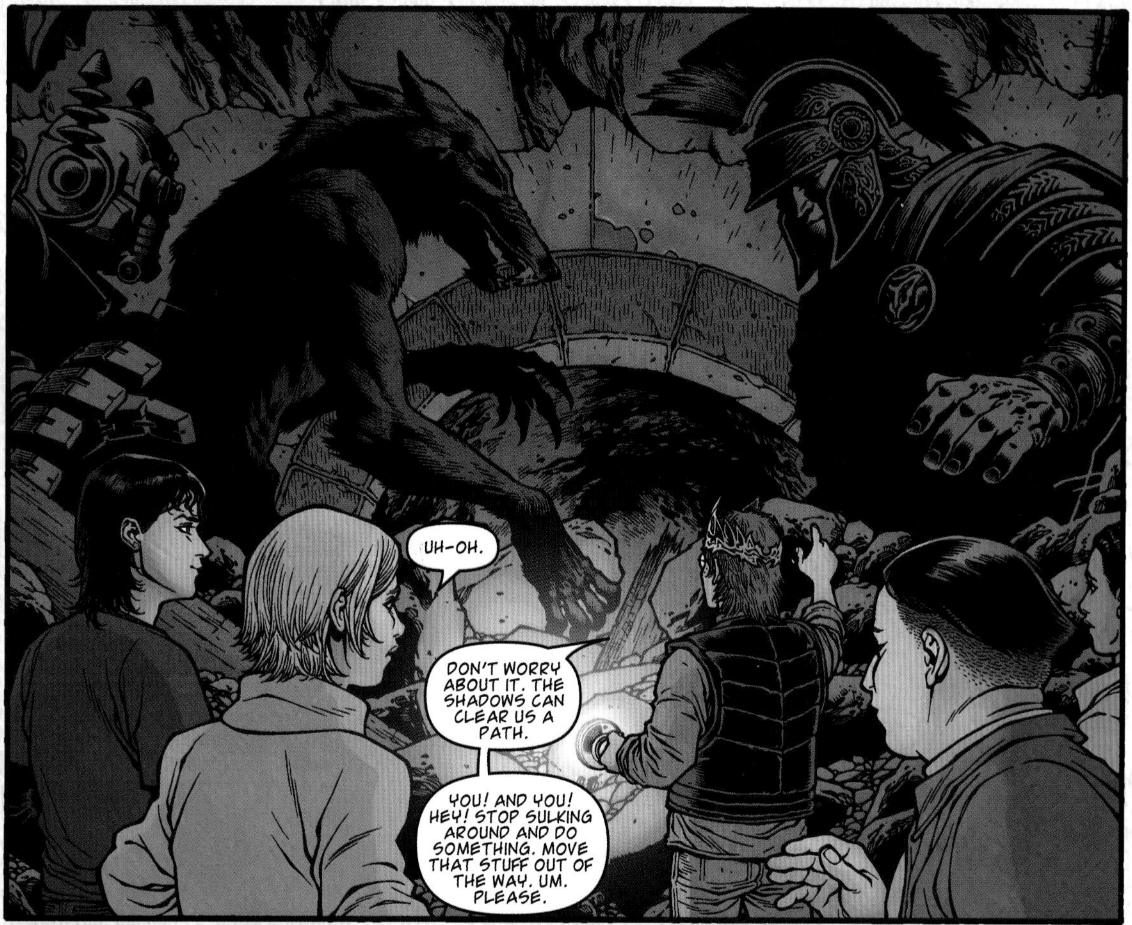
UH-OH.
DON'T WORRY ABOUT IT. THE SHADOWS CAN CLEAR US A PATH.
YOU! AND YOU! HEY! STOP SULKING AROUND AND DO SOMETHING. MOVE THAT STUFF OUT OF THE WAY. UM. PLEASE.

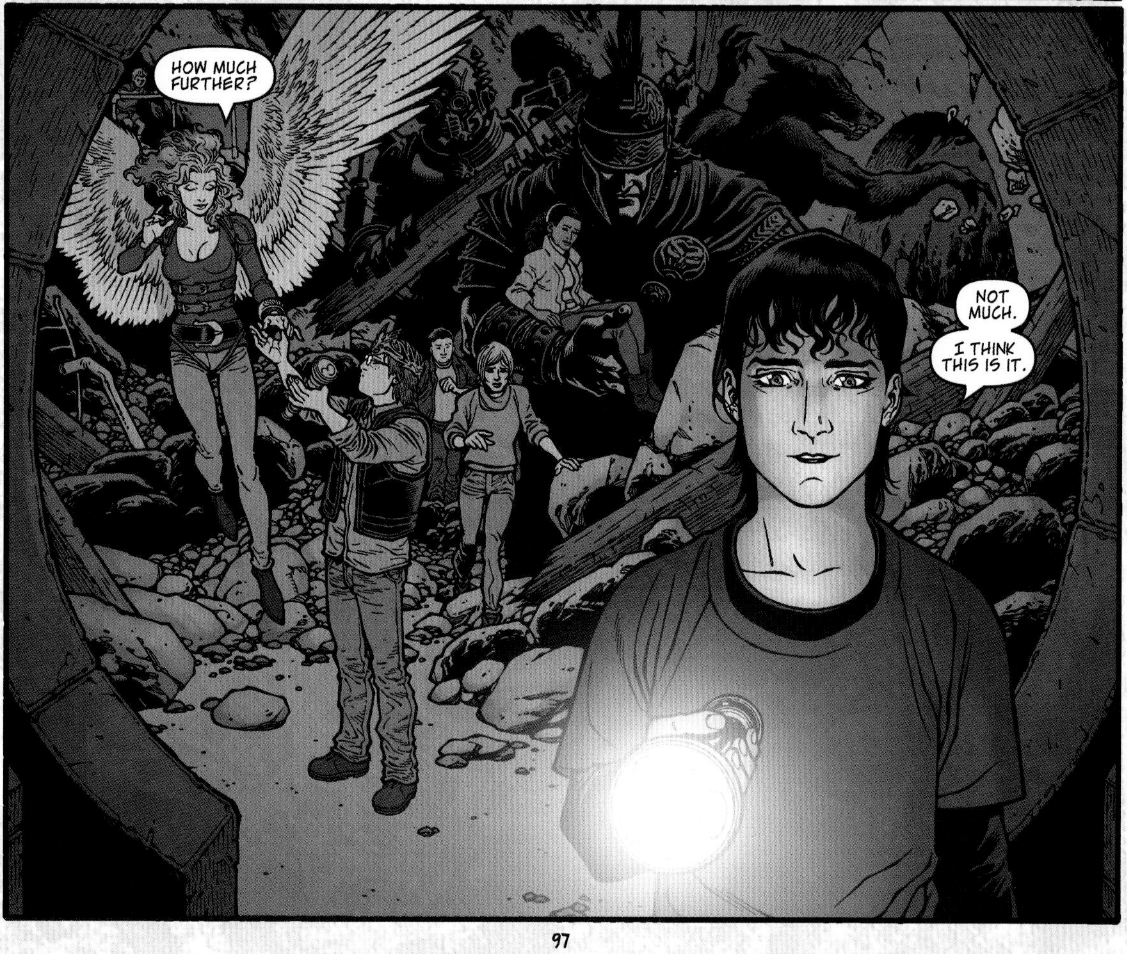
HOW MUCH FURTHER?
NOT MUCH.
I THINK THIS IS IT.

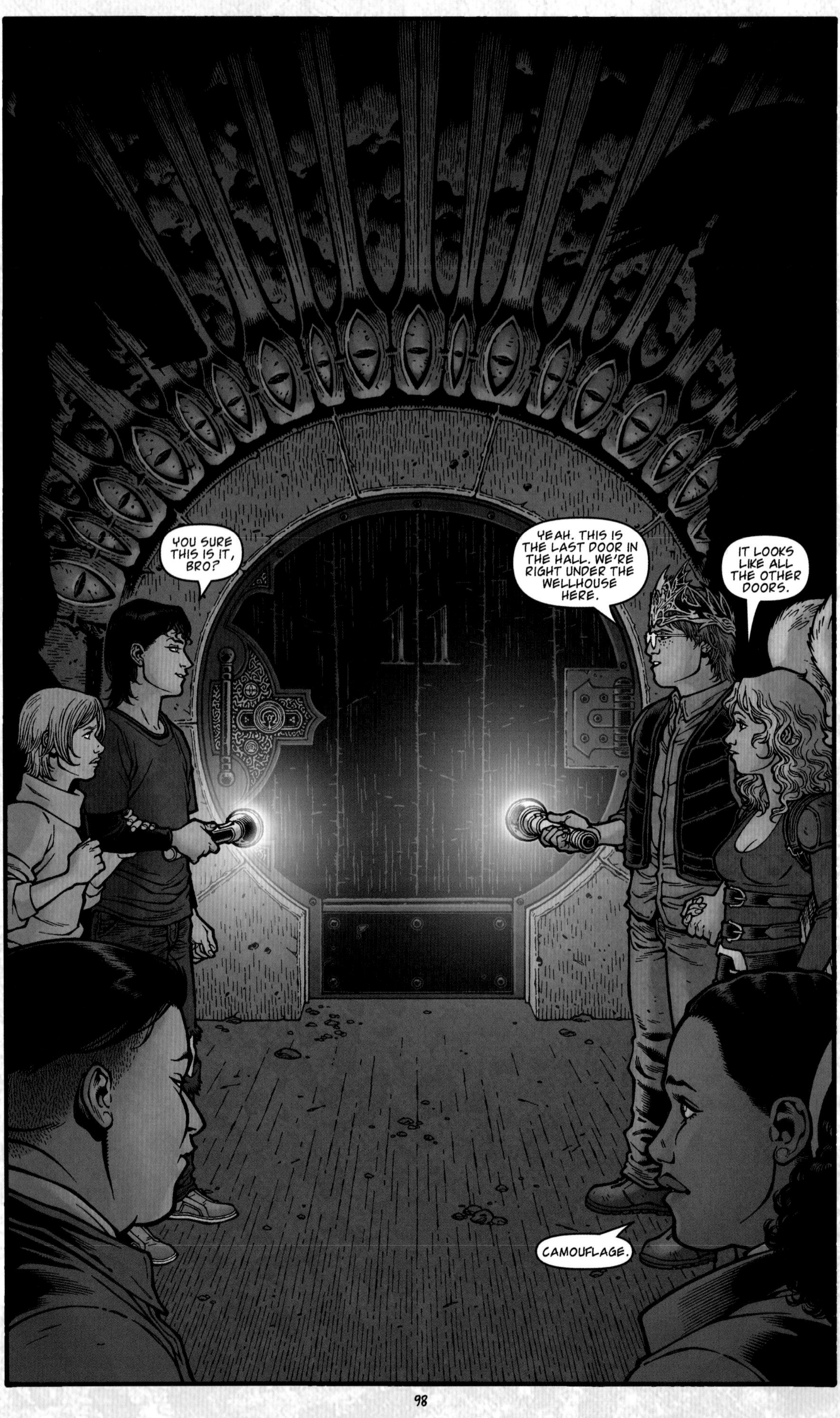
YOU SURE THIS IS IT, BRO?
YEAH. THIS IS THE LAST DOOR IN THE HALL. WE'RE RIGHT UNDER THE WELLHOUSE HERE.
IT LOOKS LIKE ALL THE OTHER DOORS.
CAMOUFLAGE.
11

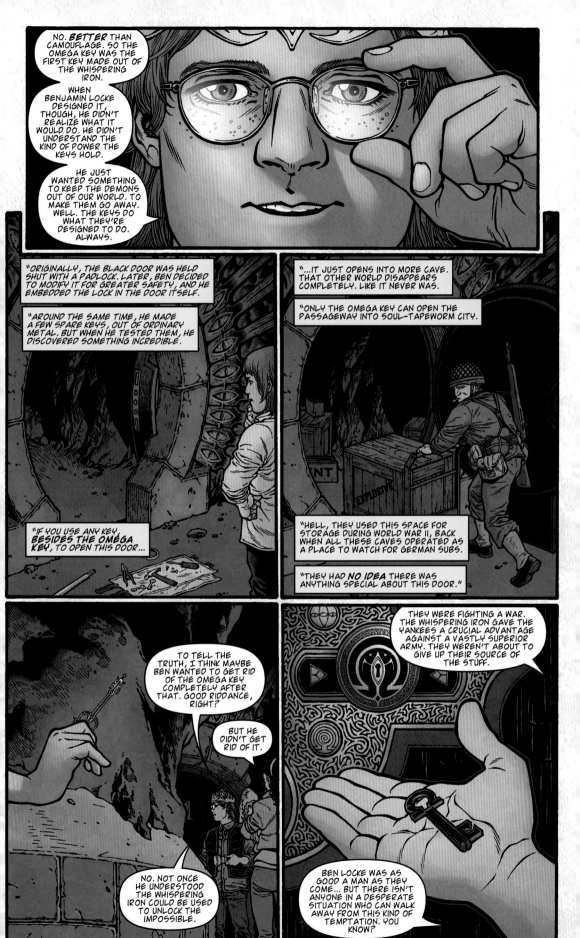

NO. *BETTER* THAN CAMOUFLAGE. SO THE OMEGA KEY WAS THE FIRST KEY MADE OUT OF THE WHISPERING IRON.

WHEN BENJAMIN LOCKE DESIGNED IT, THOUGH, HE DIDN'T REALIZE WHAT IT WOULD DO. HE DIDN'T UNDERSTAND THE KIND OF POWER THE KEYS HOLD.

HE JUST WANTED SOMETHING TO KEEP THE DEMONS OUT OF OUR WORLD. TO MAKE THEM GO AWAY. WELL. THE KEYS DO WHAT THEY'RE DESIGNED TO DO. ALWAYS.

"ORIGINALLY, THE BLACK DOOR WAS HELD SHUT WITH A PADLOCK. LATER, BEN DECIDED TO MODIFY IT FOR GREATER SAFETY, AND HE EMBEDDED THE LOCK IN THE DOOR ITSELF.

"AROUND THE SAME TIME, HE MADE A FEW SPARE KEYS, OUT OF ORDINARY METAL. BUT WHEN HE TESTED THEM, HE DISCOVERED SOMETHING INCREDIBLE.

"IF YOU USE ANY KEY, *BESIDES THE OMEGA KEY*, TO OPEN THIS DOOR...

"...IT JUST OPENS INTO MORE CAVE. THAT OTHER WORLD DISAPPEARS COMPLETELY. LIKE IT NEVER WAS.

"ONLY THE OMEGA KEY CAN OPEN THE PASSAGEWAY INTO SOUL-TAPEWORM CITY.

"HELL, THEY USED THIS SPACE FOR STORAGE DURING WORLD WAR II, BACK WHEN ALL THESE CAVES OPERATED AS A PLACE TO WATCH FOR GERMAN SUBS.

"THEY HAD *NO IDEA* THERE WAS ANYTHING SPECIAL ABOUT THIS DOOR."

TO TELL THE TRUTH, I THINK MAYBE BEN WANTED TO GET RID OF THE OMEGA KEY COMPLETELY AFTER THAT. GOOD RIDDANCE, RIGHT?

BUT HE DIDN'T GET RID OF IT.

NO. NOT ONCE HE UNDERSTOOD THE WHISPERING IRON COULD BE USED TO UNLOCK THE IMPOSSIBLE.

THEY WERE FIGHTING A WAR. THE WHISPERING IRON GAVE THE YANKEES A CRUCIAL ADVANTAGE AGAINST A VASTLY SUPERIOR ARMY. THEY WEREN'T ABOUT TO GIVE UP THEIR SOURCE OF THE STUFF.

BEN LOCKE WAS AS GOOD A MAN AS THEY COME... BUT THERE ISN'T ANYONE IN A DESPERATE SITUATION WHO CAN WALK AWAY FROM THIS KIND OF TEMPTATION. YOU KNOW?

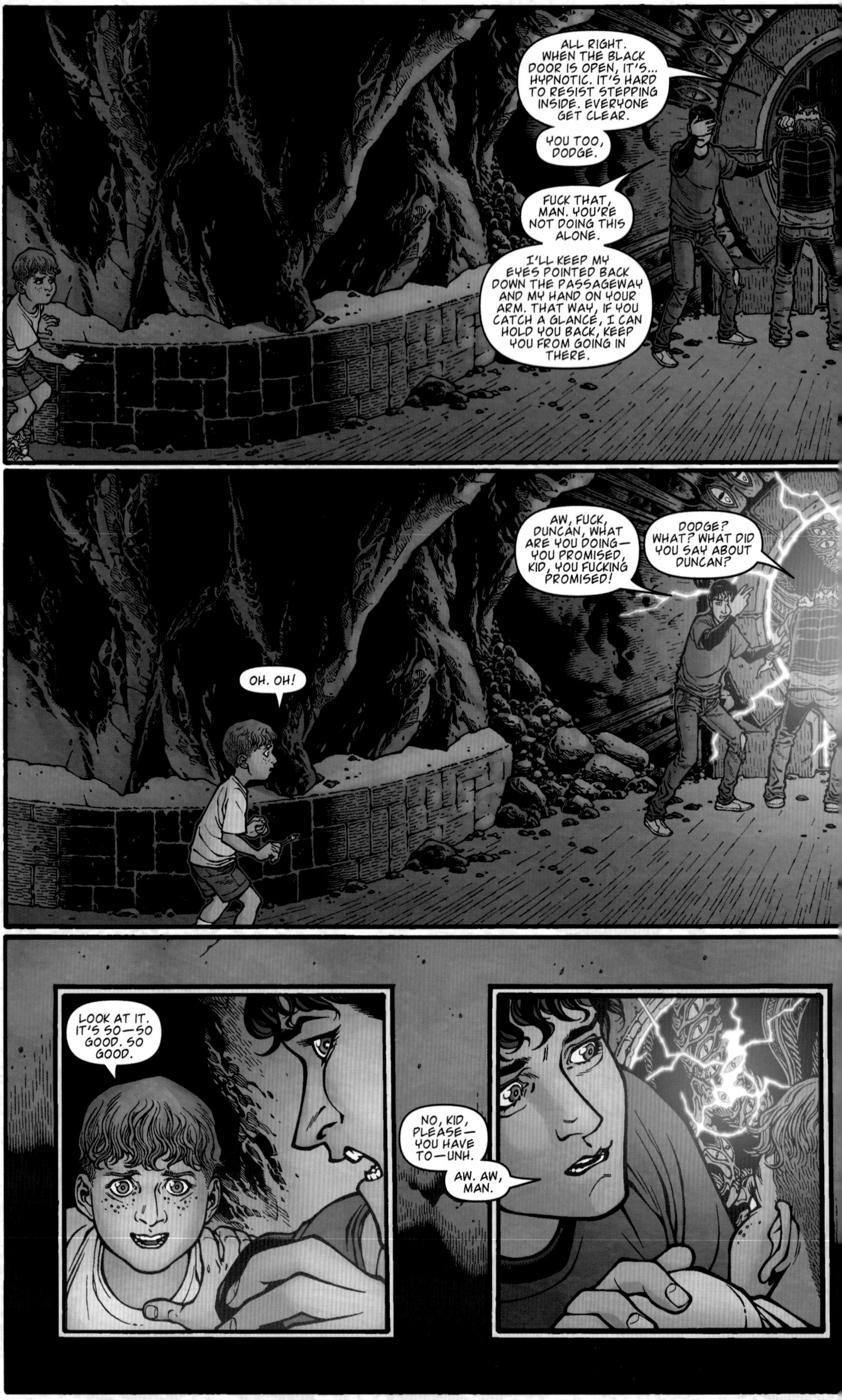
ALL RIGHT. WHEN THE BLACK DOOR IS OPEN, IT'S... HYPNOTIC. IT'S HARD TO RESIST STEPPING INSIDE. EVERYONE GET CLEAR.
YOU TOO, DODGE.
FUCK THAT, MAN. YOU'RE NOT DOING THIS ALONE.
I'LL KEEP MY EYES POINTED BACK DOWN THE PASSAGEWAY AND MY HAND ON YOUR ARM. THAT WAY, IF YOU CATCH A GLANCE, I CAN HOLD YOU BACK, KEEP YOU FROM GOING IN THERE.
AW, FUCK, DUNCAN, WHAT ARE YOU DOING— YOU PROMISED, KID, YOU FUCKING PROMISED!
DODGE? WHAT? WHAT DID YOU SAY ABOUT DUNCAN?
OH. OH!
LOOK AT IT. IT'S SO—SO GOOD. SO GOOD.
NO, KID, PLEASE— YOU HAVE TO—UNH.
AW. AW, MAN.

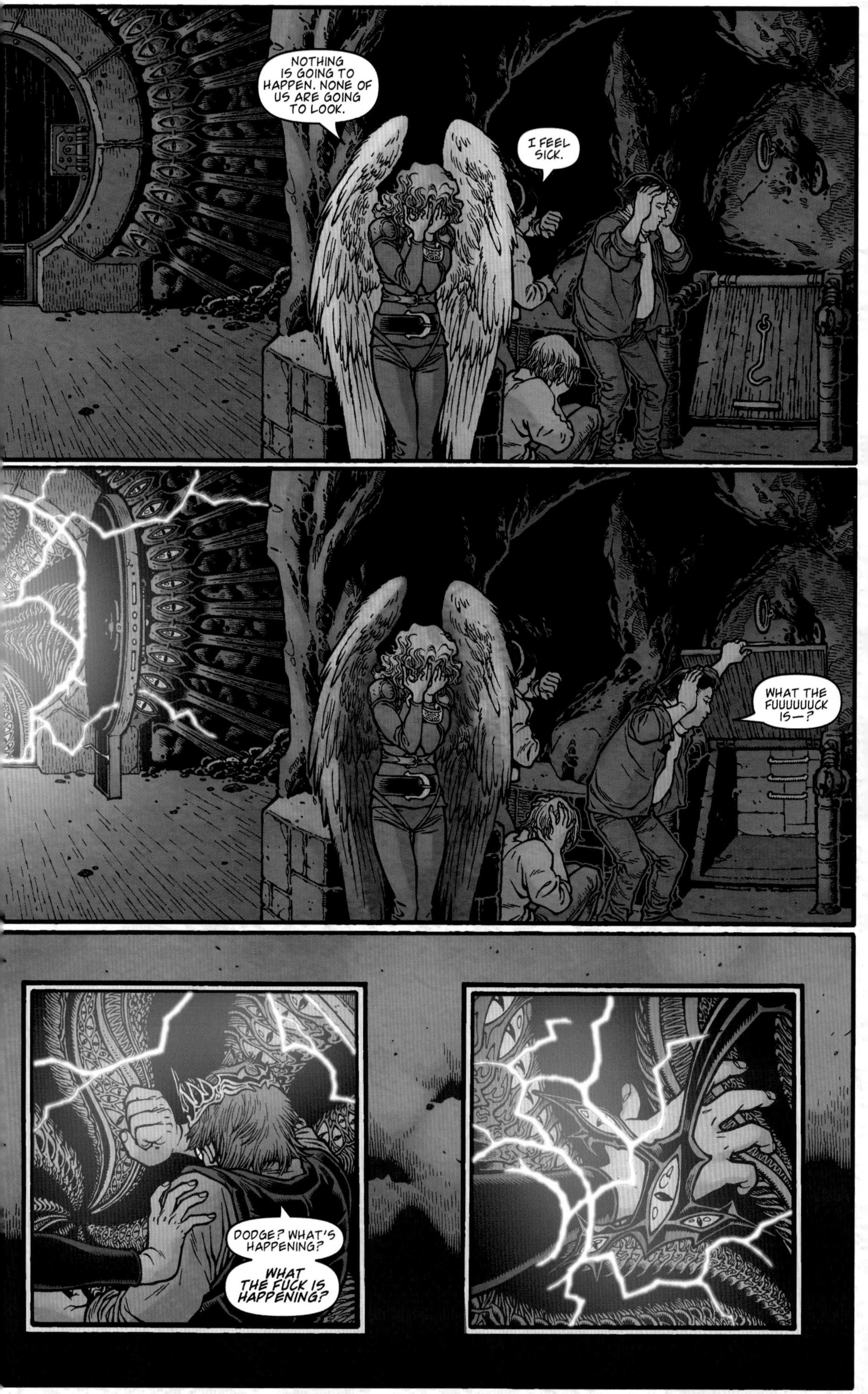
NOTHING IS GOING TO HAPPEN. NONE OF US ARE GOING TO LOOK.
I FEEL SICK.
WHAT THE FUUUUUUCK IS—?
DODGE? WHAT'S HAPPENING?
WHAT THE FUCK IS HAPPENING?

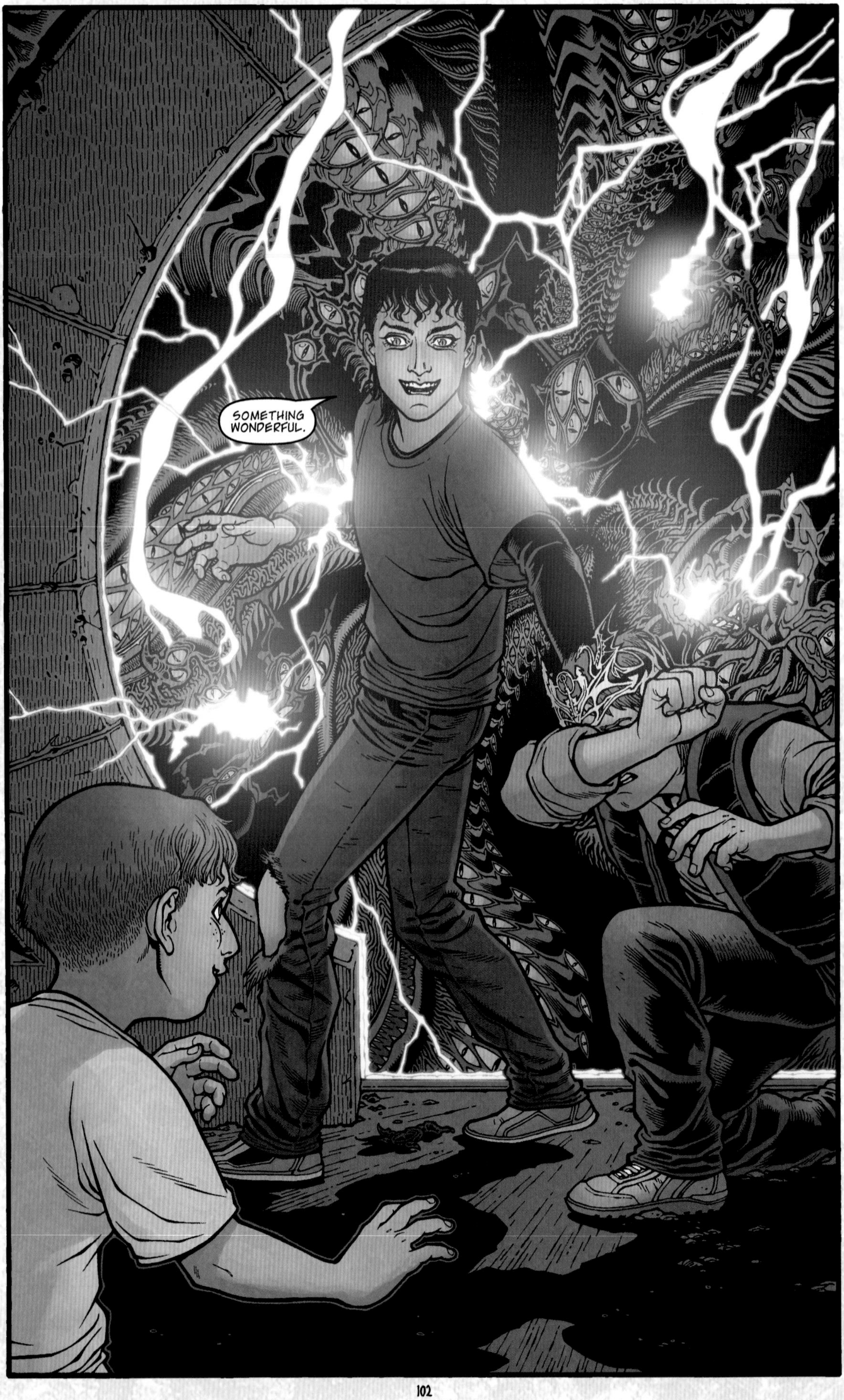
SOMETHING WONDERFUL.

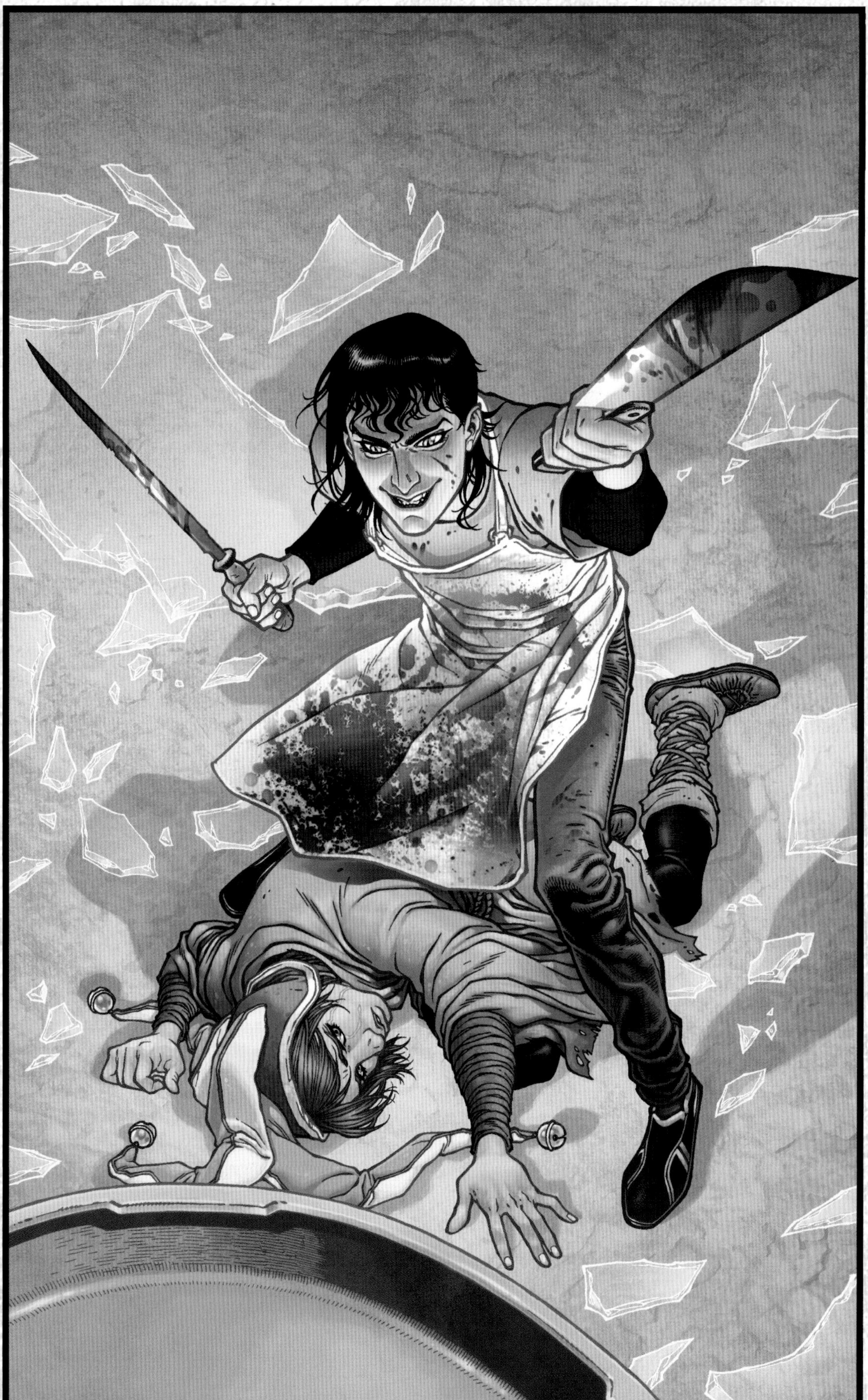

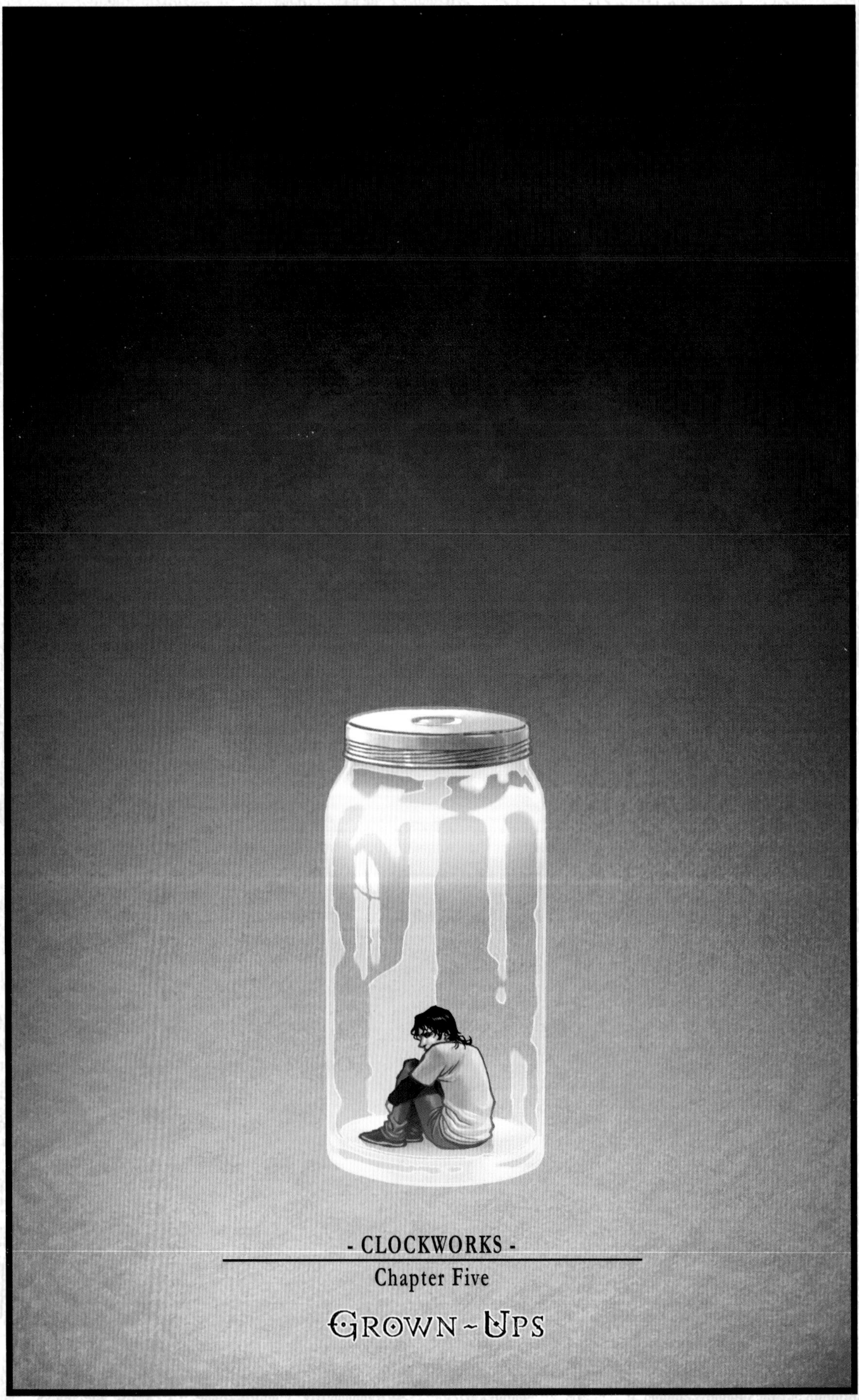

- CLOCKWORKS -

Chapter Five

GROWN-UPS

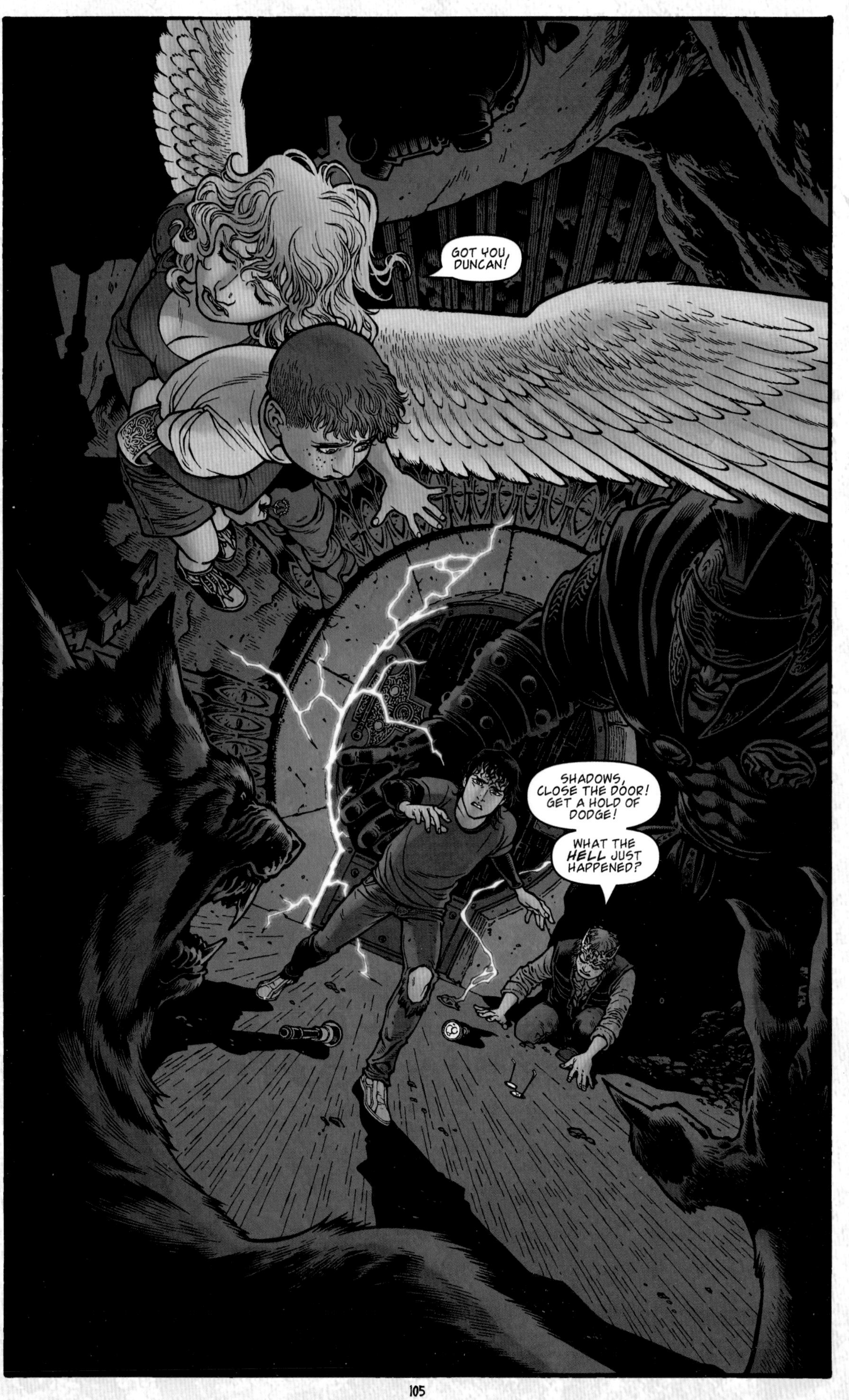

GOT YOU, DUNCAN!
SHADOWS, CLOSE THE DOOR! GET A HOLD OF DODGE!
WHAT THE HELL JUST HAPPENED?

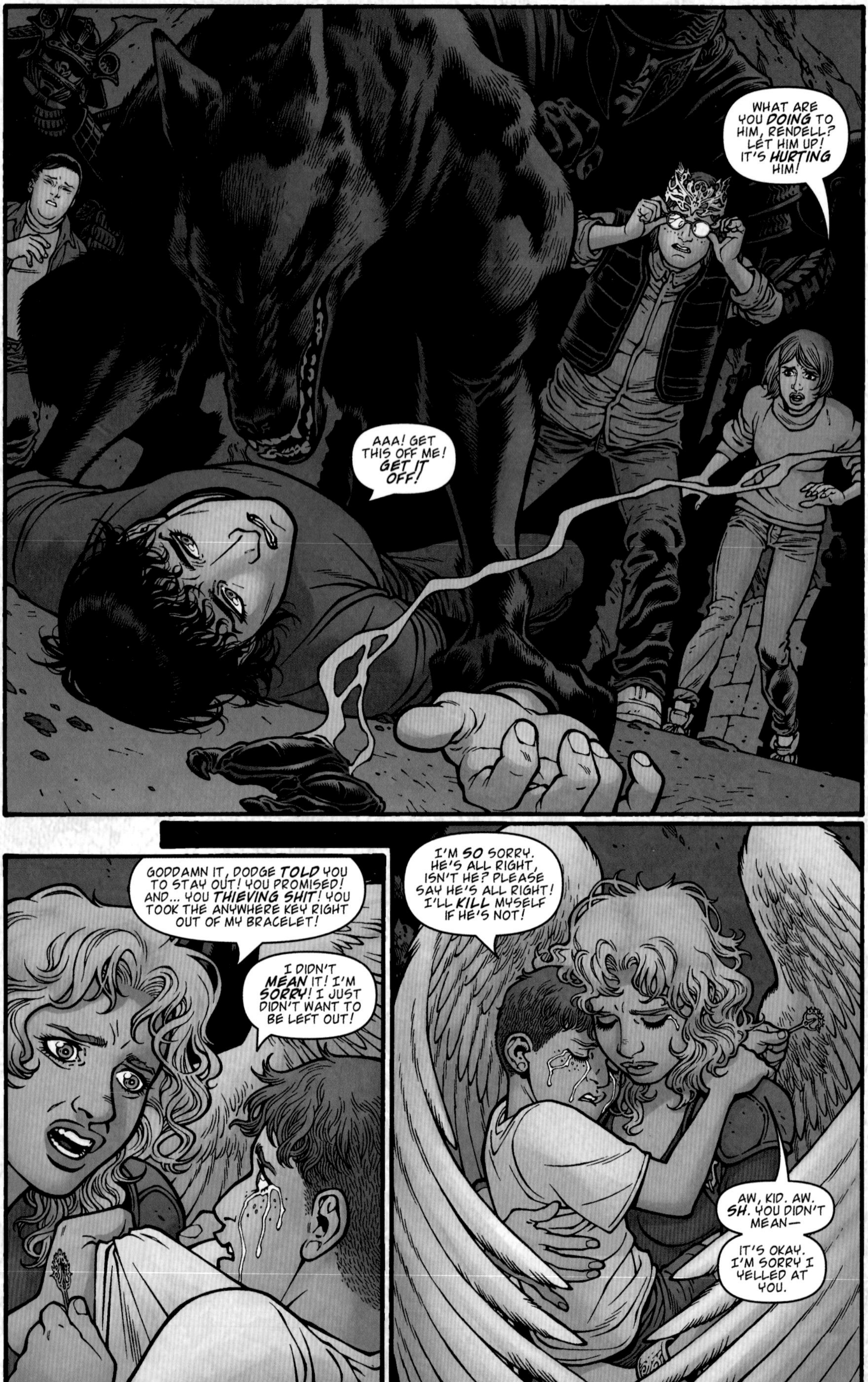
WHAT ARE YOU DOING TO HIM, RENDELL? LET HIM UP! IT'S HURTING HIM!
AAA! GET THIS OFF ME! GET IT OFF!
GODDAMN IT, DODGE TOLD YOU TO STAY OUT! YOU PROMISED! AND... YOU THIEVING SHIT! YOU TOOK THE ANYWHERE KEY RIGHT OUT OF MY BRACELET!
I DIDN'T MEAN IT! I'M SORRY! I JUST DIDN'T WANT TO BE LEFT OUT!
I'M SO SORRY. HE'S ALL RIGHT, ISN'T HE? PLEASE SAY HE'S ALL RIGHT! I'LL KILL MYSELF IF HE'S NOT!
AW, KID. AW. SH. YOU DIDN'T MEAN—
IT'S OKAY. I'M SORRY I YELLED AT YOU.

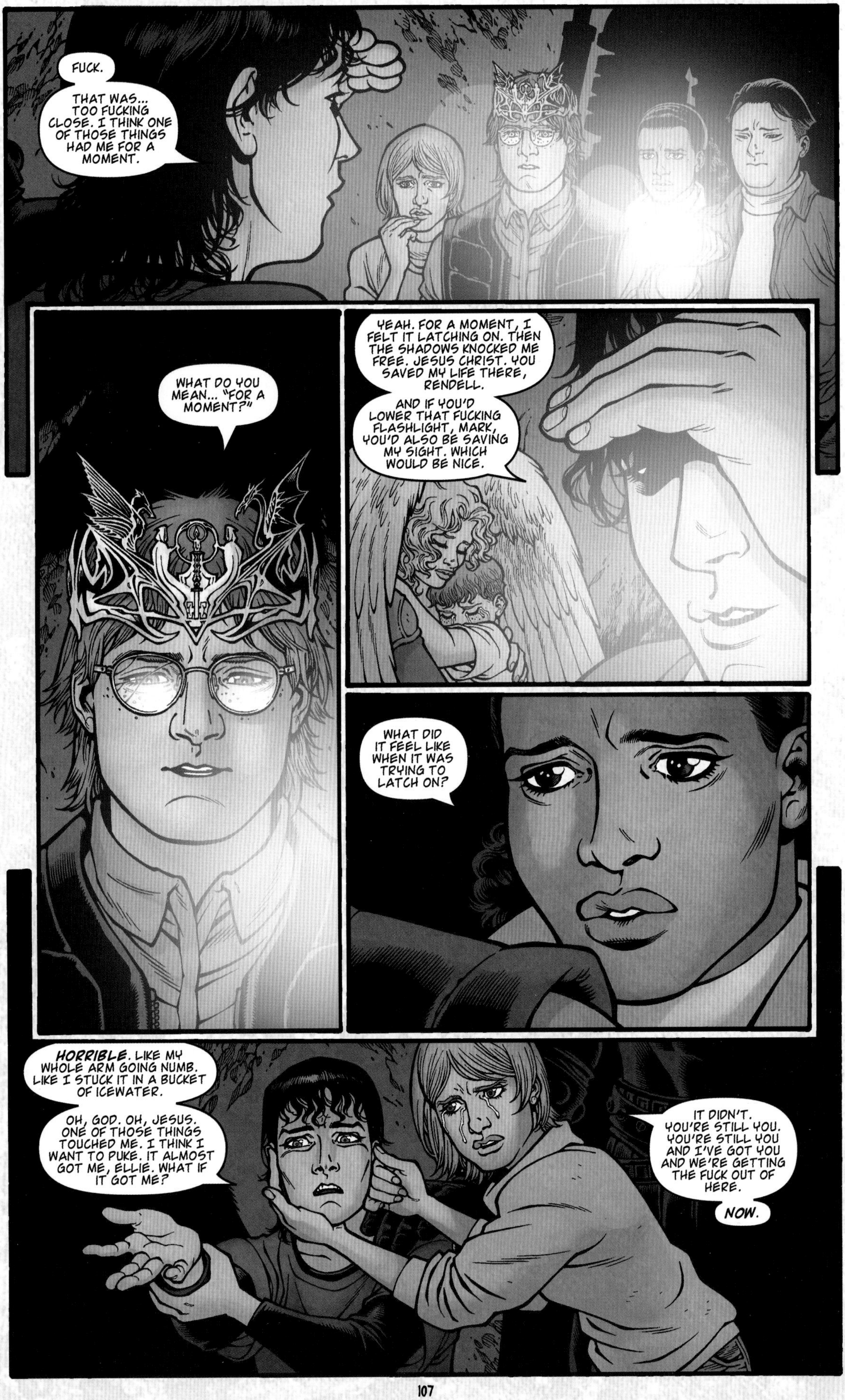

FUCK.
THAT WAS... TOO FUCKING CLOSE. I THINK ONE OF THOSE THINGS HAD ME FOR A MOMENT.
WHAT DO YOU MEAN... "FOR A MOMENT?"
YEAH. FOR A MOMENT, I FELT IT LATCHING ON. THEN THE SHADOWS KNOCKED ME FREE. JESUS CHRIST. YOU SAVED MY LIFE THERE, RENDELL.
AND IF YOU'D LOWER THAT FUCKING FLASHLIGHT, MARK, YOU'D ALSO BE SAVING MY SIGHT. WHICH WOULD BE NICE.
WHAT DID IT FEEL LIKE WHEN IT WAS TRYING TO LATCH ON?
HORRIBLE. LIKE MY WHOLE ARM GOING NUMB. LIKE I STUCK IT IN A BUCKET OF ICEWATER.
OH, GOD. OH, JESUS. ONE OF THOSE THINGS TOUCHED ME. I THINK I WANT TO PUKE. IT ALMOST GOT ME, ELLIE. WHAT IF IT GOT ME?
IT DIDN'T. YOU'RE STILL YOU. YOU'RE STILL YOU AND I'VE GOT YOU AND WE'RE GETTING THE FUCK OUT OF HERE.
NOW.

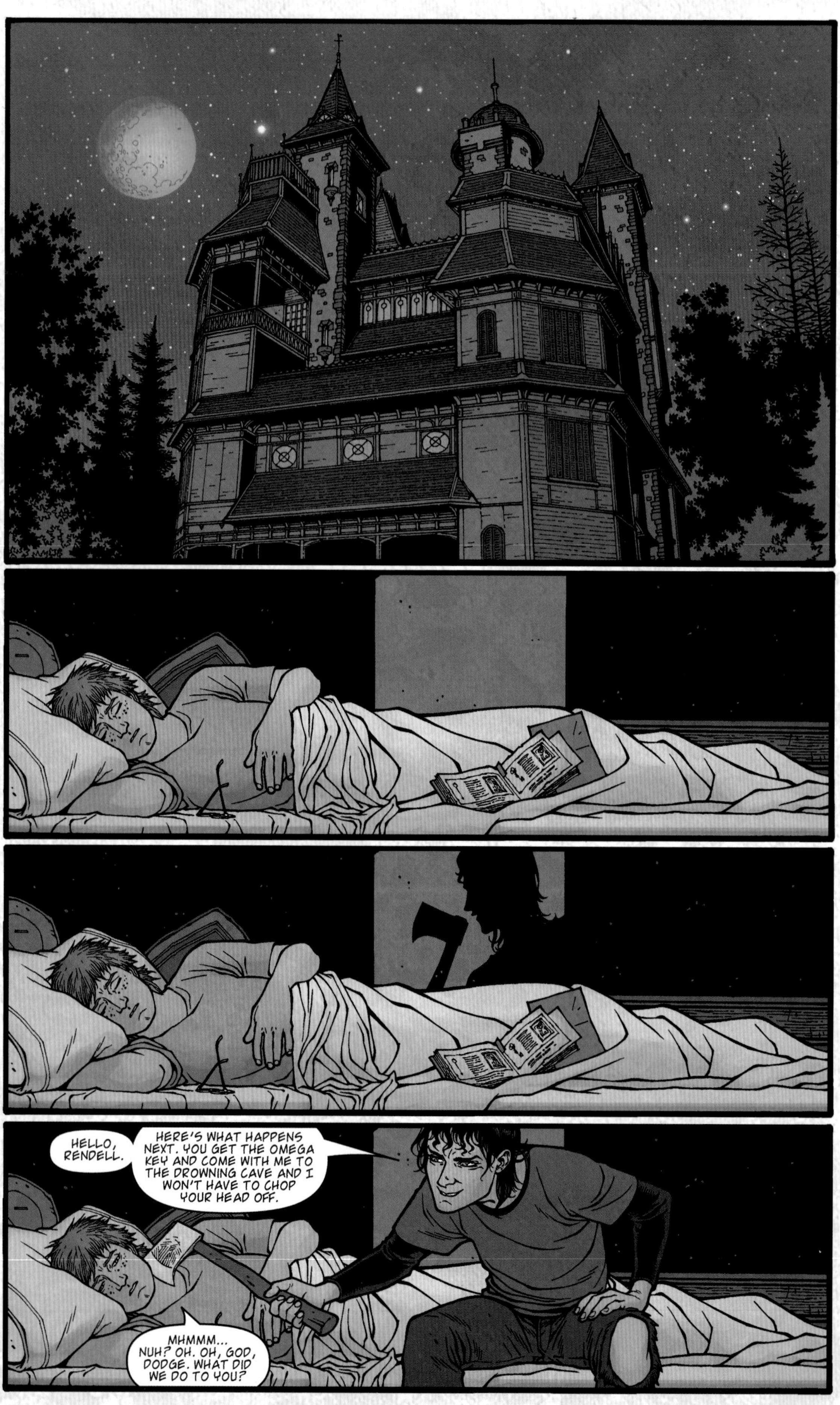
HELLO, RENDELL.
HERE'S WHAT HAPPENS NEXT. YOU GET THE OMEGA KEY AND COME WITH ME TO THE DROWNING CAVE AND I WON'T HAVE TO CHOP YOUR HEAD OFF.
MHMMM... NUH? OH. OH, GOD, DODGE. WHAT DID WE DO TO YOU?

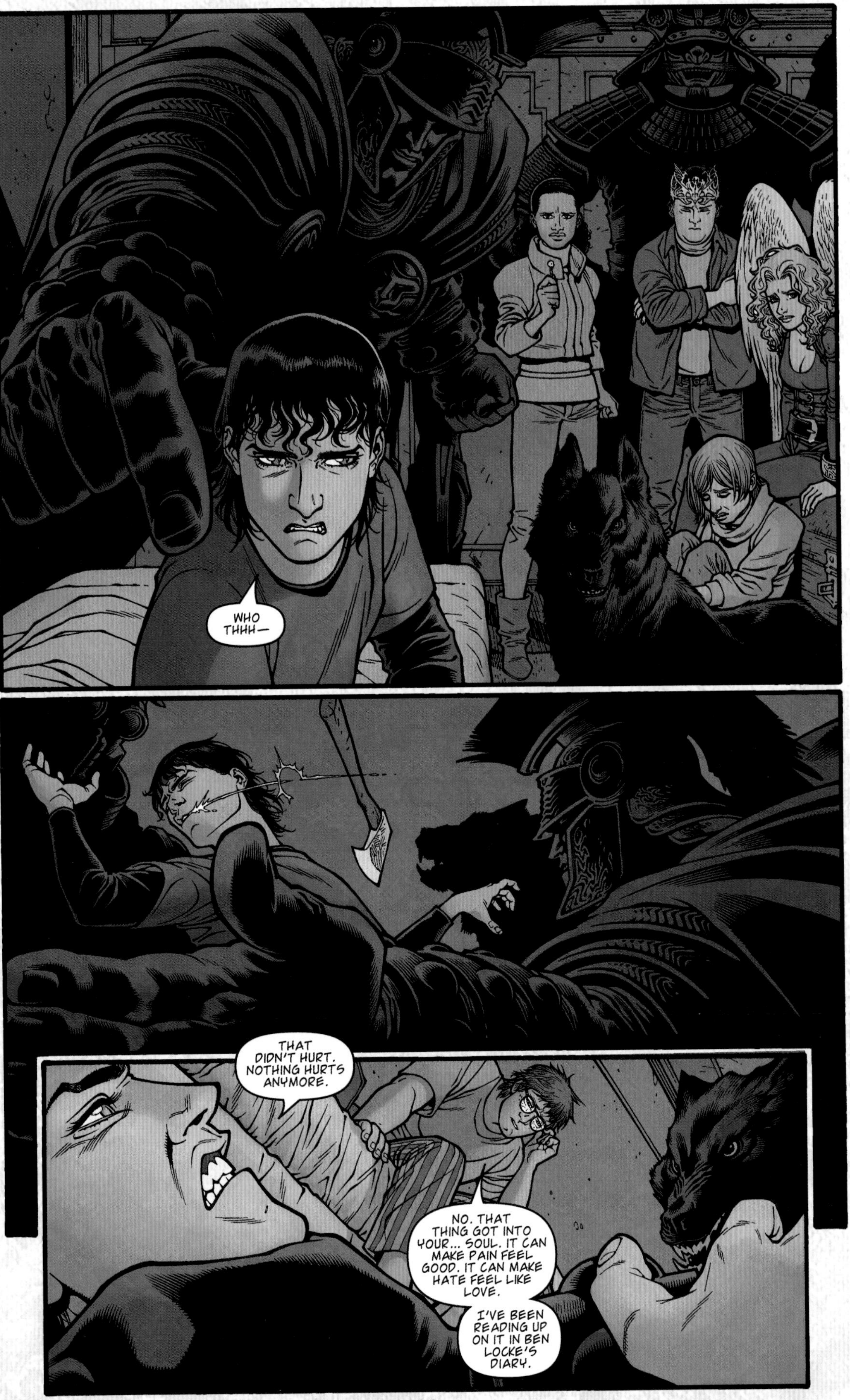
WHO THHH—
THAT DIDN'T HURT. NOTHING HURTS ANYMORE.
NO. THAT THING GOT INTO YOUR... SOUL. IT CAN MAKE PAIN FEEL GOOD. IT CAN MAKE HATE FEEL LIKE LOVE.
I'VE BEEN READING UP ON IT IN BEN LOCKE'S DIARY.

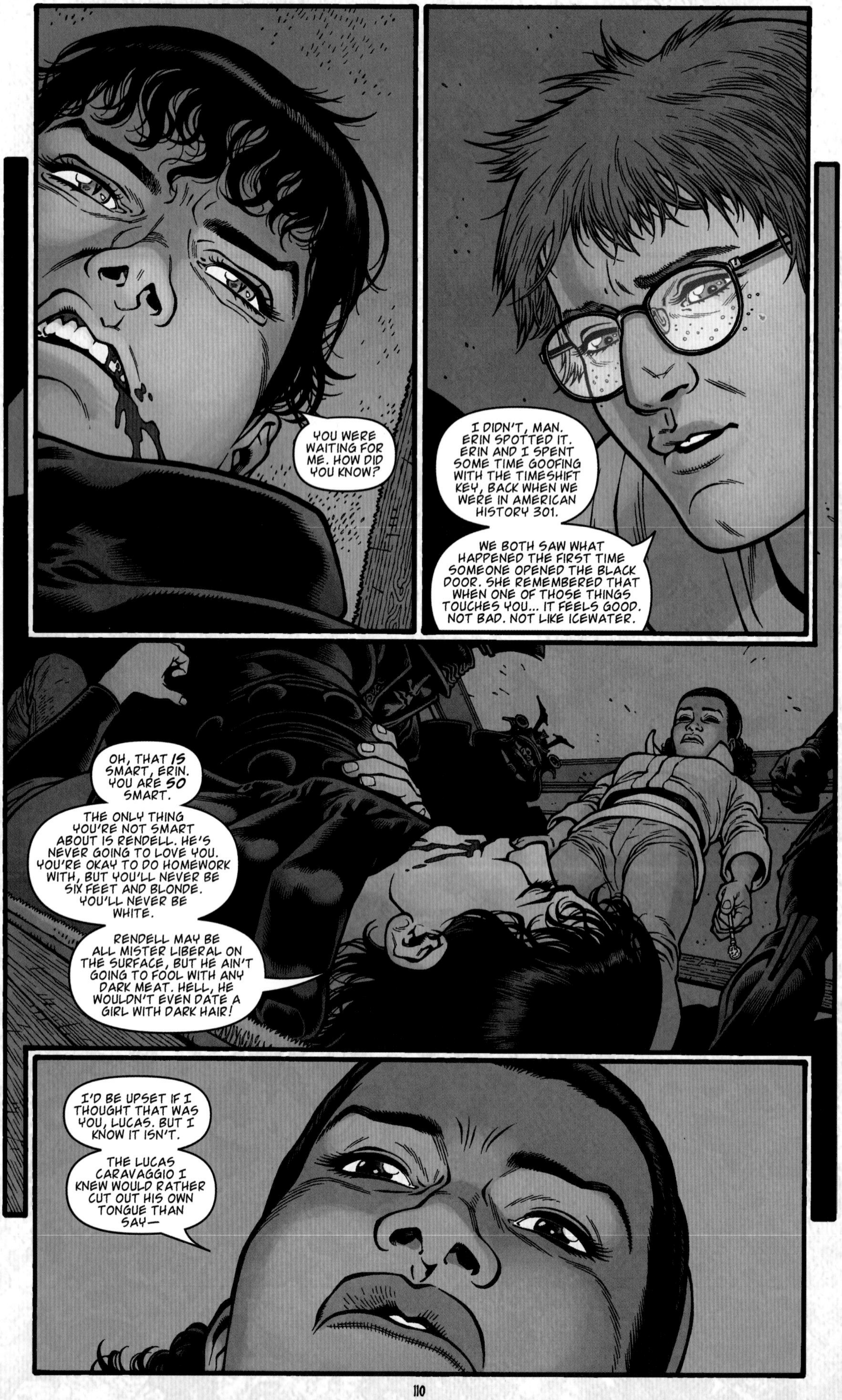
YOU WERE WAITING FOR ME. HOW DID YOU KNOW?
I DIDN'T, MAN. ERIN SPOTTED IT. ERIN AND I SPENT SOME TIME GOOFING WITH THE TIMESHIFT KEY, BACK WHEN WE WERE IN AMERICAN HISTORY 301.
WE BOTH SAW WHAT HAPPENED THE FIRST TIME SOMEONE OPENED THE BLACK DOOR. SHE REMEMBERED THAT WHEN ONE OF THOSE THINGS TOUCHES YOU... IT FEELS GOOD. NOT BAD. NOT LIKE ICEWATER.
OH, THAT IS SMART, ERIN. YOU ARE SO SMART.
THE ONLY THING YOU'RE NOT SMART ABOUT IS RENDELL. HE'S NEVER GOING TO LOVE YOU. YOU'RE OKAY TO DO HOMEWORK WITH, BUT YOU'LL NEVER BE SIX FEET AND BLONDE. YOU'LL NEVER BE WHITE.
RENDELL MAY BE ALL MISTER LIBERAL ON THE SURFACE, BUT HE AIN'T GOING TO FOOL WITH ANY DARK MEAT. HELL, HE WOULDN'T EVEN DATE A GIRL WITH DARK HAIR!
I'D BE UPSET IF I THOUGHT THAT WAS YOU, LUCAS. BUT I KNOW IT ISN'T.
THE LUCAS CARAVAGGIO I KNEW WOULD RATHER CUT OUT HIS OWN TONGUE THAN SAY—

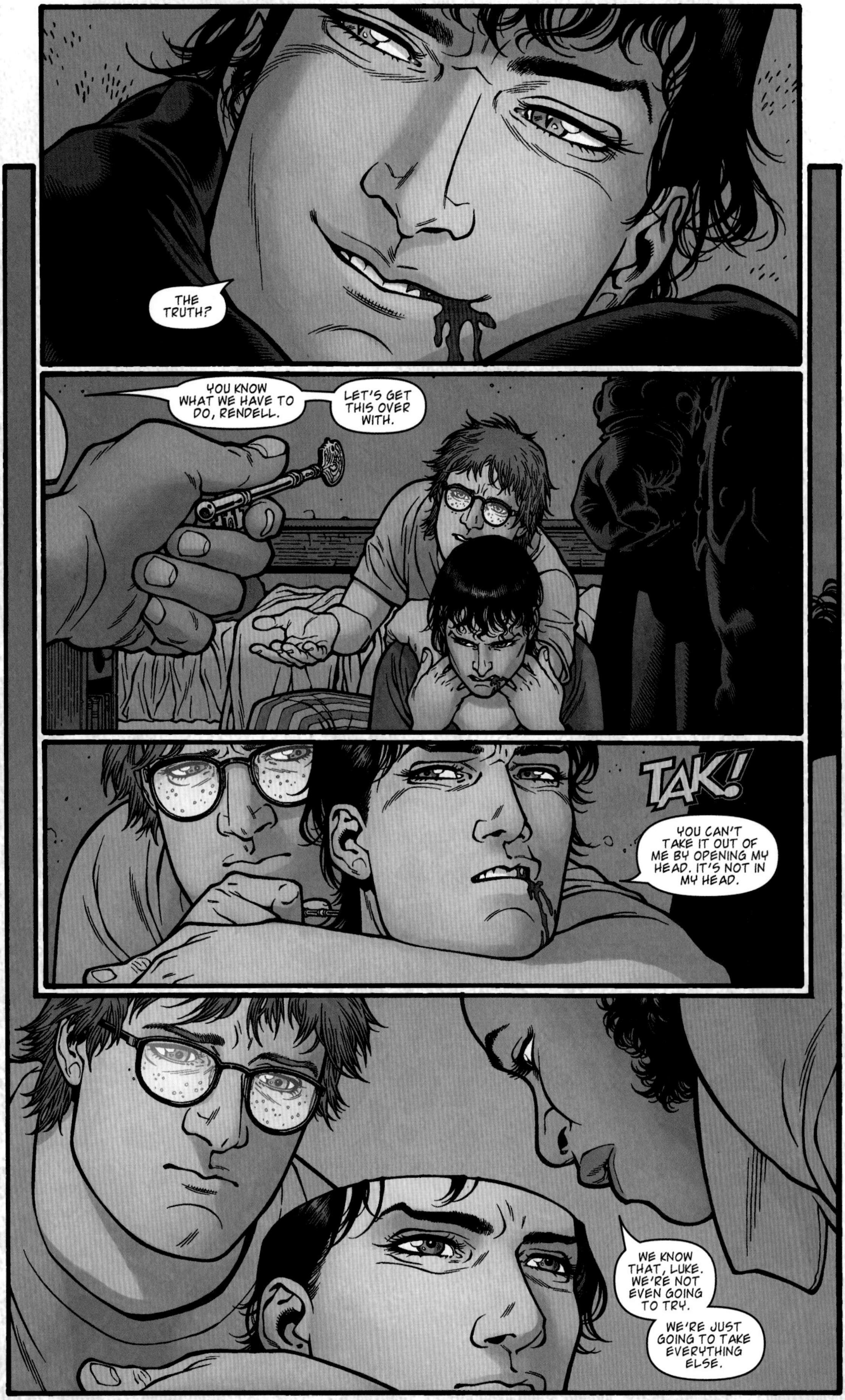

THE TRUTH?
YOU KNOW WHAT WE HAVE TO DO, RENDELL.
LET'S GET THIS OVER WITH.
TAK!
YOU CAN'T TAKE IT OUT OF ME BY OPENING MY HEAD. IT'S NOT IN MY HEAD.
WE KNOW THAT, LUKE. WE'RE NOT EVEN GOING TO TRY.
WE'RE JUST GOING TO TAKE EVERYTHING ELSE.

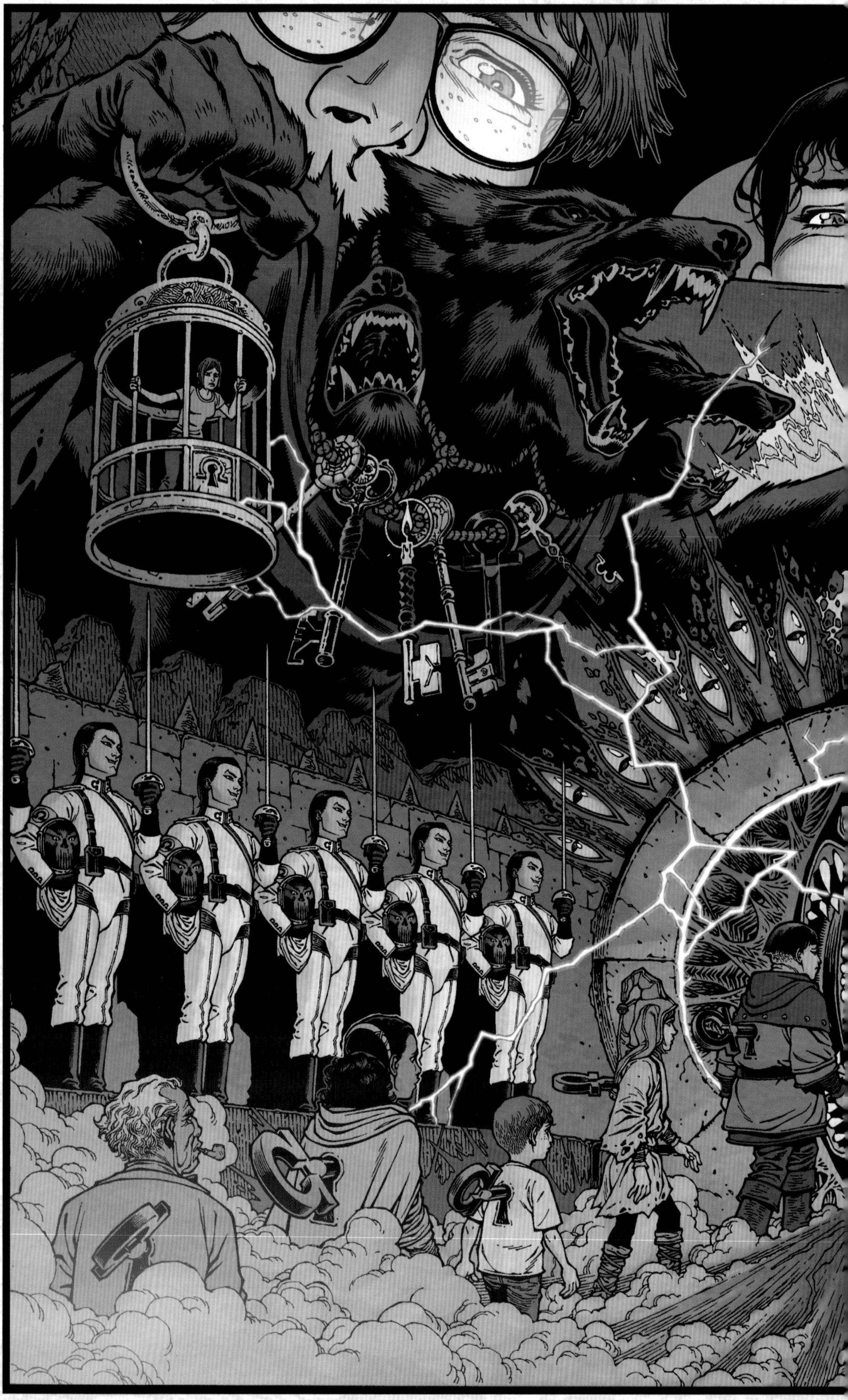

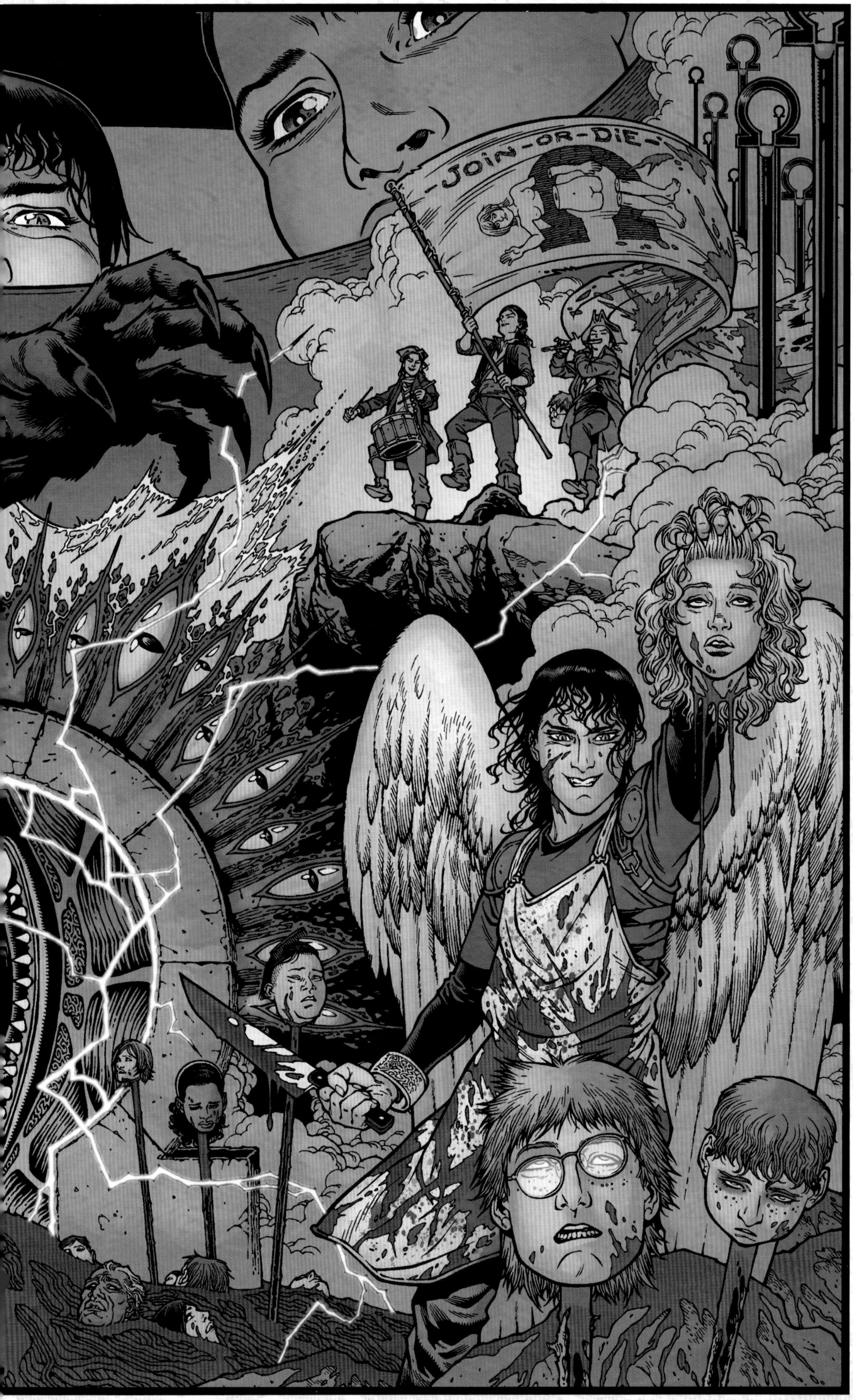
-JOIN-OR-DIE-

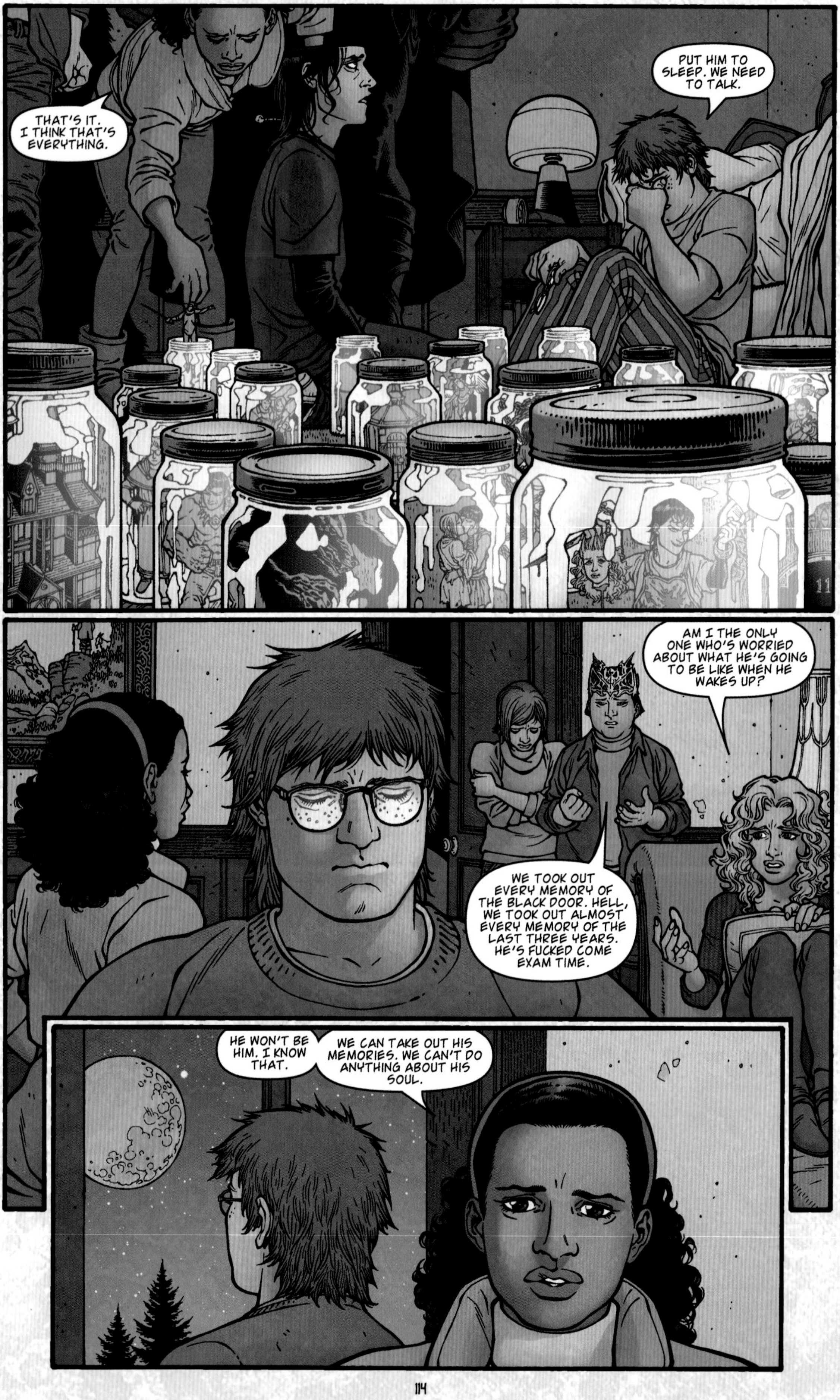
THAT'S IT. I THINK THAT'S EVERYTHING.
PUT HIM TO SLEEP. WE NEED TO TALK.
11
AM I THE ONLY ONE WHO'S WORRIED ABOUT WHAT HE'S GOING TO BE LIKE WHEN HE WAKES UP?
WE TOOK OUT EVERY MEMORY OF THE BLACK DOOR. HELL, WE TOOK OUT ALMOST EVERY MEMORY OF THE LAST THREE YEARS. HE'S FUCKED COME EXAM TIME.
HE WON'T BE HIM. I KNOW THAT.
WE CAN TAKE OUT HIS MEMORIES. WE CAN'T DO ANYTHING ABOUT HIS SOUL.

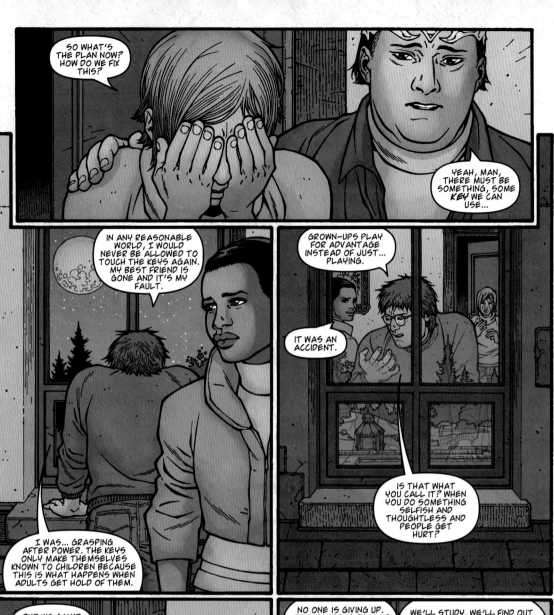

SO WHAT'S THE PLAN NOW? HOW DO WE FIX THIS?

YEAH, MAN, THERE MUST BE SOMETHING, SOME *KEY* WE CAN USE...

IN ANY REASONABLE WORLD, I WOULD NEVER BE ALLOWED TO TOUCH THE KEYS AGAIN. MY BEST FRIEND IS GONE AND IT'S MY FAULT.

I WAS... GRASPING AFTER POWER. THE KEYS ONLY MAKE THEMSELVES KNOWN TO CHILDREN BECAUSE THIS IS WHAT HAPPENS WHEN ADULTS GET HOLD OF THEM.

GROWN-UPS PLAY FOR ADVANTAGE INSTEAD OF JUST... PLAYING.

IT WAS AN ACCIDENT.

IS THAT WHAT YOU CALL IT? WHEN YOU DO SOMETHING SELFISH AND THOUGHTLESS AND PEOPLE GET HURT?

BUT WE CAN'T JUST GIVE UP. IF WE DON'T FIX HIM...

...HE WON'T EVEN REMEMBER HE LOVES ME.

NO ONE IS GIVING UP. THIS HOUSE IS FULL OF OLD JOURNALS. THERE'S A LOT OF INFORMATION ABOUT THE KEYS, ABOUT THE CAVE.

WE'LL STUDY. WE'LL FIND OUT EVERYTHING WE CAN ABOUT THE DEMONS. MAYBE THERE'S SOME WAY TO REVERSE THIS. IN THE MEANTIME, THOUGH, WE NEED TO BE CAREFUL.

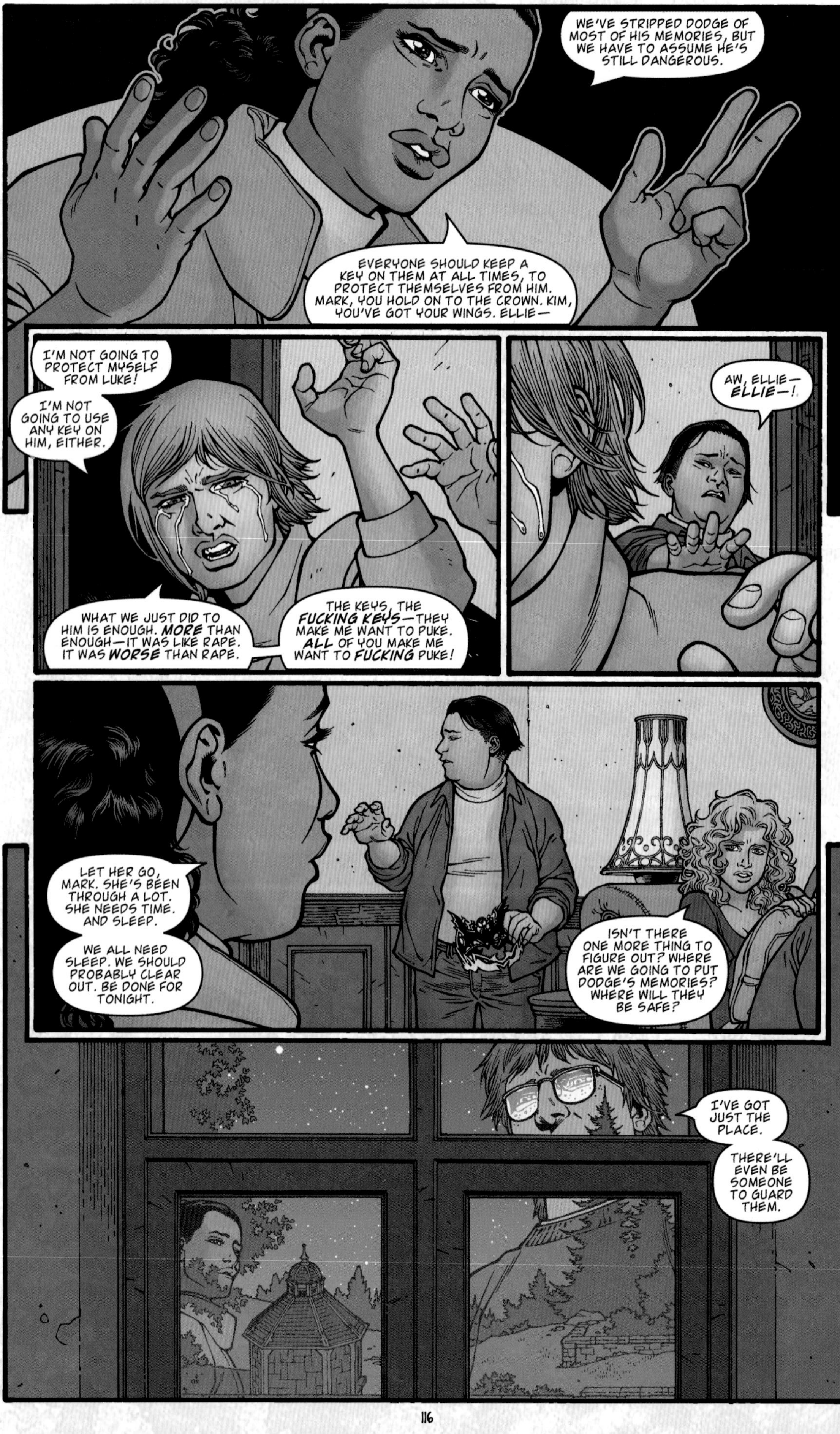

WE'VE STRIPPED DODGE OF MOST OF HIS MEMORIES, BUT WE HAVE TO ASSUME HE'S STILL DANGEROUS.
EVERYONE SHOULD KEEP A KEY ON THEM AT ALL TIMES, TO PROTECT THEMSELVES FROM HIM. MARK, YOU HOLD ON TO THE CROWN. KIM, YOU'VE GOT YOUR WINGS. ELLIE—
I'M NOT GOING TO PROTECT MYSELF FROM LUKE!
I'M NOT GOING TO USE ANY KEY ON HIM, EITHER.
WHAT WE JUST DID TO HIM IS ENOUGH. *MORE* THAN ENOUGH—IT WAS LIKE RAPE. IT WAS *WORSE* THAN RAPE.
THE KEYS, THE *FUCKING KEYS*—THEY MAKE ME WANT TO PUKE. *ALL* OF YOU MAKE ME WANT TO *FUCKING* PUKE!
AW, ELLIE— *ELLIE*—!
LET HER GO, MARK. SHE'S BEEN THROUGH A LOT. SHE NEEDS TIME. AND SLEEP.
WE ALL NEED SLEEP. WE SHOULD PROBABLY CLEAR OUT. BE DONE FOR TONIGHT.
ISN'T THERE ONE MORE THING TO FIGURE OUT? WHERE ARE WE GOING TO PUT DODGE'S MEMORIES? WHERE WILL THEY BE SAFE?
I'VE GOT JUST THE PLACE.
THERE'LL EVEN BE SOMEONE TO GUARD THEM.

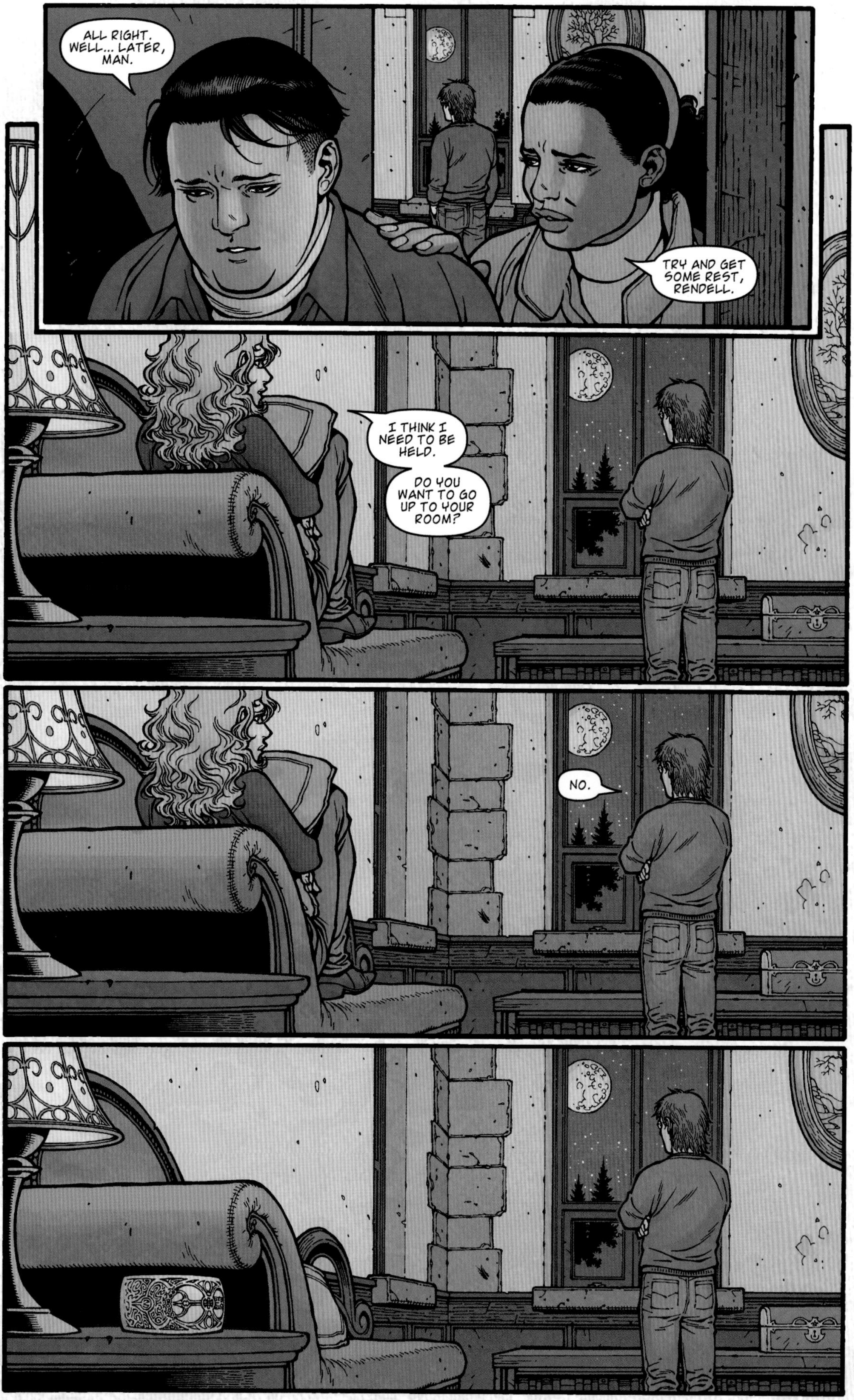
ALL RIGHT. WELL... LATER, MAN.
TRY AND GET SOME REST, RENDELL.
I THINK I NEED TO BE HELD.
DO YOU WANT TO GO UP TO YOUR ROOM?
NO.

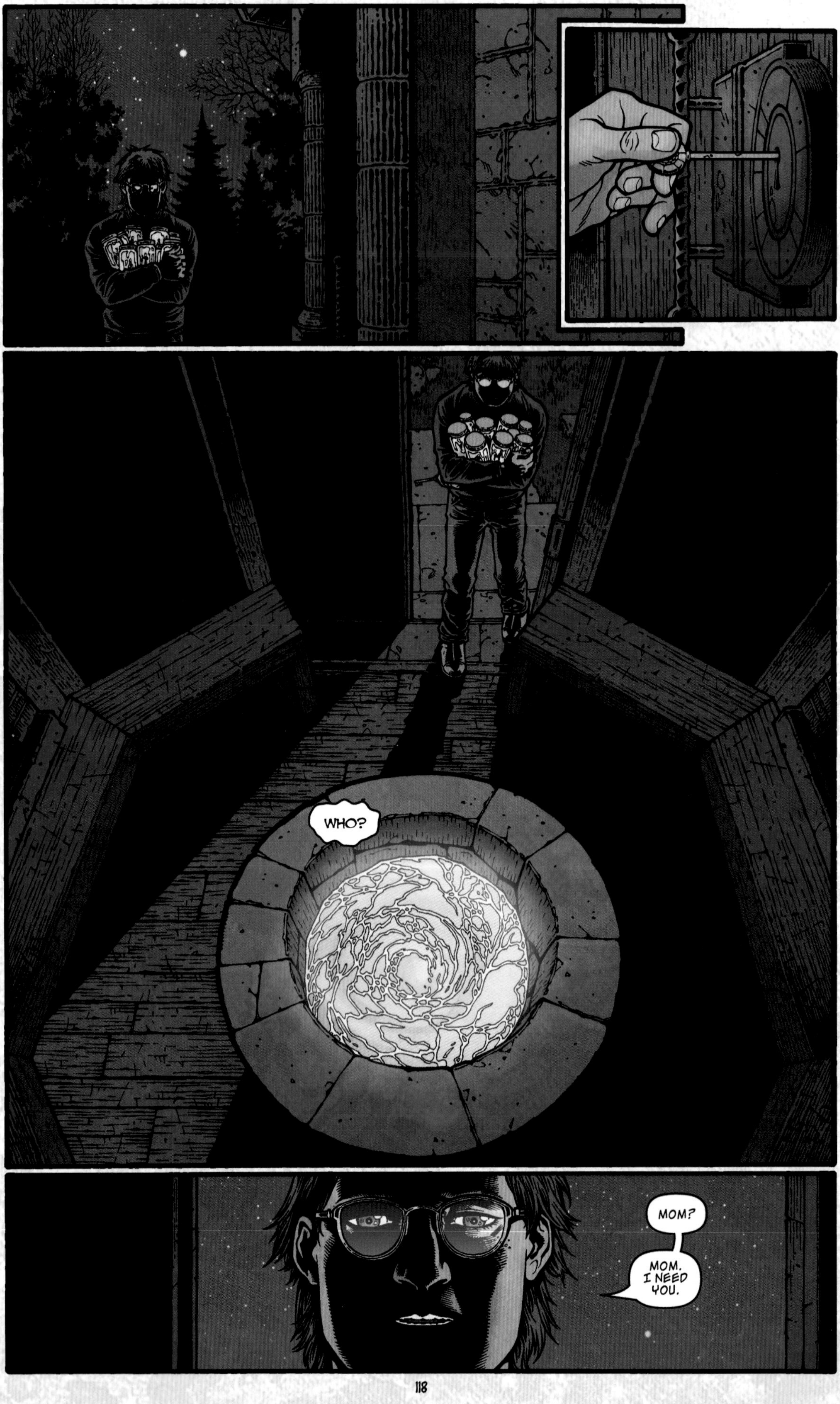
WHO?
MOM?
MOM. I NEED YOU.

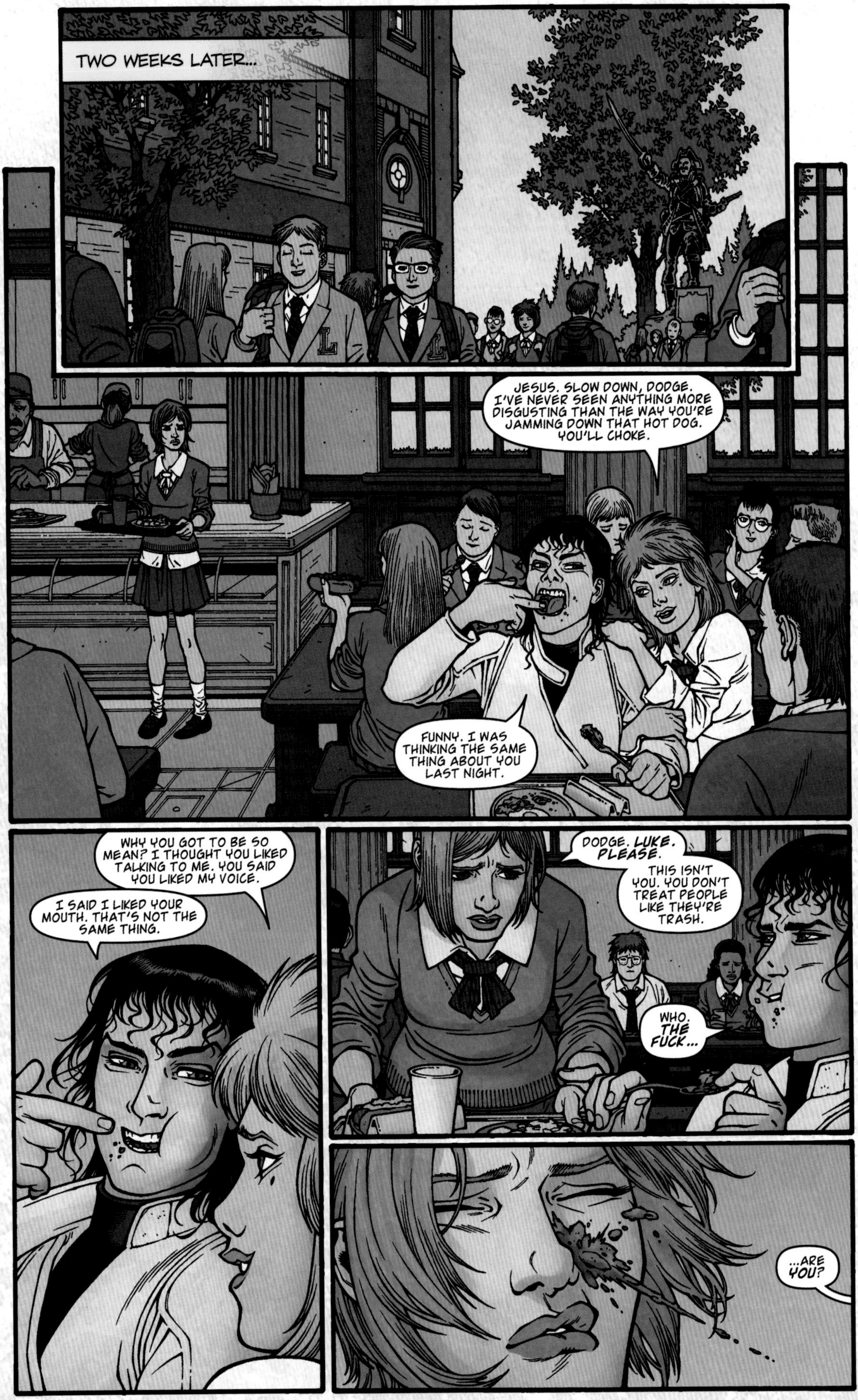
TWO WEEKS LATER...
JESUS. SLOW DOWN, DODGE. I'VE NEVER SEEN ANYTHING MORE DISGUSTING THAN THE WAY YOU'RE JAMMING DOWN THAT HOT DOG. YOU'LL CHOKE.
FUNNY. I WAS THINKING THE SAME THING ABOUT YOU LAST NIGHT.
WHY YOU GOT TO BE SO MEAN? I THOUGHT YOU LIKED TALKING TO ME. YOU SAID YOU LIKED MY VOICE.
I SAID I LIKED YOUR MOUTH. THAT'S NOT THE SAME THING.
DODGE. LUKE. PLEASE.
THIS ISN'T YOU. YOU DON'T TREAT PEOPLE LIKE THEY'RE TRASH.
WHO. THE FUCK...
...ARE YOU?

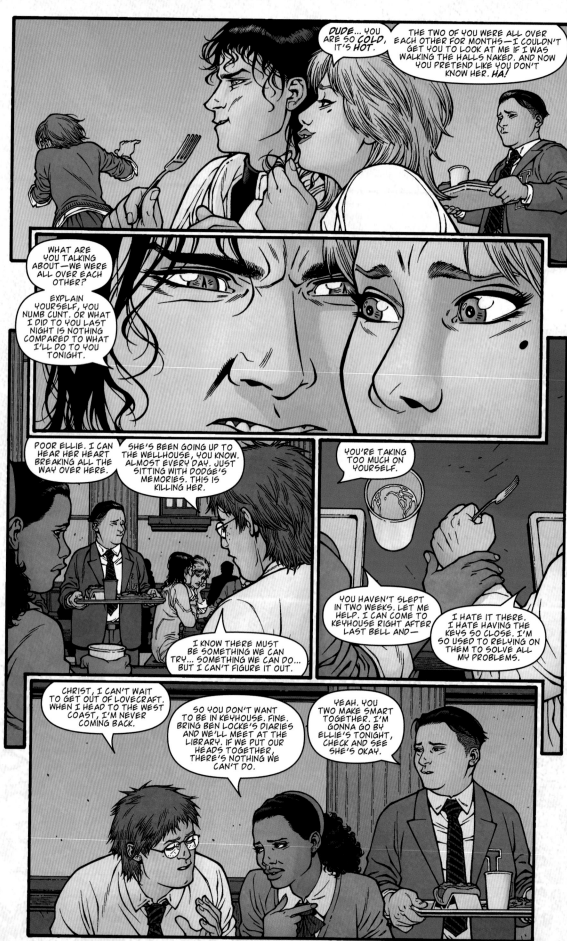

DUDE... YOU ARE SO *COLD*, IT'S *HOT*.

THE TWO OF YOU WERE ALL OVER EACH OTHER FOR MONTHS—I COULDN'T GET YOU TO LOOK AT ME IF I WAS WALKING THE HALLS NAKED. AND NOW YOU PRETEND LIKE YOU DON'T KNOW HER. *HA!*

WHAT ARE YOU TALKING ABOUT—WE WERE ALL OVER EACH OTHER?

EXPLAIN YOURSELF, YOU NUMB CUNT. OR WHAT I DID TO YOU LAST NIGHT IS NOTHING COMPARED TO WHAT I'LL DO TO YOU TONIGHT.

POOR ELLIE. I CAN HEAR HER HEART BREAKING ALL THE WAY OVER HERE.

SHE'S BEEN GOING UP TO THE WELLHOUSE, YOU KNOW. ALMOST EVERY DAY. JUST SITTING WITH DODGE'S MEMORIES. THIS IS KILLING HER.

YOU'RE TAKING TOO MUCH ON YOURSELF.

I KNOW THERE MUST BE SOMETHING WE CAN TRY... SOMETHING WE CAN DO... BUT I CAN'T FIGURE IT OUT.

YOU HAVEN'T SLEPT IN TWO WEEKS. LET ME HELP. I CAN COME TO KEYHOUSE RIGHT AFTER LAST BELL AND—

I HATE IT THERE. I HATE HAVING THE KEYS SO CLOSE. I'M SO USED TO RELYING ON THEM TO SOLVE ALL MY PROBLEMS.

CHRIST, I CAN'T WAIT TO GET OUT OF LOVECRAFT. WHEN I HEAD TO THE WEST COAST, I'M NEVER COMING BACK.

SO YOU DON'T WANT TO BE IN KEYHOUSE. FINE. BRING BEN LOCKE'S DIARIES AND WE'LL MEET AT THE LIBRARY. IF WE PUT OUR HEADS TOGETHER, THERE'S NOTHING WE CAN'T DO.

YEAH. YOU TWO MAKE SMART TOGETHER. I'M GONNA GO BY ELLIE'S TONIGHT, CHECK AND SEE SHE'S OKAY.

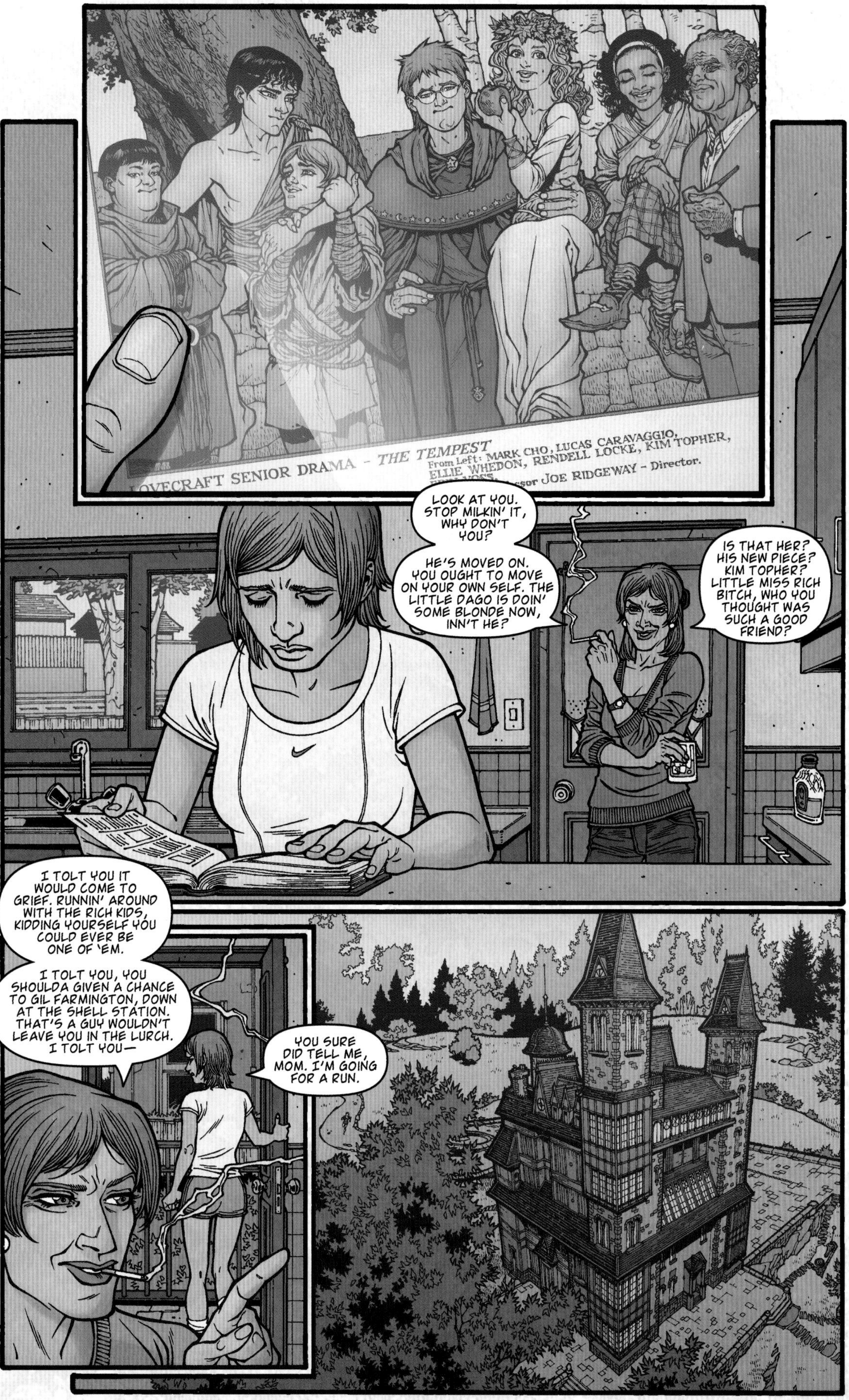

LOVECRAFT SENIOR DRAMA - THE TEMPEST
From Left: MARK CHO, LUCAS CARAVAGGIO, ELLIE WHEDON, RENDELL LOCKE, KIM TOPHER,
JOE RIDGEWAY - Director.
LOOK AT YOU. STOP MILKIN' IT, WHY DON'T YOU?
HE'S MOVED ON. YOU OUGHT TO MOVE ON YOUR OWN SELF. THE LITTLE DAGO IS DOIN' SOME BLONDE NOW, INN'T HE?
IS THAT HER? HIS NEW PIECE? KIM TOPHER? LITTLE MISS RICH BITCH, WHO YOU THOUGHT WAS SUCH A GOOD FRIEND?
I TOLT YOU IT WOULD COME TO GRIEF. RUNNIN' AROUND WITH THE RICH KIDS, KIDDING YOURSELF YOU COULD EVER BE ONE OF 'EM.
I TOLT YOU, YOU SHOULDA GIVEN A CHANCE TO GIL FARMINGTON, DOWN AT THE SHELL STATION. THAT'S A GUY WOULDN'T LEAVE YOU IN THE LURCH. I TOLT YOU—
YOU SURE DID TELL ME, MOM. I'M GOING FOR A RUN.

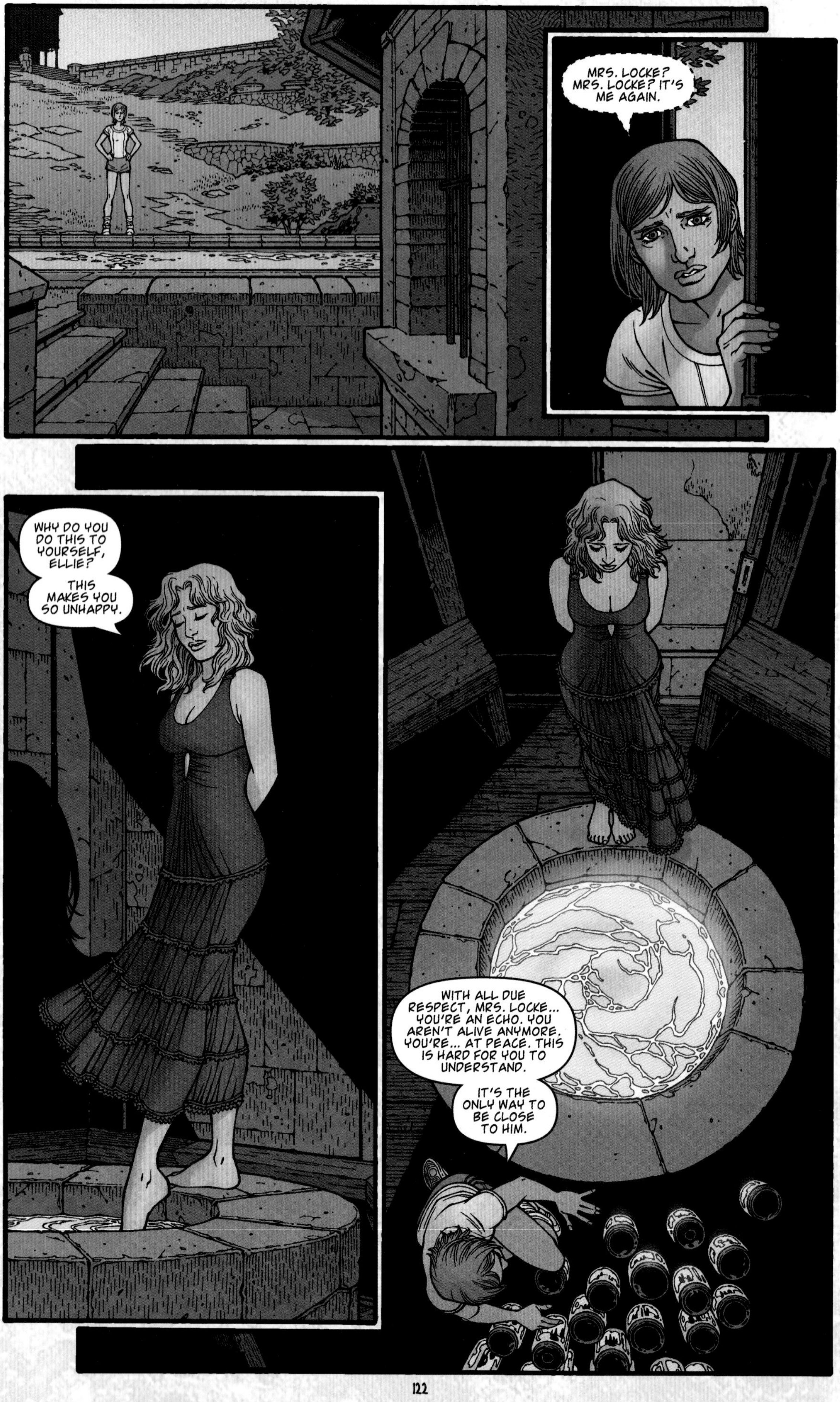
MRS. LOCKE? MRS. LOCKE? IT'S ME AGAIN.
WHY DO YOU DO THIS TO YOURSELF, ELLIE?
THIS MAKES YOU SO UNHAPPY.
WITH ALL DUE RESPECT, MRS. LOCKE... YOU'RE AN ECHO. YOU AREN'T ALIVE ANYMORE. YOU'RE... AT PEACE. THIS IS HARD FOR YOU TO UNDERSTAND.
IT'S THE ONLY WAY TO BE CLOSE TO HIM.

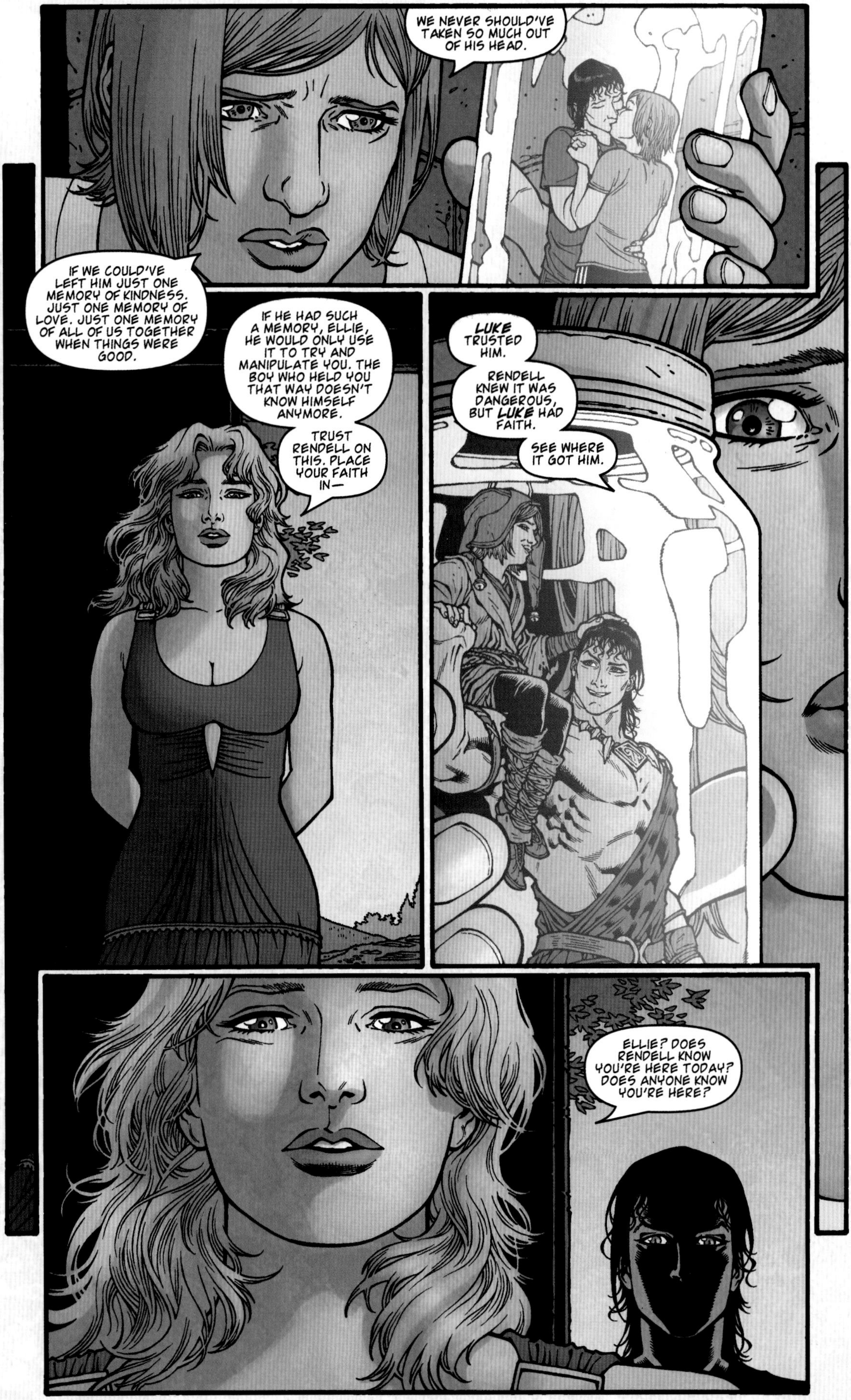

WE NEVER SHOULD'VE TAKEN SO MUCH OUT OF HIS HEAD.
IF WE COULD'VE LEFT HIM JUST ONE MEMORY OF KINDNESS. JUST ONE MEMORY OF LOVE. JUST ONE MEMORY OF ALL OF US TOGETHER WHEN THINGS WERE GOOD.
IF HE HAD SUCH A MEMORY, ELLIE, HE WOULD ONLY USE IT TO TRY AND MANIPULATE YOU. THE BOY WHO HELD YOU THAT WAY DOESN'T KNOW HIMSELF ANYMORE.
TRUST RENDELL ON THIS. PLACE YOUR FAITH IN—
LUKE TRUSTED HIM.
RENDELL KNEW IT WAS DANGEROUS, BUT ***LUKE*** HAD FAITH.
SEE WHERE IT GOT HIM.
ELLIE? DOES RENDELL KNOW YOU'RE HERE TODAY? DOES ANYONE KNOW YOU'RE HERE?

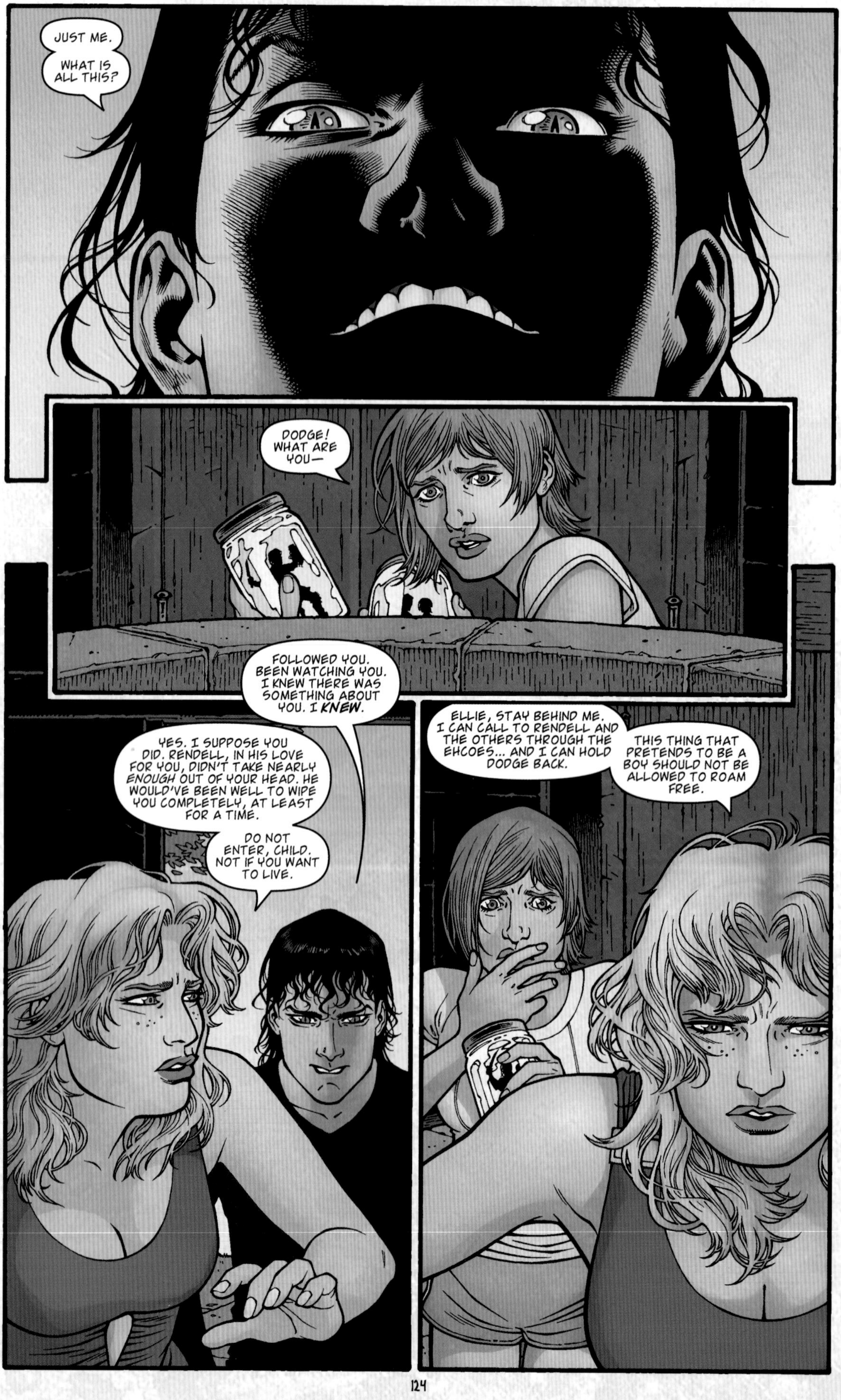
JUST ME.
WHAT IS ALL THIS?
DODGE! WHAT ARE YOU—
FOLLOWED YOU. BEEN WATCHING YOU. I KNEW THERE WAS SOMETHING ABOUT YOU. I *KNEW*.
YES. I SUPPOSE YOU DID. RENDELL, IN HIS LOVE FOR YOU, DIDN'T TAKE NEARLY *ENOUGH* OUT OF YOUR HEAD. HE WOULD'VE BEEN WELL TO WIPE YOU COMPLETELY, AT LEAST FOR A TIME.
DO NOT ENTER, CHILD. NOT IF YOU WANT TO LIVE.
ELLIE, STAY BEHIND ME. I CAN CALL TO RENDELL AND THE OTHERS THROUGH THE EHCOES... AND I CAN HOLD DODGE BACK.
THIS THING THAT PRETENDS TO BE A BOY SHOULD NOT BE ALLOWED TO ROAM FREE.

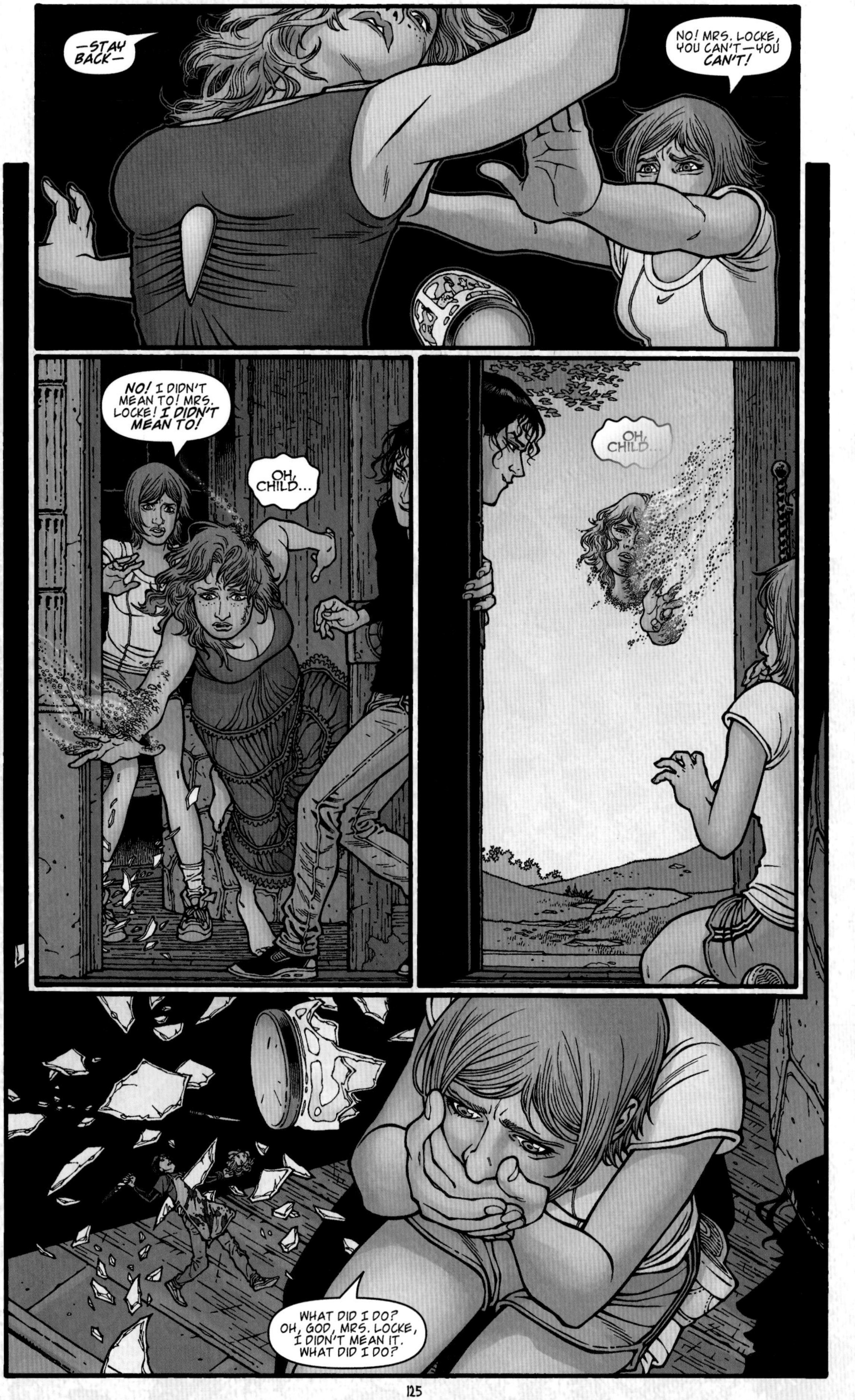
—STAY BACK—
NO! MRS. LOCKE, YOU CAN'T—YOU CAN'T!
NO! I DIDN'T MEAN TO! MRS. LOCKE! I DIDN'T MEAN TO!
OH, CHILD...
OH, CHILD...
WHAT DID I DO? OH, GOD, MRS. LOCKE, I DIDN'T MEAN IT. WHAT DID I DO?

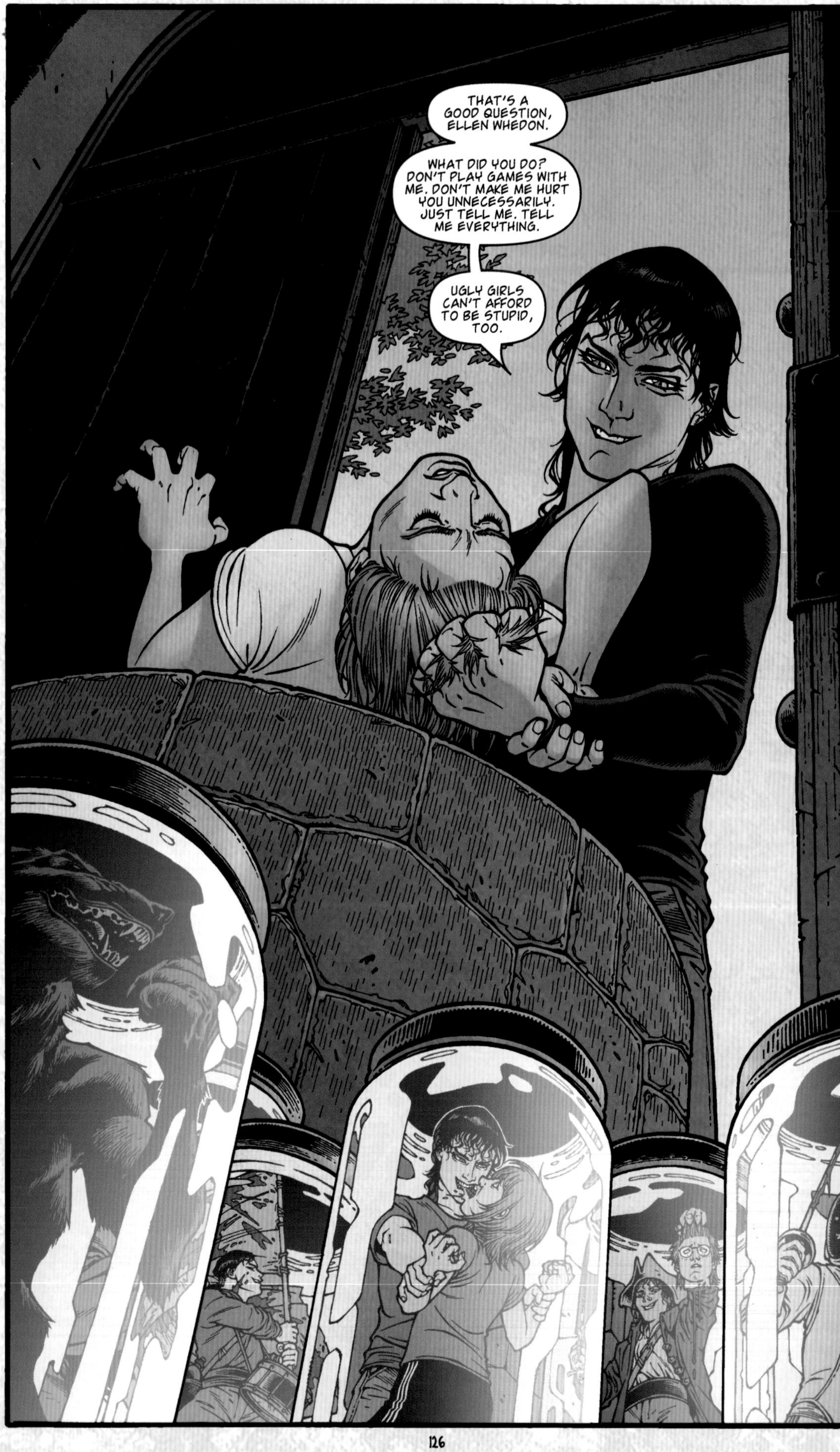
THAT'S A GOOD QUESTION, ELLEN WHEDON.
WHAT DID YOU DO? DON'T PLAY GAMES WITH ME. DON'T MAKE ME HURT YOU UNNECESSARILY. JUST TELL ME. TELL ME EVERYTHING.
UGLY GIRLS CAN'T AFFORD TO BE STUPID, TOO.

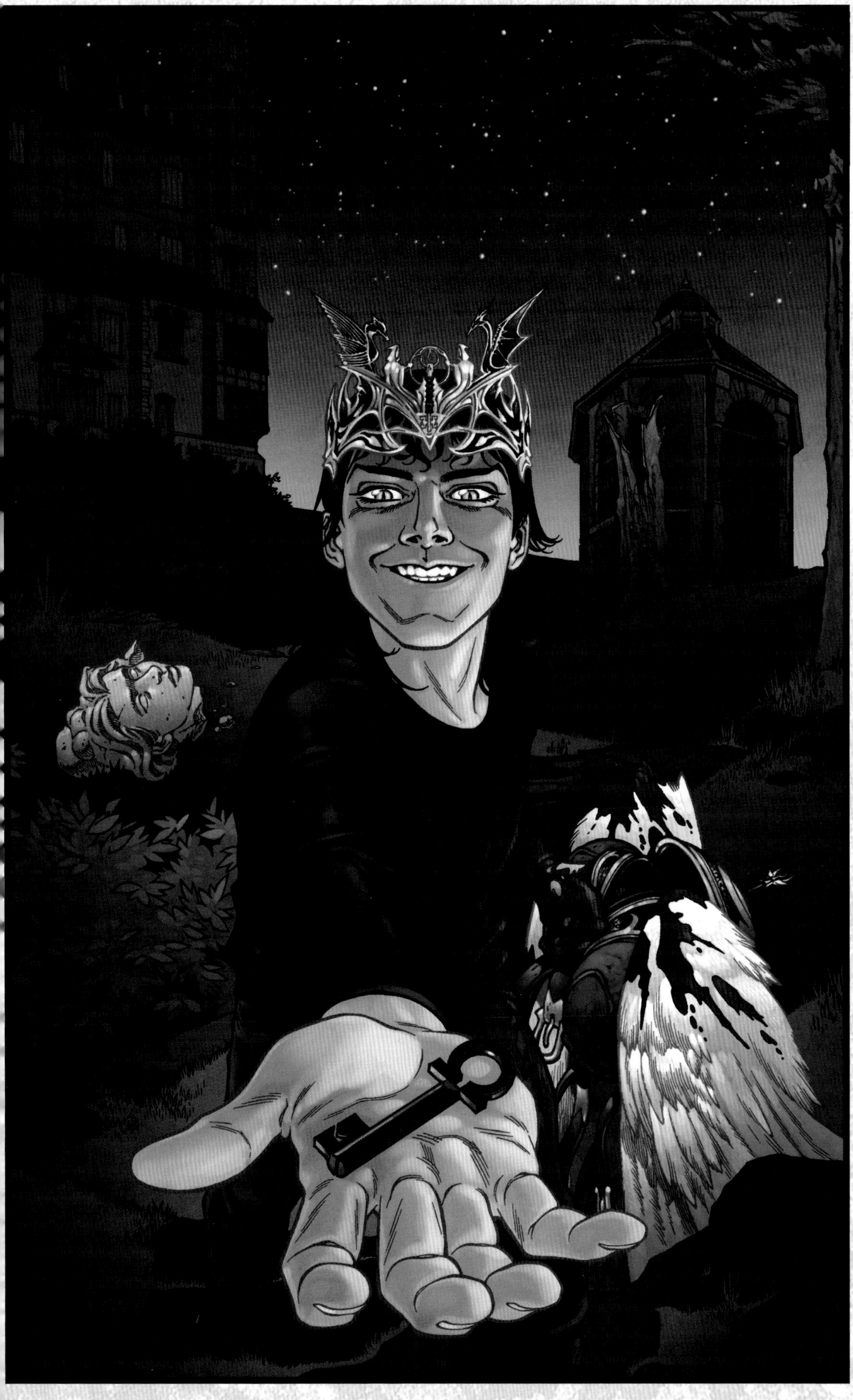

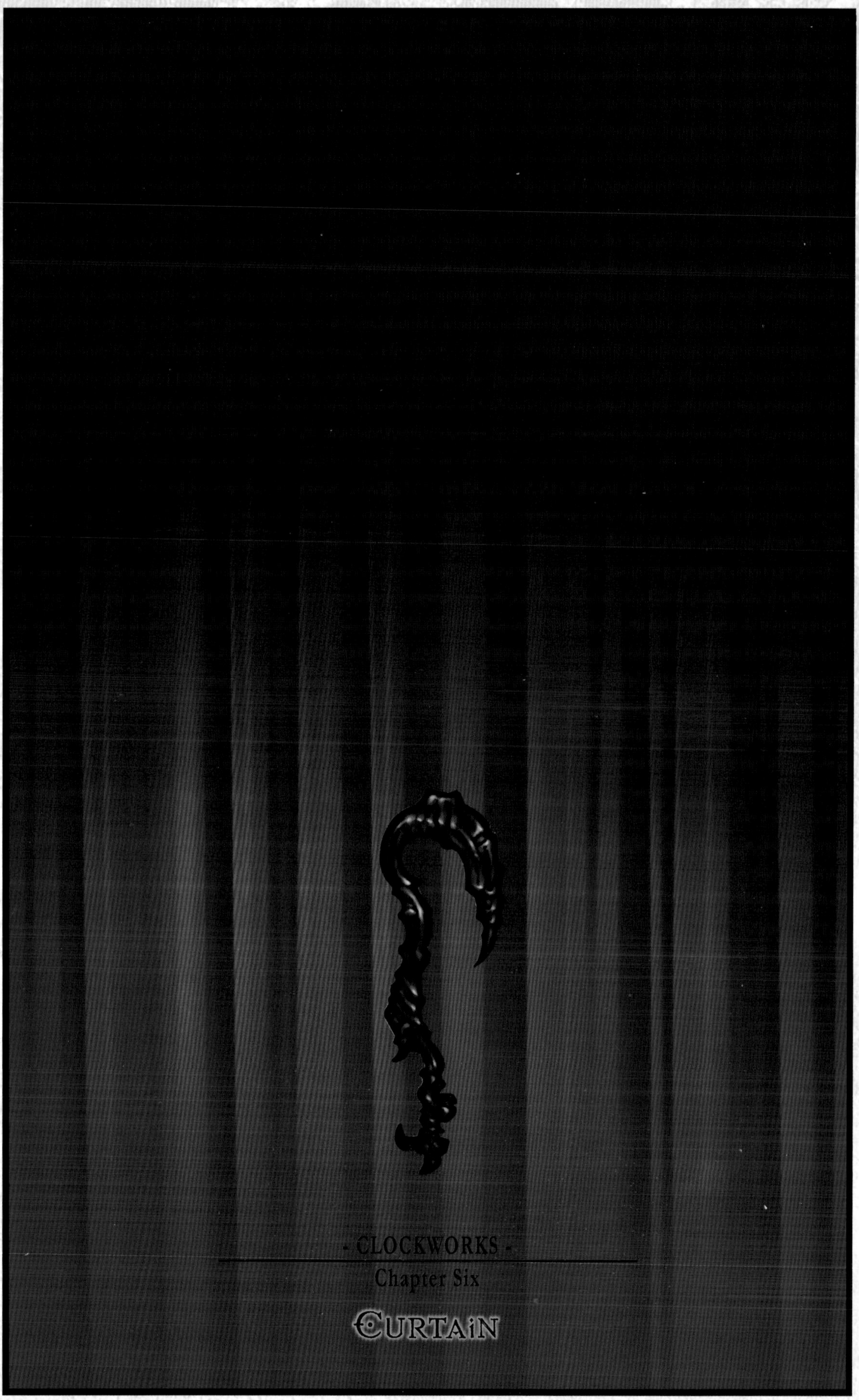
- CLOCKWORKS -
Chapter Six
CURTAIN

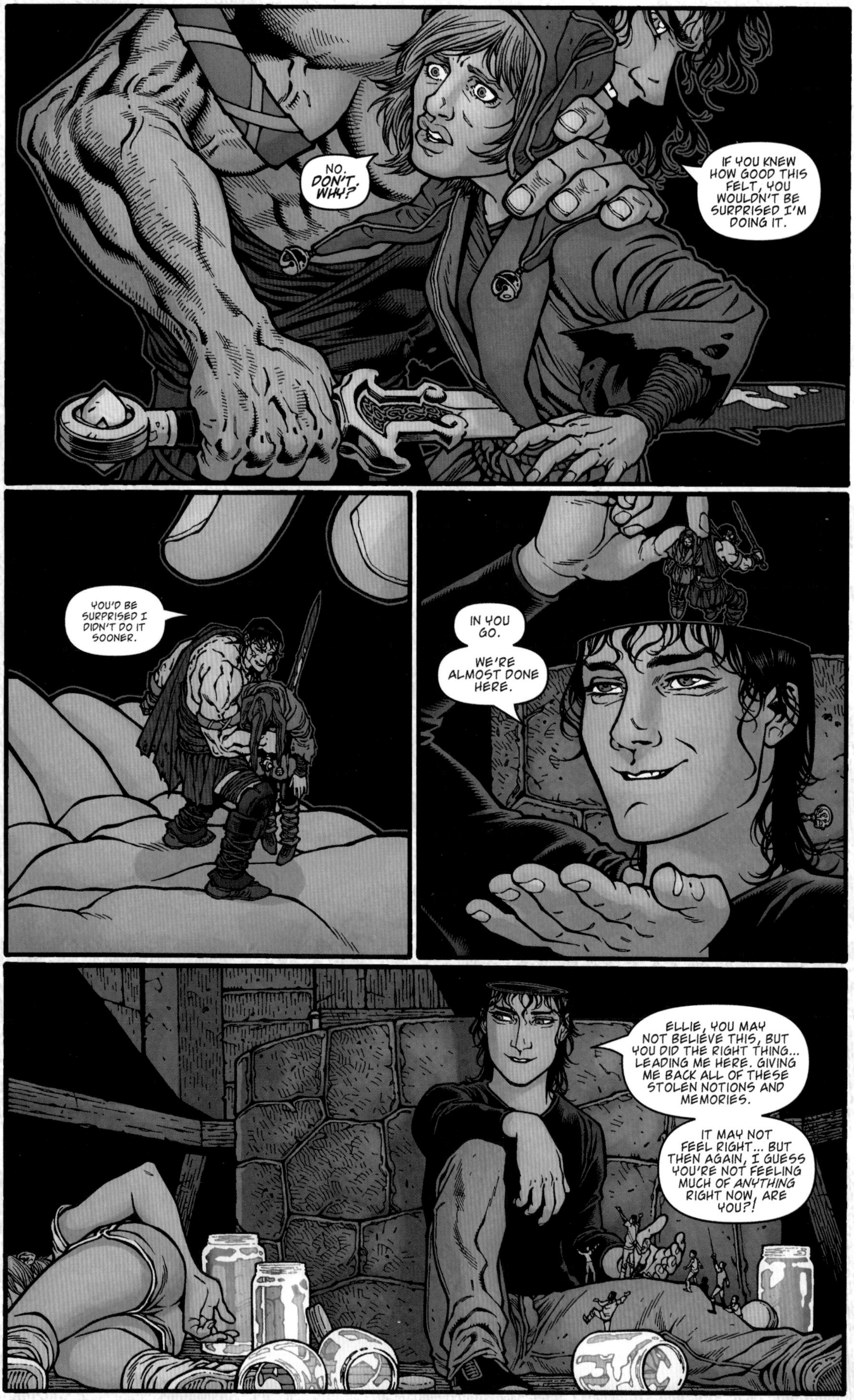
NO. *DON'T. WHY?*
IF YOU KNEW HOW GOOD THIS FELT, YOU WOULDN'T BE SURPRISED I'M DOING IT.
YOU'D BE SURPRISED I DIDN'T DO IT SOONER.
IN YOU GO.
WE'RE ALMOST DONE HERE.
ELLIE, YOU MAY NOT BELIEVE THIS, BUT YOU DID THE RIGHT THING... LEADING ME HERE. GIVING ME BACK ALL OF THESE STOLEN NOTIONS AND MEMORIES.
IT MAY NOT FEEL RIGHT... BUT THEN AGAIN, I GUESS YOU'RE NOT FEELING MUCH OF *ANYTHING* RIGHT NOW, ARE YOU?!

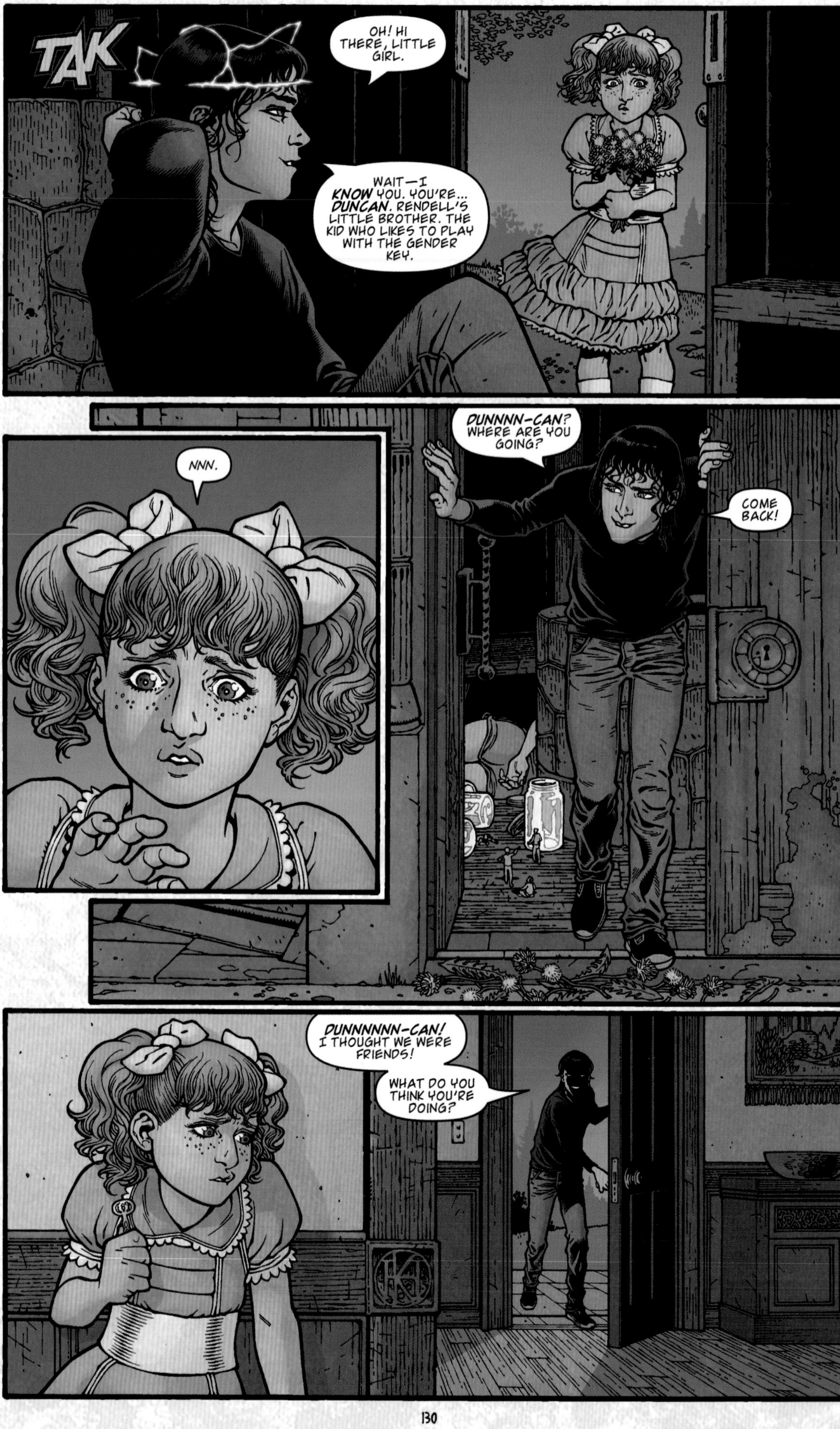
TAK
OH! HI THERE, LITTLE GIRL.
WAIT—I KNOW YOU. YOU'RE... DUNCAN. RENDELL'S LITTLE BROTHER. THE KID WHO LIKES TO PLAY WITH THE GENDER KEY.
NNN.
DUNNNN-CAN? WHERE ARE YOU GOING?
COME BACK!
DUNNNNNN-CAN! I THOUGHT WE WERE FRIENDS!
WHAT DO YOU THINK YOU'RE DOING?

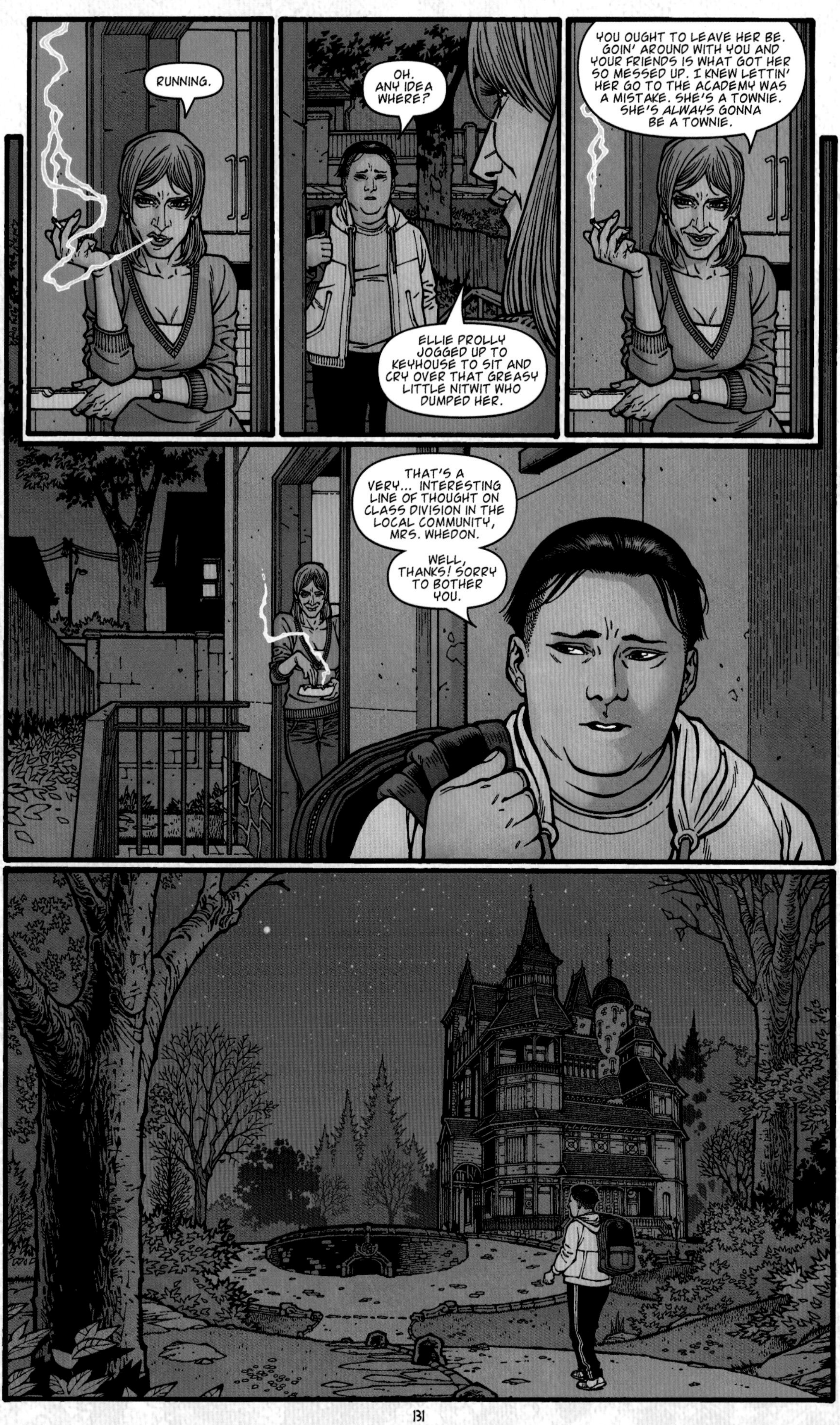
RUNNING.
OH. ANY IDEA WHERE?
ELLIE PROLLY JOGGED UP TO KEYHOUSE TO SIT AND CRY OVER THAT GREASY LITTLE NITWIT WHO DUMPED HER.
YOU OUGHT TO LEAVE HER BE. GOIN' AROUND WITH YOU AND YOUR FRIENDS IS WHAT GOT HER SO MESSED UP. I KNEW LETTIN' HER GO TO THE ACADEMY WAS A MISTAKE. SHE'S A TOWNIE. SHE'S ALWAYS GONNA BE A TOWNIE.
THAT'S A VERY... INTERESTING LINE OF THOUGHT ON CLASS DIVISION IN THE LOCAL COMMUNITY, MRS. WHEDON.
WELL, THANKS! SORRY TO BOTHER YOU.

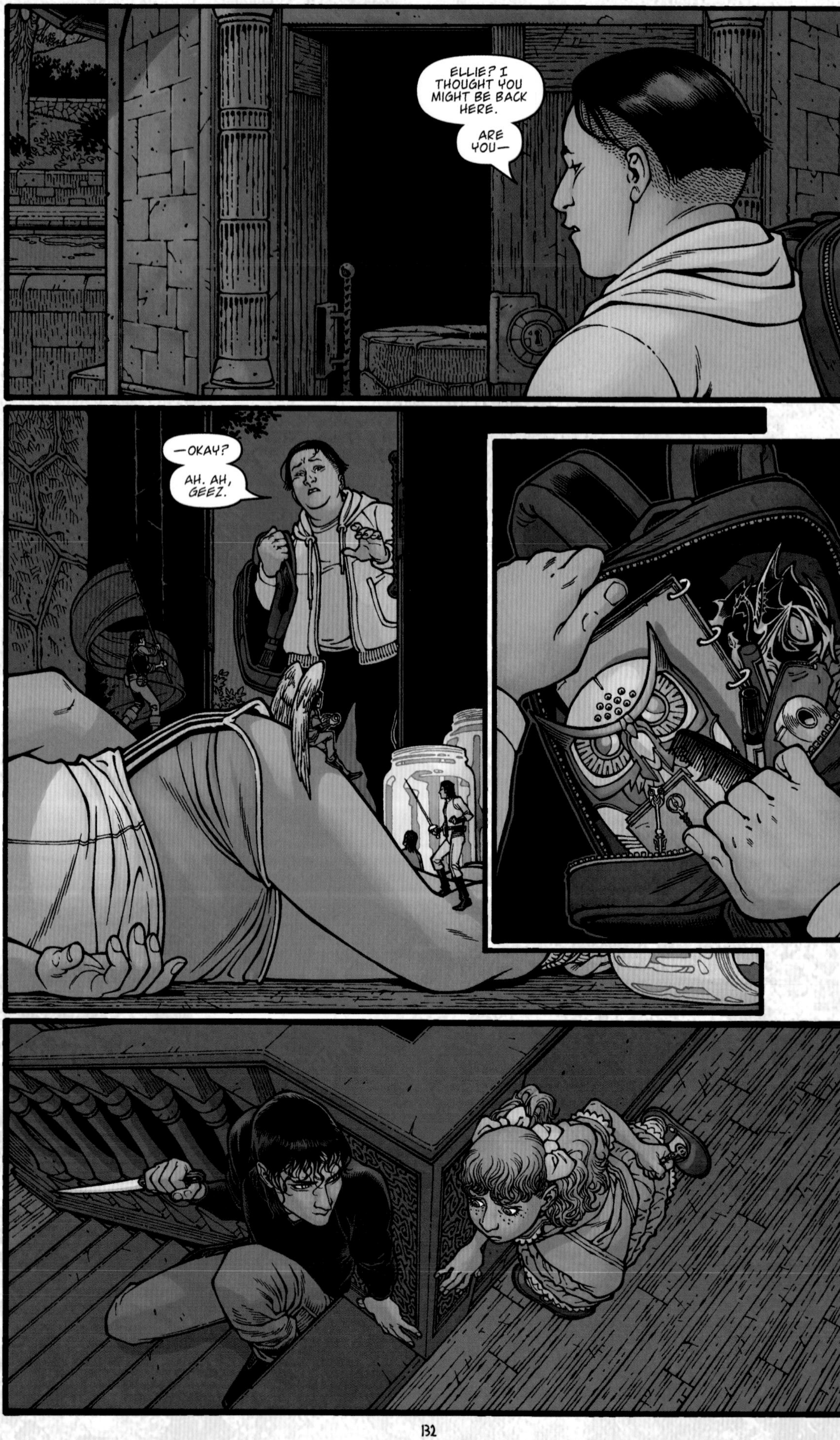
ELLIE? I THOUGHT YOU MIGHT BE BACK HERE.
ARE YOU—
—OKAY?
AH. AH, GEEZ.

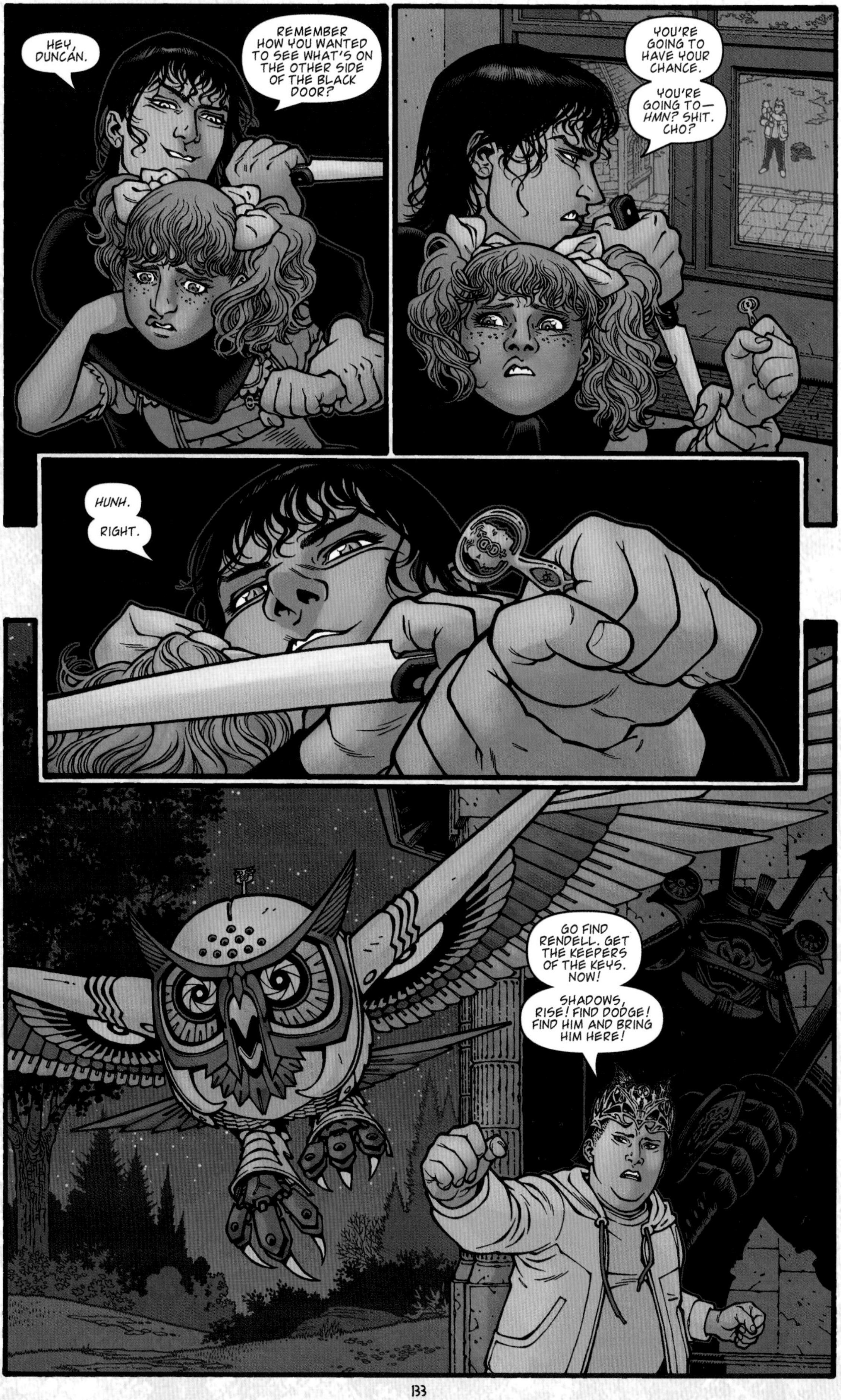
HEY, DUNCAN.
REMEMBER HOW YOU WANTED TO SEE WHAT'S ON THE OTHER SIDE OF THE BLACK DOOR?
YOU'RE GOING TO HAVE YOUR CHANCE.
YOU'RE GOING TO— HMN? SHIT. CHO?
HUNH.
RIGHT.
GO FIND RENDELL. GET THE KEEPERS OF THE KEYS. NOW!
SHADOWS, RISE! FIND DODGE! FIND HIM AND BRING HIM HERE!

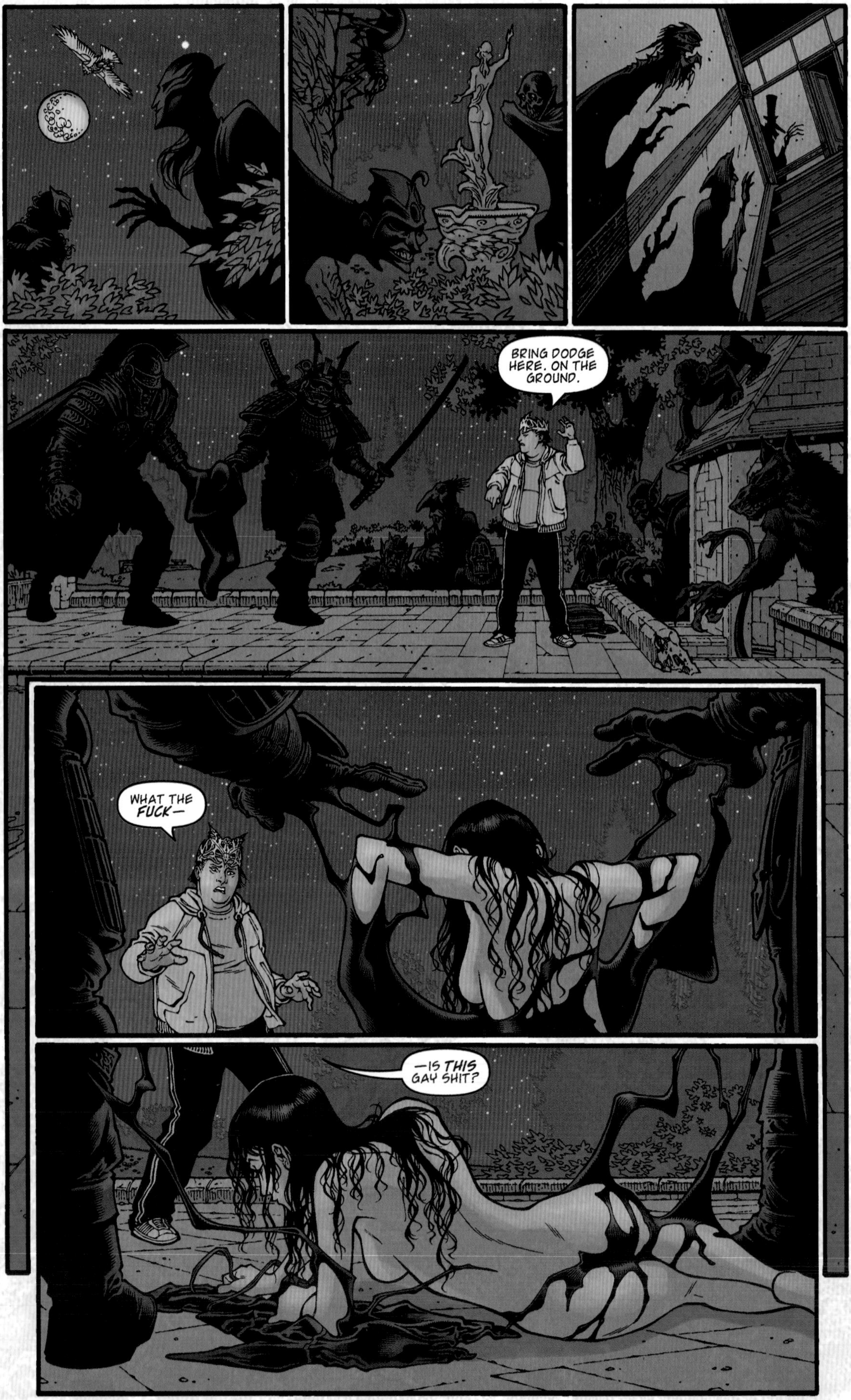
BRING DODGE HERE. ON THE GROUND.
WHAT THE FUCK—
—IS THIS GAY SHIT?

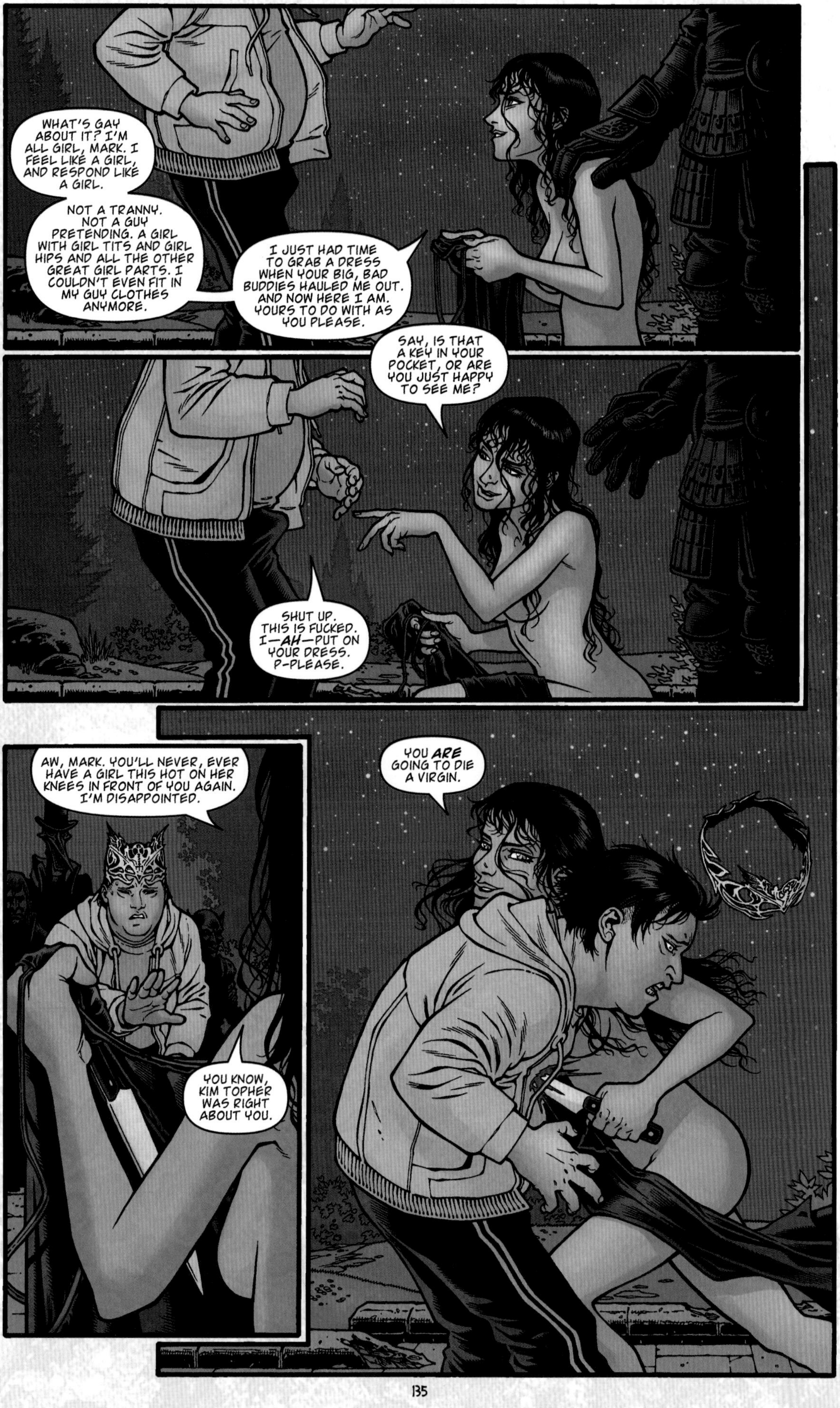
WHAT'S GAY ABOUT IT? I'M ALL GIRL, MARK. I FEEL LIKE A GIRL, AND RESPOND LIKE A GIRL.
NOT A TRANNY. NOT A GUY PRETENDING. A GIRL WITH GIRL TITS AND GIRL HIPS AND ALL THE OTHER GREAT GIRL PARTS. I COULDN'T EVEN FIT IN MY GUY CLOTHES ANYMORE.
I JUST HAD TIME TO GRAB A DRESS WHEN YOUR BIG, BAD BUDDIES HAULED ME OUT. AND NOW HERE I AM. YOURS TO DO WITH AS YOU PLEASE.
SAY, IS THAT A KEY IN YOUR POCKET, OR ARE YOU JUST HAPPY TO SEE ME?
SHUT UP. THIS IS FUCKED. I—AH—PUT ON YOUR DRESS. P-PLEASE.
AW, MARK. YOU'LL NEVER, EVER HAVE A GIRL THIS HOT ON HER KNEES IN FRONT OF YOU AGAIN. I'M DISAPPOINTED.
YOU KNOW, KIM TOPHER WAS RIGHT ABOUT YOU.
YOU ARE GOING TO DIE A VIRGIN.

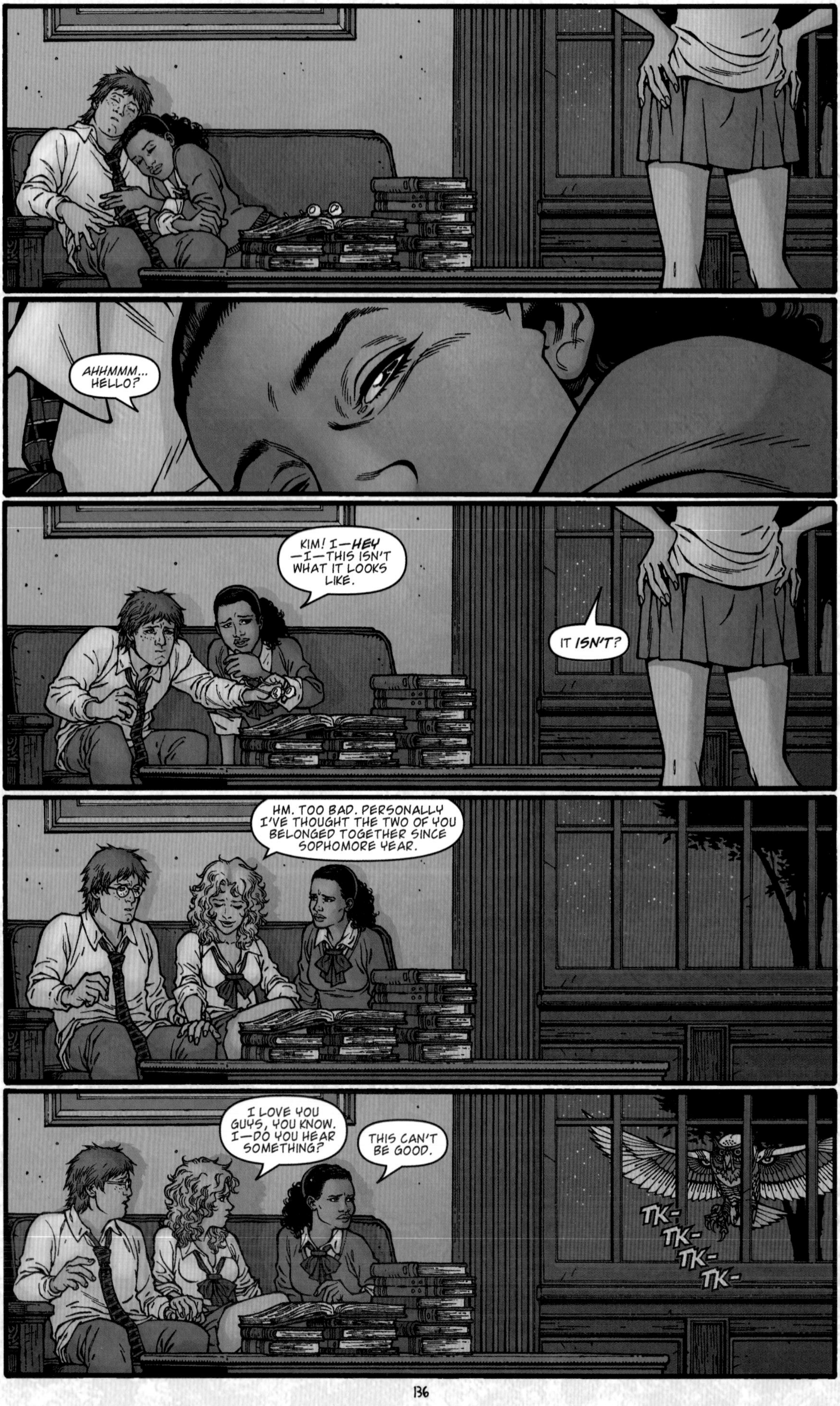
AHHMMM... HELLO?
KIM! I—HEY —I—THIS ISN'T WHAT IT LOOKS LIKE.
IT ISN'T?
HM. TOO BAD. PERSONALLY I'VE THOUGHT THE TWO OF YOU BELONGED TOGETHER SINCE SOPHOMORE YEAR.
I LOVE YOU GUYS, YOU KNOW. I—DO YOU HEAR SOMETHING?
THIS CAN'T BE GOOD.
TK- TK- TK- TK-

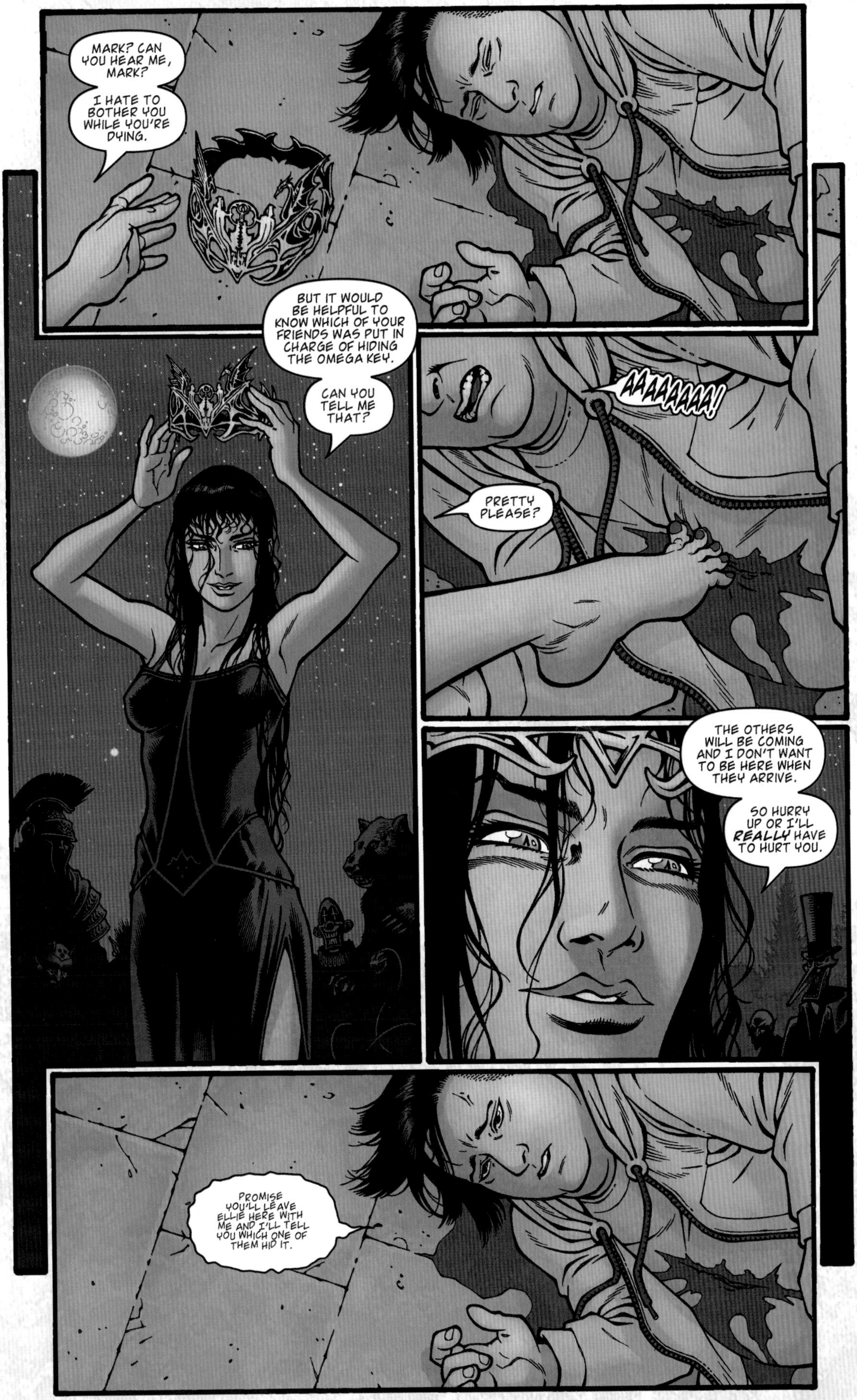

MARK? CAN YOU HEAR ME, MARK?
I HATE TO BOTHER YOU WHILE YOU'RE DYING.
BUT IT WOULD BE HELPFUL TO KNOW WHICH OF YOUR FRIENDS WAS PUT IN CHARGE OF HIDING THE OMEGA KEY.
CAN YOU TELL ME THAT?
AAAAAAAA!
PRETTY PLEASE?
THE OTHERS WILL BE COMING AND I DON'T WANT TO BE HERE WHEN THEY ARRIVE.
SO HURRY UP OR I'LL REALLY HAVE TO HURT YOU.
PROMISE YOU'LL LEAVE ELLIE HERE WITH ME AND I'LL TELL YOU WHICH ONE OF THEM HID IT.

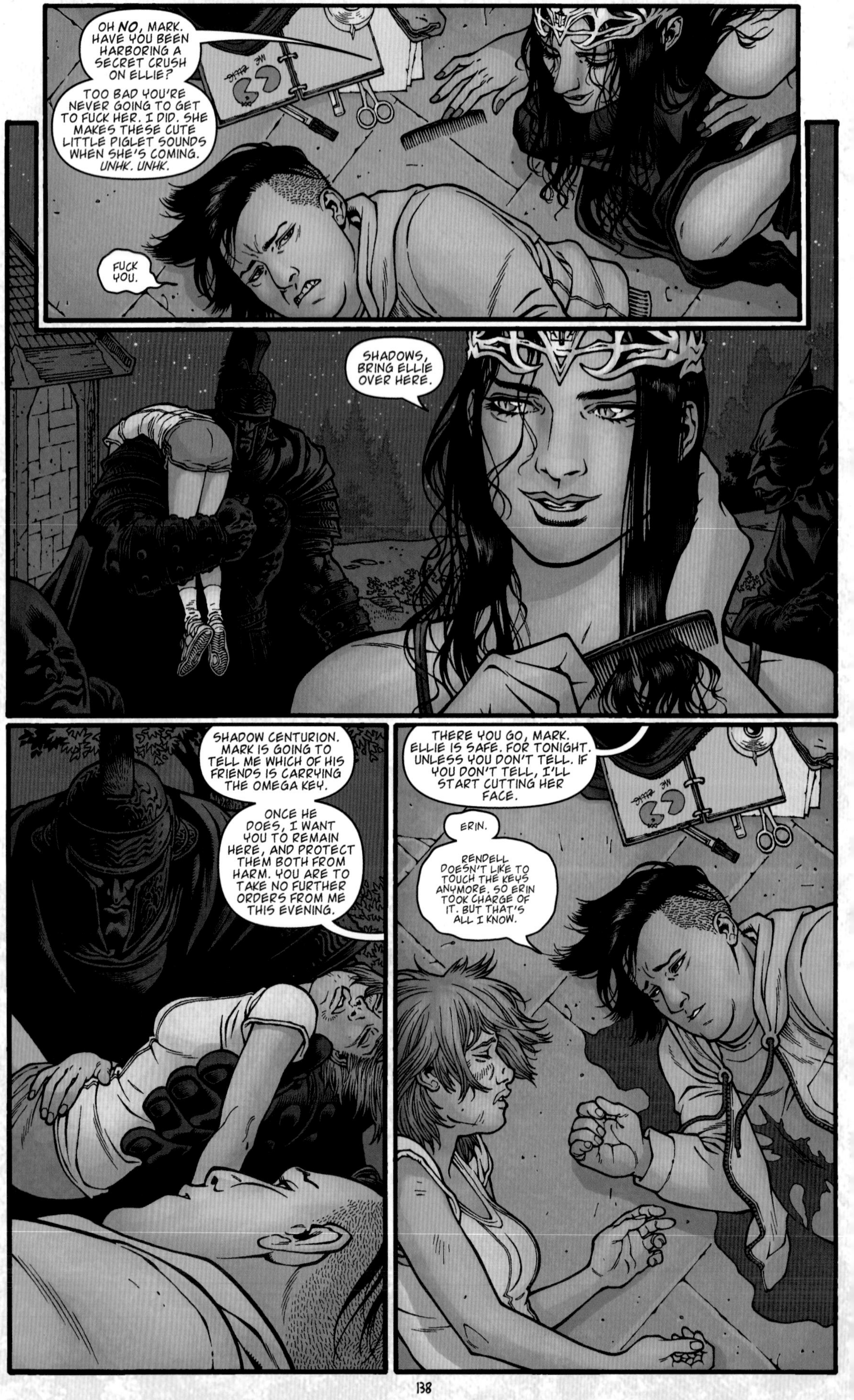

OH NO, MARK. HAVE YOU BEEN HARBORING A SECRET CRUSH ON ELLIE?
TOO BAD YOU'RE NEVER GOING TO GET TO FUCK HER. I DID. SHE MAKES THESE CUTE LITTLE PIGLET SOUNDS WHEN SHE'S COMING. UNHK. UNHK.
FUCK YOU.
SHADOWS, BRING ELLIE OVER HERE.
SHADOW CENTURION. MARK IS GOING TO TELL ME WHICH OF HIS FRIENDS IS CARRYING THE OMEGA KEY.
ONCE HE DOES, I WANT YOU TO REMAIN HERE, AND PROTECT THEM BOTH FROM HARM. YOU ARE TO TAKE NO FURTHER ORDERS FROM ME THIS EVENING.
THERE YOU GO, MARK. ELLIE IS SAFE. FOR TONIGHT. UNLESS YOU DON'T TELL. IF YOU DON'T TELL, I'LL START CUTTING HER FACE.
ERIN.
RENDELL DOESN'T LIKE TO TOUCH THE KEYS ANYMORE. SO ERIN TOOK CHARGE OF IT. BUT THAT'S ALL I KNOW.

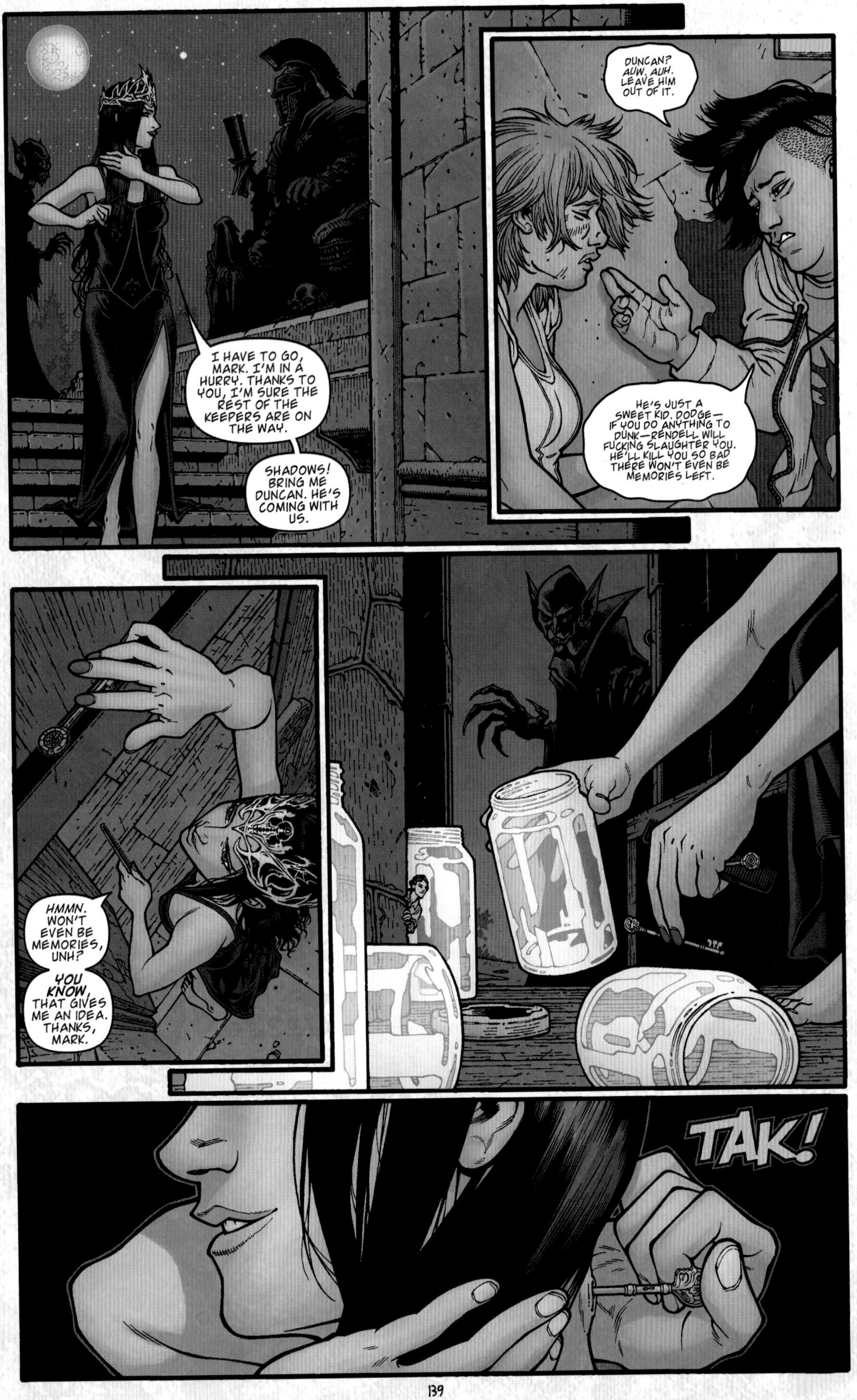
I HAVE TO GO, MARK. I'M IN A HURRY. THANKS TO YOU, I'M SURE THE REST OF THE KEEPERS ARE ON THE WAY.
SHADOWS! BRING ME DUNCAN. HE'S COMING WITH US.
DUNCAN? AUW. AUH. LEAVE HIM OUT OF IT.
HE'S JUST A SWEET KID. DODGE— IF YOU DO ANYTHING TO DUNK—RENDELL WILL FUCKING SLAUGHTER YOU. HE'LL KILL YOU SO BAD THERE WON'T EVEN BE MEMORIES LEFT.
HMMN. WON'T EVEN BE MEMORIES, UNH?
YOU KNOW, THAT GIVES ME AN IDEA. THANKS, MARK.
TAK!

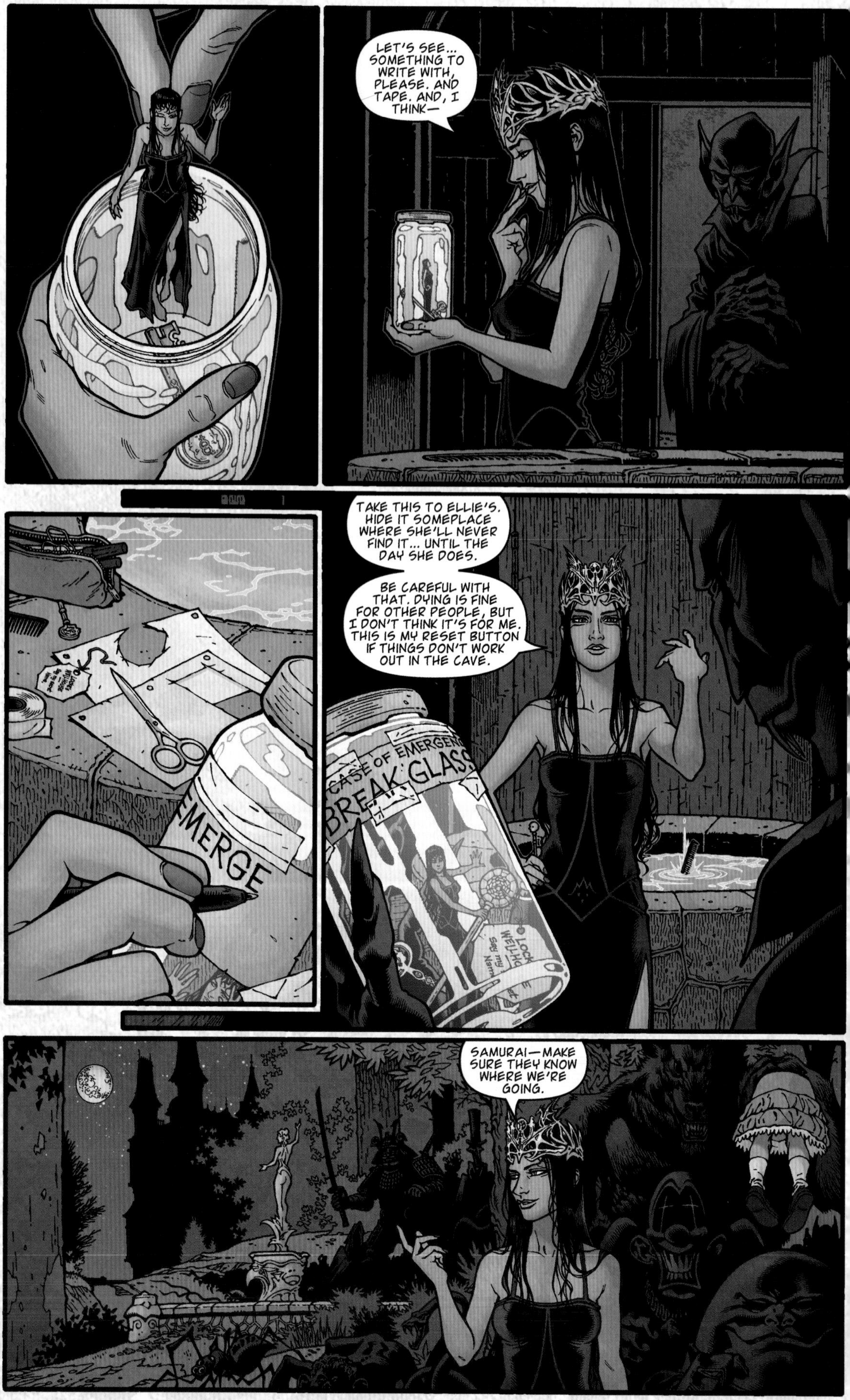

LET'S SEE... SOMETHING TO WRITE WITH, PLEASE. AND TAPE. AND, I THINK—
EMERGE
TAKE THIS TO ELLIE'S. HIDE IT SOMEPLACE WHERE SHE'LL NEVER FIND IT... UNTIL THE DAY SHE DOES.
BE CAREFUL WITH THAT. DYING IS FINE FOR OTHER PEOPLE, BUT I DON'T THINK IT'S FOR ME. THIS IS MY RESET BUTTON IF THINGS DON'T WORK OUT IN THE CAVE.
BREAK GLASS
SAMURAI—MAKE SURE THEY KNOW WHERE WE'RE GOING.

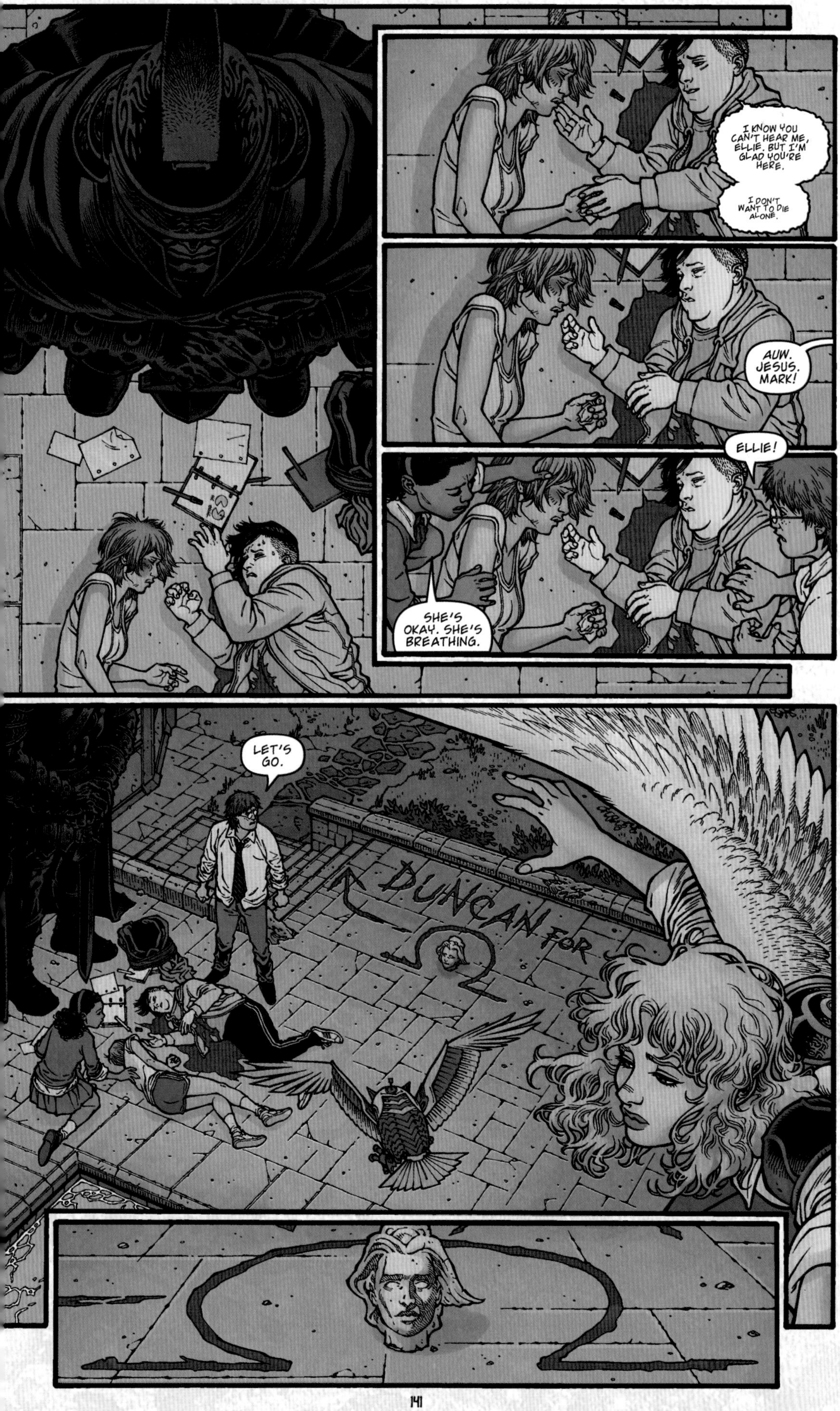
I KNOW YOU CAN'T HEAR ME, ELLIE. BUT I'M GLAD YOU'RE HERE.
I DON'T WANT TO DIE ALONE.
AUW. JESUS. MARK!
ELLIE!
SHE'S OKAY. SHE'S BREATHING.
LET'S GO.
DUNCAN FOR

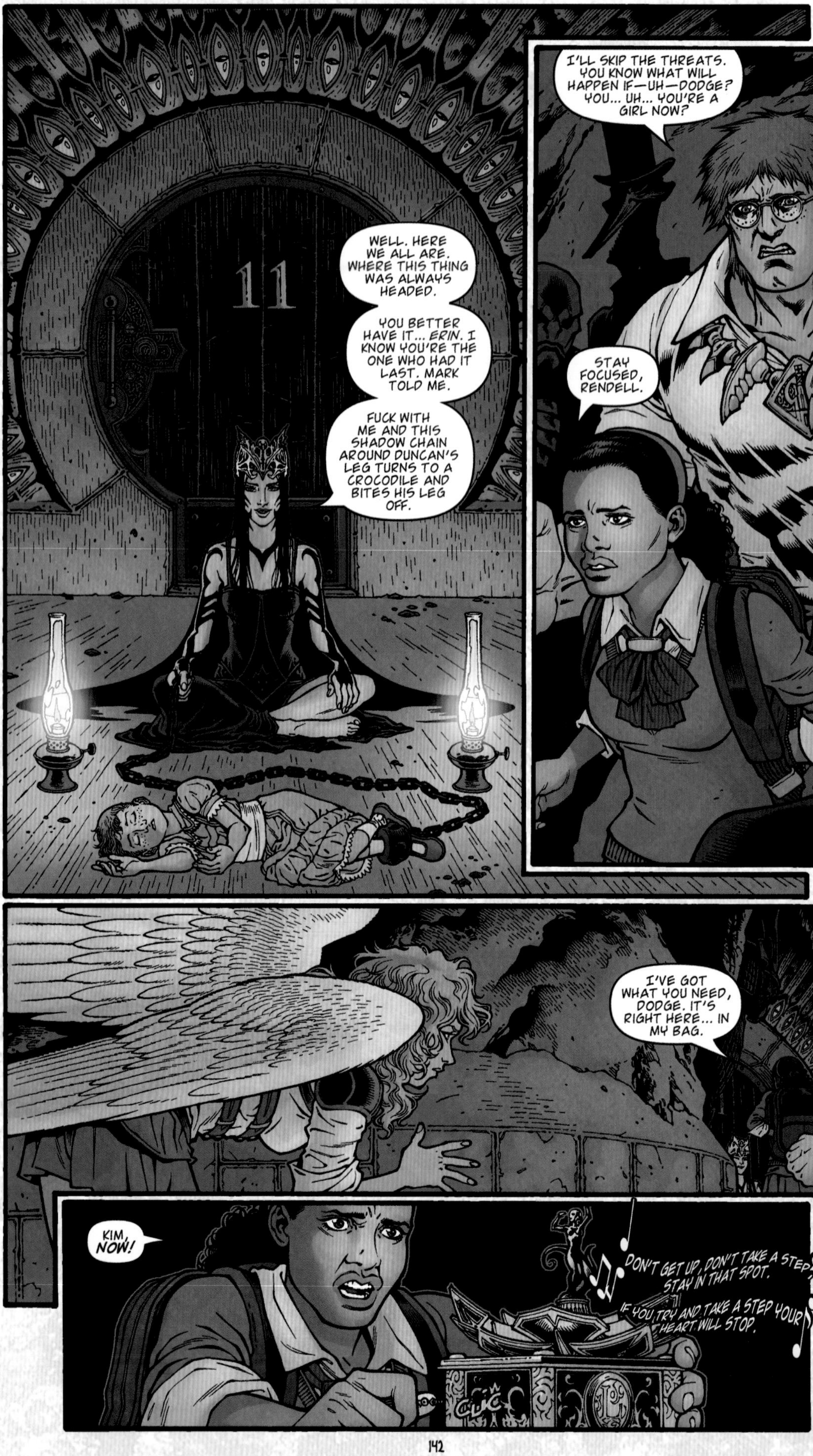
WELL. HERE WE ALL ARE. WHERE THIS THING WAS ALWAYS HEADED.
YOU BETTER HAVE IT... ERIN. I KNOW YOU'RE THE ONE WHO HAD IT LAST. MARK TOLD ME.
FUCK WITH ME AND THIS SHADOW CHAIN AROUND DUNCAN'S LEG TURNS TO A CROCODILE AND BITES HIS LEG OFF.
I'LL SKIP THE THREATS. YOU KNOW WHAT WILL HAPPEN IF—UH—DODGE? YOU... UH... YOU'RE A GIRL NOW?
STAY FOCUSED, RENDELL.
I'VE GOT WHAT YOU NEED, DODGE. IT'S RIGHT HERE... IN MY BAG.
KIM, NOW!
DON'T GET UP, DON'T TAKE A STEP, STAY IN THAT SPOT.
IF YOU TRY AND TAKE A STEP YOUR HEART WILL STOP.

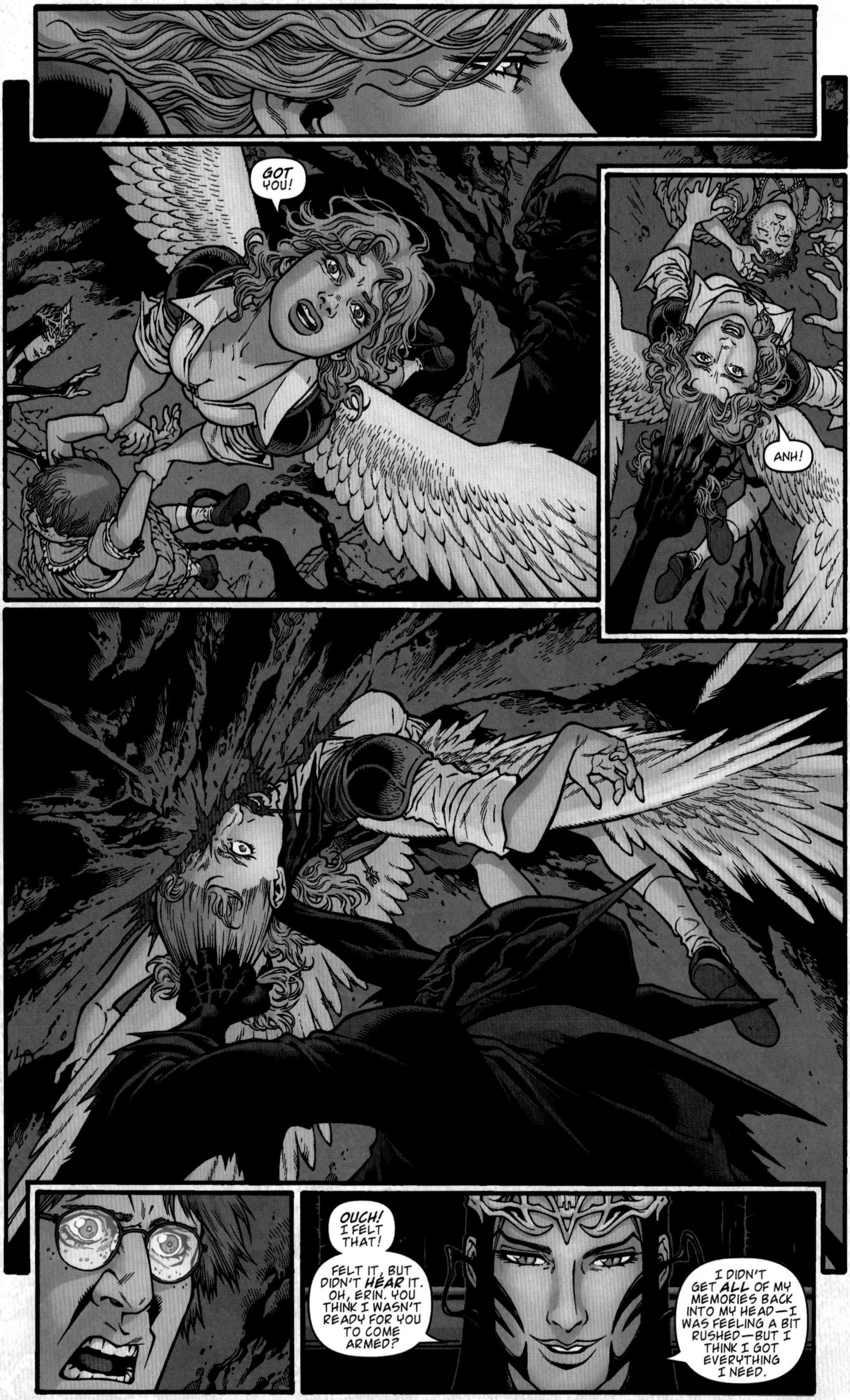
GOT YOU!
ANH!
OUCH! I FELT THAT!
FELT IT, BUT DIDN'T HEAR IT. OH, ERIN. YOU THINK I WASN'T READY FOR YOU TO COME ARMED?
I DIDN'T GET ALL OF MY MEMORIES BACK INTO MY HEAD—I WAS FEELING A BIT RUSHED—BUT I THINK I GOT EVERYTHING I NEED.

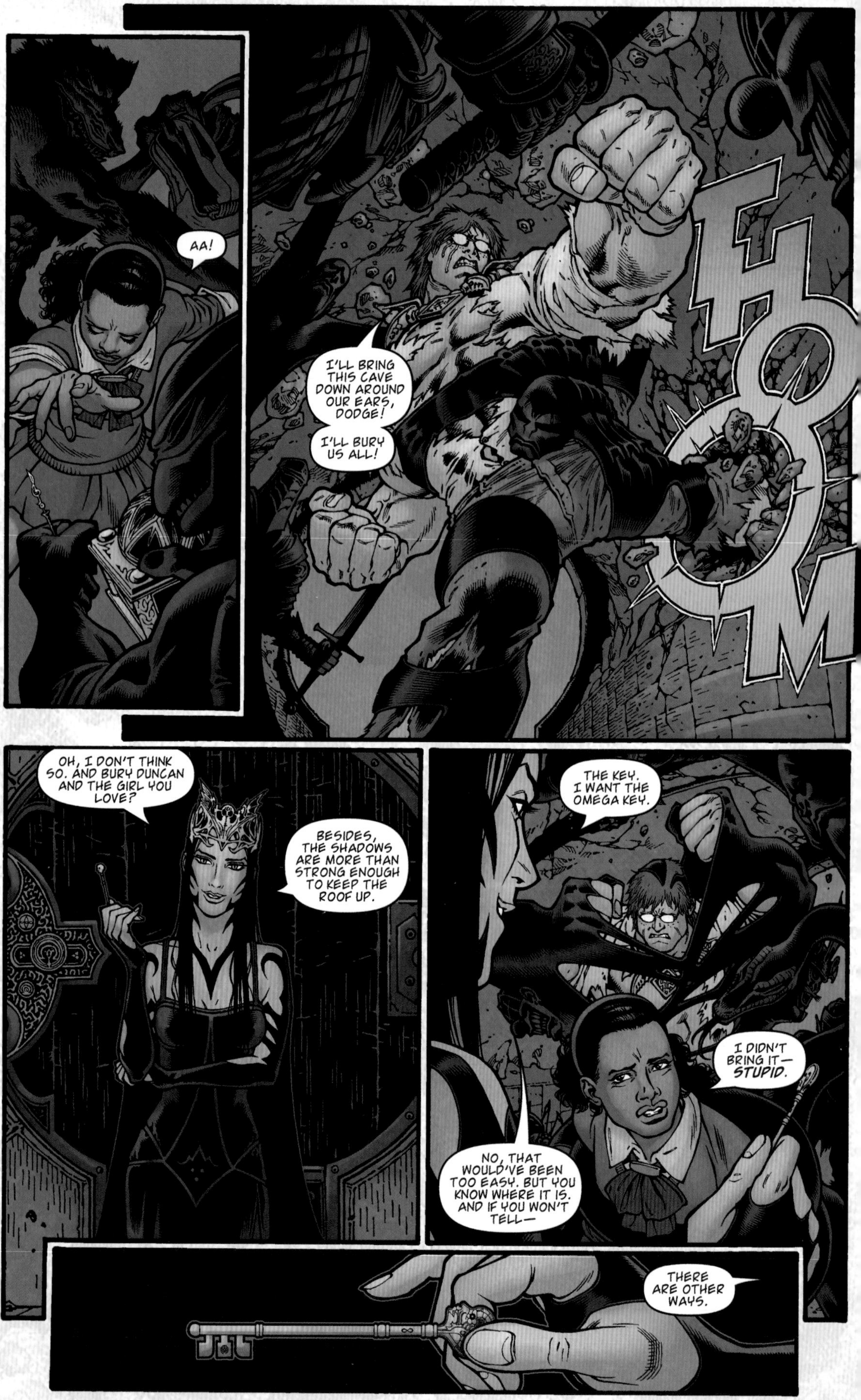

AA!
I'LL BRING THIS CAVE DOWN AROUND OUR EARS, DODGE!
I'LL BURY US ALL!
OH, I DON'T THINK SO. AND BURY DUNCAN AND THE GIRL YOU LOVE?
BESIDES, THE SHADOWS ARE MORE THAN STRONG ENOUGH TO KEEP THE ROOF UP.
THE KEY. I WANT THE OMEGA KEY.
I DIDN'T BRING IT— STUPID.
NO, THAT WOULD'VE BEEN TOO EASY. BUT YOU KNOW WHERE IT IS. AND IF YOU WON'T TELL—
THERE ARE OTHER WAYS.

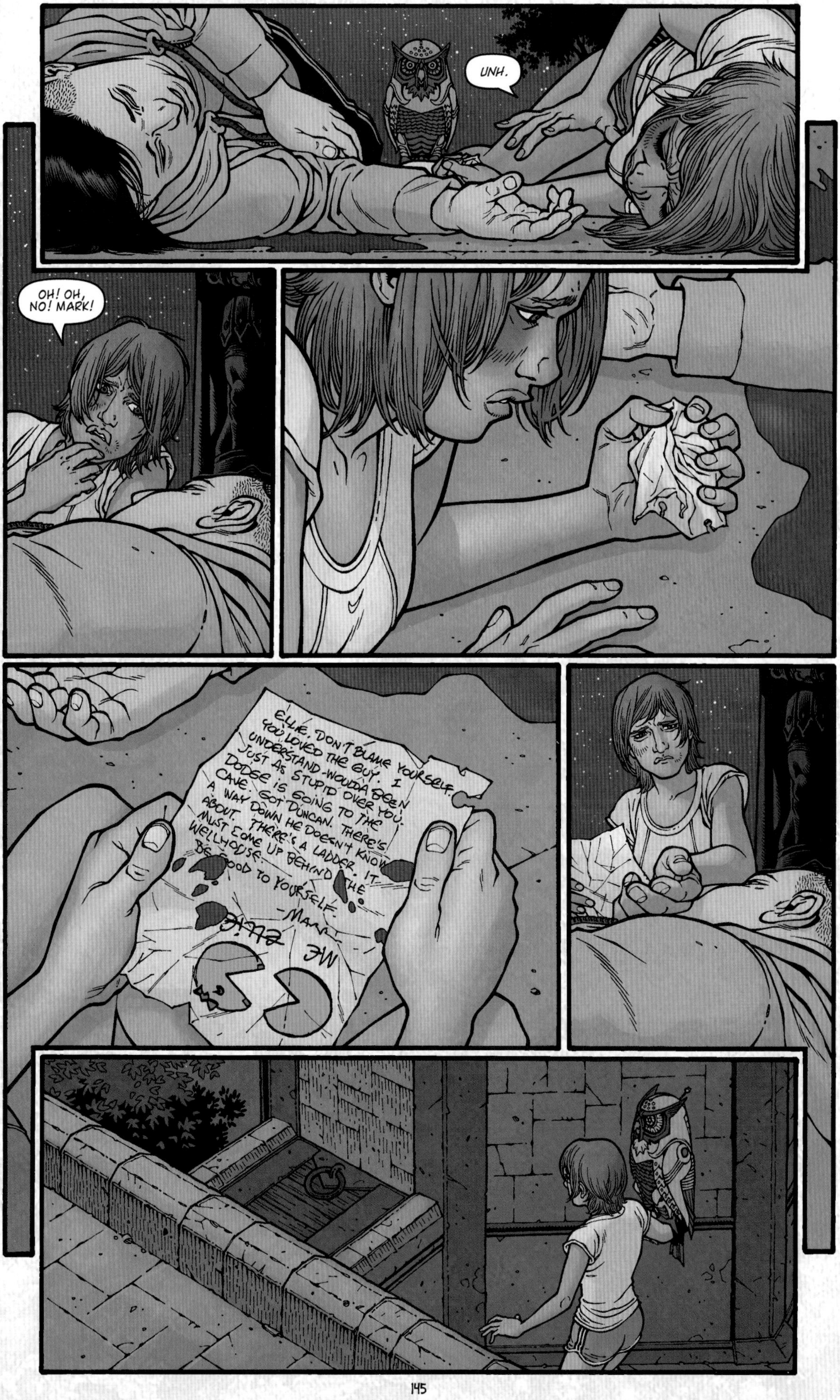
UNH.
OH! OH, NO! MARK!
ELLIE. DON'T BLAME YOURSELF.
YOU LOVED THE GUY. I
UNDERSTAND-WOULDA BEEN
JUST AS STUPID OVER YOU.
DODGE IS GOING TO THE
CAVE. GOT DUNCAN. THERE'S
A WAY DOWN HE DOESN'T KNOW
ABOUT. THERE'S A LADDER. IT
MUST COME UP BEHIND THE
WELLHOUSE.
BE GOOD TO YOURSELF.
-MARK

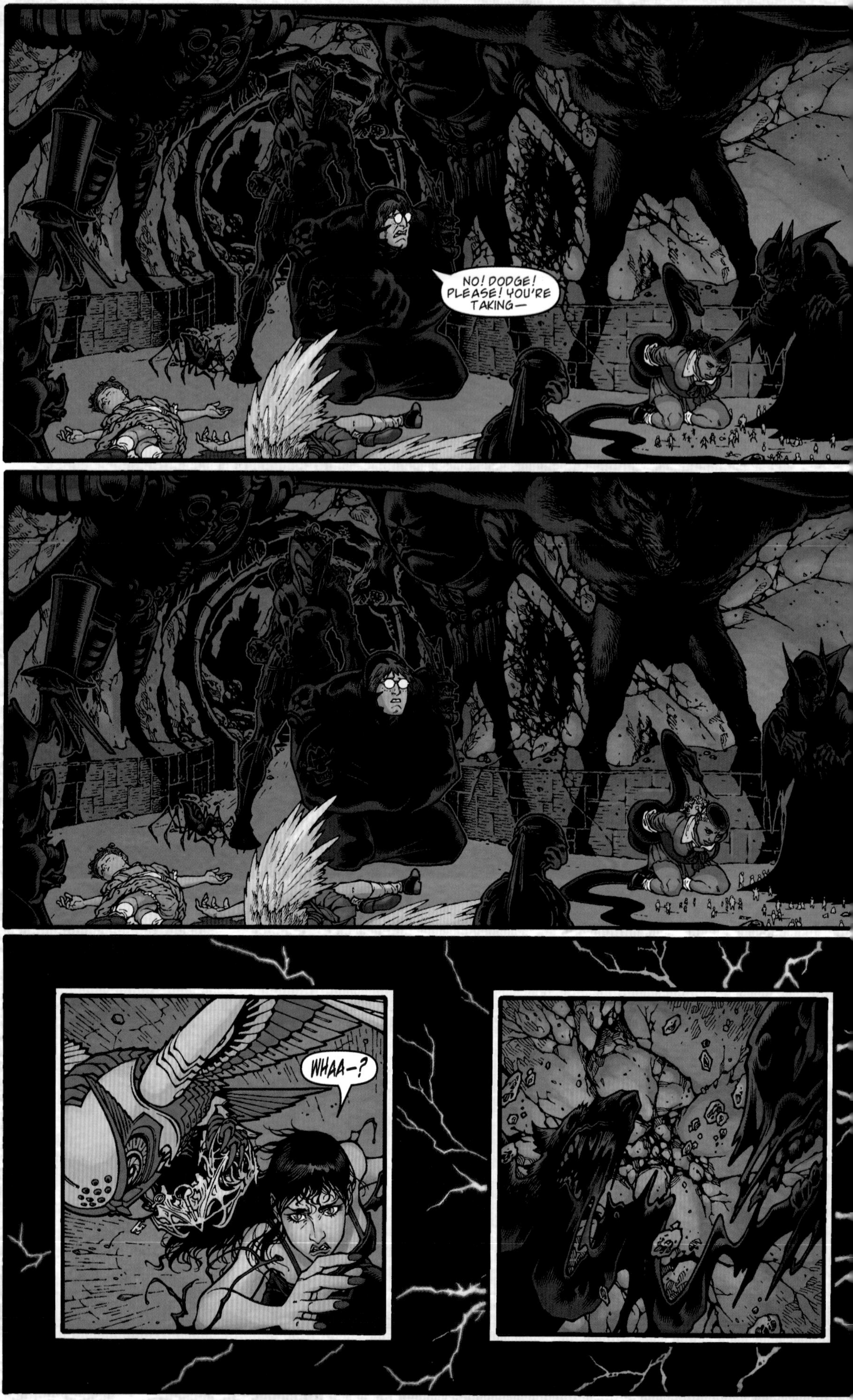
NO! DODGE! PLEASE! YOU'RE TAKING—
WHAA–?

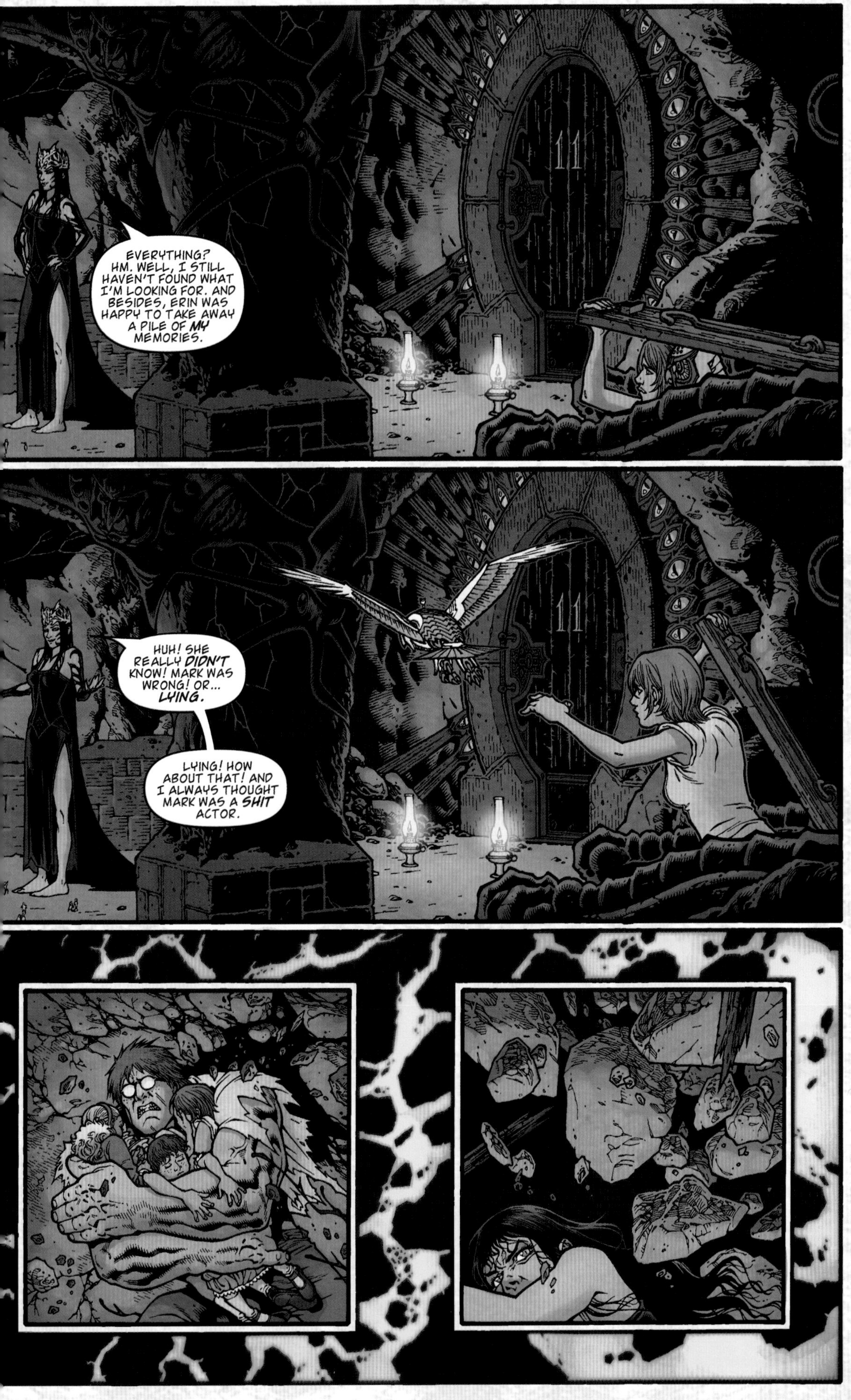
EVERYTHING? HM. WELL, I STILL HAVEN'T FOUND WHAT I'M LOOKING FOR. AND BESIDES, ERIN WAS HAPPY TO TAKE AWAY A PILE OF MY MEMORIES.
HUH! SHE REALLY DIDN'T KNOW! MARK WAS WRONG! OR... LYING.
LYING! HOW ABOUT THAT! AND I ALWAYS THOUGHT MARK WAS A SHIT ACTOR.

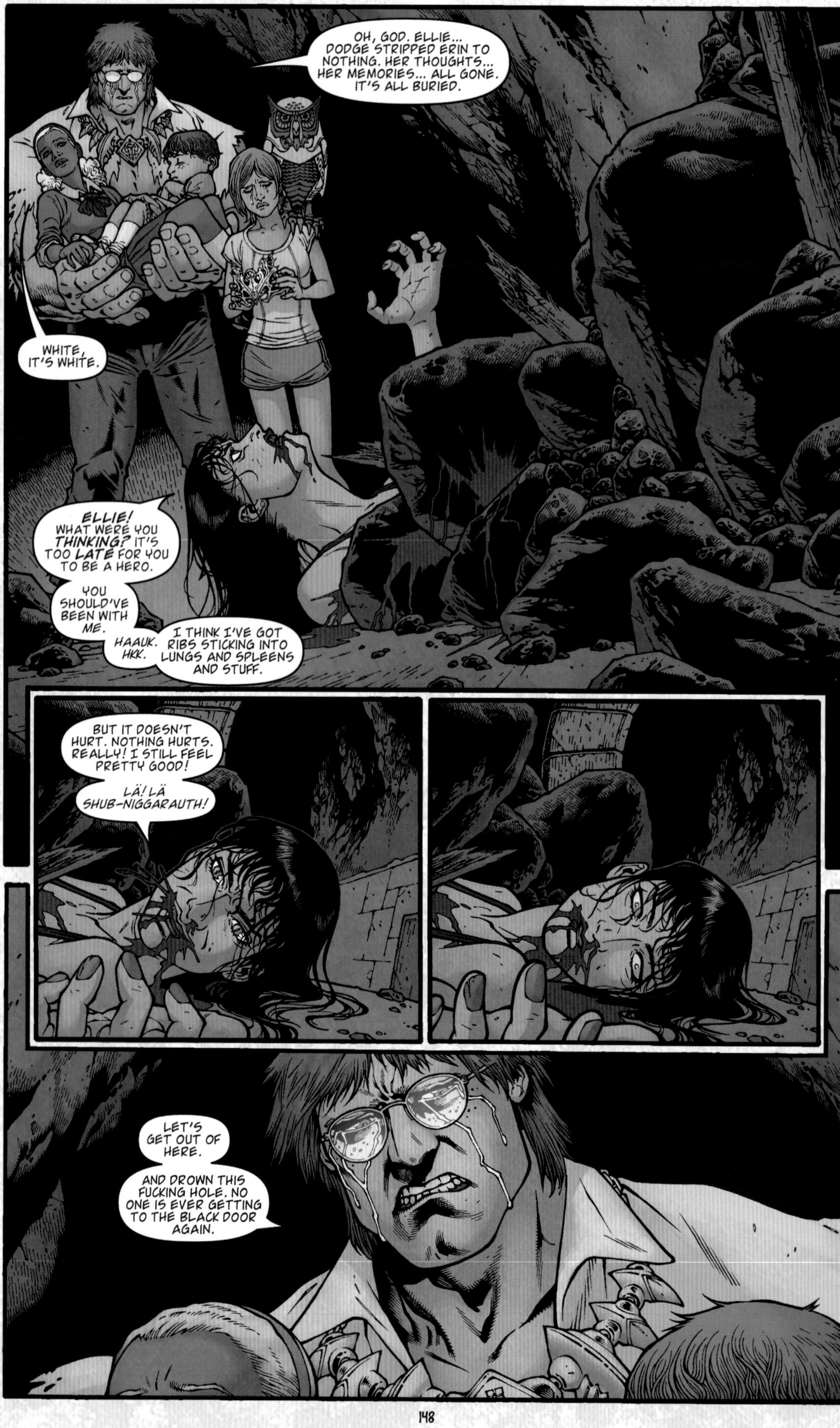

OH, GOD. ELLIE... DODGE STRIPPED ERIN TO NOTHING. HER THOUGHTS... HER MEMORIES... ALL GONE. IT'S ALL BURIED.
WHITE, IT'S WHITE.
ELLIE! WHAT WERE YOU THINKING? IT'S TOO LATE FOR YOU TO BE A HERO.
YOU SHOULD'VE BEEN WITH ME.
HAAUK. HKK.
I THINK I'VE GOT RIBS STICKING INTO LUNGS AND SPLEENS AND STUFF.
BUT IT DOESN'T HURT. NOTHING HURTS. REALLY! I STILL FEEL PRETTY GOOD!
LÄ! LÄ SHUB-NIGGARAUTH!
LET'S GET OUT OF HERE.
AND DROWN THIS FUCKING HOLE. NO ONE IS EVER GETTING TO THE BLACK DOOR AGAIN.

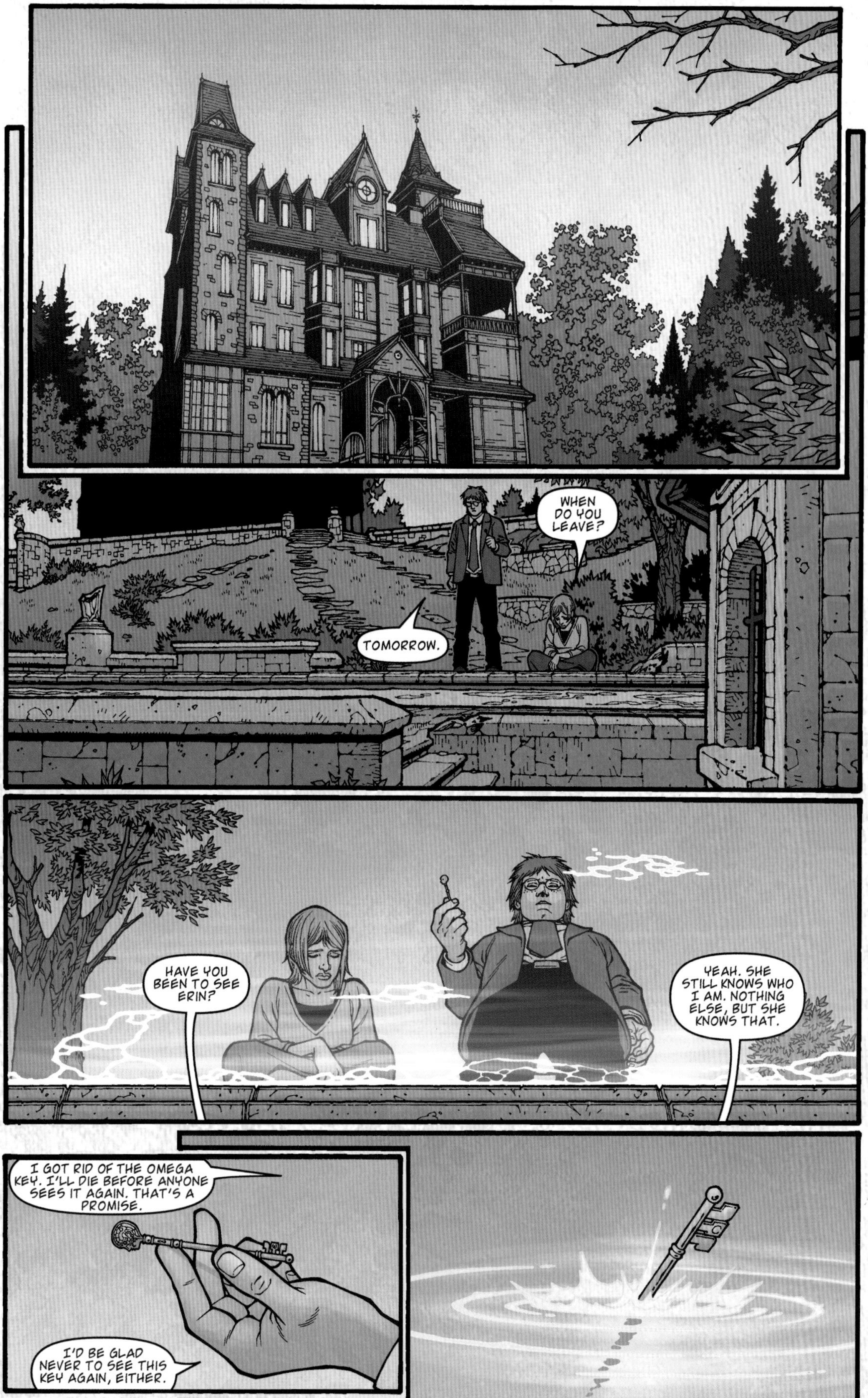
WHEN DO YOU LEAVE?
TOMORROW.
HAVE YOU BEEN TO SEE ERIN?
YEAH. SHE STILL KNOWS WHO I AM. NOTHING ELSE, BUT SHE KNOWS THAT.
I GOT RID OF THE OMEGA KEY. I'LL DIE BEFORE ANYONE SEES IT AGAIN. THAT'S A PROMISE.
I'D BE GLAD NEVER TO SEE THIS KEY AGAIN, EITHER.

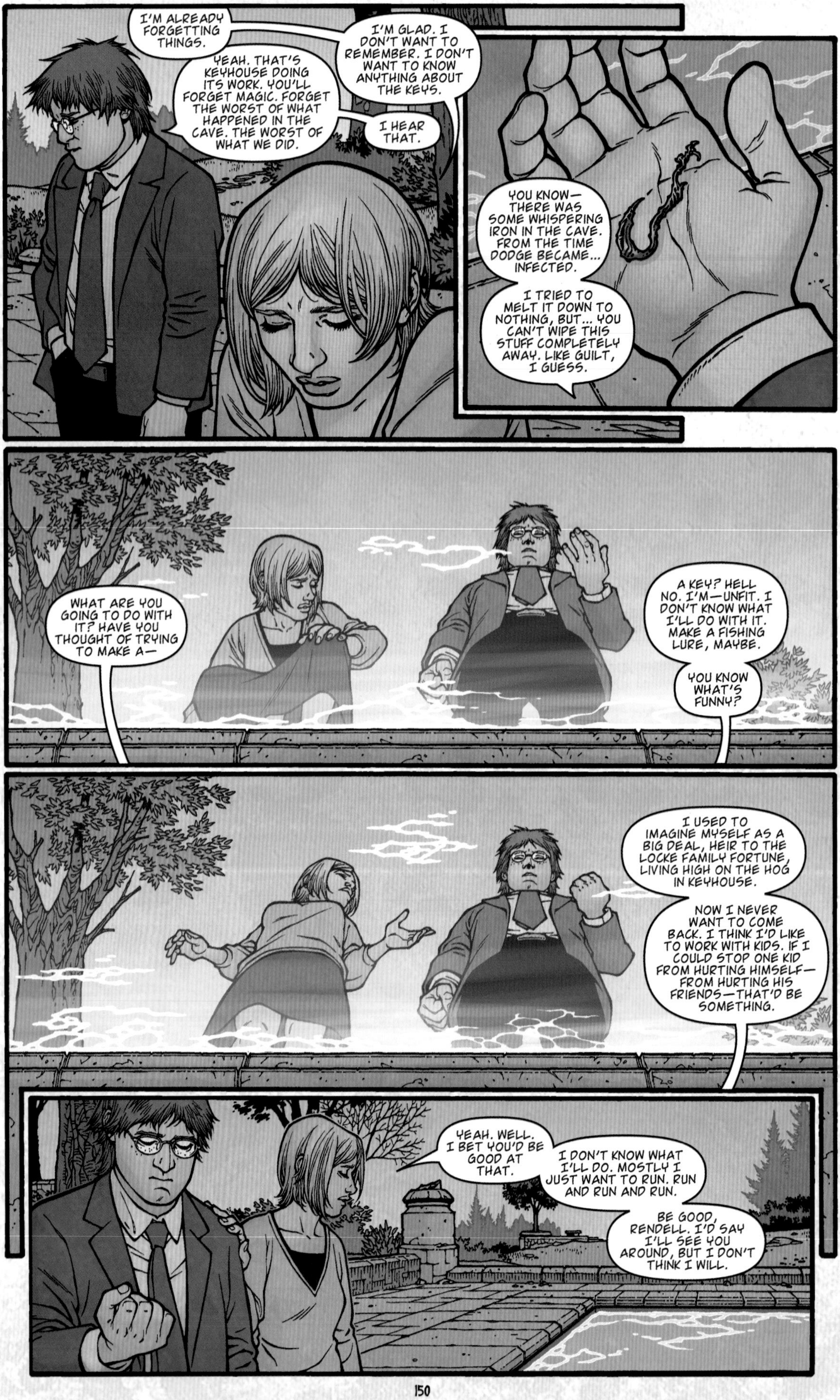
I'M ALREADY FORGETTING THINGS.
YEAH. THAT'S KEYHOUSE DOING ITS WORK. YOU'LL FORGET MAGIC. FORGET THE WORST OF WHAT HAPPENED IN THE CAVE. THE WORST OF WHAT WE DID.
I'M GLAD. I DON'T WANT TO REMEMBER. I DON'T WANT TO KNOW ANYTHING ABOUT THE KEYS.
I HEAR THAT.
YOU KNOW— THERE WAS SOME WHISPERING IRON IN THE CAVE. FROM THE TIME DODGE BECAME... INFECTED.
I TRIED TO MELT IT DOWN TO NOTHING, BUT... YOU CAN'T WIPE THIS STUFF COMPLETELY AWAY. LIKE GUILT, I GUESS.
WHAT ARE YOU GOING TO DO WITH IT? HAVE YOU THOUGHT OF TRYING TO MAKE A—
A KEY? HELL NO. I'M—UNFIT. I DON'T KNOW WHAT I'LL DO WITH IT. MAKE A FISHING LURE, MAYBE.
YOU KNOW WHAT'S FUNNY?
I USED TO IMAGINE MYSELF AS A BIG DEAL, HEIR TO THE LOCKE FAMILY FORTUNE, LIVING HIGH ON THE HOG IN KEYHOUSE.
NOW I NEVER WANT TO COME BACK. I THINK I'D LIKE TO WORK WITH KIDS. IF I COULD STOP ONE KID FROM HURTING HIMSELF— FROM HURTING HIS FRIENDS—THAT'D BE SOMETHING.
YEAH. WELL. I BET YOU'D BE GOOD AT THAT.
I DON'T KNOW WHAT I'LL DO. MOSTLY I JUST WANT TO RUN. RUN AND RUN AND RUN.
BE GOOD, RENDELL. I'D SAY I'LL SEE YOU AROUND, BUT I DON'T THINK I WILL.

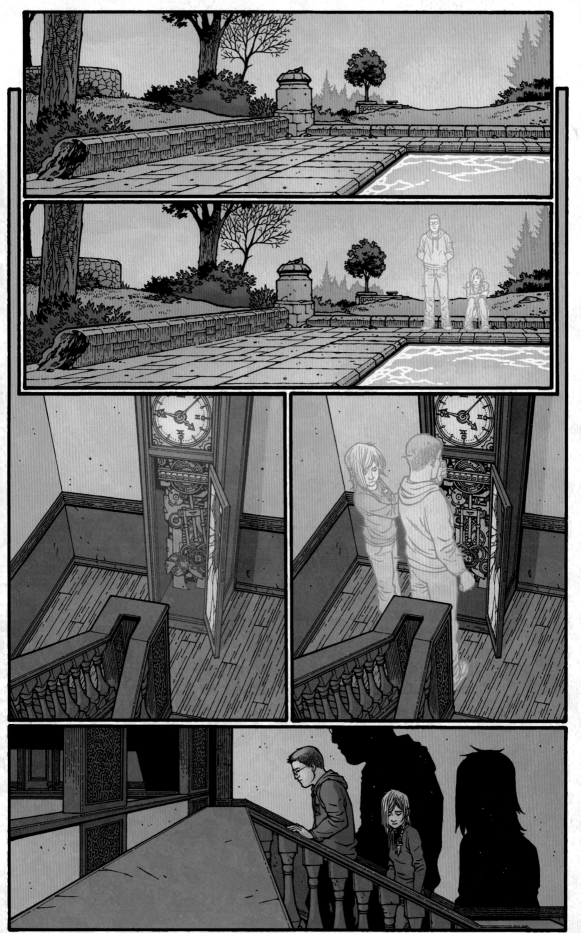

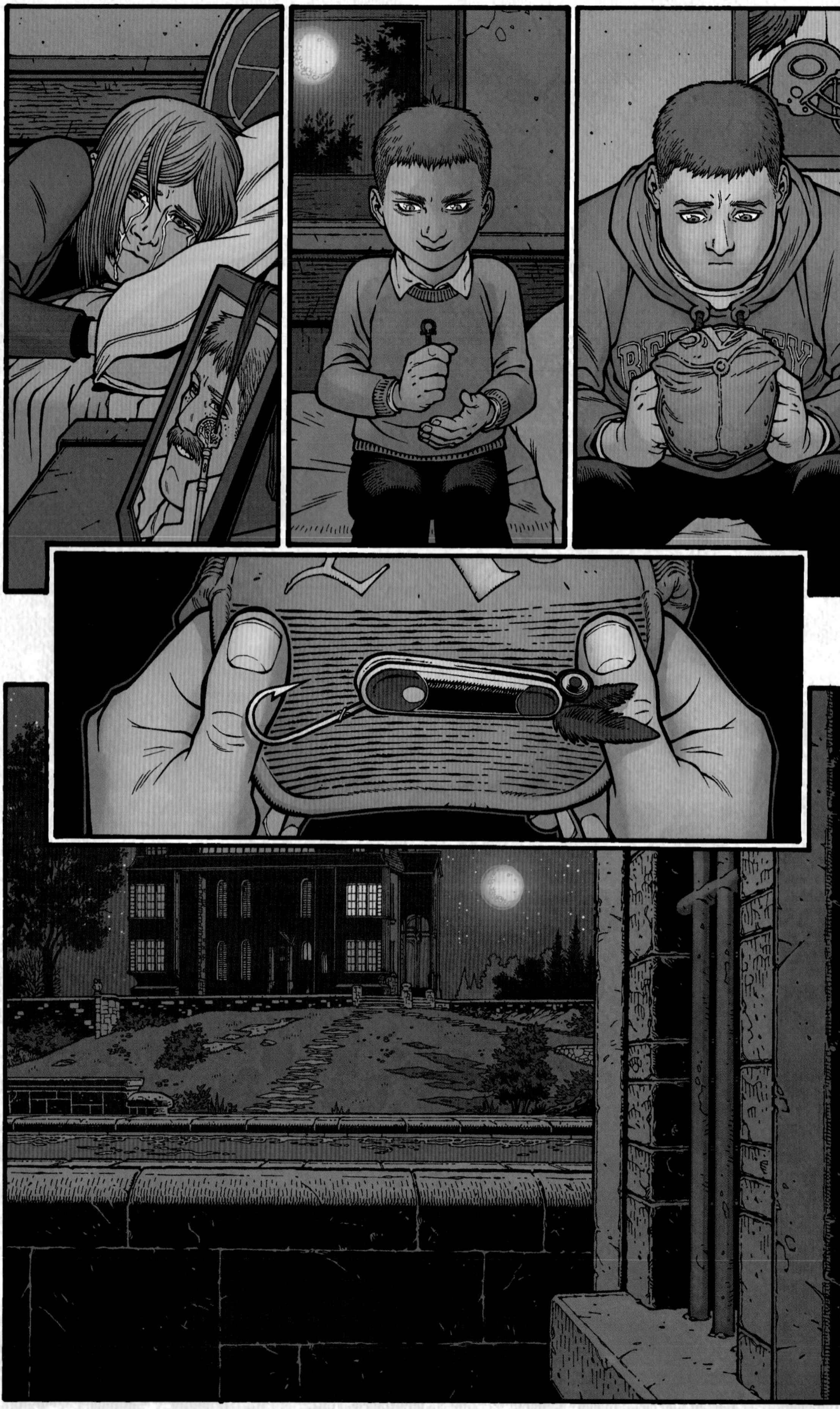

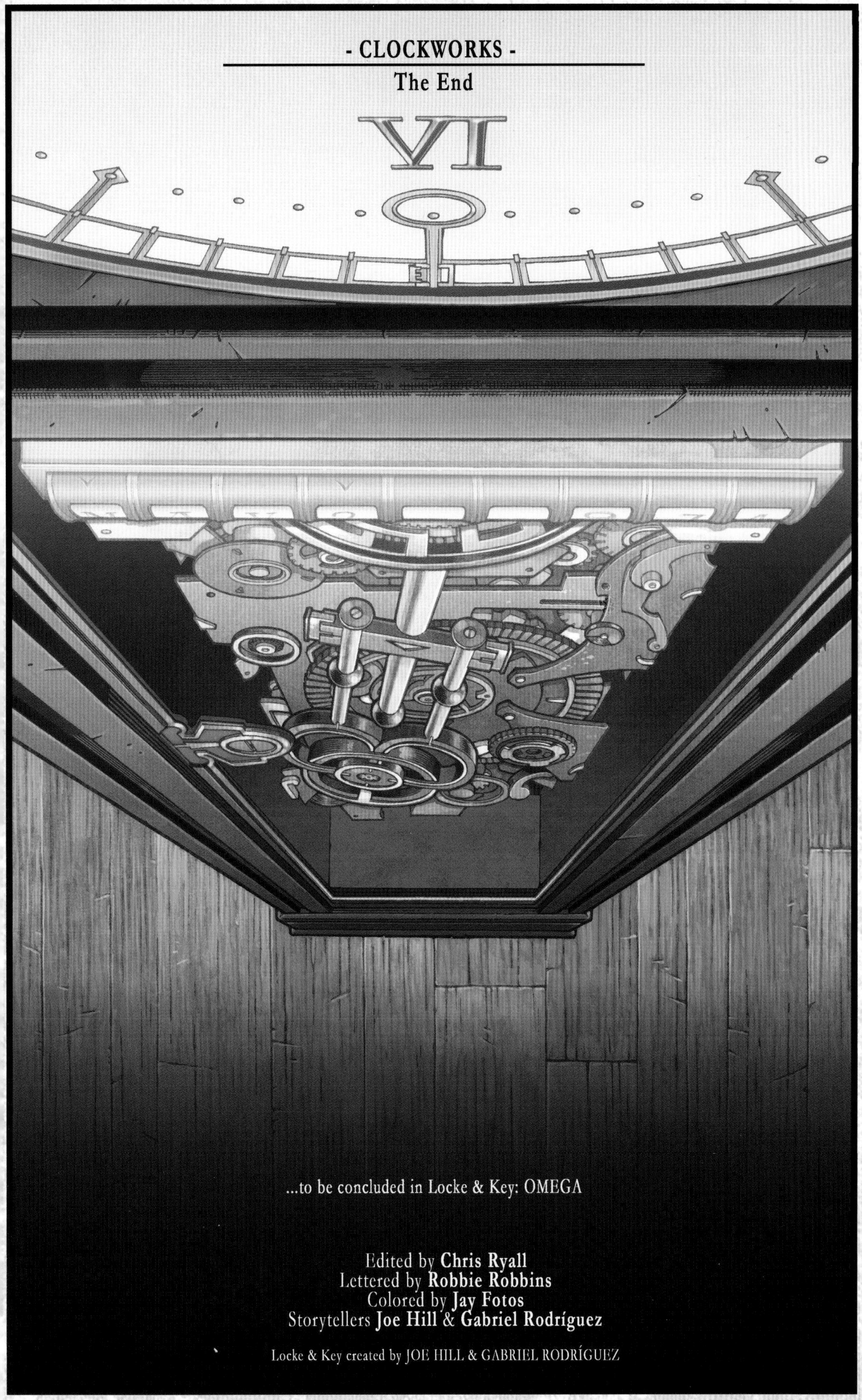
- CLOCKWORKS -
The End
...to be concluded in Locke & Key: OMEGA
Edited by **Chris Ryall**
Lettered by **Robbie Robbins**
Colored by **Jay Fotos**
Storytellers **Joe Hill** & **Gabriel Rodríguez**
Locke & Key created by JOE HILL & GABRIEL RODRÍGUEZ

The Known Keys

(Excerpts from the diary of Benjamin Pierce Locke, 1757 - 1799)

ΩMeGa Ke

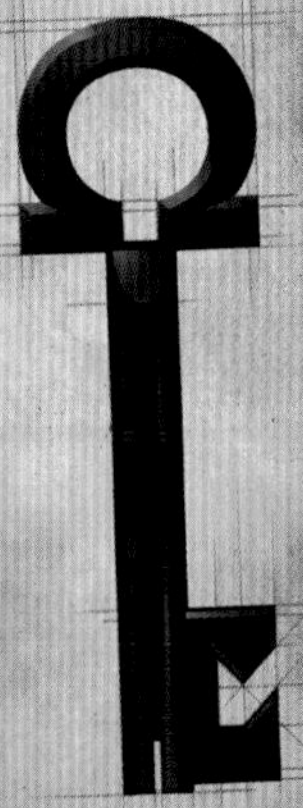

in our
& I resolv
hazzarded such a
long I work'd in a
till finallie t'was c
oh how I feerd!
in the gath
straiked ou
held the d
beig'd
Gon
ha

GHoST KeY

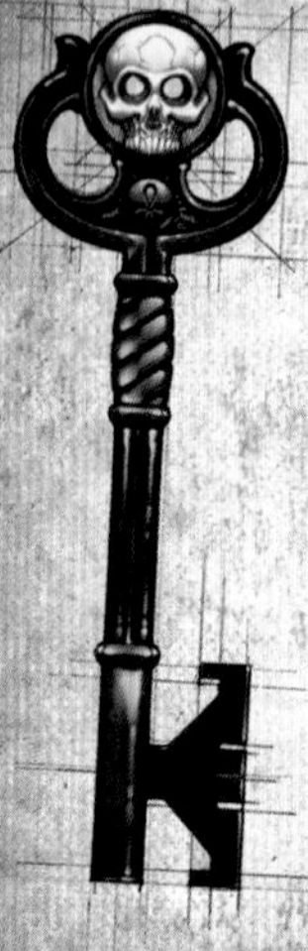

onlee in occaisonull daith do I find peece now, for with the bode caste aisyde, it is possibull for one to know his own ETERNAIL SOULE. My spairt cannot leeve the grounds of Keyhowse, but heyre I walke laik an aingel! I aim everywhare and nowhare at once, from the tall's towair, to the deepst caves. It is hard to dreem thair could be any dore more terryble or wondairfulle than that wych dyvydes deth from lyfe, yet my expairances at the thraishold of the black dore have teach'd me thair are worse things than to dyye...

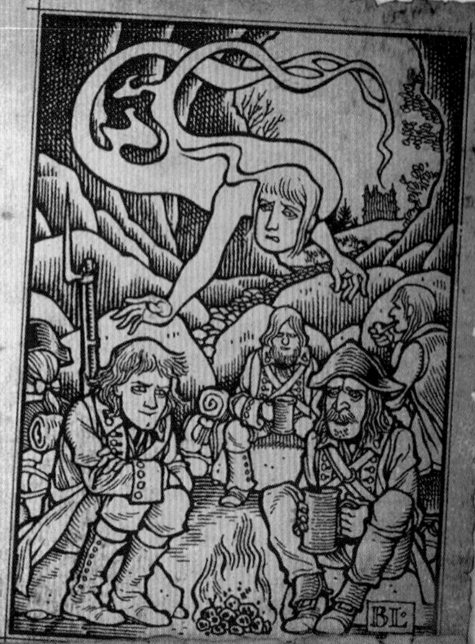

BL

eCHo KeY

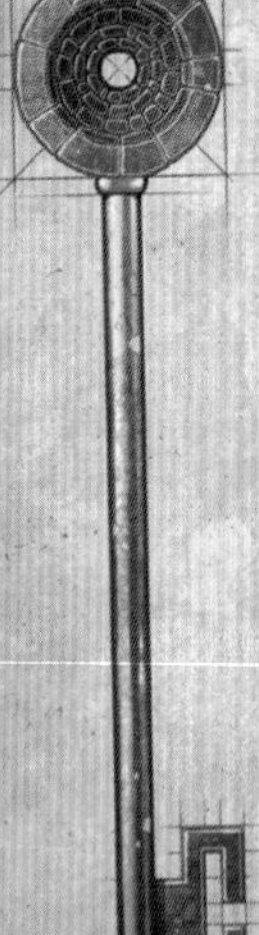

whence I unlock'd the dore I heerd a voice that saimed to ecko from the well & it aisk'd me who I sot & I spake of my brother. No sooner had the words pass'd my lips thence he ROSE from the WELL like a spairt & yet was living flaish, allthohe had dyed in the Drowning Caves not 6 weeks beefor. He clasp'd me to his bosom & sayd why do ye look so unhappy to see me brother, but I wast in feer for my allmaighty SOUL & fled to the howse & pray'd thair to the LORD

But in that grait howse, an ecko of my voice was all the reeply I receivd

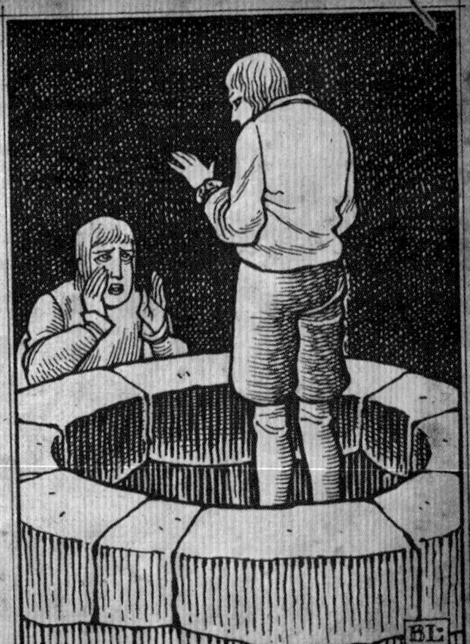

BL

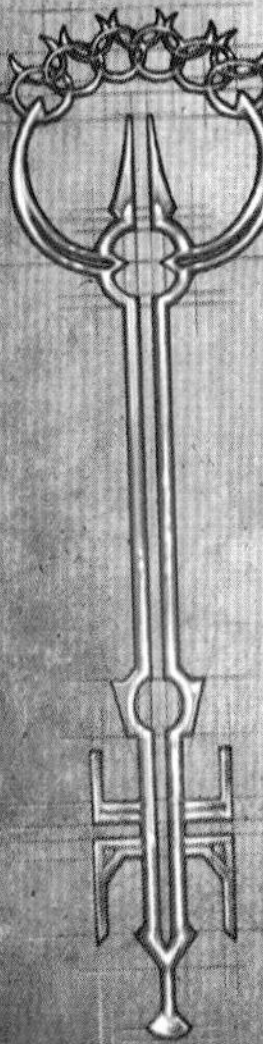

aNYWHeRe KeY

us'd the key to anyplaice againe, to return to Boston, & gaither intelaigents for Crais. Tis an act of terryble wychcraift, but better I do it, than my sister, who is obssaissed with REVENGING herself upon the RED-COATS, for thair violence agin our faither & brother & belov'd maither. Aye, my dredd of beeing called to accounnt someday by SATAN HIMSELF is a trifling concern when maiched with my desyre to rid the worlde of the devylls who taik the King's Coyne to do raip & murdur...

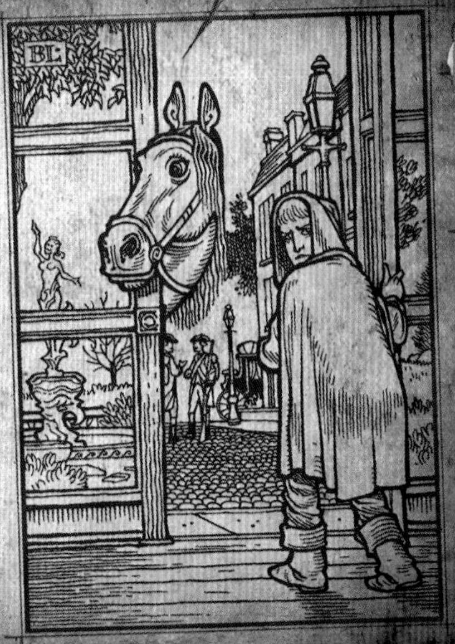

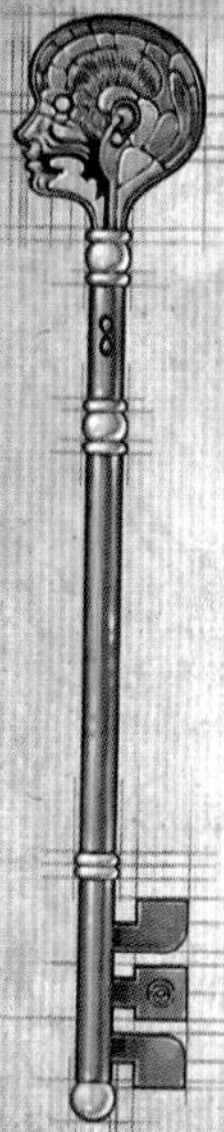

HeaD KeY

of alle the keys I have forged from the WHISP'RING IRON, 'tis the key that opens the human mind I most regrait. Miranda hast a pervairse fasinaytion whist the key & hast us'd ait to fill her head with all thair is to know about WAR & the SLAIYING of MEN, & she carrys an arsanall whist her whairever she goes. Yet I am less in dred of what she has put in than what she hast remov'd. Sometimes it is as if she is now without FEER and indeed is herself more man than I!

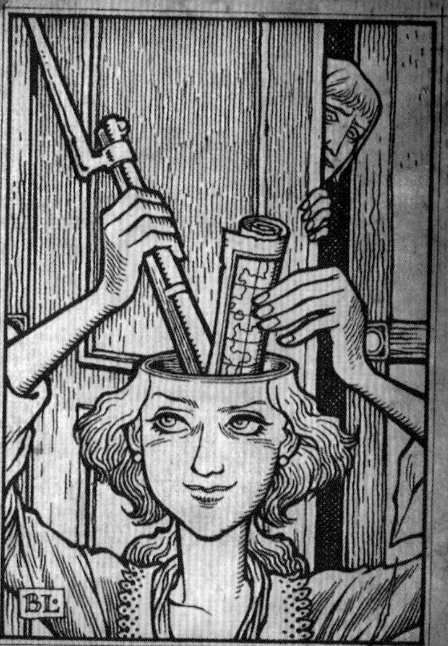

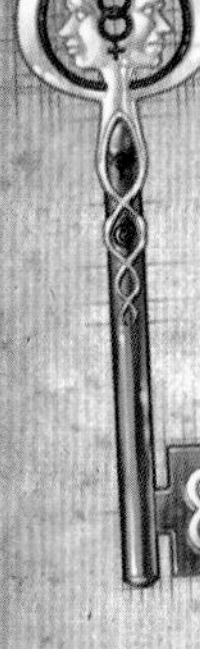

GeNDeR KeY

my sister—or should I now say my brother!—fights the shadow war with Crais in the streets of Boston whilst I wait at home, like a helpless maiden, praying to the ALLMAIGHTY! for her safe return. When first I fashin'd the key, I imagained she maight trainsform to a boy to protect her, if necessaire, from the unsavorie lusts of ENGLISHMEN should the King's foot-soldiers return to Lovecraft to abuse God fairing womain. Never did I think she wouldst WILLENGLY caist off the wardrobe of her femininitie for this ruggaid liberation among men...

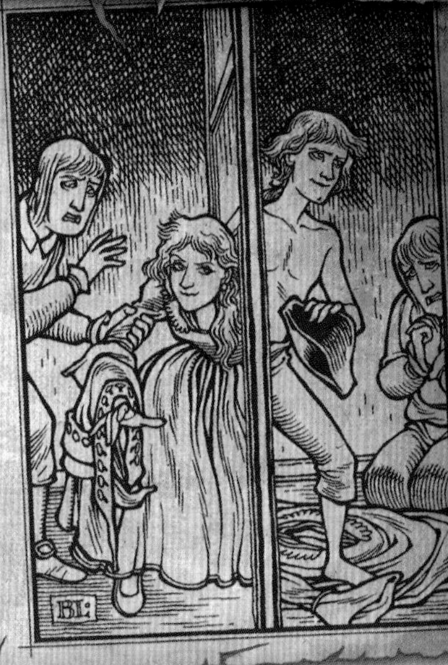

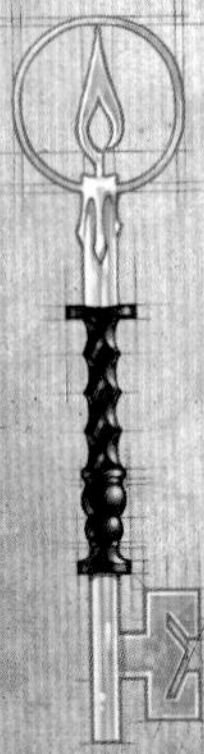

SHaDoW KEY

O Wycked Night! Damn'd be Crais & Damn'd be the Redcoats & Damn'd be my own foole self. Miranda tis griev'sly hurt & lingers on the thaishold of deth! The Redcoats pursued her & the tattr'd reminante of Crais's companie into the caves but I drove them back with the aide of the lyving shadows. If she dies I wouldst rather be a shadow myself than remain in thys diabolicall world, knowing she wouldst never have been at riske if not for me!

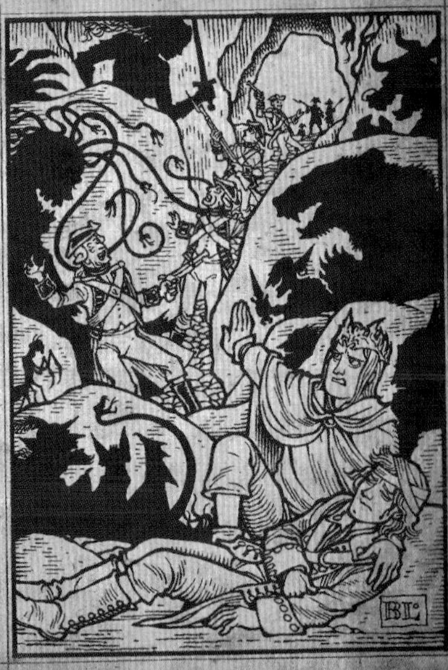
BL

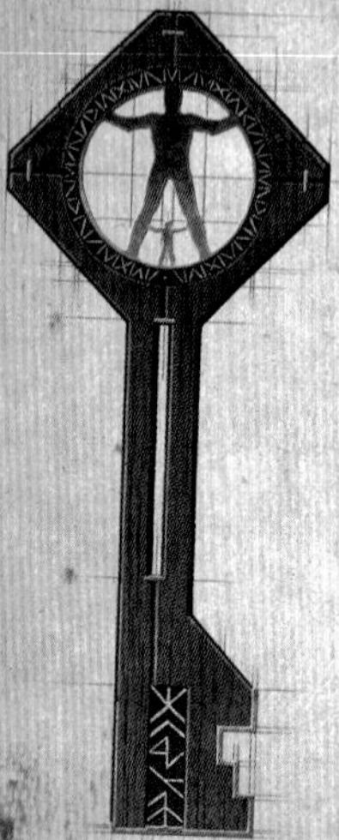

GiaNT KEY

she is dying & thair is nothing I can do to save her!
The Redcoats return'd to assalle the house & claym her & I admitte I lette my fury & miserie get the better of me. I used the giant's key to multiplie my syze, so that my body was as vaste as my hayte & I turn'd upon a wholle regiment & ~ O GOD forgive me! ~ did detestably murther them alle!

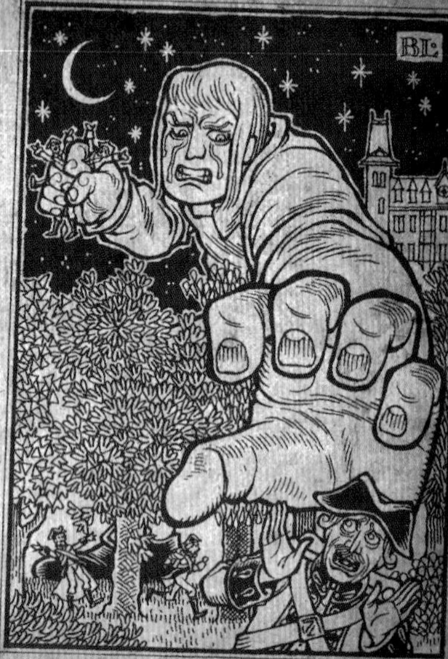
BL

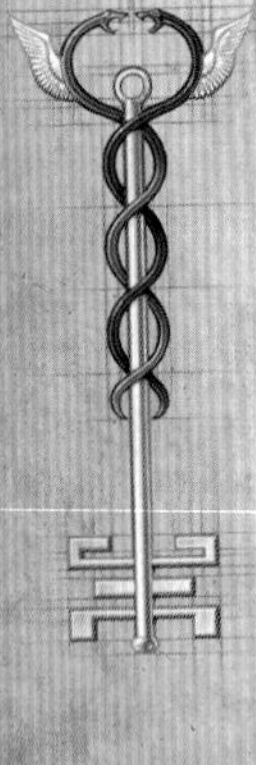

MeNDiNG KEY

the Iron whispr'd to me laste night & I work'd in a fever alle day, mayking a cabinet & forging a new key out of that dreadfull metal that is not metal. Yet if the devil may pervairt Holie Scripture to serve his purposes, so may the rihteous at times turn the DEVYLLS TOOLS to do the work of SWEET JESU! For the key & cabinet I fashin'd could be used to mend fraicturd objykts ~ shatter'd plattes, crack'd eggs & broken sistairs. Bless'd be THE LORD, Miranda hast recovr'd! I only wish she wouldst remembair her place & become the demure & modestte girlle she once was, but fear her love for Crais will emperille her againe soon enough...

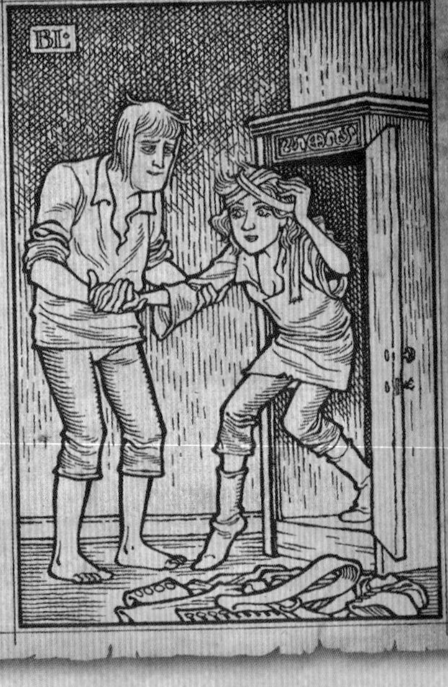
BL

Animal Key

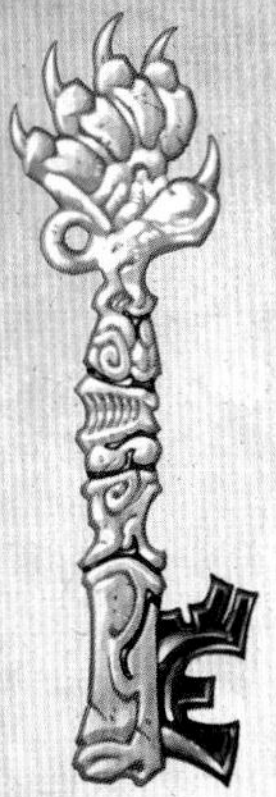

September 9th, 1851~

...Ulysses said he would fly all the way to Hell if he had to, to find Delacorte for me. Clint said he would probably only be required to fly to Georgia, but that the two places were much alike, except Georgia is a bit hotter. We have fought a thousand times, my brothers and I, but this morning I felt I could not love any living souls more. Ulysses stepped through the door, and emerged on the other side, a golden eagle. He gave me a short, lordly look, and took to the skies...

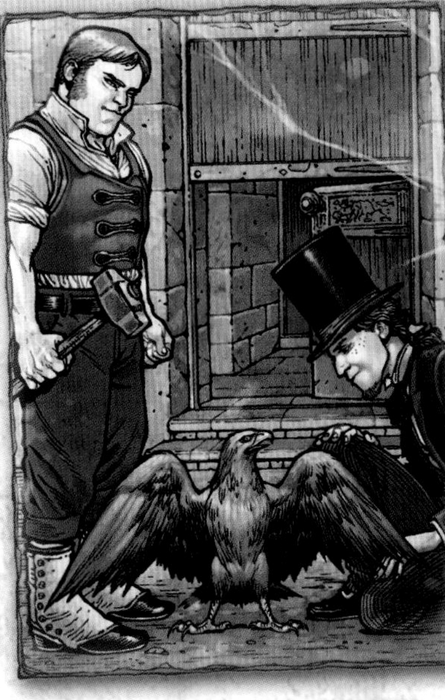

Music Box Key

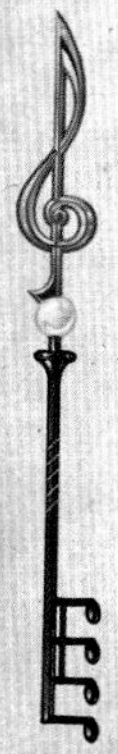

November 3rd, 1851~

...he was dying fast from his injuries and knew it. He said he would go to glory and take his secrets with him. Ulysses said that if our Lord meant to open the Gates Of Heaven to a B---- like him, he would prefer to throw in with the Devil. Clint hissed and seemed ready to strike again, but I restrained him. I knew if Hammersmith died, I would likelynever see Delacorte again, and so I turned the Key in the Music Box, and the tune began to play. A miniature version of myself turned around and around, and sang:

...tell us who paid you for the girl...
...do it now before you leave this world...

Hammersmith's eyes widened, and he began to speak...

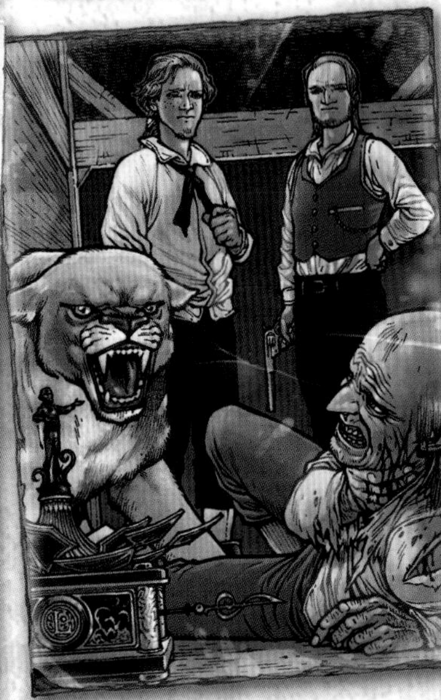

Skin Key

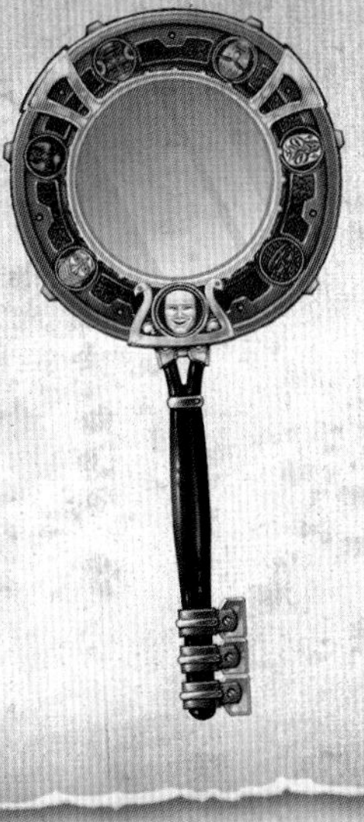

November 5th, 1851~

...I looked into the mirror, and turned it, so I became of the African race, and my skin was dark as coal. And it is a wonderment to me. All my thoughts had, until then, been bent on finding Delacorte and beseeching her to become free and white like myself. But when I saw my black features in the mirror, I was surprised to find I liked my own face better than I had ever liked it before. Ulysses considered me for the longest of times, before offering me my hat and saying: «Remember to keep your eyes down, Harland. You have the White Man's habit of meeting another man's gaze, but you will fare poorly if you behave that way here in Georgia.»

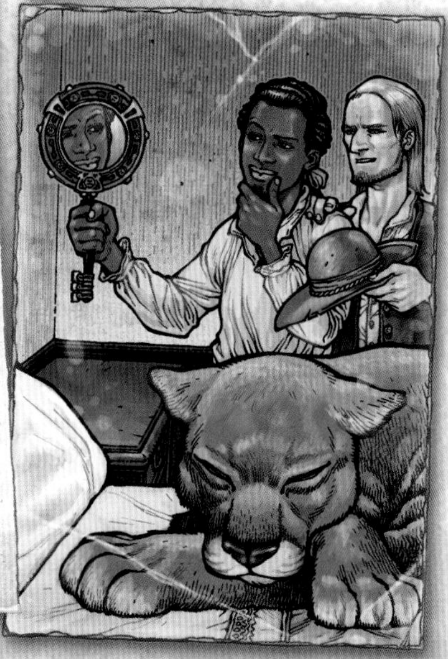

CHAIN KEY & THE GREAT LOCK

Something troublesome has happened. The Brougham Boys broke into the house this Sunday morning, while we were at church, and while attempting to enter the catacombs, triggered the Great Lock. I sorted them out with the Head Key, but I fear this is only the prelude to some new threat. The damnable thing is that they were sent with orders to break into the wine cellar, although they had no idea what they would find when they forced their way in. Someone must have some idea what I keep there, though, and someone is after it…

THE KEY TO THE MOON

There is nothing left to be done for little Ian. By the time the last fall apples are picked, his life will be wrenched from him in the most agonizing fashion, and no operation or final treatment will do anything to stop it from happening. Yet I think he hardly minds the pain that racks him nightly; nor has he any great terror of death. My brave boy! What he cannot bear is his own knowledge of all the vistas he will never see, all the people he will never meet, all the grand deeds he will never witness. It sickens me as well. I have asked Harland if he can fashion a key that can open a door in reality, a space between this life and the next. I am imagining a kind of balcony, high above the humorous tragedies and sad comedies of this earth, a place beyond pain, where the dead may gather to enjoy the great show of life below.

TIMESHIFT KEY

…Occasionally people will ask me about Ian, wanting to know how I am managing without him. I tell them honestly that I see him everyday, that he is with me always, here in this house. This usually earns me a consoling, worried look, but it is the perfect truth. With the aid of Harland's ingenious Timeshift Key and Clock, I am able to revisit all of the best days of Ian's life, as I wish. Of course I may also return Ian to our world with the Echo Key… but a human soul that has had its time on our earth longs for the warmth and comfort of That Other Place, and I know that bringing him back is something I would be doing for me, not for him. So I leave him be. I wonder, sometimes, what would happen if a truly twisted soul were to be reanimated with the Echo Key - someone with designs on the world of the living. Fortunately, I safeguard that key too closely for…

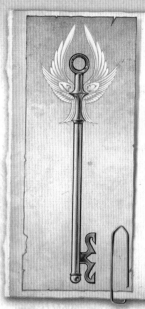

Engels-Schlüssel

4. Juni 1942

Mein Gott. Mein Gott! Bei Tagesanbruch war ich draußen und suchte nach dem kleinen Joe. Es stürmte und regnete in Strömen. Alles kam mir krank und unwirklich vor — wie in einem Albtraum. Ich rannte und rannte, völlig verzweifelt, und es war mir scheißegal, was er Jean über mich erzählte. Wenn er tot war, wollte ich selbst auch sterben. Und dann sah ich etwas Unglaubliches — etwas, das es gar nicht hätte geben dürfen, und ich bekam vor Überraschung und Staunen ganz weiche Knie. Ich sah Jean durch den Regen hinauffliegen, den zerschlagenen Körper ihres Bruders in der Armen. Sie trug das Gurtzeug mit den Flügeln, und hintendrin steckte der Schlüssel. Ich schwöre, sie ist geflogen! Und dabei sah sie so wunderschön aus wie eine Trauertaube.

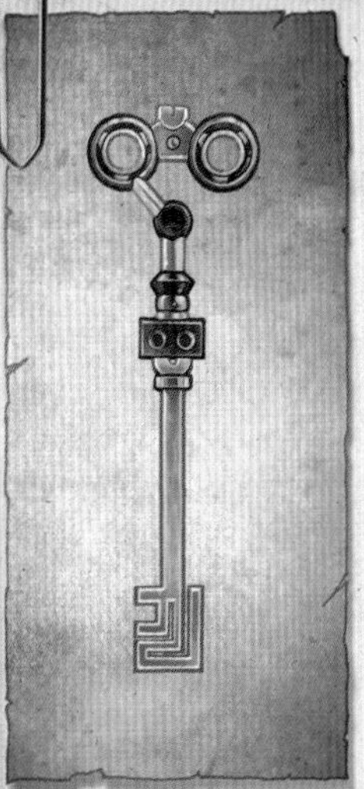

Philosophoscope Key

July 3rd, 1942

...Hannes asked me to come with him, in his quiet inflected English. I told him I liked it better when I thought he was mute because at least then he couldn't tell me lies. But I took his hand and went with him. He walked me to the Philosophoscope in the tower. Once I realized where we were going, Johnnie, I didn't want to go, and couldn't help myself. Once I realized what he was going to show me. He put the Key in, and shifted the lever to TrueLove and asked me to look. Oh Johnnie. How I have lied to myself for months. He knew what I would see somehow even when I didn't... that I would see him...

Herkules-Schlüssel

13. Juli 1942

Die Hälfte der 8. Armee und ein schier endloser Haufen SS-Männer warteten da auf mich! Ich schleuderte Eric gegen die Mauer und hörte, wie seine Rippen brachen, als wäre jemand auf ein Bündel Zweige gesprungen. Ich muss zugeben, das hörte sich wie Musik in meinen Ohren an!
Mit der anderen Hand schlug ich nach den Soldaten, und sie flogen wie Streichhölzer durch die Luft. Der Herkules-Schlüssel setzte all die Kraft in mir frei, die ich als verdammter Krüppel nie gehabt hatte. Aber der Sturmbannführer wusste, wie er mich fertigmachen konnte!

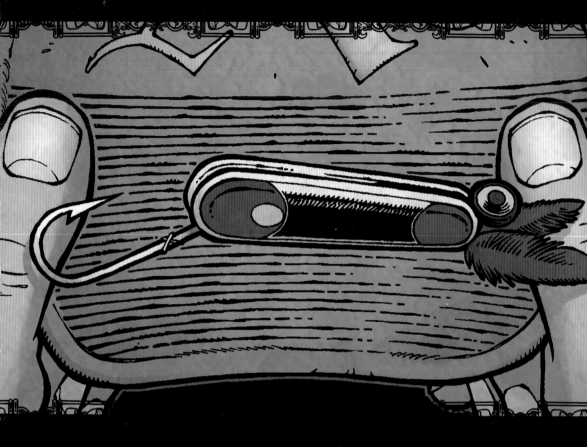

B I O G R A P H I E S

Joe Hill's first professional fiction submission was a SPIDER-MAN script, which he sent to Marvel Comics in 1984, at the age of twelve years old. It was turned down, but Joe received a handwritten note from then editor-in-chief Jim Shooter. It was impossible to read. He likes to believe it said, "You rock, kid! This is talent, baby!" Although it is possible the note actually said, "You rot, kid! This is toilet paper!" Twenty years later, Joe sold his first comic script… an eleven-page story for *Spider-Man Unlimited*. Shortly after saw the publication of his first novel, the *New York Times* best-selling HEART-SHAPED BOX. He is also the author of HORNS and a book of stories, 20th CENTURY GHOSTS. He's won some prizes, most recently the 2011 Eisner Award for Best Writer. Hill and his separated-at-birth twin Gabriel Rodriguez have been working on the award-winning ongoing supernatural saga, LOCKE & KEY, since 2007.

Try to keep up with his active Twitter stream: @joe_hill

Gabriel Rodriguez was born in Santiago in 1974. He is a Chilean architect, and long-time comic-book lover, whose life took an unbelievable turn when, in 2002, he got the chance to collaborate for the first time with IDW Publishing. Breaking in to the comics industry with *CSI* and soon working on *Clive Barker's The Great and Secret Show*, *Beowulf*, and *George A. Romero's Land of the Dead*, in 2007 Rodriguez met Joe Hill and the two bonded like brothers. Together, they created the twisted but wonderful world of LOCKE & KEY. Rodriguez currently lives in Chile with his lovely wife Catalina and their wonderful children.

Follow his antics on Twitter: @GR_comics